The Garden of Priapus

The Garden of Priapus

SEXUALITY AND AGGRESSION IN ROMAN HUMOR

REVISED EDITION

Amy Richlin

New York Oxford
OXFORD UNIVERSITY PRESS
1992

Oxford University Press

Oxford New York Toronto
Delhi Bombay Calcutta Madras Karachi
Kuala Lumpur Singapore Hong Kong Tokyo
Nairobi Dar es Salaam Cape Town
Melbourne Auckland

and associated companies in
Berlin Ibadan

First published in the United States in 1983
by Yale University Press, New Haven.

First issued in revised paperback edition
by Oxford University Press, 1992.

Published by Oxford University Press, Inc.,
200 Madison Avenue, New York, New York 10016

Library of Congress Cataloging-in-Publication Data
Richlin, Amy, 1951–
The garden of Priapus : sexuality and aggression in Roman humor /
Amy Richlin.—Rev. ed.
p. cm. Includes bibliographical references and index.
ISBN 0-19-506873-4 (paper)
1. Latin wit and humor—History and criticism. 2. Erotic poetry,
Latin—History and criticism. 3. Aggressiveness (Psychology) in
literature. 4. Satire, Latin—History and criticism.
5. Priapus (Greek deity) in literature. 6. Sex in literature.
7. Invective. I. Title.
pA6095.R53 1992
877'.01093538—dc20 91-26716

9 8 7 6 5 4 3 2 1

Printed in the United States of America
on acid-free paper

PARENTIBUS OPTIMIS LEPIDISSIMISQUE

Preface

This book began as a means of determining the place of Juvenal 2, 6, and 9 relative to Juvenal's satire as a whole and to the rest of Roman satire. The works read in this endeavor proved interesting enough in their own right that the analysis of them here takes up much more space than the analysis of Juvenal 2, 6, and 9; still, the initial aim informs the book. Thus the book largely ignores several areas only tangential to the study of satire. I presume that an analysis of sexual humor in Roman comedy and of all Roman sexual graffiti and erotic art will be most missed; both areas provide ample material for further books, and I hope these books will be written. The date and the problem of Greek versus Roman in comedy, and my lack of expertise as an epigrapher, excluded these areas from the present study. A third area not covered here includes authors later than Juvenal, except for some episodes in Apuleius; Lucian, Apuleius, Tertullian, Ausonius, Claudian, and others all clamor for attention.

To find out more about Roman humor I have borrowed theories from other disciplines, especially from psychology and anthropology. I found both fields stimulating and illuminating for reading ancient texts, and I hope the present study will be viewed not as an aberration or a trespass but as a valid and promising direction for classical philology. The scope of this book has dictated that no one author be treated in depth; moreover, several important phenomena—Roman sexual mores, sexuality in Roman religion, and the relationship between the Roman ideals of the military, the monetary, and the sexual—are only adumbrated in these pages.

Several problems of terminology need to be stated clearly at the outset. First, in the analysis of Roman homosexuality two great differences from current norms will be noticed: (1) The Romans made little mention of female homosexuality, and so lesbianism will rarely be mentioned here. (2) Roman invective assumed that there was only one main kind of male homosexual, pathic (those who were penetrated); these are often identified as effeminate. Men who penetrated other males (usually boys) were generally assumed to be bisexual; free men who penetrated adult males were either punishing them or engaging in a rare form of homosexuality. Hence the term *pathic* will often appear here, designating a man who only enjoys being penetrated. The word *puer,* "boy," will be used of the boys who appear in literature as sex objects. The notion of homosexual reciprocity appears in Latin literature only rarely and in extreme cases.

The translations throughout are my own and render primary obscenities in Latin by their English equivalents. Ancient and some modern works are abbreviated throughout according to the conventions of classical philology, and I have generally used the forms listed in the second edition of the *Oxford Classical Dictionary.* In a few cases I use abbreviations other than those listed there: *AP* for the *Anthologia Palatina* (collected Greek epigrams); Cat. for Catullus; *D.* for the *Digest* (of Roman law) and *C.* for the *Codex; S.* for Horace's *Sermones* (satires); *AA* for Ovid's *Ars Amatoria; Pr.* for the *Carmina Priapea; VA* for the *Virgilian Appendix.* In quoted texts I use the following symbols to mark different problems in ancient texts: angle brackets set off words conjectured by the editor; square brackets indicate material lost from an inscription and filled in by the editor; daggers set off material believed by the editor to be corrupt and not yet satisfactorily emended.

Finally, on the texts themselves. Two that appear repeatedly may need some introduction: for the *Carmina Priapea* I have used Mueller's text, in his edition of Catullus, Tibullus, and Propertius (Leipzig, 1892); for the three Priapics of the *Catalepton* and the long Priapic "Quid Hoc Novi Est?" I have used the Oxford edition of the *Virgilian Appendix* (1966), edited by Clausen et al. This last poem will appear as Oxford *VA* "Quid Hoc Novi Est?" or in some shortened version of this cumbrous handle. I have used Marx's edition of Lucilius, and Gow and Page's editions of poems from the *Greek Anthology* where available, but have retained the traditional numberings. In referring to Freud's *Jokes and Their Relation to the Unconscious,* I have used the pagination of the Norton edition for the convenience of students.

Acknowledgments

What a pleasure it is to be able to thank the people to whom this book brought me. Since 1982 I have had a new source of support in the sisterhood of the Women's Classical Caucus, whose members have challenged me to go further and helped out along the way. In addition, I want to thank Sandra Joshel for her mythic bibliography and sense of humor; Terri Marsh for her grasp of theory and sense of honor; Molly Myerowitz Levine for peripatetic exegesis; and Suzanne Dixon, Mary-Kay Gamel, and Diana Robin for broadening my horizons. Special thanks to Gordon Williams for his unfailing support and kindly ear: *tibi cano et Musis.* Not only here but in all that I do I am inspired by the courage, work, and vision of two remarkable classicists and feminists: Judith Hallett and Marilyn Skinner.

To my new colleagues at the University of Southern California, both in Classics and the Program for the Study of Women and Men in Society, heartfelt thanks—especially to Lois Banner, to Donald McGuire and Carolyn Dewald of the 1990 Writing Group, and to the much-missed Jeffrey Henderson. You have given me a wonderful place to work.

This edition was made possible by the imagination, initiative, and energy of Rachel Toor, now of Duke University Press. A research leave from the University of Southern California gave me the time I needed, for which I am most grateful.

Above all, thanks to everyone who told me they had used the book and found it helpful; there can be no words more heartwarming to a writer. And thanks to Lon, for the distractions.

Los Angeles A.R.
October 1991

Contents

Introduction

> [S]aid Mr. Sensible, with a rather chilly smile, ". . . A gentleman's knowledge of the ancient authors is not that of a pedant: and I think you have misunderstood the place which philosophy ought to hold in the reasonable life. We do not memorize *systems*. What system can stand? What system does not leave us with the old refrain—*que sais-je?* It is in her power to remind us of the strangeness of things—in the brown charm of her secluded meditations—above all, in her decorative function—that philosophy becomes instrumental to the good life. We go to the Porch and the Academy to be spectators, not partisans."
>
> —C. S. Lewis, *The Pilgrim's Regress*

The revised edition of a book, a great and unexpected pleasure to any writer, offers a chance to think about what it has meant. This introduction reflects the critical turmoil of the past decade in the academy at large and, to a lesser extent, within the field of Classics. I write here for very different groups of readers: for Latinists, and for classicists generally; for young classicists just starting out, who may never have read theory; for the feminists in Classics; for feminists generally; for theorists of culture and literature; and for historians of sexuality. This essay thus serves the double function of introducing readers to a debate in theory and of participating vigorously in that debate; in what follows I will sometimes turn to speak to one group or another. The book itself is for everyone, and I am glad it is in your hands.

Toward a History of Sexuality

This book was originally published in 1983 and was written and researched during 1981–82. It was conceived as a study of Roman sexual humor, and the title reflected that original goal. But the scope and implications of the project grew so that it came to encompass much broader cultural phenomena than humor alone: the construction of gender in Roman and other societies; the function of ideology in maintaining class barriers and hierarchies; the interrelation between aggression and sexuality. I took Rome as a paradigm for a type of hierarchical system common among human beings; and I now see the instance of Rome as also important because of its historical position, for the phenomena I discuss call into question current attempts to barricade off periods of history from one another. In writing, I used comparative studies from anthropology and from behavioral and Freudian psychology, while my political analysis was shaped by the feminist critique of the pornographic. I hoped when the book was first published that it would not only change the way classicists looked at Roman satire but would, in general, provide a historical perspective for the study of humor and of sexuality, which I defined as interrelated discourses of aggression. As it turned out, the history of sexuality was to loom large in the theoretical landscape of the 1980s. Thus, the book's revision in the 1990s launches it into several discussions among feminists and other theorists: on the relation between literature and history; on the political implications of Foucault's theories, the New Historicism, and postmodernism in general; on the history of sexuality; and on the history and nature of the pornographic.

A central place in these discussions has been taken by Michel Foucault's late work, the three volumes of his projected *History of Sexuality* (1978, 1985a, 1986). Since the second and third volumes dealt with Greek and (ostensibly) with Roman cultures, attention from nonclassicists has turned toward antiquity, especially because of the picture Foucault drew of an ancient sexuality different in kind from modern sexuality. This picture, however, is distorted, based on information that is far from complete; the reissue of *The Garden of Priapus* will serve to fill in some missing pieces.

The main problems posed by Foucault's second volume (Greek) and third (some Roman, mostly later Greek) include the following:

1. Although the whole project is called *The History of Sexuality,* Foucault states early on that he sees his history as that of the desiring subject, who is male (1985a: 5–6, 22); women figure in these pages only as objects, and that rarely; adult passive homosexual males (a Greco-Roman category) are ignored, their marginality reinscribed. By adopting the point of view of his sources, Foucault ends by replicating their omissions (Henry 1991). Moreover, he meets his sources dressed in their Sunday best; it is hard to recognize in Foucault's contemplative, self-disciplined, married pederasts the men who made so many jokes about rape and ugly women. Insofar as this is a history of sexuality at all, it is a history of *male* sexuality, and a partial one at that. Naomi Schor (1989: 54–58) perceives Foucault's project to be shaped by his own restricted definition of sexuality as the nineteenth-century bourgeois discourse on sex, and gives him credit for "scrupulous attention . . . to the gender of the enunciating subject" (54); I can only say that when I read these books I sense not consciousness but silence, a failure to ask where women's subjectivity was. Coincidentally, Foucault effaces the relevant work of feminist scholars (Martin 1988: 7; cf. Richlin 1991c).

2. Although the whole project is called *The History of Sexuality,* Foucault states early on that he does not believe, exactly, that sexuality existed prior to the nineteenth century—or maybe the eighteenth—but in any event it was not always there (1985a: 3–5). As noted by Schor, Foucault's definition of sexual-

ity is not the commonly held one (something like "sexual behavior and ideas about it") but something more like "the abstract ideas about human sexual nature generated in modern Europe." The important implication is that sexual norms are locally determined. His title, then, is a paradox, for it is not what it seems; Foucault, in keeping with his earlier projects, is really writing a *pre*-history of sexuality, a history of the ideas that came together and resulted in the construct "sexuality." It is as if, say, religion, law, and medicine were what might be called first-order social constructs, while sexuality was a second-order social construct, culturally specific and historically delimited. But the problem here goes beyond that of a misleading title; Foucault's whole claim, which has startled and attracted so many scholars (e.g., Schor; the introduction to Halperin et al. 1990), rests on arguments from a silence that Foucault has himself created by means of selective reading. The texts from the Roman period that Foucault does look at are recommendations for physical, spiritual, and moral health directed at an elite audience, more philosophical than sexual (Martin 1988); his project is the equivalent of reconstructing the sexual attitudes of the eighteenth through the twentieth centuries in Europe and America by analyzing the works of some fashionable European psychologists and nutritionists, all but a few from the twentieth century. The results are not so much wrong as incomplete: *Whose* sexual attitudes? When? Did people take this seriously? What people? What other information is available?

These questions lie outside the defined limits of Foucault's project. He wanted to know whether he could find harbingers of Christian asceticism in pagan philosophy; if so, "one would thus find, formulated by a few austere philosophers isolated in the midst of *a world that did not itself appear to be austere,* the outline of a new ethics, destined, in the following centuries, to take more stringent forms and to gain a more general validity" (1986: 235; my italics). That italicized world has no part in Foucault's book. *The Garden of Priapus* displays what Foucault left out and should provide nonclassicists with a clearer and much more detailed idea of what Roman social realities might have been like.

3. For, in addition to the distortions arising from Foucault's lack of attention to gender and idiosyncratic choice of sources, a third, more serious problem lies in his lack of general knowledge about Greece and Rome and in his erasure of the individuality of Roman culture.[1] In the third volume he collapses Hellenistic into Roman, Republic into Empire, and all the emperors into each other, skipping a hundred years of civil war and the drastic social changes that accompanied it. In fact, with some exceptions, he skips the first eight or nine hundred years of Roman culture altogether, focusing on the high Empire (second century A.D.) and concluding that it marked a change—primarily, as far as I can see, because he was unfamiliar with any earlier Roman periods. The text is full of unattached comparisons. For example, Foucault claims that "the 'question of pleasure' . . . had become more insistent" (1986:

39). Than at what earlier time? Than in Greece six hundred years earlier, it seems. Indeed, most of the sources in this volume are Greek, not Roman. It is strange that the champion of local peculiarities of history should carry on like this, but it is a fact. Ironically, he was only able to make his argument for the difference between antiquity and the present by leaving out major differences between Greece and Rome, between Empire and Republic. The discussion of marriage is framed (1986: 147–49) as if Rome of the high Empire could profitably be compared directly with fifth-century B.C. Athenian society, without consideration of earlier Roman society; and as if Plutarch (a Greek from Boiotia) and Pliny (a wealthy Roman from Cisalpine Gaul) shared the same culture. The world depicted here is unrecognizable to a reader of Tacitus or Martial or Catullus, and it is not Roman.[2]

Meanwhile, indelible and grand, the title of the series continues to persuade readers that the books actually constitute a history of sexuality in the commonly understood sense of the word. Foucault was questioned about this in a late interview (1985b: 9–11); he at first acknowledged "a kind of gap which opens up between the title of the book and its content," but in subsequent responses stated his topic to have been sexuality. It is too easy to forget that Foucault was dealing with only a small part of the word's common meaning, a meaning he would not himself have accepted but one that he occasionally seems to use.

The kind of sexuality left out of antiquity by Foucault (1986: 39) is connected with what we might call the "obscene": genital and copulative practice and language perceived by their subjects as shaming. There was no dearth of such words and events in Roman culture; *The Garden of Priapus* gives an indication of the wealth of pertinent material available from the late Republic and early Empire: literary and forensic texts both in Latin and Greek—love poetry and speeches as well as satire; nonliterary texts (graffiti, gossipy anecdotes, lampoons, rhetorical exercises, personal letters)—the scrawls of the semiliterate as well as the epistles of Cicero; accounts of incidents the authors believed had actually taken place or had seen. Where Foucault's texts take an almost ascetic stance toward sex, these texts manifest a Rabelaisian interest in the physical body, with the male genitalia serving as a source of bellicose pride, and the female genitalia as a source of (male) disgust. In these texts rape and the threat of rape are a means of communication; sexual self-identity is an obsession; and both male and female homosexuality are named phenomena. Women and boys are equally objectified, though women, albeit rarely, write themselves. The institutions of empire and slavery, and of an elaborate but permeable class system, haunt the texts. I chose the figure of the ithyphallic god Priapus, who threatens to rape thieves who enter his garden, as a synecdochic embodiment of the sexuality consciously constituted in these Roman texts: male, aggressive, and bent on controlling boundaries.

This Priapic figure is familiar, especially to those who read feminist theory, for it is a type that can be found in many other cultures. Feminists have described cultures under patriarchy—that is, most cultures—as dominated by institutions associated with precisely Priapus' characteristics: male, aggressive, controlling boundaries. On the symbolic level, a talking phallus situated in the middle of a walled garden surely makes a good sign for phallogocentrism.

In short, while Rome is definitively *itself,* with definable characteristics, the *otherness* of antiquity has been greatly overstated: Priapus is peculiarly Roman; Priapic attitudes are not. As Clifford Geertz has said, "Understanding a people's culture exposes their normalness without reducing their particularity" (1973: 14; see also Lloyd 1990: 1–38). Foucault's treatment of the abstraction "sexuality" as a purely modern construct is wrong; the extensive Roman efforts to define the obscene formed part of a traditional Roman moral system (see chapter 1). In the desire to set the modern off from other periods, Foucault leaves out much in Roman culture that resembles modern institutions.

He also leaves out much that cries out for political analysis. What are we to make of a humor, and a sexual poetics, in which an ithyphallic male stood at the center of a protected space and threatened all intruders with rape? The feminist interpretation of sexual behavior as enactments of gendered hierarchies of power seems to me to provide the best analytical model for these Roman texts and history. When I argue here that forms of misogyny and phallic thinking characterized Roman culture *in the same way* as they have both earlier and later cultures, and that these forms are essentially related to humor, my thesis places me among those feminists who use "patriarchy" to denote the very *longue durée* of institutionalized oppression of women (e.g., Lerner 1986). One message of *The Garden of Priapus* is that Greek and Roman societies, though they have sometimes been looked to by those searching for a prepatriarchal golden age, are neither outside of, nor do they predate, patriarchy—the "ancient" world is not different in kind. Another is that humor itself is a patriarchal discourse.

The construct of patriarchy has often been called into question, in part by feminist historians reluctant to accept what looks like a steady-state model (see Scott 1989: 87, 91–92). But models should not be rejected simply for the reason that they are inconvenient; in any case, even if the most extreme biological determinist model turned out to be true, it would not imply the impossibility of change. Action demands knowledge, however inspiring myth may be. And it seems to me that in the West the bottom line for women has remained unchanged throughout recorded history (though what came *post* is not necessarily *propter*); the same holds true for many non-Western cultures. Certainly the material in *The Garden of Priapus* looks patriarchal. On the other hand, this model is not incompatible with historicism; it is possible that we have here only an unusually *longue durée,* and one that has begun to change over the last two centuries (see Schor 1989: 58).

I should note that I make these claims in full cognizance of recent critiques by women of color of the construct *patriarchy.*[3] The term is problematic; first, when theorists imply it is adequate to describe all cultures; second, when theorists imply that the oppression of women by men takes precedence over all other forms of oppression, or when they ignore other types of oppression altogether; third, and more generally, it is the kind of construct that obscures differences and implies that all women are members of one class. A better term for the institution would be "hierarchy," and it seems to me that feminism, if it is to work, must be a subset of anarchism (see Richlin 1991b *sub fin.*). *The Garden of Priapus* deals with xenophobia and homophobia as much as with misogyny, treating them all as manifestations of the same power structure. Roman literature, like Greek (see duBois 1982), was obsessed with the Other and found it in women and (enslaved or conquered) foreigners equally; in fact, in a move now familiar from postcolonial studies, these cultures not only saw the female as foreign but the foreign as female (see the discussion of Edward Said's *Orientalism* in Hartsock 1990: 161). Just as work on Rome can benefit from subaltern studies, so those performing the autopsy on the empires of the West may find a useful anatomical precedent in Rome.

The subject-verb-object model that is sometimes applied to sexuality (see Scott 1989: 86) has obvious applications in the analysis of imperialism, and I discuss both contexts (see chapter 3) in connection with the model of the structure of humor: joker-audience-butt (see also Richlin 1991b). Interestingly, though the structure remains fixed, the identity of each position can change much more readily for imperialism than for gender: Etruria-owns-Rome becomes Rome-owns-Etruria, while the bottom position in a model for gender *qua* gender is female (see de Lauretis 1987: 38). In Rome, as in other imperialist cultures, an upper-class woman could own a male slave or far outrank a lower-class male; for class, as for empire, the bottom position would then tend to be feminized. The problem lies in the structure more than in the identities—hence hierarchy is a more adequate term than patriarchy—but the identities have historically not been arbitrary, and patriarchy is not an inadequate term by any means (see Bordo 1990: 149).

Such a set of claims places this book alongside some—but not all—feminist work, and in opposition both to some postmodernist and to traditional work on gender in Greek and Roman cultures.[4] This is a current critical debate with larger implications for how we read the past; sides are drawn according to whether a critic believes it is possible to see sameness along with difference across history or cultures. In the history of sexuality, the sides have been aligned, respectively, with essentialism and social constructionism; "essentialism" in this context is the idea that there is an essential female (or male) nature, while social constructionism argues that gender is a product of social conditioning.

(This schema is needlessly binary, and a synthesis seems both possible and desirable; here I simply present these ideas as an introduction to the debate.) The controversy has been important to both feminist theory and gay history. The positions are far from monolithic: some essentialists are misogynistic (Aristotle), while others are radical feminists (Mary Daly, Adrienne Rich); some social constructionists are liberals (John Stuart Mill, NOW), working for reform, while others are radicals (Monique Wittig), dynamiting gender. In general, the historical abuses of essentialism have given it a bad name because of the many who have claimed that women are essentially *worse* than men (St. Paul, Aquinas, Freud), thereby justifying oppression. Foucauldians tend to be extreme social constructionists, arguing that gender varies locally from society to society; they avoid any evaluative analysis, which becomes impossible (see Foucault 1980: 97). But this poses obvious political problems. Yet "essentialist" has lately become the thing not to be. The point is, surely, that both essentialism and social constructionism can be used to support varying positions within the political spectrum. Each comes with drawbacks, but so does the rejection of either.[5]

An ongoing dialogue within the feminist camp has explored the pros and cons of each stance. If we agree that there is no such thing as male or female, then how do we explain crimes regularly committed by men against women? How can we explain the recurrence of misogyny in unrelated cultures? How can we notice misogyny at all? But if we were to agree that male and female are ineluctable categories, then how will social change be possible? Or if we talk about "women," who is "we," and what women? This debate can lapse into Olympian heartlessness, as in Gayatri Spivak's grudging "strategic essentialism" (1988), or in the exhortation to "risk essentialism" (see Fuss 1989). Who is risking what? In the context of postmodernism, theorists risk embarrassment if they posit that a class of women exists. The risk is easily seen to be more real for the theorists than for the women. The battles of the academy hardly touch the lives of their putative objects, of whom it might be said, as of the countrymen of Yeats' Irish airman, "No likely end could bring them loss / Or leave them happier than before." In the context of color, though, theorists erase difference when they posit a class of women; academic women must reconcile theory with difference, the class of women with solidarity among women.[6] As is true for all academics, the material (political, ethical) implications of the theory we generate are always with us. What we *can* do is produce sound theory that is designed to mesh with action.

Feminist history, then, is an ethical history, one that tries not only to take gender into account but to create consciousness of the material reality of oppression. As has been amply noted, this can put feminism and Foucault at cross purposes, just as it can place women of color at odds with postmodernist theory in general. Feminism has the goal of social change; Foucauldian scholarship tends to lose its social agenda, winding up in positions of nihilism or of contemplation of the text.[7]

How does *The Garden of Priapus* fit into this set of political and intellectual concerns? It can be described as fundamentally essentialist and materialist in its assumptions. It is essentialist in its claim that elements of Roman culture bear a noncoincidental resemblance to similar phenomena in other cultures. It is materialist in its claim that these elements existed as such—not just in my subjective view or in the texts that fossilize them—and affected the lives of real Romans.

Some essentialism is necessary to cross-cultural and transhistorical models (Bordo 1990; Janan 1991). A common Foucauldian claim is for the local peculiarity of each culture; but I would argue that, for example, the *Priapea* shares significant features with the *National Lampoon.* I have throughout this study adduced comparable ethnographic material from cultures widely scattered across space and time. I believe that these phenomena recur, together with similar social and political structures, just as the chemical elements recur in the physical world. Their essence does not make them immutable or omnipresent. I am claiming not that Roman sexual practices were identical with modern ones but that the definitions of masculinity constructed within Roman culture recur, as does the Roman definition of empire. This cannot be explained by means of constructionism (see Gilmore 1990).

Materialism, even positivism, is necessary to any account of oppression. A common postmodernist claim is for the basic unknowableness of events; but I believe it is possible to trace connections between the texts and real events as Roman people lived them, and I have tried to do so (see esp. Appendixes 1 and 2). Political analysis is not possible without such an axiom (see Bordo 1990: 144; Hartsock 1990: 171), nor can experience be accounted for otherwise. The labor of history is to map a hyperbola, approximating the reality it can never touch (see Richlin 1990). The very subjectivity of slaves, women, and various Others can only be extrapolated, but it is nonetheless to be sought after. Roman culture involved real oppression and suffering, which can be deduced from the texts with reasonable certainty—for example, from accounts of the punishments for adulterers (flogging, rape, mutilation, death), or the infibulation of slaves (which involved a pin through the foreskin), or from invective against old women, foreigners, and passive male homosexuals.

Thus *The Garden of Priapus* runs counter to many postmodernist tenets. Although it shares with Foucauldian work a focus on the power inherent in discourse, its gender-based analysis is not found in Foucault and only patchily in the new Foucauldian work on Greek and Roman sexuality. In an oddly similar way it also runs counter to the ideology of the field of Classics itself, which resolutely claims to be apolitical. In general, feminist analyses of sexuality in antiquity have asked different questions and come up with different answers from those of both Foucauldians and mainstream classicists.

Feminist Work Within Classics

As a feminist work within Classics, *The Garden of Priapus* stands on embattled ground. Indeed, the advances of feminist scholarship throughout the academy are somewhat illusory; when I look outside my own field with admiration, I soon recognize the same old problems (see Aisenberg and Harrington 1988, Jardine 1987). The percentage of women in the field grows, but slowly, and the percentage of feminists grows at an even slower rate, and not at institutions that nurture research. Moreover, like women themselves, the study of women and gender has never played a central role in Classics; the field "Women in Antiquity" is still considered a subfield, and little systematic mainstreaming has taken place.[8]

Nonetheless, a substantial body of scholarship has been generated (for surveys, see: Culham 1986; Skinner 1986, 1987a; and Fantham 1986). Not all this work is explicitly feminist, and still less of it utilizes feminist theory, but it does serve two solidly feminist ends: the recovery of the realities of ancient women's lived experience and the feminist critique of ancient texts (most of which are male-authored). Like feminist scholarship in general, this work has an explicit agenda. It is activist in that it seeks to change what it can in our own culture—the college curriculum, the classroom experience of students, common beliefs about history. It is revisionist in that it seeks to make ancient women visible and to question the traditional canon; indeed, the most recent debate in the field concerns the value of using literary texts at all in the struggle to find ancient women (*Helios* 17.2 [1990]). It is materialist in its insistence that there *was* a reality that the few and biased texts we have veil from our eager view, and that we need to learn about the conditions of ancient women's lives. And it is the product of women who have been activists in their lives as well as in their scholarship, many involved in the Women's Classical Caucus of the American Philological Association—another (not very) muted group within a patriarchy.

Despite reactions from the field at large ranging from bemused to hostile (see Skinner 1987b), the stream of publications increases. I would like to make special mention of Judith Hallett's *Fathers and Daughters in Roman Society* (1984), Eva Keuls' *The Reign of the Phallus* (1985), Page duBois' *Sowing the Body* (1988), Suzanne Dixon's *The Roman Mother* (1988), Jane Snyder's *The Woman and the Lyre* (1989), and the many articles of Marilyn Skinner as of particular interest to the student of Greek and Roman gender. I list them (and wish I had room for many more) especially because this work is too little known outside of Classics, despite general interest in gender in Greece and Rome; although historians both of women and of culture like to use Greek and Roman cultures (usually lumped together as "antiquity") as *terminus post quem* in arguments about the persistence of norms, they tend to be unaware of the feminists who write within the field of Classics. Feminists generally, it is true, have been suspicious of Classics as an especially "old boy" field. Thus feminist classicists have felt the pressure of conflicting loyalties, caught between a field that deplores their politics and a politics that deplores their field (see Skinner 1985, 1986, 1987a; Hallett 1985).

The Garden of Priapus takes its place in the field of Women in Antiquity through its analysis of the sexual attitudes of Roman males, for the nature of the extant texts makes direct consideration of the construction of female sexuality highly problematic (but see Richlin 1984, forthcoming; Hallett 1989). The book includes an extensive treatment of the Roman concept of female beauty and the objectification of both women and boys (see chapter 2), along with a section on the realities of adultery at Rome (see appendix 1). Moreover, the book represents a major departure from the way classicists have traditionally approached texts like Juvenal's sixth satire (against women), which basically had been to use them as direct evidence for what Roman women were like. Most of all, this book considers the implications of the ideological construction of Roman male sexuality for nondominant Romans: women, slaves, foreigners, boys—the penetrated.

Philology, the New Historicism, and the Foucauldian Theory of Sexuality in Antiquity

Mainstream classicists have continued to be suspicious of theory of any kind, maintaining the claim to have no political agenda. Work of this kind first pushed me down the perilous path of theory, as I read whole studies of Priapic poetry that asked only about whether it was derived from Archilochus and never commented on the content. It was the analysis of this content that I thought would be recognized as the book's major contribution. Instead, it was greeted with comments like this: "Though R. suggests that her approach is a valid and promising direction for classical philology (p. ix), its essential preoccupation with moral judgement renders it inapplicable to that field" (Kay 1985).

At first, comments of this sort looked to me like a simple inability to recognize feminism; indeed, it has been a common practice within Classics to assign feminist books to reviewers who know nothing about feminism in order to achieve a more objective reading. In fact, however, this reviewer has pointed to the exact location of the split between feminist and some other approaches. Philology agrees with Mr. Sensible that "we go to the Porch and the Academy to be spectators, not partisans." Curiously, for a group that would agree with Allan Bloom that reading Plato makes men better (i.e., moral), philologists are reluctant to ask any political (i.e., moral) questions *about* Plato—I suppose because it makes Plato look worse. I need hardly note that this amounts to partisanship by omission. Feminists, as we have seen, are committed partisans and routinely ask political questions about Plato. Thus, the "preoccupation with moral judgement" (e.g., asking what are the social implications of worshiping a personified phallus) was basic to the book; defining such questions as "inapplicable" to Classics depends on who is defining Classics. Naming is a powerful prerogative. In this way positivist scholars (especially those working in England), when they have glanced at Greek and Roman gender and sexuality, have attempted to define feminist work out of existence, along with the questions such work raises.

Ironically, Foucault's work on gender in antiquity, far better known than that of the theory-spurning positivists within Classics, winds up in more or less the same position theirs does, namely, with Mr. Sensible: women are in their proper place and antihierarchical value judgments are avoided. These phenomena accordingly recur in the work of two groups heavily influenced by Foucault: the New Historicists and the constructionist historians of Greek and Roman sexuality.

The New Historicism replicates Foucault's exclusion of the political analysis of gender and his rejection of moral judgment. Yet there is a certain overlap between New Historicist and feminist praxis. A recent listing of the assumptions of the New Historicism (Veeser 1989: xi) includes the following:

- that every expressive act is embedded in a network of material practices [Louis Montrose's "the historicity of texts," 1989: 20];
- that every act of unmasking, critique, and opposition uses the tools it condemns and risks falling prey to the practice it exposes;
- that no discourse . . . gives access to unchanging truths nor expresses inalterable human nature [Montrose's "the textuality of history"].

The first principle is clearly in keeping with what feminist scholars do and is partly subsumed by the women's movement slogan "the personal is political." The second principle repeats Audre Lorde's axiom "the master's tools will never dismantle the master's house" (1984), although she was suggesting that we might try to find or invent other tools and get that house dismantled, whereas the New Historicism often contents itself with contemplating its tools and groaning—epistemologoskepsis. The third principle, however, precludes much feminist work, since what it means in practice is that what actually happened is inaccessible to us, and that each historical enclave is allowed to have its own set of rules, largely in order to compare it favorably with the New Historicists' bugbear, capitalism. (New Historicists cluster in modern and early modern Europe and America.) Anything that occurred before the modern era must be better, also (paradoxically) not capable of assessment by current standards. There is no place here for moral judgment or questions of real experience; historians of women, colonialism, and the Third World are out of luck.[9] The way lies open for a treatment of the Watts riots as well-wrought urn. Meanwhile, just as Foucault and the philologists elide feminist work, so here again work by feminist critics disappears, even where New Historicists reinvent it (Newton 1988; Richlin 1991c).

The late 1980s has seen a burst of work on the construction of sexuality in Greek and Roman cultures, much of it influenced by Foucault and following New Historicist patterns (Winkler 1990; Halperin 1990; Halperin, Winkler, and Zeitlin 1990; Brown 1988; Konstan and Nussbaum 1990; both Winkler and Zeitlin had previously published work in the New Historicist journal *Representations*). The title of the collection *Before Sexuality,* as well as the title of Halperin's *One Hundred Years of Homosexuality,* let the reader know that we are here on familiar Foucauldian ground.[10] Both Winkler and Halperin devote a great deal of attention to the social constructionist/essentialist debate in an effort to show that the concept of "a homosexual" did not exist in "ancient" society (see esp. Halperin 1990: 8, 17–40; Winkler 1990: 17–23). Yet in so doing, as Micaela Janan has pointed out (1991), they often resort to cross-cultural comparisons (e.g., to Melanesian initiation rites), a move that would be invalid if each cultural locus were indeed unique. As might by now be expected, this Foucauldian work tends to look away from feminist writing on gender in antiquity, although it presents much that is of value to feminist scholars (see esp. Winkler 1990: 101–209; Halperin 1990: 113–51; also several pieces in Halperin et al. 1990), and Winkler at least sometimes writes from a feminist position.

But that position rests uneasily beside analyses of gender like Winkler's treatment of "men's ideologies" in "ancient societies" (1990: 6):

> The more we learn about comparable gender-segregated, pre-industrial societies, particularly in the Mediterranean area, the more it seems that most of men's observations and moral judgments about women and sex and so forth have minimal descriptive validity and are best understood as coffee-house talk, addressed to men themselves. Women, we should emphasize, in all their separate groupings by age, neighborhood, and class, may differ widely from each other and from community to community in the degree to which they obey, resist, or even notice the existence of such palaver as men indulge in when going through their bonding rituals.

This sounds good; let's take a look at two examples of this "palaver" from Rome, an ancient Mediterranean society:

> hic ego nu[nc f]utue formosa fo[r]ma puella
> laudata a multis, set lutus intus erat.
>
> Here I have now fuckid a gril beatiful too see,
> praised by many, but there was muck inside.
> [Pompeiian graffito, discussed on p. 82]

bidens amica Romuli senis memor
paratur, inter atra cuius inguina
latet iacente pantice abditus specus

A two-toothed mistress who remembers old Romulus
is ready, amidst whose dark loins
lies a cave hidden by a flaccid paunch
[section of a poem from the *Virgilian Appendix*, discussed on p. 115]

The poem, with its elevated style, resembles the misspelled graffito in its content, and both might be presumed to resemble the "coffeehouse talk" Winkler has in mind. It is long past the time when it should be necessary to reiterate that such ideology, which can be paralleled in antiquity in sources from Hesiod to Tertullian, affected women and tallied with women's material circumstances and cannot adequately be described as "addressed to men themselves." In a way these texts have a high "descriptive validity," in that they represent feelings that were present to men and women even when not voiced. It is highly misleading to build a model that puts this ideology into a delimited space which women had the option of ignoring (a rhetorical ploy, in fact, common among Roman writers; see chapter 1), for the coffeehouse contained its whole society, and the women had to live there, too.

Part of the problem is that Winkler is here thinking "Athens" and writing "ancient societies." Oddly for a group of classicists, the Foucauldians (like Foucault) tend to look away from Rome as they look away from women; although these scholars follow Foucault in using some Roman imperial sources, their usual topic or reference point is the culture of fifth-century B.C. Athens, to the degree that they leave Rome out of what they call "ancient" culture. At the same time, they combine the Foucauldian habit of bracketing off cultures with an explicit valorization of the studied culture, as opposed to our own. This is especially visible in Winkler's work, which blurs Athens into what he calls variously "ancient" or "Mediterranean" culture, positing its structural identity with modern "Mediterranean" culture and its opposition (and superiority) to what he dubs "NATO" culture (1990: 13; see also 27, 73). Such a tendency to accentuate the positive, at least elsewhere and in the past, contrasts sharply with the tendency in *The Garden of Priapus* to focus on the violence of sexual politics in both ancient and modern societies.

But that focus should perform an important service of reminding, and I hope the book's reissue will make that happen. The experience of the penetrated, especially of the *cinaedus* (adult male passive homosexual), always obscure, has disappeared in the Foucauldian effort to redefine ancient sexuality. (It is thought-provoking that penetration and writing seem to be interdependent.) Oppression vanishes along with the transhistorical framework (see Janan 1991; Bordo 1990). Marilyn Skinner has pointed out to me that phallic thinking plagued Roman men, like Catullus, with much-evidenced anxiety. Though I consider this later (see chapters 3 and 6), my emphasis here is on the fact that phallic thinking affected others besides the thinkers, and that those others had a real existence which we can try to discern if only by reflected light (see Boswell 1980): Roman women had to live in a world in which Juvenal's sixth satire was funny, and Juvenal's second satire pretty much rules out the possibility that life was happy for the Roman berdache.[11] Still, Winkler's formulation of invective against *cinaedi* as the "bluff" of male groups does at least balance what might be seen as an excessive literal-mindedness or bipolarity in *The Garden of Priapus.* I hope those interested in gay history will read this book in conjunction with those by Winkler, Halperin, and Boswell.

Through the Garden and Back

Since writing *The Garden of Priapus,* I have focused more directly on Roman women (Richlin 1984, 1991b, 1992, forthcoming). One thing I would add to the book would be a consideration of the questions of women's humor and the possibility of subversive humor (now treated, for Roman women, in Richlin 1992). The question of whether there can be subversive humor is part of the larger question of whether there can be subversive discourse, which receives a shaky but repeated "yes" in the Foucauldian school. Yet, on the one hand, Foucault wound up arguing that power infuses everything, so that the oppressed, oppressors, and chains are all codependent (e.g., 1980: 95–98)—an idea incongruent with feminist political critique, almost Sadeian.[12] On the other hand, the New Historicists find shifting complexities in everything, so there is a kind of free-floating subversion (see critique in Fish 1989). This constitutes a kind of suppression-by-acclamation of the experience of the oppressed. And what is subversion, anyway? Does it change anything? It is indeed hard to see how an oppressed group, which by definition has less power, could transform anything without a whole new language—a problem often discussed within feminism (see Lorde 1984, Jehlen 1981; see also Hebdige 1979). Political gains have been made by means of confrontation, not by inverted commas. While some discourse may be suited to transcending patriarchy, I doubt that humor is one of them (pace Walker 1988)—certainly not in Rome.

With the collection *Pornography and Representation in Greece and Rome,* I have continued to pursue an interest in the theory of the pornographic, which has been one of the more challenging areas of recent critical theory (see bibliography in Richlin 1991a). Another thing I would add to *The Garden of Priapus* if I could would be an integration of this vast body of theory into the book as a whole; in particular, recent work on the structure of fantasy would be useful in theorizing the positions of the joke teller, his audience, and their object. The model set up by Laplanche and Pontalis postulates an oscillation among the positions of subject/verb/object, so that part of the pleasure of the joke to teller and audience would be an imagined sharing of the experience of the object.[13] According to the terms I set out later (see chapters 1 and 3), this would imply a pleasure not only in staining but in being stained—temporarily (see p. 59). In turn, the book's connection of sexuality with aggression provides material for the feminist debate on the nature of the pornographic. A historical perspective might be useful to feminist theorists (cf. Hoff 1989), especially in countering the tendency to associate pornography with the modern. Finally, several of the pieces in *Pornography and Representation in Greece and Rome* include material highly pertinent to *The Garden of Priapus,* especially Henry on Athenaeus, Joshel on the rape of Lucretia and Verginia in Roman ideology, Myerowitz on Roman erotic art, and Parker on erotic handbooks.

The world of Foucault and the New Historicists is the world in which feminists live; this is increasingly becoming the kind of history we all write. We think in the same terms even when we disagree. The mantle of privilege has fallen from the elite text; methods and issues are borrowed from anthropology; the goal is a holistic view of a given society, seeking subjectivity in bottom as well as top positions; and societies are seen in their relation to other societies. Thus *The Garden of Priapus,* though it originated in a different critical space from Foucauldian work, exhibits some similar traits, a true Foucauldian child of its time (what Skinner 1986 calls "postclassicist"). I accept wholeheartedly the approach that melds anthropology with history; I define humor as a discourse of power; I view texts as artifacts; I am seeking to piece together social norms by juxtaposing different kinds of evidence that seem to describe different realities, and I am examining what produces those disparities.

Indeed, I share the spirit of fascinated exploration less problematically evinced by the work of Winkler et al. Despite my Catonian finger-shaking, I have to admit I like Roman culture, which has been my imaginary home for so long. The experience of putting together the additions to this volume reminded me of what delighted me when I first wrote the book: rummaging around in anecdote collections and fragments—the Roman lumber room—which I still love; construing Roman satire in a social context; juxtaposing graffiti and the speeches of the forum; reading Lucilius as an author rather than an antecedent; reading Horace without kid gloves; and reading the parts of Juvenal and Catullus that used to be left out. This seemed to me not only delightful but important; I wanted so much to say, "Look what's here!" I hope the publication of the book in a paperback edition will make it available to those I most wanted to reach—the students.

Where I differ from Foucauldian and New Historicist scholars, as well as from some postcolonial scholars, is in my focus on material that implies sameness rather than otherness, continuity rather than disjunction, universality rather than social construction. Mr. Sensible—with his denial of systems and his decorative, meditative, secluded philosophy—seems to me to have a cold heart;

I go to the Academy to be a partisan, not a spectator. Still the most surprising thing to me about *The Garden of Priapus* is the concluding synthesis (see pp. 210–13). Written without any awareness of postmodernist theory, indeed, formed largely by the experience of teaching Roman law from the standpoint of Bakunin, it raises the questions "of what determines a hierarchy, whether a non-hierarchical structure is possible, and whether humor is possible without a hierarchy. . . ." It concludes:

> The figures who evoked Priapus' most savage threats and most disgusted invective—the ugly woman, the randy *vetula* [old woman], the weak *cinaedus,* the foreigner—no longer find Priapus funny; nor can Priapus be accepted as a model any more. Male and female cannot remain polar opposites. The *vetula* who says "I am not that" perhaps will found another mode, a new world without the comparative degree, in which laughter and cruelty cannot cooperate.

Nothing I have read since writing those lines make me want to change them.

The issues in this book about humor are very serious. I wrote this book on campuses where gang rape and assaults on women are common occurrences. A friend of mine was raped and murdered the year after it was published. Cultures where rape is a joke are cultures that foster rape. We need to know our history and our present.

I began the book without politics and finished it a feminist in principle; the experience of having written the book completed the process, so that now I am a feminist in practice. Like Alice in the garden of Priapus, I gained a firsthand knowledge of phallogocentrism. It has been an interesting trip. To my companions and teachers on the road I owe deep thanks; their courage has been my inspiration.

Notes

Many thanks to Judith Hallett, Sandra Joshel, Marilyn Skinner, and especially to Diana Robin for their critical reading of this essay, with which I am sure each of them will still disagree on many points. I also benefited from the insights of David Fredrick in his work-in-progress on Roman gender.

Portions of this introduction appear in slightly different form in Richlin 1991c.

1. For further discussion and additional sources, see Halperin 1990: 63–64; see also duBois 1988: 2, 189–90; and especially Henry 1991, who critiques Foucault in the context of feminist work on the pornographic in Greek and Roman cultures.

2. Foucault's interview in *Raritan* (1985b) bears further witness to his tendency to blur Rome into Greece (e.g., his apparent identification of Seneca as Greek, 3); and to the huge gaps in Foucault's knowledge of Greek and Roman culture (e.g., his response that from the fourth century B.C. to the second century A.D. "there is hardly any conception of love which would have been qualified to represent . . . experiences of madness or of great amorous passion"—news to readers of the Greek Anthology, Apollonius Rhodius, Catullus, Vergil, and so on; he attributes the "emergence of the amorous delirium" to Ovid, 6). This interview is full of statements like "the question

of style was central to experience in antiquity" (2). Whose experience? What is "antiquity"? In the confines of this endnote I suggest that Foucault's work on antiquity is so ill-informed that it is not really worth reading.

3. For a strong statement, see hooks 1984; also Moraga 1986, especially on the "simultaneity of oppression" (180, 187, tracing the idea back to the Combahee River Collective Statement [April 1977]); see also Brooks-Higginbotham 1989.

4. I see my arguments here as close to those forcefully put by Bordo 1990, Hartsock 1990, and Pierce 1991. For the hazards of postmodernism in anthropology, see Mascia-Lees et al. 1989. For surveys of feminism and the essentialist/constructionist debate, see Tong 1989; de Lauretis 1990c. For a lucid overview of the debate in gay history as it applies to the study of ancient sexuality, see Boswell 1990; see also the discussion in Halperin 1990: 41–53. On radical feminist constructionism, see Butler 1990: 1–34; see also de Lauretis 1990b.

5. This point is briefly stated by Fuss 1989: 20, but she disappointingly devotes her extended discussion of essentialism largely to a demonstration that all constructionist positions entail a degree of essentialism. For advocacy of a " 'resistance postmodernism' that has refused to abandon the project of emancipation or to allow for the easy dismissal of systems and totalities," see Ebert 1991.

6. See Schor 1989: 57–58, de Lauretis 1990a, hooks 1984: 43–65, Lugones 1991, Moraga 1986; see also Haraway 1990 on "affinity" as a combining principle.

7. For feminist critiques of Foucault, see Martin 1988; de Lauretis 1987: 12–18, 34–38; and Hartsock 1990; see also Spiegel 1989. On women of color and postmodernism, see Christian 1988. For a defense of the political usefulness of Foucault's theories, see Hekman 1990: 175–90 (not, to me, cogent). For an attempt at balance between critique and appropriation, see Diamond and Quinby 1988: ix–xx.

8. As the term is used in women's studies, "mainstreaming" denotes efforts to take the topic of "women and . . ." out of curricular ghettoes and integrate issues of class, race, and gender in the curriculum as a whole—even to problematize the epistemology that formed the curriculum in the first place. See, e.g., O'Barr 1989; on the field of history, see Scott 1989: 83–84. For a dramatic demonstration of the nonintegration of feminism into Classics graduate departments, one need only consult the lists of doctoral dissertations in the United States and Canada published in the *Newsletter* of the American Philological Association; in 1989–90, 53 percent of Classics dissertations were written by women, 12.8 percent were directed by women, and only one dissertation had the word "woman" or "feminine" in the title or indicated any investigation of gender.

9. See Porter 1990 on Greenblatt's erasure of the existence of the Algonkian Indians apart from texts about them, an example of what she dubs "Colonialist Formalism"—the application of formalist principles to the social text. According to Graff (1989: 173), the "refusal to totalize or speak for the other [does] not necessarily confer political innocence"; see Lugones 1991 on the use of disclaimers by white feminists to avoid dealing with difference.

10. See Halperin et al. 1990: 3–7, which poses—without resolving—the question of whether there was sexuality in antiquity.

11. On the berdache, see Williams 1986; the word is used of males in Native American cultures who adopted androgynous gender roles. Williams demonstrates that gender crossing in Native American societies was generally accepted, thereby reminding me that all cultures are not identical with Rome. See Bartky 1990: 7, 42, on the political function of "pessimism."

12. Foucault does have feminist fans even on this point; e.g., Diamond and Quinby (1988: xi) see possibilities in Foucault's idea of "reverse discourse," while Walkowitz 1989 claims a Foucauldian model of power for her work-in-progress. For critiques see

Lentricchia 1989: 235–40; Graff 1989: 169; see also Nelson 1987; and see sources cited in note 7.

13. For Laplanche and Pontalis—and studies branching off from their work and related work—see Burgin et al. 1986; for an application to Ovid, see Richlin 1991b.

Bibliography

Aisenberg, Nadya, and Mona Harrington. 1988. *Women of Academe: Outsiders in the Sacred Grove.* Amherst: The University of Massachusetts Press.

Bartky, Sandra Lee. 1990. *Femininity and Domination: Studies in the Phenomenology of Oppression.* New York: Routledge.

Bordo, Susan. 1990. "Feminism, Postmodernism, and Gender-Scepticism." In *Feminism/Postmodernism,* ed. Linda J. Nicholson: 133–56. New York: Routledge.

Boswell, John. 1980. *Christianity, Social Tolerance, and Homosexuality.* Chicago: The University of Chicago Press.

———. 1990. "Concepts, Experience, and Sexuality." *differences* 2.1: 67–87.

Brooks-Higginbotham, Evelyn. 1989. "The Problem of Race in Women's History." In *Coming to Terms,* ed. Elizabeth Weed: 122–33. New York: Routledge.

Brown, Peter. 1988. *The Body and Society: Men, Women and Sexual Renunciation in Early Christianity.* New York: Columbia University Press.

Burgin, Victor, James Donald, and Cora Kaplan, eds. 1986. *Formations of Fantasy.* London: Methuen.

Butler, Judith. 1990. *Gender Trouble: Feminism and the Subversion of Identity.* New York: Routledge.

Christian, Barbara. 1988. "The Race for Theory." *Feminist Studies* 14.1: 67–80.

Culham, Phyllis. 1986. "Ten Years After Pomeroy: Studies of the Image and Reality of Women in Antiquity." *Helios* 13: 9–30.

de Lauretis, Teresa. 1987. *Technologies of Gender.* Bloomington: Indiana University Press.

———. 1990a. "Feminism and Its Differences." *Pacific Coast Philology* 25.1–2: 24–30.

———. 1990b. "Eccentric Subjects: Feminist Theory and Historical Consciousness." *Feminist Studies* 16: 115–50.

———. 1990c. "Upping the Anti (sic) in Feminist Theory." In *Conflicts in Feminism,* ed. Marianne Hirsch and Evelyn Fox Keller: 255–70. New York: Routledge.

Diamond, Irene, and Lee Quinby, eds. 1988. *Feminism & Foucault: Reflections on Resistance.* Boston: Northeastern University Press.

Dixon, Suzanne. 1988. *The Roman Mother.* Norman: Oklahoma University Press.

duBois, Page. 1982. *Centaurs and Amazons: Women and the Prehistory of the Great Chain of Being.* Ann Arbor: University of Michigan Press.

———. 1988. *Sowing the Body: Psychoanalysis and Ancient Representations of Women.* Chicago: The University of Chicago Press.

Ebert, Teresa L. 1991. "Postmodernism's Infinite Variety." Review of *Feminism/Postmodernism,* ed. Linda J. Nicholson. *The Women's Review of Books* 8.4: 24–25.

Fantham, Elaine. 1986. "Women in Antiquity: A Selective (and Subjective) Survey, 1979–84." *Echos du Monde Classique* 30: 1–24.

Fish, Stanley. 1989. "Commentary: The Young and the Restless." In *The New Historicism,* ed. H. Aram Veeser: 303–16. New York: Routledge.

Foucault, Michel. 1978. *The History of Sexuality,* trans. Robert Hurley. New York: Random House [= vol. 1].

———. 1980. *Power/Knowledge,* trans. Colin Gordon et al. New York: Pantheon.

———. 1985a. *The Use of Pleasure,* trans. Robert Hurley. New York: Random House [= *The History of Sexuality,* vol. 2].

———. 1985b. "Final Interview." *Raritan* 5.1: 1–13.

———. 1986. *The Care of the Self,* trans. Robert Hurley. New York: Random House [= *The History of Sexuality,* vol. 3].

Fuss, Diana. 1989. *Essentially Speaking: Feminism, Nature and Difference.* New York: Routledge.

Geertz, Clifford. 1973. "Thick Description: Toward an Interpretive Theory of Culture." In his *Interpretation of Cultures:* 3–30. New York: Basic Books.

Gilmore, David D. 1990. *Manhood in the Making.* New Haven: Yale University Press.

Graff, Gerald. 1989. "Co-optation." In *The New Historicism,* ed. H. Aram Veeser: 168–81. New York: Routledge.

Hallett, Judith P. 1984. *Fathers and Daughters in Roman Society: Women and the Elite Family.* Princeton, N.J.: Princeton University Press.

———. 1985. "Buzzing of a Confirmed Gadfly." *Helios* 12: 23–37.

———. 1989. "Female Homoeroticism and the Denial of Roman Reality in Latin Literature." *Yale Journal of Criticism* 3: 209–27.

Halperin, David M. 1990. *One Hundred Years of Homosexuality.* New York: Routledge.

Halperin, David M., John J. Winkler, and Froma I. Zeitlin, eds. 1990. *Before Sexuality: The Construction of Erotic Experience in the Ancient Greek World.* Princeton, N.J.: Princeton University Press.

Haraway, Donna. 1990. "A Manifesto for Cyborgs: Science, Technology, and Socialist Feminism in the 1980s." In *Feminism/Postmodernism,* ed. Linda J. Nicholson: 190–233. New York: Routledge.

Hartsock, Nancy. 1990. "Foucault on Power: A Theory for Women?" In *Feminism/Postmodernism,* ed. Linda J. Nicholson: 157–75. New York: Routledge.

Hebdige, Dick. 1979. *Subculture: The Meaning of Style.* London: Methuen.

Hekman, Susan J. 1990. *Gender and Knowledge: Elements of a Postmodern Feminism.* Boston: Northeastern University Press.

Henry, Madeleine. 1991. "The Edible Woman: Athenaeus' Concept of the Pornographic." In *Pornography and Representation in Greece and Rome,* ed. Amy Richlin: 250–68. New York: Oxford University Press.

Hoff, Joan. 1989. "Why Is There No History of Pornography?" In *For Adult Users Only: The Dilemma of Violent Pornography,* ed. Susan Gubar and Joan Hoff: 17–46. Bloomington: Indiana University Press.

hooks, bell. 1984. *Feminist Theory from Margin to Center.* Boston: South End Press.

Janan, Micaela. 1991. Review of David M. Halperin, *One Hundred Years of Homosexuality. Women's Classical Caucus Newsletter* 16.2.

Jardine, Alice. 1987. "Men in Feminism: Odor di Uomo or Compagnons de Route?" In *Men in Feminism,* ed. Alice Jardine and Paul Smith: 54–61. New York: Methuen.

Jehlen, Myra. 1981. "Archimedes and the Paradox of Feminist Criticism." *Signs* 6: 575–601.

Joshel, Sandra R. 1991. "The Body Female and the Body Politic: Livy's Lucretia and Verginia." In *Pornography and Representation in Greece and Rome,* ed. Amy Richlin: 112–30. New York: Oxford University Press.

Kay, N. 1985. "Roman Obscenity." *Classical Review* n.s. 35.2: 308–10.

Keuls, Eva. 1985. *The Reign of the Phallus.* New York: Harper.

Konstan, David, and Martha Nussbaum, eds. 1990. *Sexuality in Greek and Roman Society.* Special issue of *differences* (2.1).

Lentricchia, Frank. 1989. "Foucault's Legacy—A New Historicism?" In *The New Historicism,* ed. H. Aram Veeser: 231–42. New York: Routledge. Excerpted from his *Ariel and the Police* (Madison: University of Wisconsin Press, 1988: 86–102).

Lerner, Gerda. 1986. *The Creation of Patriarchy*. New York: Oxford University Press.
Lewis, C. S. 1958[1933]. *The Pilgrim's Regress*. Grand Rapids, Mich.: Wm. B. Eerdmans.
Lloyd, G. E. R. 1990. *Demystifying Mentalities*. Cambridge: Cambridge University Press.
Lorde, Audre. 1984. "The Master's Tools Will Never Dismantle the Master's House." In her *Sister Outsider:* 110–13. Trumansburg, N.Y.: The Crossing Press.
Lugones, María C. 1991. "On the Logic of Pluralist Feminism." In *Feminist Ethics,* ed. Claudia Card: 35–44. Lawrence: University Press of Kansas.
Martin, Biddy. 1988. "Feminism, Criticism, and Foucault." In *Feminism & Foucault: Reflections on Resistance,* ed. Irene Diamond and Lee Quinby: 3–19. Boston: Northeastern University Press.
Mascia-Lees, Frances, Patricia Sharpe, and Colleen Ballerino Cohen. 1989. "The Postmodernist Turn in Anthropology: Cautions from a Feminist Perspective." *Signs* 15: 7–33.
Montrose, Louis A. 1989. "Professing the Renaissance: The Poetics and Politics of Culture." In *The New Historicism,* ed. H. Aram Veeser: 15–36. New York: Routledge.
Moraga, Cherríe. 1986. "From a Long Line of Vendidas: Chicanas and Feminism." In *Feminist Studies/Critical Studies,* ed. Teresa de Lauretis: 173–90. Bloomington: Indiana University Press.
Myerowitz, Molly. 1991. "The Domestication of Desire: Ovid's *Parva Tabella* and the Theater of Love." In *Pornography and Representation in Greece and Rome,* ed. Amy Richlin: 131–57. New York: Oxford University Press.
Nelson, Cary. 1987. "Men, Feminism: The Materiality of Discourse." In *Men in Feminism,* ed. Alice Jardine and Paul Smith: 153–72. New York: Methuen.
Newton, Judith Lowder. 1988. "History as Usual? Feminism and the 'New Historicism.' " *Cultural Critique* 9: 87–121.
O'Barr, Jean F., ed. 1989. *Women and a New Academy: Gender and Cultural Contexts.* Madison: University of Wisconsin Press.
Parker, Holt N. 1991. "Love's Body Anatomized: The Ancient Erotic Handbooks and the Rhetoric of Sexuality." In *Pornography and Representation in Greece and Rome,* ed. Amy Richlin: 90–111. New York: Oxford University Press.
Pierce, Christine. 1991. "Postmodernism and Other Skepticisms." In *Feminist Ethics,* ed. Claudia Card: 60–77. Lawrence: University Press of Kansas.
Porter, Carolyn. 1990. "History and Literature: 'After the New Historicism.' " *New Literary History* 21: 253–72.
Richlin, Amy. 1984. "Invective against Women in Roman Satire." *Arethusa* 17.1: 67–80.
———. 1990. "Hijacking the Palladion." *Helios* 17.2: 175–85.
———, ed. 1991a. *Pornography and Representation in Greece and Rome.* New York: Oxford University Press.
———. 1991b. "Reading Ovid's Rapes." In Richlin 1991a: 158–79.
———. 1991c. "Zeus and Metis: Foucault, Feminism, Classics." *Helios* 18.2: 1–21.
———. 1992. "Julia's Jokes, Galla Placidia, and the Roman Use of Women as Political Icons." In *Stereotypes of Women in Power: Historical Perspectives and Revisionist Views,* ed. Barbara Garlick, Pauline Allen, and Suzanne Dixon: 65–91. Westport, Conn.: Greenwood Press.
———. Forthcoming. "Making Up a Woman: The Face of Roman Gender." In *The Female Head,* ed. Wendy Doniger and Howard Eilberg-Schwartz.
Schor, Naomi. 1989. "Dreaming Dissymmetry: Barthes, Foucault, and Sexual Difference." In *Coming to Terms,* ed. Elizabeth Weed: 47–58. New York: Routledge.

Scott, Joan. 1989. "Gender: A Useful Category of Historical Analysis." In *Coming to Terms,* ed. Elizabeth Weed: 81–100. New York: Routledge.

Skinner, Marilyn. 1985. "Classical Studies vs. Women's Studies: *duo moi ta noemmata.*" *Helios* 12: 3–16.

———. 1986. "Rescuing Creusa: New Methodological Approaches to Women in Antiquity." *Helios* 13: 1–8.

———. 1987a. "Classical Studies, Patriarchy and Feminism: The View from 1986." *Women's Studies International Forum* 10: 181–86.

———. 1987b. "Des Bonnes Dames et Méchantes." *Classical Journal* 83: 69–74.

Snyder, Jane McIntosh. 1989. *The Woman and the Lyre: Women Writers in Classical Greece and Rome.* Carbondale: Southern Illinois University Press.

Spiegel, Gabrielle M. 1989. "History, Historicism, and the Social Logic of the Text in the Middle Ages." *Speculum* 64: 59–86.

Spivak, Gayatri. 1988. "Subaltern Studies: Deconstructing Historiography." In her *In Other Worlds:* 197–221. New York: Routledge.

Tong, Rosemarie. 1989. *Feminist Thought: A Comprehensive Introduction.* Boulder, Colo.: Westview Press.

Veeser, H. Aram. 1989. "Introduction." In *The New Historicism,* ed. H. Aram Veeser: ix–xvi. New York: Routledge.

Walker, Nancy A. 1988. *A Very Serious Thing: Women's Humor and American Culture.* Minneapolis: University of Minnesota Press.

Walkowitz, Judith [with Myra Jehlen and Bell Chevigny]. 1989. "Patrolling the Borders: Feminist Historiography and the New Historicism." *Radical History Review* 43: 23–43.

Williams, Walter L. 1986. *The Spirit and the Flesh: Sexual Diversity in American Indian Culture.* Boston: Beacon Press.

Winkler, John J. 1990. *The Constraints of Desire: The Anthropology of Sex and Gender in Ancient Greece.* New York: Routledge.

The Garden of Priapus

CHAPTER 1

Roman Concepts of Obscenity

In the course of this book the word *obscene* will be used many times, and the question immediately arises whether the Romans had a concept corresponding to that denoted by "obscene," and, if so, how it did or did not tally with the modern concept. "Obscenity" today includes explicitly sexual literature, visual arts, dress, and actions; sometimes it includes material that is merely suggestive, and usually it includes scatological material as well. The idea is that all this material ought not to be seen and that it is "dirty" or "perverse." Did the Romans feel that literature could be prurient—could excite sexual passion? If so, did they think this was bad or to be restricted? Did they have similar feelings about sexual words, objects, and actions?

In modern times literature on sexual topics is considered erotic if artistic and obscene if not, where artistry has implied the exclusion of certain words and images; the value of such literature has been the subject of violent debate and has fluctuated sharply in the present century.[1] Although the Romans seem to have drawn a similar kind of line—we read of writers of pornography who did not have the status of Roman literati[2]—it was in a different place. Form counted for a good deal: if an epigram was elegantly shaped and had some sort of point, it was art. This elegance is often the only difference between literature and graffiti. Martial, for example, whose epigrams are always beautifully made, juxtaposes epigrams on the most formal subjects—epitaphs, epithalamia, odes to the emperor—with epigrams whose content is crudely sexual. This cannot have been an offensive practice, since Martial's professed goal in life was to live as well as he could on patronage. Catullus provides a more sublime example of the same phenomenon: he makes explicit sexuality and crude invective into major components of his poetry, using this material to put the dark distances into his chiaroscuro.

Both these poets, as well as others who used sexual material in their works, were conscious that it had a special nature; such material is common in epigram, some lyric, satire, some drama, and in prose invective at all levels, and writers of these sorts of literature often comment on the content of their work and on the way they choose their words. The idea of "obscenity" was thus familiar to the Romans even if their definition and practical application of it were not the same as ours. The term *obscenum* itself had a strong religious sense, and this, as will be seen, may have promoted the special treatment of sexual material in Latin literature. The feeling that the material was special produced a convention of *apologiae* in poetry and a series of strictures on decorum in prose. The inhibition was strong enough to generate a charge in certain words, equivalent to the English "four-letter words," and an association of ideas of staining, wrongdoing, and ugliness with most sexual concepts.

Apologiae

The simplest *apologiae* were disclaimers—statements that, however obscene the subject matter of the work at hand, the author himself had sound morals. Many of these *apologiae* model themselves on Catullus 16, sometimes even quoting the lines that seem most pertinent: "nam castum esse decet pium poetam / ipsum, versiculos nihil necesse est," "for it is right for a pious poet to be chaste / himself, but there's no need for his little verses to be so" (5–6). Catullus, as will be seen, is not really making a straightforward defense here; but the pedestrian Martial (1.4, 11.15) and the egregious Pliny (*Ep*. 4.14) both appealed to these lines, apparently seriously, to excuse themselves and defend their personal lives. Martial begins his first book of epigrams with a fivefold introduction: first a lengthy prologue in prose (discussed below), then an introduction of himself (1.1), an address by the book to the reader (1.2), an address by the author to the book (1.3), and finally an ingratiating address to Domitian (1.4). This poem concludes (1.4.7–8):

innocuos censura potest permittere lusus:
lasciva est nobis pagina, vita proba.

Your censorship can permit innocent games;
my page is lascivious, my life upright.

Martial has a serious need to acknowledge the official moral position and to make a distinction between the fiction of his books and the reality of his own life. Similarly, at 11.15.11–13, after a glowing description of the bacchanalian surroundings proper to his book, he dissociates himself from the whole:

versus hos tamen esse tu memento
Saturnalicios, Apollinaris:
mores non habet hic meos libellus.

But do remember that these verses are
Saturnalian, Apollinaris;
this book does not have my morals.

And Pliny, who actually quotes Cat. 16.5–8, does so to lend authority to his argument that sober men of high political rank *(summos illos et gravissimos viros)* had, like him, written light verse. Both Martial and Pliny perceive their audiences as welcoming erotic verse but as needing to be reassured of the author's real respectability. The effect is to remove the erotic poetry itself as far from reality as possible.

This attitude is a naive one, the premise being that all literature is a factual account of the author's life. In fact the idea is common in Roman criticism, on the principle *talis oratio, qualis vita*.[3] This theory claims not that reading obscene literature influences mores for the worse but that an obscene way of life influences literary style for the worse. Explaining why the youth of the day are no good as orators, the elder Seneca says (*Controv.* 1, Intro. 8–9):

> Torpent ecce ingenia desidiosae iuventutis nec in unius honestae rei labore vigilatur; somnus languorque ac somno et languore turpior malarum rerum industria invasit animos: cantandi saltandique obscena studia effeminatos tenent, [et] capillum frangere et ad muliebres blanditias extenuare vocem, mollitia corporis certare cum feminis et inmundissimis se excolere munditiis nostrorum adulescentium specimen est. Quis aequalium vestrorum quid dicam satis ingeniosus, satis studiosus, immo quis satis vir est? Emolliti enervesque quod nati sunt in vita manent, expugnatores alienae pudicitiae, neglegentes suae.

> Look, the intellects of our lazy youth are asleep, nor do they wake up for the exercise of a single respectable occupation; slumber and languor and, what is more disgusting than slumber and languor, the pursuit of wicked things has invaded their spirits: the obscene pursuit of singing and dancing keeps them effeminate, and curling the hair and shrilling the voice into womanish cajoleries, competing with women in the softness of the body and cultivating themselves with the foulest elegances, that is the pattern of our young men. Who of your agemates is what I might call intellectual enough, diligent enough, rather, who is enough of a man? Softened up and emasculate as they were born they remain all their lives, laying siege to other people's chastity, careless of their own.

The *obscena studia* of singing and dancing, depilation, and high or soft voices, as well as bisexual promiscuity, were standard accusations made by invective against effeminate homosexuals; here, as elsewhere, these men debauch others' wives *(alienae pudicitiae)* and also allow themselves to be used as women *(suae)*. Such ambivalence and external attributes also characterize the effeminate literati of Persius 1, who are made by the satirist to typify the style of poetry he deplores.

The elder Seneca blames the style of life he deems effeminate for a decline he perceives in the quality of oratory; interestingly enough, the younger Seneca, discoursing in the same vein, took as a notorious example of the connection between effeminacy in life and in literary style Maecenas, a contemporary of the elder Seneca (*Ep.* 114.4, 6):

> quomodo Maecenas vixerit notius est quam ut narrari nunc debeat, quomodo ambulaverit, quam delicatus fuerit, quam cupierit videri, quam vitia sua latere noluerit. quid ergo? non oratio eius aeque soluta est quam ipse discinctus? non tam insignita illius verba sunt quam cultus, quam comitatus, quam domus, quam uxor? magni vir ingenii fuerat, si illud egisset via rectiore, si non vitasset intellegi, si non etiam in oratione difflueret. . . . non statim cum haec legeris hoc tibi occurret: hunc esse qui solutis tunicis in urbe semper incesserit (nam etiam cum absentis Caesaris partibus fungeretur, signum a discincto petebatur); hunc esse qui in tribunali, in rostris, in omni publico coetu sic apparuerit ut pallio velaretur caput, exclusis utrimque auribus, non aliter quam in mimo fugitivi divitis solent; hunc esse cui tunc maxime civilibus bellis strepentibus et sollicita urbe et armata comitatus hic fuerit in publico: spadones duo, magis tamen viri quam ipse; hunc esse qui uxorem milliens duxit, cum unam habuerit? haec verba tam improbe structa, tam neglegenter abiecta, tam contra consuetudinem omnium posita ostendunt mores quoque non minus novos et pravos et singulares fuisse.

> How Maecenas lived is so notorious it need not be restated here—how he walked, how refined he was, how he loved to be seen, how unwilling he was that his vices should remain hidden. What then? Isn't his oratory as dissolute as he himself was unbuttoned [literally, "loose-belted"]? Aren't his words as clearly stamped as his dress, as his companions, as his house, as his wife? He would have been a man of great intellect if he had gone about it in a more straightforward way, if he had not avoided being understood, if he hadn't flowed off in all directions even in his public speaking. . . . When you read this [of Maecenas'], doesn't this at once occur to you: this is a man who always went downtown with his shirt open (for even when he was performing the function of the absent Caesar, the soldiers' password for the day was received from one unbuttoned); this is a man who in the tribunal, on the speaker's platform, in every public gathering appeared with his head veiled in an opera cloak, with his ears sticking out on each side, just like the fugitive slaves of the rich man in the burlesque show; this is a man whose retinue, at that time when the civil wars were raging most fiercely and the city was in an uproar and up in arms, was, in public, as follows: two eunuchs, still more virile than himself; this is a man who took a wife a thousand times, when he had one already. These words so improperly put together, so carelessly thrown out, positioned so much against the common custom, demonstrate that his morals too were no less strange and depraved and idiosyncratic.

Whereas the elder Seneca had claimed to perceive this connection in a whole generation, the younger one makes the same point about only a single outstanding case in an earlier time—Maecenas, patron of Horace and Vergil, close friend of Augustus. Like the young men decried by the elder Seneca, Maecenas appears effeminate and commits adultery; he also demonstrates ambivalent qualities as commander-in-chief, carrying out the function in the wrong style. Likewise it is the style of his writing that is censured here—a slightly different connection from that in Martial and Pliny, who say they fear that simply writing on sexual topics will be taken to indicate moral failings on their part. But the two axioms—content stems from life, style stems from life—are still close enough for such fears to be justified, and these *apologiae* may be the most sincere in all Latin literature.

Such *apologiae* leave the author uncomfortably on the defensive; but the assumption of the offensive, though common, does not improve the author's position. Petronius, by playing with the offensive stance, comes off fairly well (*Sat.* 132.15)—the idea is that sex is known to everyone and only the puritanical object to its presence in literature, and they need not read what offends them:

quid me constricta spectatis fronte Catones
  damnatisque novae simplicitatis opus?
sermonis puri non tristis gratia ridet,
  quodque facit populus, candida lingua refert.
nam quis concubitus, Veneris quis gaudia nescit?
  quis vetat in tepido membra calere toro?
ispe pater veri doctos Epicurus amare
  iussit et hoc vitam dixit habere τέλος.

Why do you Catos look at me with wrinkled brow
  and condemn a work of novel simplicity?
The charm, not stern, of clean speech smiles,
  and what the people do, the candid tongue relates.
For who is unfamiliar with sleeping together, with the joys of Venus?
  Who forbids limbs to grow hot in the warm bed?
The father of truth himself, Epicurus, has ordered the learned
  to love, and said that life has this *telos*.

This poem follows Encolpius' mock-heroic address to his impotent phallus and, like all the literary criticism in the *Satyricon*, is somewhat vitiated by the rascality and circumstances of the speaker. Still, it applies not only to the words Encolpius has just spoken in his own defense but, of course, much more to the work Petronius is writing. The *apologia* cannot be taken at face value: the *Satyricon* is a work *novae simplicitatis* in the sense that its form and its sharp focus on low life are unusual, but it is hardly *simplex*; Petronius' *sermo* is not *purus* in any conventional sense except that he uses no outright obscenities; the events of the *Satyricon* are *quod . . . facit populus* only in a selective sense; and the idea that the author's tongue is frank *(candida)* in relating *quod facit populus* is disingenuously skewed, not at all the same as being innocent and pure, usually part of the connotation of *candidus*. The protestation of innocence here is thus tongue-in-cheek, but the basic message remains the same: the poet differentiates himself and his subject matter from that expected by a putative puritanical critic, represented by the stock figure of Cato.

Again, Martial and Pliny develop this theme fully without any Petronian ambiguities. Martial scattered his numerous *apologiae* throughout his books;[4] the introduction to book 1 of the epigrams can stand as an example:

> Spero me secutum in libellis meis tale temperamentum ut de illis queri non possit quisquis de se bene senserit, cum salva infimarum quoque personarum reverentia ludant; quae adeo antiquis auctoribus defuit ut nominibus non tantum veris abusi sint sed et magnis. Mihi fama vilius constet et probetur in me novissimum ingenium. Absit a iocorum nostrorum simplicitate malignus interpres nec epigrammata mea scribat: inprobe facit qui in alieno libro ingeniosus est. Lascivam verborum veritatem, id est epigrammaton linguam, excusarem, si meum esset exemplum: sic scribit Catullus, sic Marsus, sic Pedo, sic Gaetulicus, sic quicumque perlegitur. Si quis tamen tam ambitiose tristis est ut apud illum in nulla pagina latine loqui fas sit, potest epistula vel potius titulo contentus esse. Epigrammata illis scribuntur qui solent spectare Florales. Non intret Cato theatrum meum, aut si intraverit, spectet. Videor mihi meo iure facturus si epistulam versibus clusero:
>
> Nosses iocosae dulce cum sacrum Florae
> festosque lusus et licentiam volgi,
> cur in theatrum, Cato severe, venisti?
> an ideo tantum veneras, ut exires?
>
> I hope I have followed in my books such restraint that no one who has a clear conscience can complain of them, since their sport is made with respect for the good name even of the lowest sort of people; which principle was so ignored among the ancient authors that they abused not only real names but even great names. Let fame be cheaper for me, and may my modern cleverness win favor. All evil-minded interpreters can leave my simple jokes alone, and not rewrite my epigrams: it's wrong to exercise your ingenuity on another man's book. I would make excuses for the sportive frankness of my words, that is, the tongue of epigrams, if I were setting the style; but so writes Catullus, so Marsus, Pedo, Gaetulicus, so whoever is read all the way through. If anyone, though, is so determinedly moral that it seems wrong to him to speak plain Latin on any page, he can content himself with this introduction, or, better, with the title page. Epigrams are written for the kind of people who watch the Floralia. Let Cato not come into my theater, or, if he comes in, let him watch. I think I will be acting according to my own standards if I close my introduction with some verses:
>
> When you recognized the sweet rites of ribald Flora
> and the holiday games and freedom of the crowd,
> why have you come to the theater, straitlaced Cato?
> or is it that you've come, so you can leave?

Martial here makes a simple statement: his verses are lascivious but not harmful.[5] They should not be a target for moralistic critics, since everyone knows what they are. With a typical epigrammatic twist, Martial insinuates that any who criticize are just going out of their way to be shocked, to call attention to themselves. Where Petronius had imagined a circle of spectators watching Encolpius/him *(quid me . . . spectatis . . . Catones?)* and generalized the experience of sexual intercourse to all people *(nam quis concubitus . . . nescit?)*, Martial sees the world as more neatly divided—Cato versus *qui solent spectare Florales*. Elsewhere he takes other tacks that also make him seem uneasy with his public persona; his *apologiae* sound like excuses, without Catullus' proud belligerence or Petronius' happy warmth. He protests that other men, even nobles, have written obscene poetry (book 8, intro.) and, quoting an epigram attributed to Augustus (11.20), remarks, "absolvis . . . libellos," "You excuse my books." Here he is defending himself against a vague, putative moralist (11.20.1–2), but in the introduction to book 8 he makes a serious dedication of the book to Caesar and vows that the book will be clean in deference to its august dedicatee. He expresses a similarly simple ambivalence in making the traditional *recusatio* of writing more elevated poetry. He has his muse state that his books reflect life, and so are worth writing (8.3; cf. Ovid *Am.* 3.1). Modest in comparing his work with the great epic poetry written by his friend Silius Italicus (4.14), he begs Silius to read his poetry indulgently, as Vergil might have read Catullus'. Still he claims that his sort of poetry is more widely read than tragedy and epic (4.49). Perhaps because as an epigrammatist Martial's chief strength had to be an ability to shift personae, he never arrives at a unified formulation of the significance of his obscene verse. Instead, he provides various simple excuses in different *apologiae* for why he writes as he does, always defining the world as divided into fun and seriousness, dour censor and naughty reader, with the poet as an uncomfortable intermediary. While the *apologiae* are sometimes clever, they are rarely confident.

Pliny, who seems to have felt uncomfortable about his own output of obscene verse and performance of it in public readings, repeats Martial's arguments in two long *apologiae* (*Ep.* 4.14, 5.3). Pliny's discomfort is personal: he is worried about his reputation (although the elaborate defense really amounts to boasting of his slender muse and his little recitations, his cultivation). Like Martial, he points to his predecessors in the field, showing off, while easing his conscience, by the length of his list. He is particularly concerned to mention men of senatorial rank and to patronize Vergil, Nepos, Ennius, and Accius; he also stipulates that he has not felt bold enough to use obscene language *(nudis verbis)*. Presumably he wants to establish his claim to be considered cultured and aristocratic without aligning himself with any writers he feels to be too daring. Like Martial and Petronius, he states that such poetry is part of the human condition, but he weakens the effect by speaking of his writing as a pastime (*oblectamus otium temporis*, 4.14) and as the equivalent of any sort of harmless relaxation (*innoxiae remissionis*, 5.3). His poetry, then, is no more than an exercise in erudition, a sort of symptom of being a gentleman, and this is how Pliny wants it understood. Whereas Martial is a poet without an *ars poetica*, Pliny is a self-avowed amateur.

Such *apologiae* and such limp arguments do not lead to a very clear understanding of the place of obscenity in Latin literature. These excuses say only why it is all right for an author to deal in obscenity, why he can be forgiven, why his work is not to be associated with himself. There are *apologiae* that do much more than this—that establish a place for obscene literature, that define it, giving it quasi-religious boundaries in the quasi-religious world of Roman poetry. As the *vates* of Latin epic claims descent from Homer and inspiration from the Muses, so the poet of obscene verse claims independence for himself and separation, for his poetry, from the Muses and from all that is chaste and pure.

Ovid, at the beginning of the *Ars Amatoria*, makes an important *recusatio* (1.25–34):

non ego, Phoebe, datas a te mihi mentiar artes,
   nec nos aeriae voce monemur avis,
nec mihi sunt visae Clio Cliusque sorores
   servanti pecudes vallibus, Ascra, tuis;
usus opus movet hoc: vati parete perito;
   vera canam. coeptis, mater Amoris, ades.
este procul, vittae tenues, insigne pudoris,
   quaeque tegis medios instita longa pedes:
nos Venerem tutam concessaque furta canemus
   inque meo nullum carmine crimen erit.

I will not lie, Phoebus, and say my arts were given to me by you,
   nor am I admonished by the voice of a bird in the air,
nor were Clio and Clio's sisters seen by me
   guarding my flocks in your valleys, Ascra;
use moves this work: obey a skilled prophet;
   I shall speak true things. Mother of Love, be present to my undertakings.
Be far away, slender fillets, sign of chastity,
   and you, long flounces which cover the legs to mid-foot;
I shall hymn safe love and permitted chicanery
   and there will be no crime in my poem.

He denies a connection with the Muses and their home, insinuating meanwhile that the claims of epic poetry are lies. He then separates his work from the audience who should not read it—*matronae*, proper married women—for the important reason that he wishes to pretend to be advocating not adultery but free love with freedwomen (a joke that had been safe for Horace thirty years earlier [*S.* 1.2] but was to have grave repercussions in Ovid's own life). Like Martial, Ovid has a serious need to dissociate himself from any real sexual wrongdoing and to remove his work from reality. But he does nothing so simple. The words he chooses are significant—*este procul*, *vittae tenues*, "begone, ye slender fillets." This warning—*este procul*—was normally used by lictors clearing the area of a sacrifice from all who might profane it; in the same way, all who might contaminate them were forbidden to touch the holy priests or Vestal Virgins.[6] Here the warning is applied in reverse, to the emblems of chastity themselves—the headband and long skirt that marked and veiled a faithful wife.

This *apologia* defines poetry on sexual themes as an area, an unholy place. The theme is repeated elsewhere, not always seriously, but it is the one that defines the area belonging to Latin sexual literature. The Priapic poems include a great formulation of this delimitation (*Pr.* 2):

> Ludens haec ego teste te, Priape,
> horto carmina digna, non libello,
> scripsi non nimium laboriose.
> nec Musas tamen, ut solent poetae,
> ad non virgineum locum vocavi.
> nam sensus mihi corque defuisset,
> castas, Pierium chorum, sorores
> auso ducere mentulam ad Priapi.
> ergo quidquid id est, quod otiosus
> templi parietibus tui notavi,
> in partem accipias bonam, rogamus.

> Playing with these things with you as witness, Priapus,
> these poems suited to the garden, not a book,
> I have written none too carefully.
> Nor, still, as poets do, have I called
> the Muses to a place not for virgins.
> For I would have been lacking in feeling and in heart,
> if I had dared to lead to Priapus' prick
> the chaste sisters, the chorus of Pierus.
> Therefore, whatever it is that in my idle hours
> I have marked on the walls of your temple,
> I ask that you accept it in good part.

Here the speaker, a poet and devotee of the ithyphallic god, says he will not invoke the virgin Muses to this *non virgineum locum*—identifying the shrine, the statue of the god, and the poetry of the *Priapea* as aspects of the same thing. The *Priapea* are, after all, religious artifacts, and they belong to the area of the world demarcated as Priapus'. Paradoxically, what is *obscenus*—what would contaminate a priest or priestess and taint omens and sacrifices—is proper to this area. It seems at least probable that the primary meaning of *obscenus* is its religious one, "of ill omen," that it applies to sexual and scatological material along with other things perceived as unclean, and that this meaning extends into the world of literature, which itself is, for the Romans, quasi-religious.[7] Fittingly, the obscene area has its own bards and its own poetry.

In the *apologiae* analogies are drawn between this poetry and special religious festivals; Martial, without developing the analogy, often justifies the obscenity in his poems by stating the likeness between poetry and festival. In the introduction to book 1, quoted above, he compares his epigrams to the *ludi Florales*, the public festival that featured nude dancing, and says the audience is the same for both. He makes the analogy concrete, calling his books *theatrum meum*, "my theater." Elsewhere he says that epigrams are for special occasions: a triumph (7.8; cf. 1.4.3–4) or the Saturnalia (11.2, 11.15). All three festivals—*ludi Florales*, triumph, Saturnalia—share a peculiar attribute. In the *ludi Florales* the prostitutes, whose lascivious dress and behavior were commonly considered disgraceful or at least tawdry, were the chief participants in the central event of the festival; that is, behavior normally shunned was put on display, and all for the honor of the goddess Flora.[8] In triumphs soldiers sang obscene songs mocking their general.[9] At the Saturnalia the slaves played master for a day.[10] In all three festivals, then, the normal order of things, social and moral, was reversed. Such festivals of reversal, many involving obscenity, are found in all societies, and their function is to ward off evil from those in power (as in a triumph) and increase fertility (as in the *ludi Florales*).[11] Thus celebrations promoting license and reversed values have a great positive and conservative function in their societies; the *apologiae* in Roman sexual poetry are announcements by the poets that the obscenity in their work is to be aligned with such celebrations.

These festivals, especially the *ludi Florales* and the triumphs, were also highly theatrical. The final spectacle in the *ludi Florales* was in fact a stage production, with the prostitutes taking the part of the actors.[12] Now the theater at Rome was stigmatized in several ways: dancing, the mode of performance used in pantomime, was itself looked upon as lewd, foreign, suspicious, and perverted; actors and actresses suffered the same deprivation of civil rights as did prostitutes and pimps; actors were often considered and treated as male prostitutes, while the word *mima* (pantomime actress) was a term of opprobrium approximately equivalent to *meretrix* (prostitute). Moreover, the traditional and sublime theatrical genres of tragedy and comedy existed side by side with highly popular genres—pantomime, thought to be decadent and overly titillating, and mime, which was usually obscene, as well as Atellan and Oscan farce.[13] The theater is also a physical place that houses all these genres. Thus, when Martial and Pliny compare their work to mime (Mart. 1.4, 3.86, 8 intro.; Pliny 5.3), they are drawing an analogy among three areas, one literary and two combining written and physical art: obscene poetry, theatrical and obscene religious festivals, and the obscene theater.

In accordance with this perception of obscene poetry as a special place, Martial says that special rules exist for epigram: "lex haec carminibus data est iocosis, / ne possint nisi pruriant iuvare," "This law has been set for joking songs, / that they cannot be useful unless they itch with lust" (1.35.10–11; cf. 1 intro. and Cat. 16.7–11). And not only is there a special law for epigram, there is a special facial expression. In 1.4 Martial uses the phrase *pone supercilium*, "put aside your eyebrows"—in other words, "don't frown at my works"—and asks Domitian to read his poems with the same face he puts on to watch mime (cf. 4.14, to Silius). This appeal to the emperor seems odd when compared with Martial's praise of

Domitian elsewhere for the restoration of chastity (6.2, 6.4, 9.6); but it is no more than a sort of by-your-leave, which nevertheless is necessary, serving as a prelude that allows Martial to combine obscene epigrams with all his others, including those hymning the emperor.[14]

The same themes appear in the *apologiae* of the *Priapea*. *Pr.* 2 specifically excludes the Muses, as being virgins; *Pr.* 1 contrasts the god with Minerva, Vesta, and Diana, the virgin goddesses, and points out that Priapus is not like them. The idea of a special facial expression appears in *Pr.* 1 and 49, with the same phrase, *pone supercilium*; the reason given is that these poems are to be read in the same spirit with which one looks upon the god's phallus (*Pr.* 1). The phallus is, after all, Priapus' great and sacred attribute, and *Pr.* 9 states jokingly that Priapus' phallus is not covered because no god hides his weapons (with comparisons between the phallus and Jove's thunderbolts, Apollo's quiver, and so on). Thus the *Priapea* make the connection between the reading of the poems and the viewing of sexual organs, or at least representations of them, in addition to the connection between poems and festivals.

The boundary containing obscene poetry, along with its readers, must thereby exclude others. Two main categories of excluded people figure in *apologiae*—moralists, who are imagined as frowning but (perhaps pruriently) listening, and told to go away; and *matronae*, who are warned off but invited in. Like Petronius (*Sat.* 132.15; and cf. Horace *S.* 1.2.31–35), Martial uses the younger Cato as a figure of the stuffy, stern moralist in the introduction to book 1 (also 11.2, 11.15) and adds the Curii and Fabricii as similar figures (7.68, 11.16); he also puts his friend, the epic poet Silius Italicus, in the same category (4.14). Here the stern, warlike, and virile genre, epic poetry, puts Silius on a level with the mythic and historic heroes of Rome. All represented a sort of chaste virility; pathic homosexuals who ape Stoic ways are said to be trying to look like the Curii or other bygone patriots (cf. Juv. 2.153–58), and Cato's attitude toward sexuality was the subject of numerous anecdotes.[15] These men embody, then, not asexuality but abstinence.

Married women, likewise, are sexual but supposedly above temptation; the sorts of poems and warnings addressed to *matronae* serve as teasing come-ons for the chaste (cf. Ovid *AA* 1.25–34, above). Martial tells the reader not to read his works if they are offensive (1 intro., 11.16), addressing himself especially to matrons—these books are not for them (3.86, 5.2 by implication); but he says he knows this will only make them read the more eagerly (3.68, 11.16). He reserves books 5 and 8 for the chaste (5.2, 8.1) but changes his mind (8.3). The same sort of mock warning appears in the *Priapea*: in *Pr.* 8 the poet first warns off *matronae* and then comments that now they are all the more avid. In keeping with the hostile tone of the *Priapea*, *Pr.* 66 develops the idea further, insinuating that the addressee turns his back on the god's statue not through chastity but from a desire to feel *intra viscera* what he is afraid to see. These poems constantly focus on the border between chaste and unchaste thoughts and behavior, suggesting that even the most chaste really want to cross the border, to see what they would not ordinarily see, to feel what they would not ordinarily feel, and to read what they would not ordinarily read. This emphasizes the desirability of what is within the demarcated area while at the same time defining its boundaries more securely. The figures of *matrona* and Cato stand for the traditional values of Roman society, and by their very attributes they not only counter but presuppose and demand the existence of the obscene; *pudor* is a negative virtue, the lack of certain actions.

The poet's own viewpoint can shift with relation to this border around the unchaste. Martial's professed attitude toward his own obscenity is not constant: he makes a *recusatio* of hard-core pornography (2.86, 8 intro.) but admits that his works are obscene in comparison with others (3.69, 7.17) and even boasts of their lasciviousness (7.51, 11.16). This, too, must be a result of the switching of personae that is the epigrammatist's pride. Still, even Horace and (possibly) Vergil shifted from epode to ode, from epic to Priapic, as a deliberate change of position with respect to the bounded area, in other words, as a change in persona.

With this in mind it is appropriate to take a preliminary look at Catullus 16 and its function as *apologia*. The lines on the separation of life from work, so often quoted by other writers, are not straightforward and have a different meaning in context than out of context. The place of 16 in Catullus' book will be discussed below; for now, the way the poem operates as an *apologia* can provide a marked contrast to the more limited function of *apologiae* by other writers:

Pedicabo ego vos et irrumabo,
Aureli pathice et cinaede Furi,
qui me ex versiculis meis putastis,
quod sunt molliculi, parum pudicum.
nam castum esse decet pium poetam
ipsum, versiculos nihil necesse est;
qui tum denique habent salem ac leporem,
si sunt molliculi ac parum pudici,
et quod pruriat incitare possunt,
non dico pueris, sed his pilosis
qui duros nequeunt movere lumbos.
vos, quod milia multa basiorum
legistis, male me marem putatis?
pedicabo ego vos et irrumabo.

I will bugger you and I will fuck your mouths,
Aurelius, you pathic, and you queer, Furius,
who have thought me, from my little verses,
because they are a little delicate, to be not quite straight.
For it is proper for a pious poet to be chaste
himself, but there is no need for his little verses to be so,
which only then have wit and charm,

if they are a little delicate and not too clean,
and can arouse a lewd itching,
I don't mean in boys, but in these hairy men
who can't move a hard groin.
You, because you have read "many thousands
of kisses," think me not quite a man?
I will bugger you and I will fuck your mouths.

The distinction between the *castum . . . {et} pium poetam* and his obscene work is a paradox and a joke. Although Catullus would only be proving his virility and the weak effeminacy of Furius and Aurelius by the acts proposed in 16.1, to rape one's friends would be neither *castum* nor *pium*. Moreover, the poem itself in reality achieves a kind of public verbal rape, even if it is a joke; so much for the actual chasteness and *pietas* of the poet/Catullus. Catullus goes on, in 16, to associate *sal* and *lepor* (wit and charm), the two qualities he values most highly, with *quod prurire possit*, "what can itch with lust." Again he is joking, but the matter is highly serious, and the seriousness of Catullus' intent is amply proved by the number of his poems that do use obscene material. The separation of life and work is not only not real for Catullus (i.e., not included within the syntax of the poem); it is not even the issue at hand. The complexities of 16 serve well to prove the seriousness of Catullus' concern with obscene poetry. Later poets or poetasters may have quoted it defensively because of discomfort with the implications of their material for their own lives; Catullus has no such naive worry.

Decorum in Prose

The area of obscenity in Latin literature seems to have included poetry much more comfortably than it did prose. Indeed, formal verse satire, because of the fiction of the genre—that its content derived from the poet's indignation—needed no *apologiae* at all. With the exception of the *Satyricon* and Apuleius' *Metamorphoses*, little Latin prose dealt with sexual material as poetry did—that is, as erotica or enjoyable satire. The one genre that often used sexual material was rhetoric, but the relationship was not wholly comfortable and distinctions were made between what could and what could not be said in a courtroom, despite the fact that the fiction of the genre was the same as that for formal verse satire. The issue is not merely one of place: poetry could certainly be public, but somehow the rules for the public courtroom were different from those for the readings of poetry. The central issue concerned the persona of the speaker: the satirist's dignity was limited to satire, but the orator's had to extend to nonsatiric contexts as well.

Despite the fact that character assassination was one of the primary goals of any orator on the offensive, all Roman writers on rhetoric agree that a speaker had to choose his words carefully. Malicious gossip and political invective attack the same kinds of sexual behavior that form the staple content of epigram and satire, perhaps in a more circumlocutory fashion but with the same impact; the process of innuendo is very much a deliberate one in formal rhetoric. While the final implications could be that the man under attack had formerly been a pathic homosexual prostitute, that the woman under attack was an adulteress, or that either habitually indulged in oral sex (these being the most serious sorts of sexual accusation in the Roman scheme of things), Cicero, the elder Seneca, and Quintilian[16] all comment that the orator should not use obscene language or even define the putative sins explicitly. Of course, the pretense of delicacy achieved by such *praeteritio* only leaves the audience's imagination free either to invent greater horrors or to leave the meaning murky and sinister.

In the *Philippics* Cicero leaves little unsaid about Antony's alleged depravities, while always using formal language and professing his own reluctance to state the full truth (2.44–47):

> Sumpsisti virilem, quam statim muliebrem togam reddidisti. Primo vulgare scortum, certa flagitii merces, nec ea parva; sed cito Curio intervenit, qui te a meretricio quaestu abduxit et, tamquam stolam dedisset, in matrimonio stabili et certo collocavit. Nemo umquam puer emptus libidinis causa tam fuit in domini potestate quam tu in Curionis. Quotiens te pater eius domu sua eiecit, quotiens custodes posuit, ne limen intrares! cum tu tamen nocte socia, hortante libidine, cogente mercede per tegulas demitterere. Quae flagitia domus illa diutius ferre non potuit. Scisne me de rebus mihi notissimis dicere? Recordare tempus illud, cum pater Curio maerens iacebat in lecto, filius se ad pedes meos prosternens lacrimans te mihi commendabat. . . . Ipse autem amore ardens confirmabat, quod desiderium tui discidii ferre non posset, se in exilium iturum. . . . Sed iam stupra et flagitia omittamus; sunt quaedam, quae honeste non possum dicere; tu autem eo liberior, quod ea in te admisisti, quae a verecundo inimico audire non posses.

> You assumed the *toga virilis*, which you at once turned into a woman's toga. First you were a public whore, and the price of your shame was fixed, nor was it small; but soon Curio intervened, who led you away from the prostitution business and, as if he had given you your bridal gown, established you in a steady and fixed marriage. No boy bought for the sake of lust was ever so much in the power of his master as you were in Curio's. How many times his father threw you out of his own house, how many times he posted guards to keep you from crossing the threshold! But you, with night as your ally, your lust urging you on, and your payment compelling you, were let down through the rooftiles. These shames that house could bear no longer. Don't you know I'm talking about things well known to me? Recall that time, when Curio the father was grieving, lying in bed, and his son flinging himself at my feet weeping entrusted you to me. . . . He himself, moreover, burning with love, affirmed that he could not bear the longing caused by your separation and would go into exile. . . . But now let us pass

> over your sex crimes and shameful acts; there are certain things which I cannot pronounce with decency; you, however, are that much freer, since you have allowed things to your discredit which you could not hear named by an enemy who had any sense of shame.

When Cicero says "sunt quaedam, quae honeste non possum dicere," what can he be leaving out? Without giving a graphic description of Antony's intercourse with the younger Curio, he has implied that it was habitual and passionate. The ultimate insult was to accuse someone of indulgence in oral intercourse, and presumably Cicero means to imply this for Antony. But the weight of the sentence is on the neat paradox, "You have done things that a man of good morals cannot even name," and on the contrast between Cicero, who is *honestus* and *verecundus*, and Antony, who is not. It is like a sort of reverse legerdemain, in which the spectators are encouraged to watch the magician's hands so that they will not realize a magic trick is going on. For Cicero has in fact explicitly stated quite shocking things about Antony: that he wore a woman's toga (the garb of a female prostitute), that he did prostitute himself, and that Curio kept him as a wife, even smuggling him into his family home. While most of the language is formal, *scortum* is quite strong, like "slut" or "whore"; Cicero's *verecundia* is not such that it cloaks Antony's activities but that it covers them with a thin, alluring gauze. However, his *verecundia* does observe rules: he does not describe sexual acts in so many words and he avoids naming certain things or acts.[17]

Cicero's attack on Antony here accords fairly well with his own dicta in the *De Oratore*. In an extended discussion of the place of wit in rhetoric (*De Or.* 2.216–91), Cicero includes not only many anecdotes illustrative of types of humor but some speculation on the limits and decorum of humor in the courtroom. The issue, as in the passage against Antony, touches on the speaker's dignity: the speaker must temper his jokes to the people involved, the topic, and the occasion, "ne quid iocus de gravitate decerperet"—"lest the joke detract from his dignity" (229). The discussion includes a whole section asking whether humorousness becomes an orator (235–36); the answer is that it does, within limits. The speaker should gain credibility by an appearance of restraint (242):

> Orator surripiat oportet imitationem ut is qui audiet cogitet plura quam videat; praestet idem ingenuitatem et ruborem suum verborum turpitudine et rerum obscenitate vitanda.

> The orator should sneak up on the audience with his mockery so that anyone listening will imagine more than meets the eye; likewise the speaker should emphasize his gentlemanliness and modesty by avoiding foul words and obscene subjects.

Nor should the speaker indulge in buffoonery; too much exaggeration, or too much *obscenitas*, will recall the mimes (242), although anecdotes should include both *verisimilia*, "the plausible," and *subturpia*, "the off-color" (264). But the *subturpia*, though essential, must not be put in so many words; Cicero clearly draws a distinction of place, saying that the obscenity of the comedian is "non solum non foro digna sed vix convivio liberorum," "not only not proper for the courtroom but hardly for the dinner table of free men" (252).

The elder Seneca draws up a similar set of rules for the declamations of the *scholae*, even though the reputations of real people were not at stake in the set pieces of the classroom. The issue is, then, the decorum proper to an orator rather than the protection of the innocent. Seneca finds need to comment on decorum in rehashing the arguments in *Controv.* 1.2, which debates whether a priestess who has been captured by pirates, sold to a pimp, prostituted, and freed (because of her murder of a soldier and subsequent victory in the murder trial) should be made a priestess again. He concludes (*Controv.* 1.2.21–23):

> dicendum est in puellam vehementer, non sordide nec obscene. Sordide, ut Bassus Iulius, qui dixit: "extra portam hanc virginem" et: "ostende istam aeruginosam manum," ⟨vel⟩ Vibius Rufus, qui dixit: "redolet adhuc fuliginem fornicis." Obscene, quemadmodum Murredius rhetor, qui dixit: "unde scimus an cum venientibus pro virginitate alio libidinis genere deciderit?" (22) Hoc genus sensus memini quendam praetorium dicere, cum declamaret controversiam de illa quae egit cum viro malae tractationis quod virgo esset et damnavit; postea petit sacerdotium. "Novimus," inquit, "istam maritorum abstinentiam qui, etiamsi primam virginibus timidis remisere noctem, vicinis tamen locis ludunt." Audiebat illum Scaurus, non tantum disertissimus homo sed venustissimus, qui nullius umquam inpunitam stultitiam transire passus est; statim Ovidianum illud: "inepta loci," et ille excidit nec ultra dixit. Hoc autem vitium aiebat Scaurus a Graecis declamatoribus tractum, qui nihil non et permiserint sibi et inpetraverint. Hybreas, inquit, (23) cum diceret controversiam de illo qui tribadas deprehendit et occidit, describere coepit mariti adfectum, in quo non deberet exigi inhonesta inquisitio: "ἐγὼ δ' ἐσκόπησα πρότερον τὸν ἄνδρα, ⟨εἰ⟩ ἐγγεγένηταί τις ἢ προσέρραπται." Grandaus, Asianus aeque declamator, cum diceret in eadem controversia, "non ideo occidi adulteros [non] paterentur," dixit: "εἰ δὲ φηλάρρενα μοιχὸν ἔλαβον." In hac controversia de sacerdote non minus obscene dixit Murredius: "fortasse dum repellit libidinem, manibus excepit." Longe recedendum est ab omni obscenitate et verborum et sensuum. quaedam satius est causae detrimento tacere quam verecundiae dicere.

The girl should be accused strongly, but not cheaply or obscenely. It was done cheaply, as when Bassus Julius said, "this maiden outside the gate" and "hold out that tarnished hand"; or when Vibius Rufus said, "she still smells of the soot of the brothel." Obscenely, as when the orator Murredius said, "How do we know that she did not settle with those who came to her by another kind of lust in place of her virginity?" I remember a certain man of

> praetorian rank to have made this kind of implication when he expounded the *controversia* on the woman who was suing her husband for bad treatment, because she was a virgin, and she won her case; afterward she sought the priestess-hood. "We are familiar," he said, "with that kind of abstinence on the part of husbands who, even if they excuse their fearful brides their first night, nevertheless sport in neighboring areas." Scaurus, who was not only the most eloquent of men but the wittiest, and who never let pass unpunished the grossness of any man, heard him. At once that Ovidian phrase: "inexperienced girl, other place"; he stopped there, nor said anything more. Scaurus used to say, moreover, that this fault is derived from the Greek speakers, who denied themselves nothing and got away with it. Hybreas, he said, when he was speaking in the *controversia* on the man who caught the lesbians and killed them, began to describe the feelings of the husband, for whom this disreputable line of questioning should not have been made: "d'abord j'ai regardé pour voir si l'homme était naturel ou s'il a été attaché." Grandaus, likewise an Asianist speaker, when he was speaking in the same *controversia* as to whether they would not allow male adulterers to be killed for this reason, said, "si j'avais pris une amante en travestie . . ." In this *controversia* about the priestess, Murredius said no less obscenely, "Perhaps while she repulsed his lust, she held it in her hands." One must retreat from all obscenity, both of words and of sense. Certain things are more satisfactorily left unsaid, to the detriment of the case, than said, to the detriment of one's modesty.

While the attack should be strong *(vehemens)*, it should be neither sordid nor obscene. Seneca defines both terms by illustrations: sordidness apparently comes from mention of probable but disgusting physical circumstances—the streets, the grime of money, the smell of the brothel; obscenity, from any too vivid imagining of sexual intercourse. The girl's case was that she had preserved her virginity throughout her ups and downs; Murredius was hinting that she might have satisfied her customers by offering them anal intercourse as a substitute. Even more ineptly, in Seneca's view, has the speaker in 22 alluded to the same practice; perhaps the worst aspect of his approach is the opening word, *novimus*, as if calling to mind personal experience. The words *timidis* and *ludunt* present an almost erotic picture, and *vicinis* is coy without hiding anything. Seneca compares Scaurus, whom he praises as *venustissimus* in contrast with the *stultitia* of the first speaker (a "certain praetorian," who presumably should have known better). By using a very brief poetic allusion,[18] Scaurus manages to imply all of what the praetorian had said without using any explicit imagery at all, indeed without using any concrete nouns. (The poem he is quoting says that a bride's fears on her wedding night result in her allowing her husband anal intercourse; the words *inepta loci* remind the cognoscenti in the audience of that situation without any description being necessary.) Such explicitness is here called a *vitium*; and Murredius, seemingly a habitual offender in this direction, provides the final example of the obscene as explicit. By playing on *libidinem*—in the first part of the sentence it means only "lust"; in the second, as object of *excepit*, it must stand for *mentulam*—he achieves a vivid picture of the ex-priestess fondling the genitals of a soldier. Thus Seneca's conclusion, "recedendum est ab omni obscenitate et verborum et sensuum," is something of a tautology: clearly, obscene words in oratory are those that state too explicitly the picture of the sexual intercourse that is meant to be implied.

"Four-Letter Words"

Words considered obscene in English—"four-letter words" or primary obscenities[19]—would automatically be excluded from oratory by Seneca's rule. Further evidence does exist for Roman attitudes toward the use of such words, in the form of a letter from Cicero to Paetus, *Fam.* 9.22 (46–44 B.C.). The letter, which is more a jeu d'esprit on a frivolous subject than a serious analysis of Cicero's feelings about decorum, nevertheless demonstrates an inhibition on his part from actually writing down a primary obscenity. He discusses many such words, but always through the use of circumlocutions and puns. Although this may be only a game, Cicero does expressly say that his *verecundia* makes him reluctant to use such words. On the other hand, we can gather from the letter itself (9.22.2) that Paetus, in a previous letter, had used the world *mentula*, "prick." The inhibition is then to some degree a matter of personal style and preference—and Cicero is not loath to use an occasional euphemistic or suggestive obscenity elsewhere in the letters (*Att.* 2.1.5; see below, chap. 4).

Cicero frames his reply to Paetus in a discussion of the Stoic preference for unblushing bluntness in speech, which he eventually contrasts with the modest speech advocated by the Academy:[20]

> Amo verecundiam!—vel potius libertatem loquendi. Atqui hoc Zenoni placuit, homini mehercule acuto, etsi Academiae nostrae cum eo magna rixa est. sed, ut dico, placet Stoicis suo quamque rem nomine appellare. sic enim disserunt, nihil esse obscenum, nihil turpe dictu; nam, si quod sit in obscenitate flagitium, id aut in re esse aut in verbo; nihil esse tertium. in re non est. itaque non modo in comoediis res ipsa narratur (ut ille in "Demiurgo"
>
> "Modo forte—"
>
> nosti canticum. meministi Roscium:
>
> "Ita me destituit nudum."
>
> Totus est sermo verbis tectus, re impudentior) sed etiam in tragoediis. quid est enim illud
>
> "quae mulier una,"
>
> quid, inquam, est
>
> "usurpat duplex cubile?"

quid

"huius †fereit†
hic cubile inire est ausus?"

quid est

"virginem me quondam invitam per vim violat Iuppiter?"

Bene "violat"; atqui idem significat, sed alterum nemo tulisset. (2) vides igitur, cum eadem res sit, quia verba non sint, nihil videri turpe. ergo in re non est.

Multo minus in verbis. si enim quod verbo significatur id turpe non est, verbum, quod significat, turpe esse non potest. "anum" appellas alieno nomine; cur non suo potius? si turpe est, ne alieno quidem: si non est, suo potius. caudam antiqui "penem" vocabant, ex quo est propter similitudinem "penicillus"; at hodie penis est in obscenis. at vero Piso ille Frugi in annalibus suis queritur adulescentis "peni deditos" esse. quod tu in epistula appellas suo nomine ille tectius "penem"; sed quia multi, factum est tam obscenum quam id verbum quo tu usus es. quid quod vulgo dicitur "cum nos te voluimus convenire"? num obscenum est? Memini in senatu disertum consularem ita eloqui: "hanc culpam maiorem an illam dicam?" potuit obscenius? "non," inquis; "non enim ita sensit." non ergo in verbo est. docui autem in re non esse; nusquam igitur est.

(3) "Liberis dare operam" quam honeste dicitur; etiam patres rogant filios, eius operae nomen non audent dicere. Socraten fidibus docuit nobilissimus fidicen; is Connus vocitatus est. num id obscenum putas? cum loquimur "terni," nihil flagiti dicimus; at cum "bini," obscenum est? "Graecis quidem" inquies. nihil est ergo in verbo, quoniam et ego Graece scio et tamen tibi dico "bini," idque tu facis quasi ego Graece non Latine dixerim. "Ruta" et "menta" recte utrumque. volo mentam pusillam ita appellare ut "rutulam": non licet. belle "tectoriola." dic ergo etiam "pavimenta" isto modo: non potes. viden igitur nihil esse nisi ineptias, turpitudinem nec in verbo esse nec in re, itaque nusquam esse?

(4) Igitur in verbis honestis obscena ponimus. quid enim? non honestum verbum est "divisio"? at inest obscenum, cui respondet "intercapedo." num haec ergo obscena sunt? nos autem ridicule: si dicimus "ille patrem strangulavit," honorem non praefamur; sin de Aurelia aliquid aut Lollia, honos praefandus est. et quidem iam etiam non obscena verba pro obscenis sunt. "Battuit," inquit: impudenter; "depsit": multo impudentius. atqui neutrum est obscenum. stultorum plena sunt omnia. "testes" verbum honestissimum in iudicio, alio loco non nimis. et honesti "colei Lanuvini," Cliternini non honesti. quid ⟨quod⟩ ipsa res modo honesta, modo turpis? suppedit, flagitium est; iam erit nudus in balneo,non reprehendes.

Habes scholam Stoicam: ὁ σοφὸς εὐθυρρημονήσει. quam multa ex uno verbo tuo! te adversus me omnia audere gratum est; ego servo et servabo (sic enim adsuevi) Platonis verecundiam. itaque tectis verbis ea ad te scripsi quae apertissimis agunt Stoici. sed illi etiam crepitus aiunt aeque liberos ac ructus esse oportere. honorem igitur Kalendis Martiis.

Tu me diliges et valebis.

I like your modesty!—or rather, your complete freedom in speaking. But I admit that Zeno liked the latter—an intelligent man indeed, even if there is a great brawl between my Academy and him. But, as I was saying, it pleases the Stoics to call each thing by its own name. For, as they argue it, nothing is obscene, nothing foul to say; for if there is anything shameful in obscenity, it is either in the thing or in the word; there is no third possibility. It is not in the thing. Therefore not only in the works of the comic playwrights is the thing itself described (as the man says in the *Demiurgus*:

"Just now, by chance . . ."

You know the *canticum*; you remember Roscius:

"Thus she left me naked . . ."

The whole speech is discreet in wording, in its content rather more daring) but even in the works of the tragedians. For what is this:

"What one woman . . ."

what, I ask you, is

". . . enjoys a two-fold bed . . ."?

what is

"He dared to go into that one's bed . . ."?

what is

"Jupiter once molested me, a maiden, by might, against my will"?

Good thing that he said "molested," yet it means the same thing; but no one would have accepted the other word. (2) You see, therefore, that although it is the same thing, because the words are not foul, nothing seems foul. Therefore it is not in the thing.

Much less in the words. For if what is meant by the word is not foul, the word which means it cannot be foul. "Ring" [*anus*; = *podex*, "asshole"] you call by a borrowed name; why not, rather, by its own? If it is foul, don't call it even by a borrowed name; if not, then call it by its own. The writers of antiquity called a tail "penis," from which comes, because of the likeness, [the word for paintbrush,] *penicillus*; but today "penis" [*penis*; = *mentula*, "prick"] is among the obscene words. But even Piso Frugi himself complains in his *Annals* that the young men are "given over to the penis." What you call in your letter by its own name he calls, more discreetly, "penis"; but, because many have done so, the word has become as obscene as that word which you used. What about the phrase commonly used "When we [*cum nos*; = *cunnos*, "cunts"] wanted you to meet with us"? That is not obscene, is it? I remember a well-spoken consular in the senate meeting to have spoken these words: "Shall I call this fault or that one [*illam dicam*; = *il-landicam*, "th' clitoris"] the greater?" Could he have been more obscene? "No," you say, "because he didn't mean it so." Thus it is not in the word. And I have shown it is not in the thing; therefore it is nowhere.

(3) "To work on having children"—how respectably this is said; even fathers ask it of their sons. They do not dare to say the name of the work. A great lyre player taught Socrates to play the lyre; he was called "Connus." You don't think that obscene, do you? When I say "three each" I say nothing shameful; when I say "two each" [*bini*; = Greek βινεῖ, "fucks"] is it obscene? "To Greeks," you will say. Then there is nothing in the word, since I know Greek and yet I say to you "two each"; yet you act as if I were speaking Greek, not Latin. "Rue" and "mint" are both perfectly all right. I want to say "a little bit of mint [= *mentulam*]" in the same way as I say "ruelet"; I can't. "Little plasters" is fine; then say "pavement [= *pavimentulam*]" in the same way; you can't. Do you see, then, that this is nothing but silliness, and that foulness is neither in the word nor in the thing, and therefore is nowhere? (4) And so we put obscene words into respectable ones. Look—isn't "division" a respectable word? But there's an obscene one in it, to which "intermission" is similar. But these words are not for that reason obscene, are they? But we behave laughably: if we say, "He choked his father," we don't apologize; but if we say something about Aurelia or Lollia, we have to apologize. And indeed, now even words not obscene have become so; "He battered . . .," one says shamelessly; "he kneaded . . .," much more shamelessly. Yet neither is obscene. It's all full of stupidities. "Witnesses" [*testes*; = "balls"] is a totally respectable word in a courtroom, none too respectable elsewhere. And "Lanuvine bags" [*colei*; = "balls"] are respectable, "Cliternine" are not. What about the fact that the thing itself is sometimes respectable, sometimes foul? Someone farts softly, it's a disgrace; let him be naked at the baths, you will not reprove him.

There you have the Stoic school: *l'homme sage parle franchement*. What a lot from one word of yours! I'm glad you feel free to say anything to me; I preserve and will keep on preserving (for I'm used to it) my Plato-ish modesty. And so I have written to you in veiled words about those things which the Stoics handle in the most open words. But they even say that farts should be as free as belches. (Apologies to the Matronalia!)

Don't forget me, and be well.

While the letter cannot really be taken as a serious commentary on language, it makes many sensible comments (which we can take to be not particularly daring) on ways in which certain words are loaded with shame. That these words are loaded is amply attested by the letter itself and by Cicero's avoidance of the direct use of any word. Once again, the idea of place plays an important part in the analysis: the consular who, by unfortunate positioning of words, created a double entendre while speaking in the senate; the difference between breaking wind in public and nakedness in the public baths; the license allowed in the theater.

The theoretical basis of the letter (9.22.1–2) is not particularly profound and depends on a sort of logic chopping that allows Cicero to show off in paradoxes and double entendres. He states that what is obscene does not exist, since it would have to be either in the thing or in the word. Assuming that it is not in the thing, he concludes it cannot be in the word either. Cicero's premises here are of more interest than his argument: he begins by limiting *obscenum* to the verbal, giving *turpe dictu*, "foul to say," as a parallel for *obscenum* (or an implied *obscenum dictu*), although he will later adduce examples that are nonverbal. And underlying the whole letter is the fact that the place of obscenity in speech can define a philosophic discussion, however tongue-in-cheek. That the discussion will not be serious is clear from the start; this whole grandiose showpiece has apparently been touched off by Paetus' use of a single obscene word in his last letter to Cicero. Moreover, the argument is circular, although perhaps this is just a typically Academic touch. The way Cicero structures the argument allows him to cite examples from comedy, which were either explicitly sexual or highly pointed double entendres, as well as from tragedy, which, as he points out, always deals with sex crimes. He can then say that he has proved that obscenity is neither in word nor in thing, since sex crimes described in the elevated language of tragedy are not shameful, hence the thing is not shameful, so *a fortiori* the words are not. But in developing this proof he has managed (as the elegant Scaurus was to do after him) to allude to various racy scenes in comedy without sullying his page with any explicit words and has drawn parallels between the comic and tragic scenes. While this is an interesting analogy, it is simpleminded to think of tragedy and comedy as doing the same thing with the same materials; surely Cicero is drawing these two disparate bodies of materials together to raise a laugh.

The same is true of the subsequent examples he gives. Although Cicero never uses a primary obscenity in this letter, he manages to make the reader supply several, by means of plays on words—all the while maintaining his own *verecundia*. This sort of word game is titillating and can be much more amusing than explicit obscenity; in combination with appeals to chastity and pure speech, it is even funnier. Particularly the examples in which Cicero points out that an obscene word forms part of a longer but innocuous word, or of an innocent phrase, are reminiscent of deliberately obscene riddles and puns in which the reader must discover a hidden obscenity (*Pr.* 7, 54, 67, 68). The theory is sound, utilizing nuances of phonosyntactic puns;[21] but Cicero's intention cannot be merely to illustrate the theory.

He begins with the originally metaphorical obscenity *anus* ("ring"), then current for a part of the body that he says should not be mentioned at all if it is "foul," or should be called by its own name, *suo nomine*, if it is not foul. By "its own name" he presumbly means the obscene word *podex*, "asshole." This illustrates the fact that Latin did not generally turn to medical terminology as an acceptable alternative to either euphemisms or bald obscenities. Parallel with *anus* is the next example, *penis*, an old word for "(animal's) tail," which produced the slang term *penicillus*, "brush," but which was now, from the commonness of its use *sensu obsceno*, itself obscene. Again Cicero says that Paetus had called the thing denoted by *penis* "by its own name," *suo nomine*, in his letter; presumably he means Paetus had used the word *mentula*, approximately equivalent to the Engish "prick." Next follow two obscenities hidden in innocent sets of words: *cum nos* . . . ("when we . . .") is pronounced like *cunnos* ("cunts"), . . . *illam dicam* ("shall I say that one . . .") is pronounced *il-landicam* ("th' clitoris"). Returning briefly to his analysis of euphemisms, Cicero cites the phrase *liberis dare operam*, "to work on having children," and observes that no one dares to "say the name of the work," in other words, presumably, to use the verb *futuo* ("fuck").

The hidden obscenities continue: Socrates' lyre teacher, Connus, has a name that could be pronounced like *cunnus*; the word *terni* ("three each") is all right, but *bini* ("two each") is not (because it sounds like the Greek βινεῖ, "he fucks"); the words *ruta* ("rue") and *menta* ("mint") are fine, and so is the diminutive of *ruta*, *rutula*, but the diminutive of *menta* is not (it would be *mentula*); similarly, *tectoriola* ("tiny bits of plaster") is all right, but not the diminutive of *pavimenta* (which would be *pavimentula*). These examples become more and more farfetched and constitute deliberate reminders of obscenities where they need not be seen; *bini* has to be forced by a deliberate direction to be read as if it were Greek, and it is doubtful that the words for "tiny mint leaves" or "dear little paving tiles" were often needed. With the double entendre on Connus' name Cicero even casts a sly aspersion on the background of his beloved Academy.[22] He then comments, solemnly, that we ourselves put obscenities into "respectable words," *verbis honestis*, and goes on to put in a few more, pointing to obscenities in *divisio* ("division," including *visium*, "stink")[23] and *intercapedo* ("intermission," including *pedo*, "I fart").

The final series of examples concerns context, and these seem the most serious. Cicero here makes a salutary and still valid observation: that although we make no apology for a mention of murder, even of parricide, we must always apologize for a description of sexual activity, here represented by two notorious adulteresses.[24] Again Cicero cites metaphorical obscenities, this time the words *battuit* and *depsit*, "he pounded" and "he kneaded," which, in the right context, are equivalent to *futuit*. Likewise the word *testes* (which means either "witnesses" or "testicles") is acceptable in the courtroom and not elsewhere; and the word *colei* ("bags"; slang for "testicles") is all right with the adjective *Lanuvini*, apparently a common term, and not with another place-name adjective, apparently random. Here we have corroborative evidence in the number of puns made in all humorous literature on the word *testes*. The final example is in the same vein as the comparison between murder and adultery: Cicero says that to fart is a terrible gaffe, but in the baths it is perfectly all right to walk around entirely naked. All these examples are united by the idea that context or location can determine whether or not a word or activity is perceived as obscene.

The conclusion to the letter is solemn and rather fatherly in tone; although Paetus is welcome to use obscenity, Cicero will keep to the "modesty characteristic of Plato," *Platonis verecundiam*, and therefore has used "veiled words," *tectis verbis*. He then, with startling blandness, returns to the Stoics who began his discussion, noting that they wish farts to be as open as belches, and finally apologizes to the first of March—the Matronalia. It is hard not to see this conclusion, too, as tongue-in-cheek: the essay has been modest, in letter if not in spirit, and the words have been veiled, but the examples amount to a series of silly and obscene double entendres; the final allusion to the Stoics sets up an implied analogy between farts and belches on the one hand and language on the other; and the apologies to the Matronalia align this letter with the literary *apologiae* surveyed earlier, being the sort of excuse that only draws attention to the sexual intent and content of the work at hand.

If *Fam.* 9.22, then, is not a clear statement by Cicero of Roman attitudes toward obscene language, it nevertheless provides clear examples of what that language was. Cicero's list of truly *tecta verba*—the words he hints at without writing them out as such—surely constitutes a list of words commonly considered to be obscene. The very fact that Cicero writes around these words shows that the concept of limits around obscene ideas was applied to specific words, with borderline areas including periphrases or euphemisms for these words. Finally, the rough lines he does draw in *Fam.* 9.22 indicate that these words and ideas operated in different ways in different places. The philosophers could debate theory (9.22.1, 4); the theater could deal with sexual matters (9.22.1); some words acquired sexual meanings in the course of time and through usage (9.22.2); there was a danger of deliberate misconstruction of poorly ordered words (9.22.2); some words could not be used between father and son (9.22.3); convention decreed polite signaling of discussion of sexual matters, though not of other equally shocking matters (9.22.4); some innocent words were homonyms for obscene words (9.22.4); acceptable inhibitions differed for special places like the baths (9.22.4), or for the Matronalia; there seems throughout a strong connection between the idea of sexual or excretory behavior and the use of obscene and scatological language (esp. 9.22.4); above all, the letter itself, a private letter between friends, exists in the borderline area between verbalization subject to prohibition and free verbalization, but it lies closer to free verbalization, as attested by the freedom previously exercised by Paetus in writing to Cicero. This evidence demonstrates the existence of several rules governing obscene language and its use: that the word was perceived as closely connected with the thing; that usage of words as obscene developed over time; and that sexual language or behavior was acceptable in some settings (serious study, the theater, the baths), marginal in others, as in Cicero's correspondence, and unacceptable, that is, obscene, in others (between family members, to *matronae*). It was permissible in formal conversation only with apology, but then again it was always liable to be read into innocent words by those so inclined. The places singled out by Cicero here are the same kinds of places where Pliny found it appropriate to write light verse—*in vehiculo*, *in balineo*, *inter cenam* (*Ep.* 4.14).

The actual words that Cicero highlights in *Fam.* 9.22 fall into three main areas: words for genitalia, verbs for sexual intercourse, and scatological words. Each area contains some words that Cicero has written explicitly and some that he has expressed by means of periphrasis or pun. The expressions for sexual intercourse include the oblique allusion to "something about Aurelia or Lollia," *de Aurelia aliquid aut Lollia*; the metaphorical obscenities *battuit* and *depsit*, like the English "bang" and "screw"; and the more direct Greek *βινεῖ*, which always has a sexual meaning and hence is expressed here only by means of a pun on *bini*. The Latin *futuo*, the primary obscenity for sexual intercourse, presumably lurks behind the phrase *liberis dare operam*. The same sorts of levels exist for words with scatological reference, although here Cicero is slightly more explicit. The verb *pedo*, "fart," which he hides in *intercapedo*, he uses openly in the compound *suppedit*, "fart softly." On the other hand, *visium*, hidden in *divisio*, is not particularly obscene and not commonly used in Roman sexual humor. And *anus* appears instead of the "proper" name, presumbly the obscene word *podex*; nor does Cicero even hint at the obscene words for buttocks, urine, or feces.

Words for genitalia preponderate in *Fam.* 9.22; there are eight examples of such words, as opposed to only four each for scatological words and verbs for intercourse. Perhaps enabled by the lengthy historical lead-in, Cicero discusses the word *penis* without periphrasis; as he says, it was currently in use as a synonym for *mentula*. *Testes* and *colei* he can use explicitly because each had a strong nonobscene meaning, which he makes a point of emphasizing. He brings in three other words by means of puns, thereby both avoiding writing them out and inserting them forcibly into innocuous phrases: *mentula* is expressed by extrapolating diminutives for *menta* and *pavimenta*, *cunnus* by punning on *cum nos* and *Connus*, and *landica* by punning on *illam dicam*. Examples for male genitalia outnumber female five to three, with one of the three being the rarely used word *landica*.

It can be seen, then, that Cicero grows progressively more indirect as he approaches words that can be used only with a sexual meaning—primary obscenities; at the same time, he goes to great lengths to contrive a pun that will induce the reader to form these words mentally. They are thus the most highly charged and the most interesting to him and to his reader. He encourages his reader to imagine particularly the primary obscenities for the penis and for the vagina and clitoris, for heterosexual intercourse, and for the anus. From other sexual humor it can be seen what he omits altogether—the obscene words commonly in use for oral intercourse, homosexual intercourse, buttocks, and excreta. One could then postulate a scale of intensity of obscenity, in which the things Cicero leaves out altogether weigh more than the things he includes, but it will not do to press this argument from silence too heavily.

Still, from the material that will be presented in the following chapters, it is possible to make sound generalizations about the use of obscene language in Latin. That the concept of limits applied to specific words is amply attested not only by *Fam.* 9.22 but by all Roman sexual humor. The primary obscenities appear only in graffiti and in certain contexts in literature; they correspond roughly to the list of words that caused WBAI such trouble with the Federal Communications Commission in 1973[25] and include *mentula*, *cunnus*, *podex*, *cacare* ("shit"), *mingere* and *meiere* ("piss"), *futuere*, *pedicare* ("bugger"), *irrumare* ("fuck in the mouth"), *fellare* ("fellate"), and a few others whose force varies according to context. The last two mentioned here seem to have been slightly stronger than the others, largely because of the great stigma on oral intercourse in Roman culture. Metaphorical obscenities were commonly used, but Latin is not nearly as rich in them as is Greek or English. Euphemisms were common, but few in number and prim. Unlike Greek or English, Latin did not use obscene words as expletives, and it needed to borrow from Greek when it wanted to say something like "fuck off."[26] Words like *irrumare* and *futuere* always had their full sexual meaning, while both Petronius and Martial used the Greek λαικάζειν with its weakened sense ("go to hell"). On the other hand, since nouns formed from these verbs—*irrumator*, *fellator*—denoted someone who habitually engaged in such activities, they could be used as pejoratives, although the concrete sense was never very far from the surface. The strongest focus was on the genitalia, both male (mention of which almost always related to a threat or boast) and female (almost always connoting disgust); on the mouth; and on intercourse, both heterosexual and male homosexual, with some interest in excreta. There was very little interest in female homosexuality, breasts, or masturbation.[27]

Staining

A further aspect of these words must be established: that the concept of dirt and befoulment with dirt is commonly associated with them, so that the obscene is conceived of as not only delimited but intrinsically foul.[28] Perhaps the initial perception is that the things themselves—genitalia, fecal matter—are foul; next, that acts associated with these things are foul; finally, that those who engage in such acts are foul. Perceptions of genitalia as foul pervade Roman sexual humor. The phallus, although its identity as a threatening weapon (e.g., Cat. 67.21; *Pr.* 9.2, 11.3, 20.1, 25.7, 31.3, 43.1, 55.4; Diehl 1103; Mart. 11.78.6; cf. Cat. 56.7) is a positive one, is also sometimes described as red, one-eyed, and hairless (e.g., Mart. 2.33, 9.37.10). The female genitalia are almost exclusively described as disgusting—squashy and foul in texture and constitution (*lutus*, "muck," Diehl 615; cf. *VA "Quid Hoc Novi Est?"* 26–37), hairy or depilated (Diehl 691, Mart. 3.74), salty and rank (Mart. 11.21). Indeed, the castigation of female genitalia forms one of the chief concerns of invective against old women.[29]

With the perception of the genitalia as disgusting[30] can be compared the attacks on other parts of the body in invective epigram—the armpits, always malodorous, and the nose, always too long. Given these preoccupations with smell, cleanliness, appearance, and hair, it is not surprising that the strongest Latin invective is that against the *os impurum*, the unclean mouth that supposedly results from oral intercourse. Here the sexual invective overlaps with the general, so that a person accused of having a bad-smelling, decaying, stained, or suspiciously clean mouth may also be being accused of indulgence in oral sex as the cause. Since kissing (as greeting) and public bathing were common at Rome, further fears emerge in invective—of contamination by mouths or waters that have touched genitalia. In turn, the words denoting the performance of oral sex are most foul, as are those denoting performers of oral sex. Closely connected with these are the words for pathic male homosexuals and for female prostitutes, since it is commonly assumed in Roman sexual humor that pathic homosexuals enjoyed fellating other men and that the least expensive prostitutes would do anything for money; the descriptions of the whores of the alleyways often include allusions to oral sex, as in Cat. 99.10, *commictae spurca saliva lupae*, "the foul saliva of a pissed-over whore" (cf. Mart. 11.61.2–5). A correlative reason for this view of oral sex was, of course, that it represented an assertion of the dominance of the one satisfied over the one doing the satisfying; hence the threat of irrumation—oral rape—represents both a strong staining and a strong degradation of the victim, and is the ultimate threat in invective, political or literary.

A whole list of adjectives denoting contamination by filth is commonly associated with sexual things and acts in Latin literature: *spurcus*, *inquino/atus*, *putidus*, *turpis*, *lutum*, *oblimo*, *rancidus*, *immundus*, *foedus/foedo*, *taeter*, *vilis*. Again and again a connection is made between oral sex and odor, and an identification of mouth and anus. This can be done by transfer of epithets, as when Catullus, describing a thieving father and (pathic) son, says of them (33.3–4):

> nam dextra pater inquinatiore,
> culo filius est voraciore
>
> for the father has a dirtier right hand,
> and the son has a hungrier ass

Encolpius, describing his quasi-rape by the repulsive *cinaedus* at Quartilla's orgy, says "basiis olidissimis inquinavit," "he stained me with the smelliest of kisses" (*Sat.* 21.2); Martial, describing the looseness of his victim's vagina, calls her "tam laxa . . . quam turpe guttur onocrotali," "as loose . . . as the foul gullet of a pelican" (11.21.1, 10). At 97.1–2 Catullus explicitly says "non . . . quicquam referre putavi, / utrumne os an culum olfacerem Aemilio," "I think it makes no difference whether I smell Aemilius' mouth or his ass," but the comparison is strongly implied in the three examples above and in many others; the mouth is malodorous and stained, the genitals are hungry and gaping.[31] Perhaps it is the social dynamic inherent in such a perception that makes it appropriate for invective: the speaker, by perceiving the victim as stained and utterly loathsome, expresses a fear of contamination by the victim; he not only shuns the victim's touch but even asserts he can smell or see the victim's stain from a distance. The fear and loathing are real, or real enough to raise a laugh, as they are when children play games of this pattern, even if the causes cited are as irrational as those cited by children.

Negative formations like *improbus*, *impudicus*, *indecens*, *nequam/nequitia* are also commonly used in sexual contexts and appear much weaker than the words denoting staining. In fact, however, they can be used as euphemisms or code words for sexual activities seen as especially perverse. At *Pr.* 58.2 the god laconically uses *impudicus* as a euphemism for *paedicatus/irrumatus*—the "unchastity" will consist in being the victim of anal or oral rape. Overtones even more specific than these attach to the words *purus/impurus*, which almost always signify "untainted by oral sex / tainted by oral sex."[32] In an epitaph on a cunnilinctor's tongue, Martial concludes (11.61.13–14):

> partem gulosam solvit indecens morbus
> nec purus esse nunc potest nec impurus.
>
> His unseemly disease / perversion ruined his hungry part,
> and now he can't be clean or dirty.

The technical implications of the term *impurus* are developed in Seneca's *Controv.* 1.2, about the prostituted priestess; the question is whether a woman who has been a prostitute could ever be a priestess, who must be *pura*. The woman's contamination is concretely described in several different ways:

> (1.2.3) nuda in litore stetit ad fastidium emptoris; omnes partes corporis et inspectae et contrectatae sunt.
>
> She stood naked on the shore for the approval of the buyer; every part of her body was not only inspected but handled.
>
> (1.2.9) . . . contrectata es alicuius manu, alicuius osculo, alicuius amplexu.
>
> . . . You have been gone over by the hand of one, by the kiss of another, by the embraces of a third.
>
> (1.2.10) Conservarum osculis inquinatur . . .
>
> She is stained by the kisses of fellow slaves . . .
>
> (1.2.11) . . . stare in illo ordine, ex eadem vesci mensa, in eo loco vivere, in quo etiamsi non patiaris stuprum videas.
>
> . . . to stand in that parade, to eat from the same table, to live in that place, in which even if you did not suffer sex crimes, you saw them.

Her contamination consists of several levels of sexual involvement: exposure to view; thorough inspection; handling of all parts of her body; public use, including handling, kissing, and embracing (cf. Mart. 6.66); kissing by those of low status or by other prostitutes; living in the brothel, including display, eating with prostitutes, and witnessing sexual activity. In this list the problem posed by her eating with other prostitutes, seemingly the least serious, must relate to the tainting of her mouth (cf. Juv. 6.O.4–6).[33]

In the summary of this *controversia* the first speaker, Latro, considers her sexual tainting to be under the heading *an casta sit*, while *purus* refers only to her act of murder. Under chastity, he includes the question (1.2.13)

> utrum castitas tantum ad virginitatem referatur an ad omnium turpium et obscenarum rerum abstinentiam. Puta enim virginem quidem esse te, sed contrectatam osculis omnium; etiamsi citra stuprum, cum viris tamen volutata es . . .
>
> whether chastity refers only to virginity or to abstinence from all foul and obscene things. Even granted you are a virgin, you have been covered by the kisses of all; even if it stopped short of outrage, still you were tumbled together with men . . .

But a later accuser (1.2.16), a fiercer one, considers *pura* to refer to her sexual abuses:

> Hispo Romanius accusatoria usus pugnacitate negavit puram esse, non ad animum hoc referens, sed ad corpus; tractavit impuram esse quae osculum impuris dederit, quae cibum cum impuris ceperit.
>
> Hispo Romanius, using a prosecutor's aggressiveness, denied that she was *pura*, referring this term not to her spirit but to her body; he considered that a woman was *impura* who kissed *impuri* and who ate meals with *impuri*.

Hispo associates oral contamination with the word *impurus*; it seems probable, then, that *impurus* always carried at least the suggestion of the meaning "contaminated by oral-genital contact."

The concept of tainting applied to the words themselves, as well as to the things; Seneca observes (*Controv.* 1.2.7), "coram sacerdote obscenis homines abstinent," "in the presence of a priestess men abstain from obscenities," as if the words themselves could stain the holy person. The epithet *obscenus* is commonly used to describe such words, as well as all sexual matters. The strength of these words and their sexual appeal are clear, as, for example, in *Pr.* 29:

> Obscaenis, peream, Priape, si non
> uti me pudet inprobisque probris.
> sed cum tu posito deus pudore
> ostendas mihi coleos patentes,
> cum cunno mihi mentula est vocanda.
>
> I'll be damned, Priapus, if I'm not
> ashamed to use obscenities and nasty insults.
> But when you, a god, throw away your modesty
> and show me your balls openly,
> I have to say "cunt" and "prick."

Moreover, these words are often said to be exciting or seductive: proper to orgiastic dancing (Juv. 11.174), used by a helpful mistress (Ovid *Am.* 3.7.12), and improper for matrons (*Pr.* 8.1–2) or well-brought-up children to hear (Juv. 14.44–46). And like *impudicus*, *obscenus* can be used as a euphemistic substantive, as at Juv. 2.9 and 6.513, where it stands for pathic homosexuals.

This interlinking of the word with the thing manifests itself strongly in the complex of words based on the root *-fa-*, "speak," that are often applied to sexual activities: *infamis/infamia/nefas/famosus/famae non bonae*. The idea is not so much that these things are not to be spoken of; rather, by being spoken of too much—by being too gossipworthy—they demean, even stain, those involved in them. Moreover, such activities are morally wrong; besides the word *stuprum*, "sex crime," a group of words denoting crime and sin is commonly associated with sexual activities: *crimen*, *facinus*, *sceleroIscelus*, *furtum/furtivus*, *flagitium*, *pecco, vitium*, *incestus*, *dedecus*, *infidus*. Against such misbehavior stand the words that denote right behavior—*pudor* and *verecundia*, *honestus*, and so on. As noted above, *pudor* and the rest are essentially negative virtues, denoting a lack of any wrongdoing—like "purity," "stainlessness." Still, they are among the most highly esteemed virtues a Roman could have, especially a sexually attractive Roman—that is, a woman or a young boy. Perhaps, then, the perception of sex as a "sin" or "crime" attaches particularly to the debauching of such a person, and the existence of this class of terms comes from the existence of this class of (ideally) untouchable people (who, in fact, are just the ones everyone wants to touch).

The Roman concept of obscenity, then, included the restriction of certain words from certain situations and the association of ideas of staining with sexuality. This makes even more surprising the position of the *vates* of obscenity, the poets who took as their area the garden of Priapus. Were they really secure in their place? Were they not stained by the content of their work? Martial, accusing a rival poet, provides a final example of the reconciliation of the paradoxes involved in this delimited poetry (4.6):

Credi virgine castior pudica
et frontis tenerae cupis videri
cum sis improbior, Malisiane,
quam qui compositos metro Tibulli
in Stellae recitat domo libellos.

You want to be thought more chaste than a virgin maid
and to be viewed as of a delicate demeanor
when you are more indecent, Malisianus,
than the man who recites little books
composed in the meter of Tibullus in Stella's house.

L. Arruntius Stella was Martial's friend and patron, addressed with adulation in 1.7, 6.21, 6.47, 8.78, and 9.42. The description of the "reciter of little books" could very well be applied to Martial himself: he is saying, "when you are more indecent—than I!" Martial attacks his victim here by using himself as a point of comparison; yet, all in all, he is secure. He places his recitations in the house of the respected, decorous Stella, himself a serious poet.[34] If the domain of obscenity in language and literature is definitely outside the domain of the nonobscene, it is still clear that the poet of the obscene was free to travel between the two, and was a welcome visitor.

CHAPTER 2 # The Erotic Ideal in Latin Literature and Contemporary Greek Epigram

Chapter 1 has demonstrated that some Romans associated feelings of disgust and defilement with some forms of sexuality and with certain words. These feelings were a necessary ingredient in Roman sexual humor but not a sufficient determinant of the particular targets of that humor. The idea that obscenity in literature was a delimited area implies that things within that area were different and to be differentiated from things outside it; thus erotic as well as moral ideals formed a positive extreme that Roman sexual satire deliberately countered. In this bipolar system there was both a positively valued "beauty," which was praised as attractive/pursued, and a negatively valued "ugliness," which was satirized as repulsive/rejected.[1]

In addition, because the serious praise of love and a beloved were adopted by the Romans part and parcel with lyric poetry of all sorts, the erotic ideal stood not only for a belief about the objects of desire but for a belief about poetry and the poet's relation to it, about the poet's place in society, and about the relation of poetry to reality. Not all poets arrived at similar formulations of belief, conditioned as always not only by temperament but by their times; where Catullus wrote brash political poetry and highly real love poems, Ovid chose to make love poetry into an escape from epic and politics, even hinting that the mistress he addressed was a figment of his imagination (*Am.* 2.17.29). How natural to Rome this erotic ideal was, or, if it was borrowed, how popular it became, and the effect it then had on real men and women can only be guessed at, although the strong humorous reaction to it suggests that it was widely accepted. Its structural premise divides the world (represented by the poem) into two characters, the pursuing figure of the poet/*amator* and the pursued figure of the beloved. Most commonly the beloved is not felt to have a reality outside the poem corresponding with that of the real men Catullus, Horace, Propertius, Tibullus, Ovid—partly because his or her real name is kept secret and masked with a fantasy name, usually Greek.[2] Hence, while the lover in each poem is an ideal version of the poet, the beloved is an ideal version of a figure with only a vague or shifting identity—more ideal than real.

The positive erotic material that satire mocks includes the abstract and often depersonalized love poetry found in genres like elegy and lyric; but, although this was ridiculed often enough, it produced a parody of idea rather than a perversion of physical details. Roman satire delighted in exploding the ideal of the *univira*, the chaste and faithful woman, as expressed not only in epic poetry but also in New Comedy and in moral anecdotes and essays.[3] Likewise, attitudes expressed toward women and boys in satire are diametrically opposed to those of the *paraklausithyron* and the studied laments of the elegiac poets. But the physical ideal that sexual satire distorted or abused is largely found in the less lofty genres, especially epigram, which also include sexual humor; that is, although sexual humor is found in forms other than epigram, epigram includes both sexual humor and serious expressions of lust. It seems that graphic expression of desire was considered to be on a literary par with humor concerning sexuality.

Epigram commonly treats two positive descriptions of sexuality: that of a mistress and that of a beloved boy *(puer)*. It is difficult to know how widespread the practice of male homosexuality in general and pederasty in particular was at Rome (see below, appendix 2); of course, the existence of a great deal of literature inspired by or about homosexual love must be related to that question. Whatever the relationship between the poetry and the reality, it is a fact that poems to *pueri* are as common as poems to mistresses, and are similar in tone. Indeed, in the Latin erotic ideal the attributes and foibles of women and of boys form the two great conventions. This is no coincidence: almost no poetry written by Roman women or boys about their ideal loves survives or is even attested.[4] The concepts analyzed here are exclusively those of the adult males for whom women and boys were the embodiment of beauty and sexual attraction; for this reason, the stereotypes of the mistress and of the *puer* share not only some superficial characteristics but also some deeper structural ones.

Three major factors thus determine the nature of the material to be surveyed in this chapter. Most important is the exclusively adult male heterosexual/pederastic viewpoint of erotic poetry, which limited the subject to women and boys. Next is the bipolar structure that distinguishes obscene from nonobscene, and attractive from repulsive. The concepts "attractive" and "repulsive" rest on a hierarchical evaluative system with set criteria, and the examination of women or boys relative to these criteria then forms part of the content of erotic poetry. Normally, explicitly sexual material was perceived as obscene. Yet inasmuch as the area outside the obscene had a positive value in Roman society and literature while the obscene had a negative value, poetry in which women and boys were found to meet ideal criteria could straddle the boundary between obscene and nonobscene. Hence the last major factor in the material here: a confusion of styles and genres. Some satire is rather erotic; some epigrams are not only not erotic but wry, almost satiric, and some are strongly satiric. There can be strong similarities between erotic and satiric poems on similar subjects. Therefore, because it is often difficult to isolate one standpoint for a writer, it will be much more helpful to compare writers, and even genres, for technique and for what each includes and excludes. Since primarily the physical details of the erotic ideal will be of interest in the following chapters, this chapter will deal primarily with epigram, both Greek and Latin, and will make some comparison with elegy, lyric, and epic.

Pueri

The ideal of the beautiful boy *(puer)* stands first here to emphasize the fact that in Latin erotic epigram it is not to be considered secondary or ancillary to the ideal of the beautiful woman.[5] Poetry about boys, like poetry about women, often strikes the reader as extremely idealized; the serious question of the reality of the corresponding situation in life can apply to boys, then, no more than to women. Most poems avoid physical detail,[6] and the emotion expressed is highly conventional, either slavish adulation or fiery lust. The younger Pliny was inspired to write such a poem (*Ep.* 7.4) not by a boy but by another poem—a poem that, says Pliny, Cicero wrote to Tiro.

That Cicero should have written such a poem to Tiro is surprising mostly because of the nature of the poems to *pueri*: the boys are generally pictured as lovely and idle, viewed at play, in golden adolescence, whereas one thinks of Tiro as brisk, efficient, and middle-aged. Whatever Tiro looked like, he must have been past adolescence; if Cicero really lusted after him, he was employing a high degree of fiction in the poem expressing his desire. The poems to *pueri* generally imagine them as timeless, at worst threatened by burgeoning whiskers and body hair. These boys are never viewed as potential adults who will become freedmen, carry on business and government, have children, or grow old. The *pueri* in these poems are "sex objects" in the starkest sense—lovely, desirable, romantic *things*. But another feature of their character is fairly securely rooted in reality: they are generally pictured as slaves, most commonly either for sale on the auction block or pouring wine at a dinner party. That lust toward slave boys had societal approval while lust toward *ingenui* did not is implied by Cicero's tirade against Antony's youthful career in *Phil.* 2.44–47 (see above); that this was an artificially maintained barrier is attested by the fact that sexual intercourse with a freeborn youth was illegal (see below, appendix 2).

The Greek epigrams on beautiful boys current in the late Republic and early Empire had a flavor slightly different from the Roman. Most of these epigrams in the *Palatine Anthology* are in book 12, which is composed largely of poems written by Strato but does include some earlier work. Authors of poems in *AP* 12 include the eminent poet Dioscorides, the epic poet and editor of Homer, Rhianus (both late third century B.C.); the anthologist Meleager, Phanias, and Glaucus, all of whose works appeared in Meleager's *Garland* (90s B.C.); and, from the *Garland* of Philip, Automedon, Tullius Laureas (possibly Cicero's freedman), and Statyllius Flaccus.[7] The poems in *AP* 12 are generally lofty in tone, and many of them revolve around the theme "Boy, you repulse me now; do not be so cold; you will reach manhood all too soon."

AP 12.39:

> Ἐσβέσθη Νίκανδρος, ἀπέπτατο πᾶν ἀπὸ χροιῆς
> ἄνθος, καὶ χαρίτων λοιπὸν ἔτ' οὐδ' ὄνομα,
> ὃν πρὶν ἐν ἀθανάτοις ἐνομίζομεν. ἀλλὰ φρονεῖτε
> μηδὲν ὑπὲρ θνητούς, ὦ νέοι· εἰσὶ τρίχες.

> Nikandros has been put out, like a fire, and from his skin
> all the bloom has flown away, and of his graces is there left
> not even a name—a boy whom we counted among the immortals, before.
> So plan nothing beyond mortals, o young men; hairs do exist.

The hairs represent the nemesis that awaits coy boys; they will make the beloved boy unattractive to those who once courted him and will force him in turn to pursue other boys.[8] Nikandros' attributes—the blooming skin, the "charms," the attribution of divinity, even the cleverly compressed equation of him with fire—all are conventional. For although the narrators of these poems always speak of themselves as half-crazed by desire, the meticulously controlled form of the poem belies and undercuts this fiction. And despite the facts that the thwarting of the narrators' desires is usually what stimulates the poem and that the satisfaction of their desires, if blissful, is rare, still they avow with fervor their preference for boys and proclaim the love of boys to be far more enthralling than that of women (e.g., 12.17). The attitude of the poets in *AP* 12 is markedly humble and abject; as Nikandros here is "among the immortals," so elsewhere the poet rejoices in his slavery to a beloved boy (e.g., especially 12.158, 169).

The physical and psychological attributes especially valued in boys in *AP* 12 are few in number but glowingly described. Complexions and eyes (especially "sparkling") of all shades are admired (12.5, 93, 94, 159, 165, 230, 244, 249), as are sweet voices (12.7, 22, 94, 95, 122, 162) and devoted attendance (12.34). Smooth skin is of paramount importance. The threat of impending manhood symbolized by the growth of body hair and beard stressed in many poems[9] includes several drawbacks—switch of role from beloved to lover, possible interest in women, loss of overall attractiveness—but perhaps chief of these is the marring of the beauty of the anal area (12.30 [Alcaeus], 33 [Meleager], 36 [Asclepiades], 204 [Strato]). Thus, despite the fact that Strato alone wrote thirty-four of forty-seven explicitly sexual epigrams in *AP* 12 and seven out of eleven that mention the buttocks, it seems safe to assume his concern is representative even if his poems are unusually "hard core." The aesthetic involved shows up clearly in 12.40 (anon.):

> Μὴ 'κδύσῃς, ἄνθρωπε, τὸ χλαίνιον, ἀλλὰ θεώρει
> οὕτως ἀκρολίθου κἀμὲ τρόπον ξοάνου.
> γυμνὴν 'Αντιφίλου ζητῶν χάριν, ὡς ἐπ' ἀκάνθαις
> εὑρήσεις ῥοδέαν φυομένην κάλυκα.

Don't take off, o man, my little cloak, but look [at me]
as if I were a god's statue with only head and legs of marble.
If you seek the naked grace of Antiphilos, then upon thorns
you will find the rosebud growing.

The "rosebud" is the anus,[10] the "thorns" are the bristly (as in 12.36), unattractive hairs. Strato compares the anus to gold (12.6 *πρωκτός* = *χρυσός*) and, in an extended simile (12.204), says a beautiful (*καλός*) boy is to a hairy (*δασύς*) boy as a rosebud is to a bramble, a fig[11] is to a mushroom, or a lamb like curdled milk is to an ox. The beauty of the anus is explicitly related to its sexual function, and allied with the other attractive features, in 12.22 (Scythinus: *τὸ λαβεῖν ἔνδον, ἀμεμπτότατον*) and in 12.7 (Strato):

Σφιγκτὴρ οὐκ ἔστιν παρὰ παρθένῳ, οὐδὲ φίλημα
ἁπλοῦν, οὐ φυσικὴ χρωτὸς ἐϋπνοΐη,
οὐ λόγος ἡδὺς ἐκεῖνος ὁ πορνικός, οὐδ' ἀκέραιον
βλέμμα, διδασκομένη δ' ἐστὶ κακιοτέρα.
ψυχροῦνται δ' ὄπιθεν πᾶσαι· τὸ δὲ μεῖζον ἐκεῖνο,
οὐκ ἔστιν ποῦ θῇς τὴν χέρα πλαζομένην.

There is no ring in a maiden, nor kiss
quintessential, nor natural sweet fragrance of the skin,
nor that sweet talk that whores use, nor a pure
glance, while the girl who is taught these things is even worse.
And they're all freezing cold behind; but what's a bigger [problem],
there's no place to put your wandering hand.

Comparatively few Greek epigrams discuss physical love of boys even as explicitly as this, or describe their genitalia; notable exceptions are four poems by Strato comparing a boy's penis to a lizard (11.21, 22; 12.3, 207). The terms used to describe the boys' penises sound like slang or "pet" words (12.3):

Τῶν παίδων, Διόδωρε, τὰ προσθέματ' εἰς τρία πίπτει
σχήματα, καὶ τούτων μάνθαν' ἐπωνυμίας.
τὴν ἔτι μὲν γὰρ ἄθικτον ἀκμὴν λάλου ὀνόμαζε,
κωκὼ τὴν φυσᾷν ἄρτι καταρχομένην·
τὴν δ' ἤδη πρὸς χεῖρα σαλευομένην, λέγε σαύραν·
τὴν δὲ τελειοτέρην, οἶδας ἃ χρή σε καλεῖν.

Little boys' front-hangers, Diodorus, fall into three
shapes, so learn the names given to them.
Call the bloom still untouched "goo-goo,"[12]
and the one just beginning to be puffed up, "coo-coo";
the one already rolling toward your hand, call "lizard";
but the one that is more perfect, you know what you should call it.

The preferred size is apparently the largest, as can be seen by comparing this poem with those praising the "lizard" and with those weighing the virtues of boys at different ages. In 12.4 Strato starts with boys at age twelve and says each successive year is better—until sixteen is for the gods, seventeen is for Zeus, and older than seventeen is for pathics; at 12.22 sixteen is best; at 12.205 twelve is too young. In 12.251 the poet implies that a lover would not request anal intercourse of a boy who was too young (while repeating the warning that the boy's charm in this area will leave him). The charms of plump little boys are often described and are probably inherent in the frequent equation of a boy with Cupid; Meleager (12.95) even suggests that it is pleasant to fondle the breast (τιτθός) of a boy under his tunic. Still, the general rule appears to be that the more the boy seems like an adult without development of body hair, the more attractive he is.

As has been shown, it is often implied that the lover admires smaller boys and awaits the day when such a boy will be ready for anal intercourse, at the same time fearing the day when the boy will be too old for it. Many poems rave about a boy's delicious kisses, which should be deep (12.183); an anonymous poem (12.123) describes the joy of kissing a boy who is covered with blood after winning a boxing match. Two of the troop of little boys Meleager describes at 12.95 stimulate the lover manually. But anal penetration is the underlying goal, even if it is often glossed over or euphemized (12.179 πέπεισται), and both Strato (12.11, 216, 240) and Scythinus (12.232) bemoan their impotence on occasion. There are tender vignettes of sleeping with a boy (12.125, 136, 137) and sketches of foreplay (12.209). Strato fantasizes that boys will fondle his (roll-shaped) book and rub it with various attractive parts of their body—lips, thighs, breasts, buttocks (12.208). But he also fantasizes about forcing a boy (12.200) and about a wrestling master (who would have such great opportunities, cf. 12.206) raping a boy (12.222).

The poems in *AP* 12 rarely use primary obscenities, and they delight in puns, euphemisms, and periphrases (as in 12.3). πέος appears only once, used by Strato in a description of his own impotence (12.240); πυγή appears at 30.2, πυγίζειν at 240.4, 243.1, and 245.3, and βινεῖ at 245.1, in a rejection of women. μηρός, "thigh," is more common (12.37, 97, 208, 240, 247). There are some puns on στύειν; but the language of the explicitly sexual poems is more strongly suggestive than coarse.

These poems do not specify that the boys are slaves and indeed only rarely give any explicit indication of the boys' social status or circumstances. The setting seems to be a romantic fantasy world in which external realities are much less significant than ideal passions, passing time, and ideal beauty. And all three features are idealized to an exaggerated extent: the passion burns the lover alive, the beloved is as beautiful as a statue or a satin doll, and time, which will transmute the boy, is deified as Nemesis—or else the lover speculates that Zeus will take this boy as he took Ganymede. Yet particular features of this idealized stereotype bear on the relation between the poem's fiction and the poet's reality. Foremost is the consistently upheld allotment of roles: the lover humbly beseeches or humbly exults, the boy disdainfully rejects or condescendingly gives in. Yet the poets insist on the fragility, youth, and delicacy of the boys, and when they threaten adulthood, they use brawn and hairs to represent the impending doom: presumably the beseeching lover is a brawny, hairy figure. The poems thus depend on a conscious reversal of roles in which the strong, older figure, who is also the poem's creator, abases himself before the weak, younger figure, who is the poem's subject. Even Zeus, the supreme male figure, is imagined as abject (12.1, 70).

A further contradiction inherent in the poems lies in the few physical features singled out for description. Complexions, hair, and eyes are all features described as beautiful for women—and men—in epic poetry and are usually the only features described at all for women. Fragrance is an attribute of divinity. To describe the anus and buttocks in the same breath as these other, conventionally sublime features requires the use of special terms; hence the anus is a rose and the threatening hairs are thorns. The metaphor has several levels. On the visual level the rose is round and pink, the thorns are black and spiky. On the evaluative level the rosebud is costly, precious, lovely, young, associated with luxuries and revelry; the thorns are worthless, weeds to be discarded. On the physical level the rose is smooth, soft, and sweet smelling, while thorns cause pain and difficulty.

Now although the explicit elevated treatment of the anus and buttocks does not recur frequently in *AP* 12, it is implicit in poems about the threat of hairs and can be taken as typical of the underlying idealized view of the boy's anal region. This is significant; it shows that the anal region was recognized by the poet/lover as the ultimate and most attractive focus of his sexual desire, with the boy's penis (the larger the better, within limits) an important secondary characteristic—as, for example, a woman's breasts in modern western culture are considered an important initial sexual stimulus, also to be fondled. As will be seen, no such attraction was attributed to the genitalia of mistresses (the functional equivalent of the boy's anus), with or without the help of elevated metaphor.[13] A further point of difference in the treatment of different sexual roles is that the poetry gives no clue as to what the boy was to find to attract him physically to the lover. Apart from promises of gifts, the poet/lover does not boast of or even point out his own good features. In fact, the sexual objectification of boys, which seems to portray them as omnipotent, actually deprives them of any voice at all; no poem in *AP* 12 imagines a boy betrayed or hurt by his lover, no poem speaks with the voice of a boy.

Occasionally a lover complains that boys are no longer satisfied with simple presents and now demand too much money (12.42, 44, 148, 212, 214, 237, 239). Only once does a poet address a boy who is the concubine of another (12.211); here the poet says the boy should yield to him, since his master uses him only to satisfy himself and then rolls over and goes to sleep. That boys have to be bribed or paid, or are chattel, is a great point of similarity between them and women in epigram, and this issue will be taken up again below.

This collection of epigrams certainly represents a lively tradition continued in Greek from the late Republic through the Empire. The way and the milieu in which Roman literati adopted such poetry are perhaps best shown by two anecdotes in Aulus Gellius (the first repeated wholesale by Macrobius, *Sat.* 2.2.15–17). The first concerns a Greek love poem from a man to a *puer*, attributed by Aulus Gellius to Plato, in which the poet's soul leaps across to Agathon's body in a kiss. This poem is paraphrased in Latin by a friend of Gellius' whom he calls "οὐκ ἄμουσος *adulescens*" (19.11.3), a significantly hybrid term. The second anecdote (19.9) demonstrates the antiquity of this sort of emulation. Here a defender of Roman literature over Greek quotes the erotic epigrams of early Latin poets. All are extremely similar in theme to Greek erotic epigrams appearing in the anthologies, and it is noteworthy that the speaker cites four epigrams, of which two are addressed to women and two to *pueri*, without noting any difference in kind between them. The speaker, who is supposedly a Spaniard at a party, recites the poems with veiled head, remarking that Socrates cloaked his modesty thus: two poems by Valerius Aedituus—a jingly one to "Pamphila" and one on the flames of desire to "Phileros"; one by Porcius Licinus, Scipio's friend, on the flames of desire; and one by Q. Catulus, apparently the noted member of the Scipionic circle, imitating Callimachus, on how his soul has fled to "Theotimus." The names accent the Greek flavor of the poems.

There is no need here to state again the impact of Alexandrianism on Latin literature. It should merely be noted that, in addition to these early and undistinguished epigrammatists and Cicero, Catullus (24, 48, 81, 99) and Horace (*C.* 4.10; cf. 1.4.19–20) wrote serious poems to *pueri*. Indeed, the similarity of the Juventius poems to the tally of Lesbia's kisses in Catullus 5 and 7 has given rise to a long controversy as to the referent of Catullus 16.12.[14] It can clearly be seen from Gellius' second anecdote that to a Roman reader there was no practical difference between desiring a thousand kisses from your mistress or from your *puer*. Both are expressions of masculine desire—it is the elegance of the poetry and the romantic attitude of mind that are *mollis*.

Presumably the tradition of Greek epigram continued to inspire the production of similar poems in Latin, just as Pliny emulated Cicero; but, except for the odd poem by Seneca and a few serious short poems in the *Satyricon*, few of these are preserved until the oeuvre of Martial. The sheer number of such poems in Martial presupposes their popularity, and he himself provided a model for Strato.[15] Although he achieved a certain originality in creating a middle ground between erotic and invective homosexual epigram, Martial does offer many specimens of the conventional epigram to a *puer*. His poems much resemble Greek epigram—they speak of sweet kisses and haughty looks, teasing refusals, breath like perfume. In tone they are quite formal. Martial 3.65 can stand as an example:[16]

Quod spirat tenera malum mordente puella,
  quod de Corycio quae venit aura croco;
vinea quod primis cum floret cana racemis,

gramina quod redolent, quae modo carpsit ovis;
quod myrtus, quod messor Arabs, quod sucina trita,
pallidus Eoo ture quod ignis olet;
gleba quod aestivo leviter cum spargitur imbre,
quod madidas nardo passa corona comas:
hoc tua, saeve puer Diadumene, basia fragrant.
quid si tota dares illa sine invidia?

The scent of a young girl biting into an apple,
the scent of the perfume that comes from Corycian saffron;
the scent when the white vine flowers with its first grape clusters,
the scent the young grass smells of that the sheep's just cropped;
the scent of myrrh, the scent of the Arabian harvester, the scent of rubbed amber,
the scent of the fire pale with Eastern incense;
the scent of earth when it's sprinkled lightly with summer rain,
the scent of a garland that's felt locks damp with balsam:
this is the scent with which your kisses are fragrant, Diadumenos, my cruel boy.
What would it be if you gave them whole, without grudging?

The boy himself appears only in the penultimate line of the poem, implied in the first eight lines but appearing fully only as a lovely surprise in lines 9–10. This is a highly artificial and dehumanizing technique applied by Martial to exactly opposite ends in invective; in 11.21, for example, the list consists not of sweet-smelling things but of rank, dirty, loose things, and the woman attacked appears in only the first and the penultimate lines.

Most elevated of all are the poems written for formal occasions—epitaphs for *pueri* (1.88, 6.28–29, 6.68), who are inevitably compared to Hylas, and poems written to celebrate the first cutting of the beard (1.31, 4.48, 9.16, 9.36, 12.84). A common and frigid conceit is the comparison of the boy, usually a cupbearer, to Ganymede (5.55, 10.98; cf. 9.36). The formality and social acceptability, indeed, cachet, of such poetry are demonstrated by the series of poems to Earinos, Domitian's cupbearer (9.11–13, 9.16–17, 9.36). Martial is notorious for his flattery of the *princeps*, and these poems are certainly aimed to please, not overlooking the chance to compare Jupiter unfavorably with Domitian (9.36). The proximity of these poems to those praising the revival of the laws against prostitution of male children (9.8) shows how distinct the literary perceptions of different categories of pederasty were. Martial praises Domitian for protecting children from the unspeakable evils they would undergo as prostitutes; the beauties of Earinos are something else altogether—he is no prostitute but the cherished cupbearer of an emperor. The sensibility Martial adopts for his formal poetry allows him both to embroider on a conventional, fantasized sexuality in which a boy is the object of romantic love and to deplore the sordidness of prostitution. When he was writing humorously of "himself" or of Roman society, Martial's sensibility descended from this lofty plane, and he could express less noble emotions toward boys as well as mock the whole complex of romantic homosexual fantasy. This is most true of his satirical epigrams, but quite a few poems are marginal, showing admiration of *pueri* but using coarse language or crude imagery.

It is apparent from the invective poetry against adult male pathic homosexuals (below, chap. 5) that the anal area was a focus of sexual attention for Romans as well as Greeks; the one characteristic always cited as the mark of the pathic is his shaved buttocks, which are supposed to make him once again as smooth and attractive as a boy. Admiring remarks on the boy's anus in Martial are few but suggest a strongly felt sexual aesthetic (cf. especially 11.58.4) in which boys and their sexual function win out over women (12.75):

> Festinat Polytimus ad puellas;
> invitus puerum fatetur Hypnus;
> pastas glande natis habet Secundus;
> mollis Dindymus est sed esse non vult;
> Amphion potuit puella nasci.
> horum delicias superbiamque
> et fastus querulos, Avite, malo
> quam dotis mihi quinquies ducena.

> Polytimus hurries to girls;
> Hypnus unwillingly admits he is a boy;
> Secundus has a butt fed on head;
> Dindymus is soft but does not wish to be;
> Amphion could have been born a girl.
> The sweetness and haughtiness of these
> and their complaining quarrels, Avitus, I prefer
> to a dowry of five times two hundred thousand sesterces.

And in a poem reproaching a wife for being jealous of her husband's boy-concubines (12.96.7–12):

> hi dant quod non vis uxor dare. "Do tamen" inquis
> "ne vagus a thalamis coniugis erret amor."
> non eadem res est: Chiam volo, nolo mariscam:
> ne dubites quae sit Chia, marisca tua est.
> scire suos fines matrona et femina debet:
> cede sua pueris, utere parte tua.

> they give what you as a wife do not wish to give. "I do give it," you say,
> "lest the love of my husband stray wandering from my bedroom."
> It's not the same thing; I want a Chian fig, not a *marisca*;
> lest you doubt which is the Chian, yours is the *marisca*.
> The wife and woman ought to know their own limits:
> let boys use their own part, you use yours.

In 12.75 Martial rejects any wife, even a rich one, for the love of five boys with varying sexual characteristics. While two of them (lines 1, 4) resist being the object of pederasty, three (lines 2, 3, 5) are glad of it. These boys are said to be like girls, and of them Secundus, the only one with a Roman name, has *pastas glande natis*, literally "a butt fed on acorn," *glande* being slang for the glans penis. The image is similar to that employed in invective against the female genitalia, but subtly reversed: where the *cunnus* is said to devour the penis,[17] these *natis* are *pastas*, "fed on" the penis. The feeding is voluntary, and the *natis* seem like a fat, contented animal. In 12.96, where boys and wife share the husband, Martial still clearly says that the boys provide something the wife cannot, or for which she can provide only an inferior substitute. Chian products were fine and desirable, hence Chian figs would be juicy and delicious; *mariscae*, on the other hand, were coarse, tasteless figs.[18] Not only, then, is the boy's anus preferable to a woman's, or perhaps the boy to any woman; the anus itself is perceived positively, through two metaphors related to eating. The lover's penis is like an acorn, the boy's anus is like a good fig. The metaphor is more homely than the Greek metaphor of the rosebud, and the double link with eating perhaps mirrors the anal/oral connection so prevalent in Latin invective (see below).

Martial expresses a concern that the boy's adulthood not be precipitated by genital stimulation;[19] one of his more explicit epigrams reproves a lover for fondling his *puer's* penis (11.22):

> Mollia quod nivei duro teris ore Galaesi
> basia, quod nudo cum Ganymede iaces,
> (quis negat?) hoc nimiumst, sed sit satis; inguina saltem
> parce fututrici sollicitare manu.
> levibus in pueris plus haec quam mentula peccat
> et faciunt digiti praecipitantque virum:
> inde tragus celeresque pili mirandaque matri
> barba, nec in clara balnea luce placent.
> divisit natura marem: pars una puellis,
> una viris genita est. utere parte tua.

> That with your hard mouth you rub the soft kisses
> of snowy Galaesus, that you lie with a naked Ganymede
> (who denies it?), this is too much. But let it be enough;
> at least refrain from stirring up his groin with your fucker hand.
> For smooth boys this does more harm than a prick
> and fingers make and hasten the man;
> hence goat-smell, swift hairs, and a beard to amaze
> his mother, nor does he like the baths in a good light.
> Nature has divided up the male: one part is born for girls,
> one part for men. Use your own part.

This epigram, which gave its punch line to 12.96, takes the opposite tack, depriving the adult male lover of the *puer* from use of the *puer's* penis, while 12.96

kept the woman from offering her anus in place of her vagina. The lover is seemingly attracted to the penis as he is to the boy's soft kisses and divine beauty, and the penis, like the boy, must be immature. The lover's strength *(duro . . . ore)* contrasts sharply with the boy's tenderness *(mollia . . . basia, nivei)*, which in turn is contrasted with the transformed male at adulthood—rank, hairy, bearded. The narrator's attitude is ambivalent: *hoc nimiumst* is disapproving, but the point of the poem is that *pueri* should be preserved as such as long as possible. The coarse language *(fututrici, mentula)* contrasts with the rather elevated tone of lines 1–6 just as the man contrasts with the boy, and both obscene words apply to the man. The whole, then, states a more hostile, aggressive sexuality than poems to *pueri* usually do (cf. Mart. 1.58, 11.70; 2.43.13–14, 11.58, 11.73). The paradoxes of the situation pervade 11.70: here the boys are Tucca's masters *(dominos)*, but he is selling them and they are weeping; he had paid 100,000 sesterces for them; they use cajolery *(blanditiae)* while he has bitten their necks (line 4); when their tunics are lifted, there can be seen "the prick fashioned by [his] hand" *(inspicitur . . . mentula facta manu)*.

But there is an opposing aesthetic in Martial's poetry according to which the boys are admired for their large penises. In some cases (3.71, 3.73; if *grandes* = *mutuniati*, also 7.62, 12.49) this indicates that the boys, clearly identified as *pueri*, are kept to service pathic masters, a complete reversal of the norm in Greek and most Latin poetry. Indeed, Juvenal singles out one man who plays the pathic for young men for special scorn (2.50; that he is not unique is implied by 2.40–50). But it seems that boys with large penises were admired even by nonpathic men (Mart. 11.63):

Spectas nos, Philomuse, cum lavamur,
et quare mihi tam mutuniati
sint leves pueri subinde quaeris.
dicam simpliciter tibi roganti:
pedicant, Philomuse, curiosos.

You look at me, Philomusus, while I'm washing,
and you always ask why I have
smooth boys with such big cocks.
I will reply simply to you who ask:
Philomusus, they bugger the curious.

Philomusus' question implies that "Martial" (the narrator of the poem) is being serviced by these boys, but Martial would never imply such a thing about himself and threatens Philomusus with punitive anal rape by the boys.[20] Martial must have such boys for their beauty; they are not only *mutuniati* but *leves*, one of the chief attributes of the young and beautiful *puer*. If *drauci* (?"studs") can be compared with *pueri*, it may be appropriate to note here that they were said to be extremely attractive to adult pathics because of the size of their penises (Mart. 1.96, 9.27; cf. 9.59.3–6); at 11.72 "Natta" is said to call his *draucus*'s huge penis *pipinnam*, "peeper," in a manner that anticipates *AP* 12.3.

Thus Martial treats the *puer* differently on different levels. A composite picture of the erotic ideal in Martial (e.g., 4.42) would much resemble that of Greek epigram, with the added specification that the boy is a slave from the East with long, curly locks. Like the boys of *AP* 12, Martial's *puer* is lovely: on his cheeks is only a faint adolescent fuzz; he has starry eyes; he gives delicious kisses and has soft, rosy lips; he loves to play ball or other games with other *pueri*; he is smooth and soft all over. Martial describes the boy's genitalia and anus only in coarser poems, where the anus is attractive and preferred to what women can offer, and the penis, whether undeveloped or unusually large, is much admired.

The nonsexual attractions of *pueri* in Martial shed additional light on the motivation for the poet-lover's admiration. As in 12.75, the boys are difficult: they resist, thwart the poet, and argue, and boys in Martial's epigrams run away as often as those in *AP* 12 (e.g., 1.46, 2.55, 5.83). In addition, they are expensive. The gifts they demand are not as notably lavish as those exacted by mistresses (cf. Tib. 1.4.57–60, 1.9), but often the boys are imagined as on the auction block and far too costly for the poet to buy (1.58; cf. 9.59.3–6). And often they are male concubines to be bought and sold (9.21, 9.59, 11.70, 12.16, 12.33). In short, the boys are a costly and recalcitrant commodity, each a prize for the persistent male. In this they resemble both the boys of *AP* 12 and the ideal women of Latin poetry, and this in part determines the way in which both male and female objects of desire are evaluated. The boys themselves supposedly set the cash value on their physical selves (11.58.1–4):

> Cum me velle vides tentumque, Telesphore, sentis,
>   magna rogas: puta me velle negare: licet?
> et nisi iuratus dixi "Dabo," subtrahis illas,
>   permittunt in me quae tibi multa, nates.

> When you see I want it and you can feel I'm stiff, Telesphorus,
>   you ask a big price; imagine I want to say no, can I?
> And unless I've sworn and said, "I'll pay," you take away that butt,
>   that lets you get away with so much from me.

The boys are subordinate, yet the lovers are grown men who strive for their favors; perhaps the boys are valued as they provide an exotic contrast with the appearance and role of the pursuing lover. To be pursued, one has to look like a vulnerable, shimmering creature.

Mistresses

Although erotic poetry about women was lumped by the Romans with that about boys, it occurs in a greater variety of poetic forms. Even satire included idealized descriptions of sexual encounters with women; one such in Lucilius (925–27 Marx, reconstructed by Lachmann) seems uncharacteristically straight-faced, although he certainly may have undercut it:

> ⟨Cretaea nuper⟩, cum ad me cubitum venerat
> sponte ipsa suapte adducta ut tunicam et cetera
> reiceret
>
> Cretaea recently, when she had come to me to go to bed,
> was led of her own free will to throw off her underwear
> and everything else

Likewise Horace *S.* 1.2, though it concentrates on the negative aspects of making love to the wrong women, states the positive attributes of the right women.

A short and familiar list of idealized attributes can easily be drawn up for women in epic, lyric, and elegy.[21] There is a narrow limit to the description of women's beauty in epic poetry; a highly conventionalized decorum is observed. Dido, for example, has blond hair (*A.* 4.590, 698; cf. Mercury, 4.558–59). This is the only feature Vergil ever brings up seemingly for its own sake, although when she strikes her breast, it too is "lovely" (4.589), and mention of her eyes at key points in the action makes them seem an important part of her beauty. She dresses in splendid clothes (4.137–39), and overall beauty is part of her character (1.496, *forma pulcherrima*; 4.60, 192). But beauty in characters in epic is generally part of their heroic, quasi-divine status, especially when a god or goddess throws beauty over a hero or heroine like a cloak.

Beauty in love poetry is something else again. Dido and Penelope are never (paradoxically for Dido) really objects of desire, certainly not of the poet's or reader's desire. In love poetry the fiction is that the subject of the poem is the poet's desire, or its object; yet there are similarities between the features of beauty in epic and those in elegy. For even for the women in elegy who are objects of desire there is a prescribed list of attractive features, which includes the list from epic—hair, breasts, eyes.

Several descriptive passages from Ovid's *Amores* (1.5, 2.4, 2.15, 3.3) offer typical tabulations of points of beauty.[22] In 1.5, a scene of love in the afternoon that seems to have an antecedent in the Lucilius passage quoted above, Ovid singles out for praise Corinna's white neck, shoulders, arms, breasts, smooth belly, side, and thigh (lines 17–22). In 3.3 the beauty of the forsworn mistress lies in her face, hair, fairness, small foot, shining eyes, and tallness. These are the attributes Ovid praises elsewhere in the *Amores*: Corinna's hair is still lovely even after Ovid has beaten her (1.7.12–18), but she ruins it by dyeing it (1.14); her beautiful face is enhanced by a blush (2.5) but makes her cruel (2.17); she aborts her baby to keep her belly smooth (2.14.7–8). Ovid wishes to be a ring on her hand so he might touch her bosom, nipples, and naked limbs in the bath (2.15); this poem is unusually suggestive:

> tam bene convenias, quam mecum convenit illi,
> et digitum iusto commodus orbe teras!
> ....
> me gere, cum calidis perfundes imbribus artus
> ....

sed, puto, te nuda mea membra libidine surgent,
  et peragam partes anulus ille viri.

May you [the ring] fit as well as she fits me,
  and may you rub her finger, accommodating it with the right [size] circle.

. . . .

wear me [as the ring], when you pour hot showers over your limbs,

. . . .

but, I think, with you naked my members will rise with lust,
  and I, as a ring, will play the part of a man.

Again, he praises her legs and thighs, hinting at what is above them (3.2.35–36):

suspicor ex istis et cetera posse placere,
  quae bene sub tenui condita veste latent.

I suspect from those [legs] of yours that the rest, too, is nice,
  that lies well hidden under your thin clothing.

A list of the kinds of women who attract the poet (2.4) turns out to be, he says, a list of every kind of woman. His criteria are modesty/forwardness/aloofness; learning/ignorance; admiration of Ovid's poetry/scorn for it; light step/heavy; sweet singing/playing the lyre/dancing; tall/short; ill-dressed/well-dressed; white skin/blond/dark skin; black hair/yellow hair; youth/experience. Ovid also describes, with a vividness unusual in elegy, the wantonness proper to a mistress in bed (3.14.17–26): she is to take off her clothes, lie beneath her lover and press thigh to thigh, kiss with her tongue, use many positions, cries, and motions. The flame of love appears briefly at 2.16.11–12.

The list in *Am.* 2.4, of course, does not include "every kind of woman"; the list itself and the analysis of the criteria into artificial opposites are typical of the evaluative function central to Latin erotic writing. The attributes praised are of three sorts: some wholly physical and sexual, some physical but secondary, and some that have to do with the woman's personality. This last characteristic is least detailed; Ovid specifies only modesty or lack of it, learning, and attitude toward his poetry. The list of secondary physical characteristics is much more varied, including hair, eyes, complexion, foot size, pace, voice, and dress. Characteristics that relate to actual sexual experience of the woman include parts of the body: neck, shoulders, arms; breasts; smooth belly; sides and thighs. Height probably also belongs in this category, as it must be judged relative to the poet himself; the same goes for youth versus experience. This stereotype does its best to draw attention away from the primary sexual area, the genitalia, while implicitly limiting the relationship to the sexual. The woman has enough refinement to let her talk to Ovid—maybe. Her secondary characteristics are all socially visible: her hair looks good and is blond or black (not the red of a slave), her dress is subject to comment, her feet and the way she walks are on display, her eyes (like those of *pueri*) must shine, her voice is one of her tools for performance. The parts of her body that evoke desire in the poet form a sort of circle around the genitalia: from the usually visible neck, shoulders, and arms, which need to be graceful, to the usually hidden breasts, to the belly, which must show no signs of childbirth (wrinkles are considered "ugly"), to the sides and thighs. It is as if there were a blank space in the middle of the woman.

The mistress's genitalia and buttocks are simply not described; Ovid, who is much more explicit about what is beautiful in a woman than is Horace in the *Odes*, nevertheless uses the euphemistic *latus* (1.5.22) to praise Corinna's flanks ("quantum et quale," he says). Moreover, he is not specific in his description, saying only that these were Corinna's good points, not why he likes them—"quos umeros," he says (1.5.19), "quos lacertos"—and of her breasts only that they are *apta premi*, "right for squeezing." Elegy used only part of the erotic ideal available to the literary Roman; much more graphic descriptions of the beauty of a mistress were in circulation, in Greek if not in Latin, and a great many of them survive.

Greek amatory epigrams were collected in book 5 of the *Palatine Anthology*, with some in book 11. Of the epigrams in the *Palatine Anthology* on sexual and scatological themes, a great many were written or in circulation during the time span covered here. Four writers of sexual material—Asclepiades (born ca. 320 B.C.), Dioscorides (ca. end of the third century B.C.), Crates (after the death of Euphorion, probably mid-second century B.C.), and Meleager (fl. in the first decade of the first century B.C.)—had epigrams in Meleager's *Garland*, collected in the 90s B.C. The works of three others—Automedon (probably roughly contemporary with the elder Seneca), Marcus Argentarius (probably the rhetorician known to the elder Seneca), and Philodemus (the well-known philosopher, ca. 110 B.C.–ca. 40 B.C.)—were collected in the *Garland* of Philip, which was assembled in the mid-first century A.D.[23] The poets Lucillius (fl. under Nero), Nicarchus (roughly his contemporary), and Rufinus wrote most of the explicitly sexual poems in *AP* 5.[24]

The Greek epigrams in praise of women exhibit a less lofty sentimentality than do the poems to boys in *AP* 12 and are less romantic in tone than elegy is. Proclamations of enslavement are rare. It is lust that receives conventional treatment in Greek amatory epigram, and the poet always seems to have in mind the physical experience of being in bed with a woman. Common, too, are poems decrying the cold-heartedness of a mistress and wishing upon her a rapid incursion of wrinkles, sagging breasts, and gray hairs; these are similar to the poems pointing out impending puberty to a cold-hearted boy, except that the woman is threatened with senility where the boy is threatened with adulthood. A conventional and often rueful sentiment attaches to the theme of the lamp, as a gift given to a mistress and as a telltale witness of her nights in bed (*AP* 5.4, 5, 7, 8, 128, 263, 279).

The vivid, explicitly sexual epigrams on women include few primary obscenities, only βινεῖ, "fucks" (5.126), and πύγαι, "asses" (5.35, 54, 55).[25] More commonly, they develop impressionistic physical pictures of naked women through metaphors and double entendres. Five authors (Dioscorides, Meleager, Philodemus, Marcus Argentarius, and Rufinus) who wrote epigrams on assorted unusual sexual topics single out the woman's hips, buttocks, and groin for description. Philodemus, addressing the various parts of his mistress's body, hymns her buttocks, flanks, and genitalia (5.132); Meleager puns on the name of Callistion, saying she should be called "Callischion," "beautiful hips" (5.192); the later poet Rufinus has a much more elaborate and explicit pair of poems (5.35 and 36) on the premise "I was asked, like Paris, to judge the hindquarters (5.35)/crotches (5.36) of three beautiful women":

5.35:

πυγὰς αὐτὸς ἔκρινα τριῶν, εἵλοντο γὰρ αὐταί
δείξασαι γυμνῶν ἀστεροπὴν μελέων.
καί ῥ᾽ ἡ μὲν τροχαλοῖς σφραγιζομένη γελασίνοις
λευκῆι ἀπὸ γλουτῶν ἤνθεεν εὐαφίηι,
τῆς δὲ διαιρομένης φοινίσσετο χιονέη σάρξ
πορφυρέοιο ῥόδου μᾶλλον ἐρυθροτέρη,
ἡ δὲ γαληνιόωσα χαράσσετο κύματι κωφῶι
αὐτομάτη τρυφερῶι χρωτὶ σαλευομένη.
εἰ ταύτας ὁ κριτὴς ὁ θεῶν ἐθεήσατο πυγάς,
οὐκέτ᾽ ἂν οὐδ᾽ ἐσιδεῖν ἤθελε τὰς προτέρας.

I judged the asses of three; for they themselves chose [me]
to show the lightning of their naked limbs.
And one stamped with round dimples
bloomed with white softness to the touch from her buttocks;
the snowy flesh of the second, raised and parted, blushed crimson,
much redder than the ruby rose;
the third, calm, was furrowed by a noiseless wave,
of itself rolling in her soft skin.
If the judge of the goddesses had beheld these asses,
he wouldn't have wanted to look on the first ones any more.

5.36:

ἤρισαν ἀλλήλαις Ῥοδόπη Μελίτη Ῥοδόκλεια,
τῶν τρισσῶν τίς ἔχει κρείσσονα μηριόνην,
καί με κριτὴν εἵλοντο· καὶ ὡς θεαὶ αἱ περίβλεπτοι
ἔστησαν γυμναί, νέκταρι λειβόμεναι.
καὶ Ῥοδόπης μὲν ἔλαμπε μέσος μηρῶν πολύτιμος
⟨ ⟩
⟨ ⟩
οἷα ῥοδὼν †πολιῶι† σχιζόμενος ζεφύρωι·
τῆς δὲ Ῥοδοκλείης ὑάλωι ἴσος, ὑγρομέτωπος,

οἷα καὶ ἐν νηῷι πρωτογλυφὲς ξόανον.
ἀλλὰ σαφῶς ἃ πέπονθε Πάρις διὰ τὴν κρίσιν εἰδώς
τὰς τρεῖς ἀθανάτας εὐθὺ συνεστεφάνουν.

Rhodope, Melite, and Rhodocleia contested with each other
which one of the three had the best Meriones [pun on μηρός, "groin" or "thigh"],
and they chose me as judge; and like goddesses the naked women
stood there to be seen, flowing with nectar.
And the middle of Rhodope's thighs gleamed, costly,
[two lines missing]
like a bed of roses split by the bright west wind;
Rhodocleia's was like alabaster, with fluid brow,
like a newly carved statue of a god in a temple.
But knowing well what Paris suffered through his judgment,
I crowned all three immortals at once.[26]

From these two poems it can be gathered that men, or at least Rufinus, found plump buttocks attractive in women, and that to him the ideal female genitalia were depilated and polished until they seemed to shine between the thighs. Since Rufinus is the only poet to go into such detail, these may be idiosyncrasies; he praises the buttocks similarly elsewhere (5.60). But the depilation is consistent with contemporary practices.[27]

The kind of double entendre and metaphor typical of these poems is also found in Nicarchus' punning epigram against cunnilingus (11.329): he appeals to one addressee "not to cast down his eyes or indulge his tongue, for the pig [χοῖρος—a common metaphorical obscenity for the female genitalia, cf. *MM*, p. 131] has a thorn [ἄκανθαν—used here for pubic hair as for anal hair in the poems of book 12]; but you sleep in Phoenicia [φοινικίζω apparently signifying "perform cunnilingus"] and are nourished by a thigh, like Dionysus." The same kinds of puns, this time literary, are used in a much earlier epigram by Crates (11.218): Euphorion always had *Choiri*los on his lips, his poems were full of glosses/tongues, and he liked Philetas (φιλεῖν, "kissing") because he was so Homeric (Ὁμηρικός, related to μηρός). The repeated use of μηρός where it seems the genitalia themselves are meant is not so much a euphemism as an extension—or displacement—of the focus of interest from the vagina to the surrounding area; likewise, the slang term χοῖρος refers to the appearance of the depilated labia. Rufinus (5.60, 62) uses "golden apples" and "milk" to describe breasts, and "rose" (presumably) of the anus; cf. Dioscorides (5.54–56). But there is no metaphor in the Greek erotic epigrams to women that focuses on the vagina as attractive holder of the penis, no equivalent to the description of the boy's anus as beautiful. The color, consistency, and value of the vagina are not part of the erotic ideal.[28]

Greek epigram chooses for description sexual acts that have something unusual about them. Two elaborate poems (5.49, 11.328) describe a prostitute servicing three men at once, but since in at least one of them she is an old woman, the idea probably belongs with invective against old women. The picture of the dancing girl at 5.129 is much more positive, specifying her power to bring even old men to erection by her lascivious dancing and her sexual technique; descriptions of dancing girls were a commonplace, as will be seen, but Automedon's words are unusually explicit (cf. 5.131, 132). That the buttocks of women could be the focus of sexual attention is confirmed by two poems recommending anal intercourse with women: one, by Marcus Argentarius (5.116), suggests that a woman who is εὐΐσχιος can substitute for a boy, if you must have a boy (he says love of women is best); the other, by Dioscorides (5.54), says that although it is difficult to make love with a pregnant woman, anal intercourse is a fine substitute: *ἀλλὰ πάλιν στρέψας ῥοδοειδέϊ τέρπεο πυγῇ*, "but turning her over enjoy her roselike ass." He is even more enthusiastic in an explicit description of intercourse in 5.55:

Δωρίδα τὴν ῥοδόπυγον ὑπὲρ λεχέων διατείνας
ἄνθεσιν ἐν χλοεροῖς ἀθάνατος γέγονα.
ἡ γὰρ ὑπερφυέεσσι μέσον διαβᾶσά με ποσσίν
ἤνυσεν ἀκλινέως τὸν Κύπριδος δόλιχον,
ὄμμασι νωθρὰ βλέπουσα· τὰ δ' ἠύτε πνεύματι φύλλα
ἀμφισαλευομένης ἔτρεμε πορφύρεα,
μέχρις ἀπεσπείσθη λευκὸν μένος ἀμφοτέροισιν
καὶ Δωρὶς παρέτοις ἐξεχύθη μέλεσι.

Stretching out the rose-assed Doris on the bed
I became an immortal in her blooming flowers.
For she, straddling the middle of me with her extraordinary feet,
completed without swerving the marathon of Venus,
looking languidly out of her eyes; but they like leaves in the wind,
as she rolled around, trembled, crimson,
until the white flow was poured out from both of us
and Doris was spread loose with limbs relaxed.[29]

The same poet writes of the parts of the woman's body with much greater sensuality than most (5.56).

It is clear that many of the women addressed in *AP* 5 are prostitutes, if at a rarefied level. Complaints about high prices or extortionate demands for gifts are common,[30] and two of these are cast as dialogues between the man and the woman: in one (5.46) the man can afford the woman, in the other (5.101) she turns him away for not having enough money. As in poems on boys, the idea of payment can be closely connected with the sexual experience and the genitals (*AP* 5.126, Philodemus):

πέντε δίδωσιν ἑνὸς τῆι δείναι ὁ δεῖνα τάλαντα
καὶ βινεῖ φρίσσων καὶ μὰ τὸν οὐδὲ καλήν·
πέντε δ' ἐγὼ δραχμὰς τῶν δώδεκα Λυσιανάσσηι,
καὶ βινῶ πρὸς τῶι κρείσσονα καὶ φανερῶς.
πάντως ἤτοι ἐγὼ φρένας οὐκ ἔχω ἢ τό γε λοιπόν
τοὺς κείνου πελέκει δεῖ διδύμους ἀφελεῖν.

This guy gives this girl five talents for once,
and he fucks [her] shivering [with fear], and I swear she's not even pretty.
But I [give] five drachmas for twelve times to Lysianassa,
and I fuck, what's more, a better girl, and openly.
Either I've completely lost my mind, or from now on
he ought to lose his balls to the ax.

The poem's narrator feels himself to be the better man because he pays less for more and better intercourse with a prettier woman, and he uses the primary obscenity *βινεῖ* of both couples. The narrator feels the man who has paid more for such a poor experience is no man at all, does not deserve his virility, and so the appropriate treatment for him would be castration.

Such a buyer/seller relationship between man/phallus and woman resembles a master/slave relationship inasmuch as the item for sale is the woman's body. This is borne out by some external circumstances: some women are not available to the poet because they are guarded by keepers, old women (*AP* 5.101, 106, 262, 289, 294; cf. the boy's *paidagogos*, Mart. 9.27, 12.49); and occasionally the poet records that he has beaten his beloved (5.248). On the other hand, although the lovers in *AP* 5 are not nearly as abject as those of *AP* 12, they often pursue an evasive beloved and idealize their pangs of longing. Again this longing takes the ideal form of the fires of love or Cupid's arrows, though the figure of Cupid is naturally not as prominent in book 5 as it is in book 12. Where boys were compared with Ganymede, women are compared with goddesses—usually either the Graces or the three goddesses judged by Paris. There are examples of the *paraklausithyron* in *AP* 5, and although a few address boys, by far the majority address women: the *exclusus amator* who sleeps on the ground before his mistress's door and waters his wreaths with his tears certainly appears humble. Sometimes the relationship even seems equal: twice as many poems bemoan a broken vow as profess slavery, and the vow surely implies a contract between equals.[31] And there are three poems in *AP* 5 in which a woman is the speaker and reproaches a man (120, 297, 306; probably also 8).

Although all this means that *AP* 5 shows a wider range of relationships between men and women than *AP* 12 shows between men and boys, the structure of the relationship still hinges on the physical beauty of the beloved. The pursuer pursues, adopting a humble posture, as long as this beauty is expensive (attractive to many); when it is affordable, he possesses; when it is too cheap and fading, he ceases to pursue. In Greek epigram the attractive parts of the woman's body include the hips, buttocks, and groin, even if not the vagina; the beauty of these women is voluptuous, part of their sexuality. It is significant that what threatens them is old age. *Pueri* stop being attractive when they grow body hair, that is, when they turn into adult males; they have then stopped being *pueri*. Does this mean that when the women lose their attractive features and turn into crones, they have stopped being women? It would seem so. This aesthetic divides people into types, not by age alone but by age-related sexual attractions.

The poems threatening pursued women with old age occupy a middle ground between love poetry and invective against old women. They focus on the transformation of physical features from attractive to repulsive:[32]

AP 5.76:

> *αὔτη πρόσθεν ἔην ἐρατόχροος εἰαρόμασθος*
> *εὔσφυρος εὐμήκης εὔοφρυς εὐπλόκαμος·*
> *ἠλλάχθη δὲ χρόνωι καὶ γήραι καὶ πολιαῖσι,*
> *καὶ νῦν τῶν προτέρων οὐδ᾽ ὄναρ οὐδὲν ἔχει,*
> *ἀλλοτρίας δὲ τρίχας καὶ ῥυσῶδες ⟨τὸ⟩ πρόσωπον,*
> *οἷον γηράσας οὐδὲ πίθηκος, ἔχει.*

> Before, she was lovely-skinned, spring-breasted,
> fine-ankled, fine-lengthed, fine-browed, fine-locked;
> but she has been changed by time and old age and white hairs,
> and now none of her has even a dream of what it was before,
> but she has other women's hair and a wrinkled-looking face,
> not even an ape grown old has such a face.

In *AP* 5.204 the old woman is compared to a ship (and her lovers to oarsmen); all of her is slack, shaken, and soaked—back, hair, breasts, belly, genitalia, joints: "the flaccidity of her breasts droops [like] hanging sails . . . below, all of the ship is waterlogged, and in the hold the sea floods in . . ." A few poems praise women who, though old, have kept their attractive features: in 5.13 Charito, aged sixty, still has dark hair, her breasts are still like marble cones without the use of any supporting band, and her skin is unwrinkled (cf. 5.282). Philinna in 5.258 (a late poem) has breasts like apples drooping in clusters, which the poet says he likes to cup in his hands better than a girl's. But he is unique; normally a woman's loss of attractive features signals, not a move from one sexual state to another (like the boy's), but a move froms sexuality to lack of sexuality and even loathsomeness. "Woman," then, in this erotic poetry, consists of her attractive sexual attributes; the state of "womanhood" is the state of having these attributes.

Moreover, these attributes are aesthetic; they exist in the eye of the beholder. In other words, it is a man's perception of these attributes, it is Paris' judgment, that determines what is beautiful, who is beautiful, who is more beautiful. This beauty seems to be a direct stimulus for male arousal. It is, then, not surprising that a woman (5.200) dedicates her dress, wreath, and turban to Priapus.

Amatory epigrams in Martial cover a somewhat similar list of topoi, but their slant is different. Lacking are the more formal epigrams about burning up with love and reproaches for a cold mistress. Instead, there are many jocose or ribald epigrams depending on the idea that women are wanton. The harsher ones (1.34, 7.30, 9.2, 9.32, 10.68, 11.7, 11.71, 11.100) use primary obscenities; they are close to invective, though they refrain from actual censure of their targets (as Martial says in 1.34.10 "deprendi veto te, Lesbia, non futui"—"I forbid you to be caught, Lesbia, not to be fucked"). Martial sometimes (e.g., 9.2, 10.29) achieves cynical detachment by removing the woman from himself—making her the greedy mistress of his *patronus* or of some foolish man. But the bulk of the epigrams on wanton women, about forty in number, include Martial's complaints about his mistress's coyness and greediness, or his delight at her complaisance, and descriptions of his women, those supposedly attached to friends or just seen or heard of. By far the majority of these have little content and depend on a clever paradox or turn of phrase for their interest.

In general these poems entail no graphic physical description and dwell on no lascivious details; they use primary obscenities, but usually only *futuo*, and their tone is that of racy conversation, with many euphemisms (*dare*, "give," 2.56, 7.30; *facilis*, "easy," 9.32) and an occasional pun (knight/rider, 7.57).[33] Only a few poems describe sexual intercourse in a positive tone or delineate the physical properties of an attractive woman. Often the poet says, "Give me everything" (e.g., 11.50); in an unusual burst of narrative, he hints at what he means by this (9.67):

> Lascivam tota possedi nocte puellam,
>   cuius nequitias vincere nulla potest.
> fessus mille modis illud puerile poposci:
>   ante preces totas primaque verba dedit.
> improbius quiddam ridensque rubensque rogavi:
>   pollicitast nulla luxuriosa mora.
> sed mihi pura fuit; tibi non erit, Aeschyle, si vis
>   accipere hoc munus condicione mala.

> I had a sexy girl all night,
>   whose naughtiness no girl can surpass.
> Tired out by a thousand positions I asked for the boyish one;
>   before my prayers were complete and my first words, she gave it.
> I asked for something wickeder, laughing and blushing;
>   she, that decadent, promised it with no delay.
> But she was clean-mouthed, for me; she won't be for you, Aeschylus,
>   if you want
>   to accept this gift on bad conditions.[34]

The girl has little personality and serves in the poem only to respond to the narrator's requests. The tag line of the poem seems to imply that the narrator was not willing to respond in turn to the girl's requests; this is a one-sided bargain, at least physically. Similar motives prompt the poet's rejection of a skinny mistress (11.100), "quae clune nudo radat . . . / cui serra lumbis, cuspis eminet culo," "who shaves me with her naked butt . . . / from whose groin a saw sticks out, from whose ass a spear."

Mention or description of female genitalia is very rare in Martial and found only in contexts really belonging to invective. He almost never mentions breasts, and when he does the context is that of insult—the breasts are too big (1.100, 2.52, 14.66). His poems about anal intercourse with women never describe the beauty of the female buttocks or wholeheartedly recommend anal intercourse with women: 11.43 and 12.96 are against it, jokingly; 11.78 is neutral; and 11.104 is for it in a general sort of way. Yet it is clear from the group of poems describing dancing girls that undulating movement of the hips was considered alluring (*Pr.* 19, 27; Mart. 5.78, 6.71, 14.203; Juv. 11.162–70; *Copa* 1–2). The girls are always said to shimmy in a way that would arouse even a celibate or a man as old as Methuselah—for example, in *Pr.* 19:

> Hic quando Telethusa circulatrix
> quae clunem tunica tegente nulla
> †extis scitius altiusve motat†
> crisabit tibi fluctuante lumbo?
> haec sic non modo te, Priape, posset,
> privignum quoque sed movere Phaedrae.

> Here when will Telethusa the street dancer,
> who, with no underwear covering her ass
> moves higher and more skillfully than [. . .],
> shimmy for you with her rolling groin?
> She in this way could move not only you, Priapus,
> but even the stepson of Phaedra.

The single most prevalent theme in these poems is the relationship between money and sex.[35] Although some of the women are adulteresses and have an identity as *matronae*, others are slaves and/or prostitutes: one woman appears on the auction block (Mart. 6.66), a dancing girl enthralls her former master and brings a big price (6.71). Where the transaction is carried out directly between man and woman, Martial makes it clear that the payment is for the degree of sexual gratification and that it also affects the gratification. At 11.27 he asks how "Flaccus" can be aroused by a mistress who asks for such tawdry gifts—"Ferreus es, si stare potest tibi mentula," "You're made of iron, if your prick can stand up . . ." At 11.50 the narrator says he cannot refuse (because he is mad with love, *furentem*) his mistress's request for expensive presents, but he concludes, "nil tibi, Phylli, nego; nil mihi, Phylli, nega," "I deny you nothing, Phyllis—so you must deny me nothing." Similarly, generous loving on the part of the mistress ("se praestitisset omnibus modis largam," "she had offered herself freely in all positions") prompts the poet to meditate a generous gift (12.65).

Because the women's granting of themselves amounts to a kind of currency, if a *patronus* gives all his money to his mistress, the client feels the pinch (9.2, 10.29). This system, however, is not restricted to relationships in which the male is the buyer, although that is by far the more common pattern: two poems (2.34, 4.28) reproach wealthy women for cheating their dependents or themselves of all their money by spending it on lavish gifts for their young lovers.

The erotic ideal of women in Martial's poetry, then, is a sketchy one: women should undulate as they walk and be willing to engage in anal intercourse and fellatio, and they should give good value for money. The relationship between man and woman in Martial's epigrams is more that of buyer and seller than lover and beloved. Martial's epigrams in general are impersonal and depend more on wit than on content, so it is not remarkable that these women are so ill-defined. Still, it is interesting that he chose to write a good deal of elevated poetry to *pueri* and little to women. This probably has less to do with sexual preference than with a separation of the concept of the *matrona* (chaste, asexual, and a candidate for lofty treatment, e.g., 9.30) from that of the prostitute (wanton and purchasable), although the *pueri*, too, were slaves. At any rate, an erotic ideal of women certainly existed in Latin, in elegy, even if Martial chose not to use it.

The erotic ideal described in this chapter is necessarily a composite, a mosaic made up of many vignettes, most quite frivolous in tone. But the pose of frivolity does not imply that the choice of content is arbitrary, and the patterns in the content are clear. The content is determined by the central figure: the man, the poet, the narrator, the lover, the pursuer. The objects of his love are women and boys, whom he perceives as delicate (in comparison with himself) and soft (the better to receive him). They are younger than he and their assets are defined by his assessment. Their elusiveness is a function of their value and can be expressed in terms of cash value or the price of a slave; a high degree of the recognized physically attractive features produces demand and makes the object of desire harder to obtain. (A poet occasionally remarks that possession and time cheapen the object in his eyes, e.g., Mart. 10.75.) Sometimes a lover beats his beloved (Ovid *Am.* 1.7; Tib. 1.6.73, 1.10.55; cf. 2.5.101–04). Women rarely, and *pueri* never, are the narrators of erotic poems; they have no voice here. Only in epic, and sometimes in elegy, does a woman voice her feelings on love and her lover.

The physical ideal of women both differs from and resembles that of boys, and the ideals in Greek epigram are slightly different from those in Latin—mainly in that Greek epigrams describe the ideal breasts, groin, and buttocks of women, while Latin erotic poetry ignores these areas. Latin and Greek alike describe the buttocks and thighs, and sometimes the anus, of boys as beautiful and essential to beauty. Clearly Latin poets feel an inhibition in describing the sexual areas of women's bodies that they do not feel toward boys; but this inhibition, as will be seen,[36] does not apply to invective, in which the women's genitalia constitute the chief area attacked. Women's genitalia, then, are more obscene than erotic to the Romans. Where erotic poetry ignores women's genitalia, it focuses on boys' as a secondary attractive feature; apparently, the larger the penis and the closer the boy to adulthood, the more attractive he becomes. This suggests that the delight lovers take in delicate *pueri* increases the more the boys resemble men. Perhaps this is a more satisfying sort of domination, a search for "bigger game" (as when the lover kisses the boy bloody from boxing); perhaps older boys represent men (it is unlikely they represent women, given the explicit rejections of women in *AP* 12); perhaps they just represent the best physical fulfillment, if bigger equals better. The remaining characteristics of women and boys, and those that receive the most conventional treatment, are those marking them as pursued (like deer) rather than pursuing, and distinguishing them from adult males: soft, sparkling eyes, curly hair, smooth complexion, rosy color, "sweetness," graceful arms, neck, and shoulders, legs and feet.

The ideal world generated by this erotic ideal is a world of romantic fantasy, where dawn always comes too soon and youth and beauty hang poised in flight. Neither boys nor women—nor, for that matter, their lovers—have any function outside the poem. But while the lover takes his identity from the poet—the thrifty shopper in *AP* 5.126 is the creation of the philosopher Philodemus—the women and boys have no such association. And the boys have no social identity besides slavery and athletics—no future career, no family at all; the women have only their cost and marital status (single, slave, or adulteress). Just as their genitalia disappear in erotic poetry, so these women only rarely appear as mothers or possible mothers.[37] Just as moral ideals of women and young men, supported by law, held them chaste and stainless and celebrated them in anecdote and epitaph, so erotic poetry idealizes the class of women and boys with whom sexual relations were sanctioned. The relative lack of primary obscenities conforms with this idealization and titillates the reader more than blunt language could. (The formality of the language and structure of the poem makes it clear that the professed passion is a fiction: the poet shows off, the audience is genteelly stimulated.)

A last question posed by this body of material is, Why was no erotic poetry addressed by adult males to other adult males? Invective presupposes that many men admired other men as objects of erotic desire. The obvious answer is that the stigma placed on this sort of relationship precluded men from professing it in verse, or at least kept this verse from publication or survival. The result is that the adult male in Latin literature, because of the nature of the identities accepted for poet and for subject, had no serious erotic ideal at all as an object of desire; physical attributes of the adult male appear only as the "ugly" features to be dreaded by *pueri*. Instead, the adult male is the one who acts, sees, and feels. And since he speaks in the first person, his poems must appeal primarily to those who can put themselves in his shoes. This model is the twin of the model for satire, and these forms are interdependent in structure and, as will be seen, in content.

CHAPTER 3 The Content and Workings of Roman Sexual Humor

> Percidere puer, moneo: futuere puella:
> barbatum furem tertia poena manet.
> —*Carmina Priapea* 13

Descriptive Analysis: The Priapic Model

The same sort of skewing that was noted for erotic poetry at Rome applies to Roman sexual humor: it is entirely the product of male humorists. Whatever jokes were made on sexual subjects by women at Rome are lost; we can assume that at least some women enjoyed sexual humor from Sulpicia's seemingly satirical account of her own marriage.[1] Martial in particular liked to tease his female readers for their feigned shock or indifference, giving mock warnings while claiming that these only fire women to read further. Still, the material remaining from antiquity and even the nonextant sources cited by ancient authors are overwhelmingly male-oriented, and if women participated in this literature they did so on its terms, not theirs.[2]

This is no minor point to make about this material, for the male bias forms a major element in Roman satire, as well as in epigram and other, lesser humorous genres, and must be recognized in order to understand Catullus, Juvenal's sexual satires, a few poems of Horace, and certain elements in Ovid and Petronius. Different authors utilized the motives and mechanisms to be described in this chapter in different ways, but the basic standpoints available to them were limited and can be understood as a single complex.

Roman sexual humor operated at various levels of sophistication. At its simplest, this humor was no more than a release of hostile or aggressive feelings and utilized the concept set down in chapter 1: that some parts of the body, sexual acts, and people involved in such acts are bad, dirty, low, and disgusting. This idea allowed invective and jokes to be made of which the point was either the simple mention of such things or the identification of the butt of the joke with such things. Of course, much depended on the context of the telling and the cleverness of its disguise; as will be seen, the Romans found well-disguised obscenity worthy of anthologizing, while cruder statements are to be found mainly in random graffiti preserved by chance. "Well-disguised" obscenity and invective is that which was put into well-shaped verses (hence obscured by the elegance of the poetry), or puns and other word games, or surprise punch lines; the whole genre of satire can thus be viewed as a way of making obscene invective acceptable by dressing it up.

Roman sexual humor at its most sophisticated depended on the mechanism of humor in recognition, although it, too, utilized pleasure in handling foul things. At this level positive ideas are exploded, often by "staining" them with parallel but disgusting (to the users) ideas. The result is recognizable as a distorted and befouled twin of the original idea. This is a mechanism particularly suitable to a literate society, capable of mocking not only people and their ideals and common beliefs but literature itself. And this in turn means the mocking not only of especially literary ideals and conventions but also of literary forms, through the medium of parody. For if sexual satire can be understood partly as the staining of beliefs, parody is very often the staining of words.[3]

The connection between the lower and higher sorts of sexual humor may appear to be slight or coincidental, or the first might be thought to be the delight of crude and oafish men while the second appealed to clever poets and educated, sophisticated audiences. But the distinction is false: the two levels are intimately connected. One minatory figure stands at the center of the whole complex of Roman sexual humor; he will be represented here by the god Priapus. The general stance of this figure is that of a threatening male. He is anxious to defend himself by adducing his strength, virility, and (in general) all traits that are considered normal—and this is the appeal of the joke teller to his audience, as if both are confirming and checking with each other that they are all right, despite the existence of abnormalities in other people. Hence the central persona or protagonist or narrator is a strong male of extreme virility, occasionally even ithyphallic (as in the Priapic poems). Although this figure is often felt to be extreme, the audience is expected to identify with him, at least to some degree, rather than with his victims, who are described in the vilest of terms. This figure is active rather than passive and does not always restrict himself to foul descriptions of his victims, but sometimes threatens them with punishment, usually by exposure or rape, whether vaginal, anal, or oral. On a sophisticated level, he applies his hostility to ideals, exemplary figures, and sublime literature. Odd as this model may seem, it follows logically from the fact that all Roman sexual humor was male-oriented and from the axiom that mainstream sexual humor tends to confirm the "normalcy" of teller and audience. The material to be studied here and below, as well as that already examined in chapter 2, gives ample testimony that normal male sexuality at Rome was aggressive and active, also that it was directed at both male and female objects.

There is one major modification of the use of this central figure; he, too, could be stained and humiliated. He becomes an antihero in a literal sense: he is the virile, warlike male unmanned, placed in humiliating situations, defiled by disgusting acts and foul substances. The pleasure derived by teller and audience from such humor is more complex than in the normal model but is certainly related to it. Whether or not the teller identifies himself with the stained figure, the audience can either separate themselves and laugh at the figure (that is, derive comfort from being better than that figure) or identify with the figure temporarily and derive titillation from the temporary humiliation that they in fact do not expect to experience or admit as their own. It is to be emphasized that this figure is nothing other than an opposite of the Priapic figure—ineffectual, threatened, punished, and often impotent.[4]

The nature of the Priapic figure is responsible for all the patterns of Roman sexual humor. It implies that women are either wanton and complaisant or wanton and unfaithful, either beautiful and sexually attractive or ugly and sexually repulsive, either wife, mistress, slut, or crone. Other men are either stupid cuckolds or vengeful, murderous husbands; if they are young enough and beautiful enough, they are sex objects; otherwise they are pathic perverts, potential victims of the Priapus figure who prefer to fellate other men, enjoy experiencing anal penetration, or are capable of performing only cunnilingus with women. In any case, they are less sexually potent than the Priapus figure. All these patterns depend on a scale of values in which the Priapus figure is top or best and the other figures are subordinate; *militat omnis amans*, with a big gun. The image of the phallus as weapon is a common one, and the verb "fuck" has an exact correspondent in *futuo*, which is usually used with a man as subject and a woman as object.[5]

Three major points made by Freud in *Jokes and Their Relation to the Unconscious* explain much in Roman satire and lend structural support to the Priapic model. The first is that pleasure in jokes comes from economy, a sort of verbal and psychological "short-circuit" (p. 120)[6] which allows the participants to make verbal connections that are usually more difficult to make. The clearest example of this is in puns, which obviously economize by uniting two ideas in a single word (cf. also the punch lines of tendentious riddles). The most primitive manifestation of this phenomenon is the comic of movement (p. 190); we laugh at exaggerated expenditure of energy, for example, by a mime or slapstick comic, marking the difference between the exaggerated motion and the one we normally make ourselves. What has this to do with satire? At what can be its most pleasurable, this humor becomes tendentious, expressing hostility against the subject (who is now a victim). Freud differentiates among three levels of economy (p. 236): pleasure in jokes comes from economy of expenditure upon inhibitions; pleasure in the comic comes from economy of expenditure upon ideation (e.g., in a witty turn of phrase or in an Aristophanic costume); pleasure in humor comes from economy of expenditure upon feeling (for example, a "light touch" that relieves a tense dramatic situation). It seems that satire has most in common with pleasure in jokes, since its appeal comes from its treatment of feelings of hatred, which are usually expressed elsewhere only in angry scenes. Listening to satire is pleasurable, whereas angry scenes demand high expenditures of emotion and activity; and the satirist does all the work, the audience's participation consisting merely of recognition and laughter.

The second point in *Jokes* that is supremely illuminating of the process of satire is the A–B–C model (p. 133). When A, the teller, tells a tendentious joke to C, the listener, about a victim B, A buries criticism by bringing C over to his side through laughter. A has done C a favor by breaking down in an acceptable way his barriers against expressing hostility. Rather than persuading C by argument of a particular point of view, A enjoys with C a common perception of humor. Insofar as the joke succeeds, they are allies, separated from the ludicrous B (and the hostility against B is most comfortable for C if B is absent or abstract). Horace's much-quoted *sententia* "mutato nomine, de te / fabula narratur" as a principle lends a certain piquancy to Roman satire: often it seems that A suggests similarities between the victim of the satire and the audience. But surely the satire is funny only insofar as this identification can be quickly laughed off, or at worst foisted off by C_1 onto C_2 sitting next to him. This model has the added implication that sexual or other obscene subjects are the easiest path for the comic, since great pleasure can be obtained from the simple plan of having A recount to C his viewing of B in some state usually forbidden to sight. C is spared the embarrassment of the encounter but vicariously enjoys the exposure of B.

Finally, Freud makes the point that every joke calls for a public of its own (pp. 150–51). A and C must have similar inhibitions, or there will be no pleasure at all. If C has a higher barrier than A's against enjoying hostility or sexual exposure, A may not be able to breach that barrier with the joke, and C will be offended or embarrassed or both. If C has a lower barrier, A's joke may not bring much pleasure at all. If A and C have barriers in different areas altogether, C will be puzzled or unsettled by A's joke.

These basic tenets imply two further generalizations, and it is to these two points that additions may be made here. The first is from the A–B–C model and states that jokes thus become a sort of group reassurance. Freud discusses the phenomenon of the *Bierschwefel* (comic toasting) and *Kneipzeitung* (parodic newssheet at a convention) when pointing out that the critical barrier which represses pleasure in nonsense can often not be put aside without the assistance of alcohol (p. 127).[7] The cheerful mood reduces inhibitory forces and makes accessible sources of pleasure that are usually repressed; here the observation may be added that hence comes the difference in degree of obscenity in genres proper to contexts of varying formality, like epigrams, graffiti, and formal verse satire.

It seems clear that the recognized change in mood offered by alcohol (and sometimes people pretend to be drunker than they are precisely in order to speak or act outrageously) has an equivalent in the license offered by the occasion of public recitation and the elegant form of the verse satire. This corresponds to the concept of the physical area of the obscene defined in chapter 1—what Gordon Williams has called, with respect to invective in oratory, the "privileged occasion."[8] Ideas that would be horrifying even to bystanders if shouted in the face of B can be accepted with pleasure by an expectant audience. That is, the content of Juvenal 3 is basically "I hate all you lying, cheating, pushy foreigners," but, instead of a stream of billingsgate pouring from A's mouth directly onto B, we have a highly formalized poem recited under formalized circumstances to C. B is not present, or so the fiction implies; any C to whom the satire's description of B applies must either feel uncomfortable or reject the identification, but he is not likely to do what he would do in the nonformalized situation—reply in kind or punch A in the nose. The idea that the form is a disguise that palliates the content of the joke is put forth by Freud in his discussion of tendentious jokes. They are, he says, not only playful but purposeful, and the purpose is hostile; obscene riddles, for example, are perceived as both riddle and obscene (p. 133). The form (cf. especially the double entendre) packages the obscenity, and C can pretend that it is the clever word play that makes him laugh when in fact it is the expressed obscenity. If this seems too abstract, one need only think of the situation in which C's barriers are higher than A's. When C becomes offended, A can step back as if surprised and reproach C by saying, "It's only a joke!" The joke is thus an excuse: any behavior, any speech, is supposed to be allowed if it is in the form of a joke. Hence another comment of Horace's, that satire is no more than prose set into verses while an epic poem if set up as prose will still read like epic poetry (Hor. *S.* 1.4.53–62), makes a great deal of sense. The poetry of satire is more mask than architecture.

Another advantage of the license offered by formal public recitation is the reassurance it gives to participants in the group, especially the audience. All join together in laughing at B, who is safely out of hearing and thus poses no immediate counterthreat. The more pertinent a victim B is—the greater the number of Cs who are normally vexed by such a B—the greater the audience's solidarity. This is aided even more by the satirist's common mode of expression—hyperbole. One great pleasure in satire surely comes from hearing hostilities expressed that are at least as bad as anything C has ever thought himself, and very likely worse. C can feel safe and normal: here is a whole roomful of people (including the figure of authority at the front of the room, the narrator on whom all attention is focused) who obviously share his own feelings. It is a camaraderie of relieved hostility. The place of the poet in this is less straightforward. If the feelings expressed in his satire are at all genuine, he is a man who feels his place in society is threatened. By reciting he attains a place, and a glamorous one, but he is still isolated; the teller of a joke does not usually laugh. Clearly what he gains is prestige, status, and power, and a degree of acceptance that depends on how closely he identifies himself with his audience.

Of course it can also be said of the satirist's hyperbole that it fulfills the qualifications of Freud's most primitive sort of humor, the comic of movement. E. J. Kenney uses several metaphors to describe Juvenal's language, saying that he "overdoes things, takes a sledgehammer to crack a nut (or . . . shoots sparrows with a cannon)."[9] These are humorous metaphors utilizing the comic of movement, and they exactly match the comedy in exaggerated language. Such comic hyperbole is a well-known element of slang, one that distinguishes amusing conversation (at the ordinary, colloquial level) from dull conversation; but we might also say that the "amusing" language is "cool," protected language and the "dull" language is passive, undefended language. In one of the Lawrenceville stories, set at a boys' school, Dink Stover's protector urges him to defend himself against hounding and ostracism by learning to use slang, fending off his potential tormentors with a ready command of the snappy comeback; the mentor entitles his method "the superiority of the superlative over the comparative."[10] The characteristic of admired and successful repartee is its exaggeration, vividness, and exuberance—exactly the characteristics of the language of Roman satire. What is more important, successful repartee is usually characterized by hostility, well-veiled; it does not do to be too obviously on guard or too mild. This, too, is characteristic of satire.

The other secondary point of Freud's which can be developed further is his description of *Herabsetzung*, degradation of the victim who is superior. He says (p. 200) that caricature, parody, and travesty are directed against people and institutions that are usually authoritative and respected, even sublime.[11] This obviously applies to satire directed against the powerful, like the *patroni* or Domitian in Juvenal, and Memmius, Caesar, and Mamurra in Catullus. Likewise it applies to the mock heroic, in which the *vates* of satire puts the heroes of epic into degrading positions, for example, imagining Penelope in obscene terms (*Pr.* 68). And it applies to the view of figures that are usually idealized as chaste or beautiful—women and boys—as wanton or ugly. But it may be added that there is more to *Herabsetzung* than simple de-grad-ation, loss of status. A great deal of satirical *Herabsetzung* depends on staining, the covering of the victim with filth or excrement; and the audience's pleasure in this is a definite glee in wickedness, in imagining their most pompous enemy or the most coveted beauty subjected to the most disgusting punishment or the most summary rape, and in handling the filth themselves or imagining themselves as the rapists. Common types of mechanisms listed by Freud (p. 120), such as unification, similarity of sound, multiple use, modification of familiar phrases, allusions to quotations, all leading to the sort of economy he calls rediscovery of the familiar, can, especially when used in tendentious humor, utilize this sort of staining, which often gives an additional pleasure in the staining of the words themselves. (For example, Juvenal in 9.37, αὐτὸς γὰρ ἐφέλκεται ἄνδρα κίναιδος, twists a Homeric line, substituting κίναιδος, "fag," for the original σίδηρος, "sword." The joke is not only a surprise but a tainting of the epic original and a cheapening of its dignity.) Even mock epic, by imagining someone like Penelope, Hecuba, or Hippolytus in an obscene situation, in effect stains the victim. And the best model for this kind of staining in Roman satire is the model of Priapus in the garden, threatening potential thieves with rape. To expose victims as sexually abnormal—men as pathic homosexuals, women as promiscuous—is to imply sexual power over them, to threaten them as Priapus threatens thieves.

Rape is, however, more violent than any staining with filth. In the punishment of adulterers described in Roman satire, the husband had the choice of killing the adulterer, raping him in various ways, beating him, or fining him (the last a civilized substitution in which money takes the place of sexual submission—cf. the connection made in chapter 2). In Horace's description (*S.* 1.2.41–46) there is another option: the kitchen slaves urinate upon him.[12] It seems that imagined staining is only a substitute for imagined violence, the wish to humiliate a mild form of the wish to kill. If the proverbial cream pie in the face exemplifies staining, it is, then, the recognition of the familiar features through the distorting custard that creates such uproarious laughter (those eyes blinking in the whipped cream . . .); but this can be taken a disturbing step further. Would it still be funny if the features were distorted by violent means, by burning or cutting? No, it would be horrifying or moving, presumably because instead of an empathetic economy there would be an empathetic agony. But the two kinds of distortion seem to be very close, and it may be postulated that all desire to stain is a substitute for a more violent desire, to mutilate (cf. Mart. 2.83) or kill.

A less easily proved theory holds that formal satire shows a relation to primitive invective, curses, and magic.[13] Robert Elliott cites the supposed relation of Attic Old Comedy to the phallic songs, using the song "O Phales Phales" from *Acharnians* as evidence. No attempt can here be made to raise a connection between Priapic imagery or attitudes in Roman satire and forms of religious worship, although it seems a possible one, particularly with reference to gods like Mutinus Titinus[14] and Priapus and to the recurrent use of the phallus as an apotropaic sign in Roman art and life (the *fascinum*, the lamps and paving stones found at Pompeii, and so on). But it is possible to demonstrate Elliott's hypothesis satisfactorily for Roman satire in two respects. First, that of form: Roman poets adopted such traditional forms of subliterary invective as the invective list (cf. *defixiones*), name calling, and especially the dialogue or series of rhetorical questions (cf. Catullus and the claqueurs, below). That the content of both subliterary and literary invective is the same must be a result of consistent societal stimuli and tendencies, not a cause/effect relation. The second relation lies in the intention of the speaker, that is, in the model: in all kinds of Roman invective, from malevolent graffiti to satire, the speaker's perception of himself and the world is that of Priapus, the god in the garden.

> est aliquid, quocumque loco, quocumque recessu
> unius sese dominum fecisse lacertae.
>
> —Juvenal 3.230–31

The Genres of Roman Sexual Humor

It is a fact almost too obvious to mention that sexual humor is not to be found in every kind of writing that survives from Rome. As in other cultures, and probably as fixed by the culturally determined notion of the obscene, Roman sexual humor is limited to certain settings, places, meters, and forms: graffiti, most preserved *in situ*, written on walls and potsherds; political lampoons, most preserved in letters and chronicles but originally either in oral circulation or posted as pasquinades; gossip and jokes, preserved in letters and collections of anecdotes; courtroom invective, as in the published speeches of Cicero and in fragments of other speeches; mime, Atellan farce, and comedy, all limited to the theater, sometimes even to special days (as were the mimes for the Floralia); epigram, which circulated in collections written by a single author and in anthologies, and was limited in meter to the elegiac distich and in length to an average of about eight lines (although collections usually included occasional short poems in a few lyric meters and in hexameters); and satire, always the work of a single author and limited, after Lucilius, to dactylic hexameter or to the mixture of prose and verse called Menippean.

The list is long and seemingly wide-ranging, from private conversations to published works, from semiliterate scrawls on walls to the Ciceronian period. The members of the group do share a few important characteristics. As with the erotic material, all the sexual humor that has any attribution was attributed to men. The anonymous material does not differ at all from the ascribed material in its standpoint, with the possible exception of a few graffiti, and thus the whole body of material can be said to have a male narrator. Furthermore, as the Romans believed satire as a genre to be quintessentially Roman (Quint. *Inst.* 10.1.93), so the arenas of sexual humor derive from certain Roman local institutions: politics, the law courts, public spectacles, and the recital halls. All the genres are ethnocentric in that they presuppose a narrator who perceives himself and his audience as Romans and writes as a Roman. All demand inside knowledge of specifically Roman practices or personages. Yet some of this material was aimed at wide circulation; Martial, for example, often mentions how well known he has become and how his books find an audience even in the provinces (Mart. 1.1, 1.117, 3.1, 3.4, 7.17, 7.88, 7.97, 8.3, 10.9, 10.104, 11.3). But most of the humor here reached limited and Roman audiences—groups of friends, passersby, literati, or theatergoers. Perhaps it was the eclecticism and low specificity of epigram that made it widely publishable; for all Martial's touted ability to convey the flavor of the real Rome, relatively few of his poems (and none of his sexual humor) name any names.

That sexual humor was limited as to its meter is significant. Cuing is a key element in all humor—what has been called "metacommunication,"[15] an included and encoded signal that the message is humorous. The limitation on meter constitutes a form of cuing, on the same level as costume (in the theater), tone of voice, or physical venue. Some meters—the *versus quadratus* (trochaic septenarius) and scazons—were so closely associated with sexual humor or with invective that their names could be used to denote the topic.[16] Several meters were shared by erotic poetry and sexual humor, especially the hendecasyllabic and the elegiac distich. Yet the elegiac distich was a sort of all-purpose meter in that the genre of epigram used it in its portrayal of pets, children, statuary, and jewelry, epitaphs, ceremonial announcements, jingles to accompany gifts, drinking songs, and love poems. This odd canon would seem to devalue the strength of the elegiac distich as a cue—yet it is the meter of choice for political lampoons and even appears in graffiti. The use of a jingling and sometimes rhyming couplet in invective is common throughout Europe and elsewhere,[17] and so, apparently, the cue in the elegiac distich is related to that in, for example, nursery rhymes, limericks, or the Dozens. The importance of rhyming and the verse format in folk invective is that it differentiates the content from out-and-out insult, the prelude to a fight; if the format breaks down, the path to outright aggression is open. As long as the format is held, the situation remains on the level of a game.

The use of dactylic hexameter in formal verse satire is more difficult to explain; this meter belongs otherwise mainly to epic poetry, a strange coupling, and it is tempting to see in the use of the same meter for satire a deliberate travesty of the most sublime genre. If the assignment of hexameter to satire really belongs to Lucilius, or at least within late cultural history, then perhaps this is possible. And if the act was not historical but primordial, the pairing must still be significant, a unification of the sublime with the mockery of the sublime.

The persona of the narrator is similar for all the types of Roman sexual humor. Not only is he male and Roman, he is on the offensive. Where intent to injure is not present, that is, in writing that is not invective, the persistent stereotypes are clearly those that assert the normalcy and dominance of the male Roman: the prostitute, the wanton woman, the shrill wife, the old woman; the pretty young boy, the pathic homosexual, the cuckold, the old man, the foreigner, the slave (clever or otherwise). All belong to a patriarchal, propertarian society in which marriage is normal and the problems of middle-aged married men receive the greatest attention. The message of even the mildest sexual humor is: look what these others are up to. But much of this humor is not mild, and the element of threat is correspondingly great.

The Subjects of Roman Satire

Like the trial lawyer, the satirist identifies himself closely with the narrator of his invective. In many kinds of sexual humor the author is absent (as in graffiti or material published and then read privately) or at best represented (as occasionally in the theater).[18] But the trial lawyer attacks his victim in person, as if he were a participant in a slanging match in the street; the trial is a formalized version of such a contest, and the speech therefore is somewhat fictionalized, with the lawyer representing one or the other party and assuming that party's indignation, as well as asserting his own personal information. In satire the fiction goes further, with the satirist performing in a recital hall, like a stand-up comedian.[19] His experiences, his victims, are generalized or absent, but he himself is present and speaks the lines of the satire as if they were his own personal reactions to his own experiences. He stands up alone before his audience, the focus of their attention and, he hopes, the stimulus of their laughter.

It is in this way that the figure of the Roman satirist comes to take on the attributes of Priapus outlined in the first part of this chapter. In order to make his audience laugh, he embodies the common denominator of that audience, voicing and then exaggerating the hostilities of the figure perceived as normal, the middle-aged male Roman citizen. Modern stand-up comedians sometimes assume the personae of the "other"—the shrill wife, the stupid slut, the foreigner, the pathic—but Roman satire was not so theatrical: the fiction of the dialogue was as far as it got, except when the narrator actually spoke with the voice of Priapus, as in Hor. *S.* 1.8. Thus the Roman satirist spoke as a male and inveighed as a male; therefore, when he expressed hostility, he threatened as Priapus does. Of course, much of Roman satire concerns subjects other than the sexual, but all satirists include the sexual in their satire, and the attitude they take in this area extends to other areas.

If the satirist is to represent the norm, he obviously cannot directly represent the obscene as well. The obscene, as shown in chapter 1, was a demarcated area of Roman culture, set aside from other areas and off limits to certain sorts of people. In addition, things and practices considered obscene were also considered filthy or tainted. How, then, can the satirist so consistently deal with this material? First, his normative figure is also a privileged one; the area of the obscene was off limits to those who were supposed to be chaste, and that group did not include adult males. Second, the practices and areas considered tainted or filthy do not include active male sexuality or the male genitalia, although these could be called obscene (Hor. *S.* 1.2.26, 1.8.5; *Pr.* 9.1). The set of the obscene, then, includes one group that is obscene but not filthy (male genitalia, active male sexuality) and a much larger group that is both obscene and filthy (female genitalia, pathic male sexuality, oral-genital intercourse, scatological material, and so on).

If the garden of Priapus is a metaphor for the area of the obscene, then the figure of Priapus that stands at the center of the garden is an exact parallel for the figure of the satirist. Both dominate (without owning) special areas, and both threaten those within these areas. The god threatens thieves and sometimes (as does Catullus) the poet does the same, threatening potential adulterers, interlopers, arrivistes. The god threatens rape, and the satirist achieves a similar kind of sexual exposure while asserting his dominance. The god also has occasion to threaten those who come to the garden knowing his nature and hoping to be raped—those who are "pathic," both male and female (*Pr.* 25, 40, 45, 48, 51, 64, 66, 73). The god has nothing but scorn for these people; so the satirist scorns the pathic.

It is as if the phallus itself were magic, able to exist at the center of the area of the obscene without taint or injury (and it is tempting to link this idea with the use of apotropaic phalli at Rome, in everything from children's amulets to paving stones).[20] Priapus himself, after all, is a talking, deified phallus, and poems put in his mouth are no more than elaborations of the motif of the poet's conversations with his phallus (Ovid *Am.* 3.7.69–72; Hor. *S.* 1.2.68–71; Petronius *Sat.* 132.6–15; *Virgilian Appendix*, "Quid Hoc Novi Est?"). The penis, personified, is red, hairless, and one-eyed (Mart. 2.33):

Cur non basio te, Philaeni? calva es.
cur non basio te, Philaeni? rufa es.
cur non basio te, Philaeni? lusca es.
haec qui basiat, o Philaeni, fellat.

Why don't I kiss you, Philaenis? You're bald.
Why don't I kiss you, Philaenis? You're redheaded.
Why don't I kiss you, Philaenis? You're one-eyed.
A man who kisses these things, Philaenis, sucks.

These characteristics, repulsive in a woman, are nevertheless strong and threatening rather than filthy, as when Priapus refers to his phallus (Hor. *S.* 1.8.5) as *ruber . . . palus*, "[that] red pole [of mine]." The difference between male genitalia and female genitalia in this respect is instructive (Mart. 9.37.7–10):

et te nulla movet cani reverentia cunni,
  quem potes inter avos iam numerare tuos.
promittis sescenta tamen; sed mentula surda est,
  et sit lusca licet, te tamen illa videt.

and you are moved by no shame for your white-haired cunt,
  which you can now count among your grandfathers.
Still you promise me six hundred; but my prick is deaf,
  and even if it's one-eyed, it still sees you.

In this rejection of an old woman, whose defects have been listed in the first six lines of the poem, Martial allows the *mentula* to represent the man and to see the woman's ugliness and reject it on the man's behalf. Her genitalia, on the other hand, are distinct from herself and form part of her repulsiveness.

Whereas *mentula* can stand for the whole area of the obscene and sexual humor (Mart. 1.35.3–5; 3.69.1–2; 11.15.8–10), *cunnus* personified has no such validity (Hor. *S.* 1.2.69–71; *Pr.* 68.9–10; Mart. 6.45.1, 7.35.8, 11.61.9). It was shown in chapter 2 that the female genitalia have no part in the ideal of beauty and that Latin erotic literature leaves a blank in the middle of women it describes. Roman sexual humor has a special relationship with the ideal of beauty: it rejects the not-beautiful, as it rejects all that is obscene and filthy. The phallus enters vagina and anus, but it remains strong and "clean." The satirist, the hyperbolically normative figure, has the prerogative of rejecting all sexual others. He thus takes the erotic poet's privilege of judging beauty and applies it negatively, describing the bodies of women as ugly, exposing the chaste as wanton, and loathing selected other adult males as would-be Ganymedes. While not within the group of things beautiful himself, the adult male determines what is ugly in others. What is ugly disgusts him, and what disgusts him is ugly.

The simplest definition of what is ugly is that it is the reverse of what is beautiful. If smooth skin, flowing hair, unobtrusive breasts, long legs, rich new clothes, and invisible genitalia are the features of a beautiful woman, then an ugly woman will have wrinkled skin, no hair, pendulous breasts, short legs, tattered clothes, and obtrusive genitalia, and any one of these characteristics will provide grounds for attack.[21] Likewise, if what makes a boy attractive is smooth skin, the shaved skin of the pathic will be a prime target for attack.

But it is not so easy to see why Latin literature describes female genitalia only in terms of extreme loathing, or why both Latin and Greek literature reserve a whole area of invective for old people, particularly old women (see below). Perhaps the postmenopausal woman can be perceived as uncanny, a sexual neuter, and this may have been especially troublesome at Rome, where childbearing had such a high cultural value; certainly old women often appear not just as neuters but as hags, witches, sorceresses, madams, and (most significantly) as ex-wetnurses who always lead their grown-up charges astray. Yet this does not explain the stereotype of the old woman as drunken and extremely randy, and the concomitant rejection by the speaker of any desire to copulate with such a woman (as in the two Martial poems above). That old women were drunken or randy is surely not a truth of ancient society but a projection created by the desire to reject; in other words, in order to express a total aversion to intercourse with old women, sexual humor must paint them as randy. It is only in this sense that the satirist is the arbiter of right and wrong; as Priapic figure, he rejects what is sexually "wrong." It is at least possible that these women represent mothers (cf. Mart. 10.90.6, where the old woman is told she should act like Hector's mother, not his wife) and that invective against old women expressed a taboo on intercourse with much older women.

This still does not explain the loathing for female genitalia, which are ignored in Latin erotic poetry and castigated in invective as smelly, dirty, wet, loose, noisy, hairy, and so on. The attitude of invective toward the anus of the adult male pathic (discussed below) is similar, and this suggests that all pathic orifices—orifices that received and submitted to the penis—were perceived as lowly. But female genitalia in Latin invective are much worse than lowly, and no such feeling seems to have been applied to the anuses of *pueri*. (The elaborately sublime metaphors for boys' anuses in Greek epigram perhaps constitute overcompensation for feelings of repugnance, but if so, the repugnance is well hidden.) Conceivably the answer is simply that, whereas the male originators of Roman sexual humor had anuses themselves and knew what the orifice was (could "control" it), none of them had vaginas, and this basic difference produced a fear of the unknown orifice and a very strong desire to differentiate the self from it.[22] The power and necessity of the vagina in heterosexual intercourse go without saying, and its ability to act on the phallus is in some ways alarming; the need to deny its value, in a male-centered society, is therefore perhaps all the more urgent. The clitoris is mentioned only as a flaw in the appearance of ugly genitalia.[23]

The only kind of disgust comparable to that for female genitalia is that expressed for oral-genital contact (e.g., Cat. 80; Mart. 2.10, 12, 21–23, 11.95; Juv. 6.O.4–6). The idea that the mouth may have become tainted by contact with the genitals, anus, or surfaces touched by either forms a major element in Roman sexual humor and establishes the special meaning of the word *purus* (above, chap. 1). The greatest fear seems to be of assimilation of the mouth to the other orifices, so that it, too, will smell and become obscene. Although this topic received markedly idiosyncratic treatment in Roman sexual humor, the linkage between sexual and "alimentary" concepts is worldwide,[24] perhaps partly because of the connection between the strong smells of bodily secretions, effluvia, and excreta, and the smells of food. Certainly both sexual and alimentary activity usually involve penetration of the body by external elements. Since the mouth can be used for both (obscene) sexual purposes and (nonobscene) ingestion, its ambiguity is a source of concern when it must be used for other nonobscene social functions, like talking or kissing "hello," or when it touches communal eating utensils or public water in the baths. In any case, the position of the satirist is that he wishes to violate the mouths of others, which does not taint him, without ever having his own mouth tainted, much less violated. The violation of the mouth (irrumation) is thus one of the most strongly charged assertions of domination possible in Roman sexual humor, and indeed in Roman society.

It is clear that whereas erotic poetry established what objects the writer admired and wished to own, sexual humor established what the writer shunned and wished to reject. Where erotic poetry consisted of pursuer plus objects of pursuit, satire consists of satirist plus "other." The sexuality of the humorist constitutes the definition of normal sexuality; the sexuality of women and of adult male pathic homosexuals is by definition abnormal. The objects of erotic desire had no sexuality of their own but were reified projections of the pursuer's desire; any sexual desire felt by women or male homosexuals was thus out of place. The primary obscenities of Latin underscore this bias: *futuere* ("fuck"), *pedicare* ("bugger"), and *irrumare* ("fuck in the mouth") all can be found in the first person, and when they are in the active voice are almost always used with male subjects—*pedico* and *irrumo*, of course, *futuo* more tellingly. *Fellare* ("suck [cock]") is almost always used in the second or third person and is insulting. No single verb signifies oral intercourse with women, only the periphrasis *cunnum lingere*; nor is there any verb that expresses respected passive participation in anal intercourse—*pedicari* implies intent to humiliate, or at least dominate, on the part of the active participant. This lack seems all the more significant in a language that includes a verb meaning "rape someone's mouth."

This perception of the world as other, and of things as the "opposite" of what they should be, in large part determines the content of Roman satire, perhaps of all satire. The perception of ranges of behavior as monolithic opposites is not accurate but simplifies the process of rejection and the function of satire as defender of the societal status quo. Women who behave like men, homosexuals who behave like women, cripples and foreigners, those whose behavior is in any way extreme, for example, the nouveaux riches—all embody the "other," those whom the satirist wishes to differentiate from his own "normal" self. This accounts for the emphasis placed on the bad *behavior* of the patron who bilks his client or of the host who serves food that is somehow inedible—a theme that pervades satire from *Lysistrata* to the Mad Hatter's tea party. All this behavior is paradoxical, and while paradox may underlie all humor, it is what the satirist wishes to eschew publicly on behalf of his public.

Other Models for Satire: Judgmental Analysis

HUMOR IS GOOD

> Barking dogs may occasionally bite, but laughing men hardly ever shoot.
>
> —Konrad Lorenz, *On Aggression*; quoted by J. Levine, *Motivation in Humor*

Those who have attempted to analyze satire, humor, and/or erotica have, with the exception of Freud, generally tended to evaluate the function, once defined, as good or bad. The nature of the material itself, when closely examined, is unsettling, and many critics have felt it important to decide whether or not this material serves a good end. Most commonly, "good" in this context is defined as "cathartic," while those who feel the material serves bad ends base this on the idea that it exacerbates feelings that should be controlled and minimized, or rechanneled. The critics to be examined here come from four disciplines—literary criticism, anthropology, psychology, and women's studies—and take different stands. But all share a concern to justify or attack obscene and/or humorous material, incidentally demonstrating how essential apologetics are to the obscene, an area apparently not only delimited but embattled.

Mikhail Bakhtin's study of Rabelais's novels, *Rabelais and His World*, constituted an important development in scholarship on Rabelais and is one of the major essays in semiotics. A concern to justify the content of the novels permeates Bakhtin's book, and he finds two major reasons why the novels should be valued highly. First, they derive the structure of many episodes from "popular festive forms," especially the carnival or quasi-religious fair day. Second, the structure of these events constantly draws parallels between the sublime and the "material bodily lower stratum." The first element constitutes "the free winds blowing from the marketplace" (p. 272), stressing the universality of the human brotherhood, while the second reminds all men together, joyfully, of the necessity of death and the promise of regeneration death carries with it. The catharsis of satire, in Bakhtin's view, is thus a negation of the fear of death—but this is not true for all satire; he distinguishes between Rabelais's satire and "modern," "negative" satire, which is an *ad hominem* attack by one man for personal motives, in which "the satirist . . . places himself above the object of his mockery" (p. 12).[25]

Bakhtin sees in the violence of Rabelaisian satire no hostility toward its victims; the negation is "closely linked with affirmation of that which is born anew" (p. 307), and the imagery of satire "tends to embrace both poles of becoming in their contradiction and unity" (p. 203). Thus the king who is degraded to clown only foreshadows the new king (pp. 197–98), and death and senescence imply birth and youth, with death, sexual intercourse, and giving birth as the three events that unite all lives and imply each other (p. 353). Wounds and beatings, "weddings" that are really violent attacks on intruders (p. 200), victims who suffer improbable catalogues of injuries and somehow survive for more—all are part of the celebration of rebirth. Thus the grotesque is not fearsome (pp. 46–47), feces and gore do not stain (p. 224), there is no hostility toward women (p. 240), abusive language carries a friendly message (pp. 15–16, 248), and the satirized parts of the body are not considered ugly (pp. 316–17). All these features share, in satire, a quality of ambivalence: feces and gore bridge the gap between man and earth; women represent the material bodily lower stratum—they simultaneously degrade and regenerate, and counter not man but man's follies; abusive language can be used between friends and loses its original meaning when shouted at a carnival; and the physical features abused by satire are those that protrude from the body, because they are the link to the rest of the world, or those that open the way into the lower body. For in this humanistic satire man is a microcosm and includes both high and low (p. 365): the lower body stands for earth, the upper for heaven, so that the face and head are high and the genitalia are low (p. 21), although the mouth (as gateway to the low) also represented hell (p. 348).

The only significant enemy in this schema is time, which satire seeks to conquer—"to uncrown gloomy eschatological time" (p. 235). The human enemies in Rabelais's novels are the "agelasts," those who remain serious and miss their chance to perceive immortality through humor (presumably the figure of the younger Cato fills this role in Roman satire). The satirist's ability to step out of his role—the "metatheatrics" of satire—Bakhtin traces to popular festive forms (p. 265). Thus the locus of satire is in all humanity who can laugh, at any time or place.

This assessment may work for Rabelais or for satires in the age of the humanists and after, but there are serious problems in applying it to Roman satire. This would not be surprising, except that Roman satire has most of the same formal elements as do both earlier and later satire, including Rabelais's. The phenomenon of ambivalence is certainly present in Roman satire—for example, although it usually presents women as bad, they must be important to occupy such a prominent position—but the ambivalent parts do not have equal weight. The badness and disgustingness of what Roman satire perceives as bad and disgusting are strongly felt qualities, and the satirist is not celebrating or validating their part in life. He is validating his own part in life. In any case, Bakhtin's system rests on the assumption present in satire that the adult male represents what is good/high in the universe, while women and all things sexual represent what is low; this must be accepted if one is to perceive in satire a triumphant affirmation of life.

Bakhtin's list of the parts of the body singled out for ridicule (pp. 316–17) is most helpful, his extrapolations aside. He points out that the nose (always a surrogate for the phallus, he maintains) and mouth are the most important in the grotesque body, followed by head, ears, anus, belly, and buttocks; the eyes are not included unless they protrude. Satire focuses on the parts of the body involved in "eating, drinking, defecation, and other elimination, copulation, pregnancy . . .," and these are the only parts of the body for which many slang terms exist. Where *belles lettres* closed (by ignoring) all the body's orifices, the grotesque body is open, full of holes that can leak or be penetrated. But these two ways of perceiving the body exist side by side in Roman erotic literature and sexual humor; it is not a matter of the loss of traditional folk views to a wave of culture but of the coexistence of two interdependent ways of viewing a dominated world.

The same sort of admiration for a rich portrait of the panoply of life, without Bakhtin's complexity of explication, predominates in current treatment of Roman satire, which praises Horace for his moderation and Martial and Juvenal for the way they bring to life the Rome of their day.[26] But this criticism does not, by and large, evaluate or even analyze the content of the satire, and so its praise of individual authors, based on assessment of style and originality, does not seem to be intended as a serious judgment on the message of the work.

In such serious treatment of humorous material it is easy to lose sight of the fact that this material is lighthearted and funny and makes people laugh. True, most analysis of humor leads to the conclusion that what underlies the laughter is not funny at all, but not even Freud was able to account for the physiology of laughter or the feeling of physical pleasure that accompanies a laugh; that the pleasure consists in relief, in the released pressure of a lifted inhibition, does not describe the feeling of a laugh very well. Several theorists have grounded their analysis in this most common mystery. The behaviorist William Fry analyzes all humor as based on paradox, because of the nature of the semantic structure of jokes,[27] and finds that humor shares this quality with other pleasurable cultural events and practices—play, ritual, dreams, folklore, art, and so forth. Having reached the conclusion that paradox is essential to the operation of the human mind, he comments that it "adds much richness to life" (p. 132) and ends by "affirming [his] belief in the central mystery of the nature of those human phenomena of which humor is an example . . ." (p. 172).

Fry's semimystical conclusion (perhaps not unjustified, considering the difficulty of the problem of "What is funny?") stems from the most down-to-earth sort of data—observation of animal behavior. Studies analyzing animals' play (pp. 123–28) showed that play is a metaphor for other, primary behavior; the mild aggression in play manifests all the formal attributes of serious aggression, and the barrier is sometimes broken. What separates metaphorical behavior from primary behavior, Fry explains, is a system of cuing, "metacommunication," that signals to the participants that the behavior is a metaphor, is not "real." The paradox inherent in such cuing is the paradox of Epimenides (the Cretan who said, "All Cretans are liars"): the message undercuts itself. (Hence the pleasure in satire as an exposure of paradox in life. But a more disturbing application of this observation to satire can be seen in the case of satire of bias—for example, the television series "All in the Family"—in which laughter at someone else's bigotry is difficult to distinguish from secret enjoyment of that bigotry and empathy with it.) Fry suggests as examples of metacommunication the cues in practical jokes and the use of dialects, peculiar clothing, acting, and an intermittent or fixed smile by humorists. The final corollary to Fry's theory of paradoxical thought is that these processes must have a termination point—the climax or "punch line" (p. 153).

This analysis differs from Freud's in making no distinction between play and jokes of all kinds, that is, in lumping together what Freud called "nonsense" and "tendentious humor." Presumably this is based on Fry's observation of behavior, especially behavior showing that all play resembles hostile action, and on the strength of "metacommunication": a signal that "this is not real" must then be as valid in "tendentious" circumstances as it is in innocuous circumstances.

The anthropologist Johan Huizinga places an even stronger emphasis on the sheer pleasure of humor, with similar ensuing unification of all different levels of humor, art, and other forms of recreation as "play."[28] Rejecting theories that seek to determine whether play is cathartic, aimed at socialization, or aggressive, Huizinga points out that such theories assume play serves that which is not play, presumably some biological purpose (p. 2). He claims that the mystery of why play is fun can be understood only if play itself is taken to be primary, one of the main bases of civilization (p. 5). Its characteristics (pp. 5–10, 19) set it pleasantly apart from the more humdrum aspects of life: it is voluntary and free; it is extraordinary, an interlude in "real" life; it is secluded, limited, and self-contained as to time and space (place); it generates a peculiar order or form that can be evaluated only in terms of aesthetics, placing it outside the realm of good and bad.

Huizinga presumably derives this last characteristic from art, the theater, and sports, which all fall into his very broad definition of play; but if this could apply to satire and sexual humor, it would explain the difficulties of establishing whether satire is good or bad. In addition, the emphasis this places on the importance of the form of the event implies that one main function of all play is as social event, without regard to content; as applied to Roman satire, this reminds us that any public reading of satire would have been regarded by the audience in large part as an outing, attendance being a sign of intellectual status and/or an opportunity to relax with friends, the content of the satire being secondary. The Priapic model posits an attentive and receptive audience, hardly the common run.

Huizinga outlines further qualities of play: its seclusion carries with it antagonism toward trespassers, "spoil-sports" (here the agelast Cato pops up again), so that seclusion implies exclusion; it includes Mohocking, deliberate and permitted breaking of the rules, in costume (here is Fry's paradox); it is usually nonprofit, but on the mystical level, as ritual, it can be thought to serve higher ends and perhaps coerce events. (This last aspect, the use of ritual to effect one's desires, is the one Elliott applies in tracing the development of satire from curse to formal verse.) Noting the quality of "seizure" or "rapture" often found in participants in play (p. 17), Huizinga concludes that the "concept of purpose" can be rejected, that play is an end in itself—although he grants (p. 21) that the play mood is "labile," capable of being broken easily.

Apart from the fact that satirists themselves explicitly rejected rapture, in the form of inspiration by the Muse—this amounts to no more than a sort of counter-rapture—Huizinga's theory of play ignores a great deal when it ignores content. His observations and analogies between kinds of play illuminate the relationship between humor and seemingly more "serious" social institutions, and perhaps it is not necessary to jettison the concept of purpose to retain the theory of play. For surely the genesis of individual forms of play cannot be considered arbitrary, and the content of each form must have some relation to its genesis, even if the repeated form seems purely joyful, without purpose. Moreover, the playing of any such game, every time it is played, involves social choices and tensions within the hierarchy of the microcosm (i.e., the players jockey for position).

Huizinga's ideas on play foreshadow current work on the language of play and the social function of children's play. Sanches and Kirshenblatt-Gimblett, and especially Abrams and Sutton-Smith, stress the value of play in building a child's repertory of potential future responses; play is a "means of enculturation."[29] The fantasies in children's narratives give them a means of exploring the possibilities of the world they inhabit, as do, surely, the universes of children's rhymes (including such figures as Jack, Jill, and the lady with the alligator purse). Sociolinguistic analysis of different levels of playful discourse in fact demonstrates analogies between them; the study of Sanches and Kirshenblatt-Gimblett can well be compared with that of Gossen on verbal dueling by young males in a remote area of Mexico.[30] The former show that phonological structure is the generating principle of speech play and that children use semantic associations rather than paradigmatic categories to define concepts, both principles applying especially to younger children. These same two principles—phonological generation and semantic linkage—characterize Chamula verbal duels, of which the content is also extremely obscene. Both children's speech play and obscene invective interchange are considered humorous by their performers; and both act to affirm cultural norms. Especially pertinent to a consideration of Roman humor is Gossen's description of Chamula society, in which eloquence is the key to advancement in a religious and/or political career, largely the property of males.

Young Chamula males, Gossen believes, gain practice through extemporaneous, rhyming verbal duels in the kind of format that characterizes Chamula religious language (a metaphoric couplet)—as well as indoctrination in the set of norms extolled in religion, infractions of which are derided in verbal duels.

So far, this analysis of humor is fairly neutral; but the idea that play provides a "means of enculturation" belongs with a classic body of anthropological research on "rituals of reversal" and the positive effect of these rituals in their societies. As seen above, in chapter 1, ancient satirists themselves linked their work with Roman rituals of reversal—the Saturnalia, the *ludi Florales*, and the comic theater in general. The universal connection between such rituals and comedy is a strong one, often featuring clowns and ritual abuse.

Anthropologists have described several functions that these rites fulfill in their societies; all have in common that the content of the rites is not so much rejected as it is recognized. The simplest analysis is that these rites constitute a catharsis of sexual and hostile feelings; one participant/scholar maintains this is so even though the sexual language of the rites, while ordinarily forbidden, is not perceived as obscene at all.[31] Most scholars define the content of the rites as obscene and ordinarily vile within their society;[32] but it has been pointed out that this view ignores the positive, sacred meaning of the "foul" content of these rites, for example, of excrement or menstrual blood, as well as the "sacredness of transgression."[33] Makarius, who cites elements present in the *ludi Florales* and Saturnalia as well as in satire—presents of food (pp. 59–60), reverse behavior and backward speech (p. 61), reverse feasts (p. 64)—also points to what is probably the main function of rites of reversal: conservatism. While the clown takes it upon himself to act out the statement on behalf of the community (cf. also Levine, p. 82), the gist of the statement nevertheless is that doing things backward reminds the community of what forward is (p. 70). Victor Turner [34] cites numerous examples strengthening the view that reversals reinforce societal structures. Writing on Ndembu ritual, he lays down the maxim (p. 47) that "structural contradictions, asymmetries, and anomalies are overlaid by layers of myth, ritual, and symbol, which stress the axiomatic value of key structural principles with regard to the very situations where these appear to be most inoperative" (cf. also pp. 50, 85, 92–93 [on Evans-Pritchard], 176–77, 201). He extends this rule to rituals of status reversal (pp. 167–68, 169, 172), which, he notes, are often tied to the calendar, being celebrated on strictly observed dates only (cf. Ọlajubu, p. 152); in addition, after the rites are over, the group briefly elevated returns to its lowly status and may be punished. Rites of sexual reversal (pp. 183–84) also emphasize the differences between the sexes, although they may also be used to reconcile (temporarily) differences that are felt to be uncomfortable (pp. 81, 84). This conservatism also manifests itself in the public and group excoriation of chiefs, which Turner ties in with ancestor worship (pp. 100–05, 170–72), certainly an important part of Roman political status. This is essentially the function often called apotropaic.[35] McKim Marriott observed the same function in the Indian Holī festival (quoted at length by Turner, pp. 185–88).

Similar to the idea of catharsis is the idea that these rites cleanse the state, as attested for the Ashanti Apo ritual (Turner, pp. 178–81, Elliott, pp. 76–81); this may apply to the rowdy procession of flute players on the day before the cleansing of the shrine of Vesta.[36] The use of obscenity to promote fertility is less clear: among the Ndembu it occurs in what Turner calls "the fruitful contest of the sexes" (pp. 75–78) and among the Romans seemingly in the use of Fescennine verses as a harvest ritual, sung by a masked chorus.[37] Erich Segal has connected Plautine comedy with the liberating force of the Roman festivals in a restrictive society; he also stresses the dichotomy between forum and theater/*ludi* (pp. 42–69).[38]

Anthropological analysis, while it assigns to obscene humor a positive, not to say essential, place in societies, implies the relation of the concept of the obscene to unresolved inequities in socially perceived universes. Mary Douglas, who demonstrates the "impure" to be identified with the anomalous, states that ambiguity produces laughter, revulsion, and shock, on a gradient;[39] where social roles are ambiguous, the people playing such roles will be viewed as dangerous (p. 99), and where sexual roles are ambiguous, as they usually are, beliefs about sex pollution will be rife (pp. 140–79). The applicability of these rules to satire and to invective against old women in particular is obvious; but apparently beliefs in sex pollution are preferable to a lack of them, since Douglas suggests that such beliefs normally have little strength "when male dominance is accepted as a central principle of social organisation and applied without inhibition and with full rights of physical coercion" (p. 142). Moreover, the right of comedy and satire to mediate anomalies is a precarious one, dependent on the maintenance of the status quo they mock; Barber documents the dangers of the saturnalian in societies ceasing to be conservative.[40] Thus the anthropological view of humor perceives obscenity as a product of ambiguity in society, and ritual humor as a product of conservatism—a conjunction which at once conjures up Juvenal.

Yet the fact remains that games are fun and humor produces pleasurable laughter, both of which it would be folly to reject; surely both fun and laughter must be called "good" results, results that make life pleasant.

The justification of humor, especially tendentious humor, that has the most relevant current application is the idea that tendentious humor produces catharsis of hostile feelings. It is consistent with Freud's analysis to believe that laughter comes from such a release, and it would also be nice to think that the sometimes horrifying basic content of tendentious humor represents a harmless venting of spleen that might otherwise turn into violence; it would be nice to think that humor might then be deliberately used to defuse violent situations. Psychologists have therefore tried to demonstrate the cathartic effect of humor on violence by tests on human subjects. But a series of experiments from the late 1960s demonstrate the difficulty of deciding the question in any clear-cut way;[41] the only consistent findings were that contextual variables are important and that aggressive persons prefer aggressive humor (p. 15).

Levine (pp. 1–27) defines three main research models for the motivation of humor: the cognitive-perceptual, which "stresses the successful and surprising resolution of incongruity, paradox, or double-entendre"; learning theory, which sees in action, including humor, the "reduction of base drives"; and psychoanalytic theory, which sees humor as motivated by "gratification of primary unconscious drives of sex and aggression." Fry, then, falls into the first of these categories, as does Koestler, who explained humor as "bisociation," the perceiving of an idea in two ways at once (which would certainly apply to satire).[42] Both the second and third models can be used to view humor as cathartic, since behaviorists can claim humor reduces, by relieving, the basic aggressive drives, while Freudians see humor as an outlet for hostile feelings. Levine points out, however, that while humor produces a strong fellow feeling in participants, it simultaneously produces joint aggressiveness against outsiders.

Two studies produced findings indicating that humor diminishes feelings of hostility in individuals. Dworkin and Efran[43] deliberately antagonized one group of (all-male) subjects in the process of the experiment, camouflaging this in the behavior of a particularly abrasive instructor. They then had the subjects rate the humor in cartoons of varying degrees of hostility. They found that the subjects' anger was mitigated by exposure to humor and that the more hostile the humor, the greater the mitigation. Singer refined this process by using the same content for the antagonizing material and for the humor subsequently rated.[44] In the summer of 1963 he took groups of black male subjects and first exposed them to a taped speech by a segregationist, then to one of three humorous tapes, one of which satirized segregationists in a hostile manner. (This experiment comes quite close to a re-creation both of the situation of Roman satire and Freud's A–B–C model.) Singer found that the initial tape did produce anger and that the hostile humor did reduce feelings of aggression, more so with groups later in that violent summer—so that the amount of reduction of hostility seemed to depend not so much on the immediately aroused anger as on residual anger. But he felt the variables and alternate possibilities to be vast and concluded with the reflection that one reason the humor worked was that the joke itself was a message, a sign that the participants could afford to treat the content as a joke.

HUMOR IS BAD

> The secret source of humor is not joy but sorrow; there is no humor in heaven.
>
> —Mark Twain, *Pudd'nhead Wilson's New Calendar*; epigraph for G. Legman, *Rationale of the Dirty Joke*, series 2

Those who have found that the "bad" aspects of humor predominate have located this "badness" in various areas. First, they find humor not to be cathartic but a reinforcement of innate hostilities. They link humor with the "bad" qualities in human beings. And, on a practical level, they link violent fantasies with violent action, in some cases holding the fantasies to be a contributory cause of the action. If this is true, it is a grave indictment of such fantasies and must at least partially implicate sexual humor, much of which depends on extremely violent fantasy.

Levine cites two general findings that support the idea that humor harbors and fosters aggression, rather than releasing it. First, he notes (pp. 19–20) that it could be inferred from psychological experiments that the humorist, by offering sexual/aggressive humor, invites his audience to relax their inhibitions toward expressing their corresponding feelings. This applies especially to the socialization of children. He also found through his own experiments that "getting" a joke does not imply understanding its basic content, and in fact the reverse is true: individuals avoid being fully aware of the aggressive content. (This, then, excuses the Priapic audience from being fully attentive; their lack of attention is actually the condition of their acceptance of the content of satire.) Studies showed that some individuals deliberately masked preferences for aggressive humor, to appear more socially acceptable, until they had consumed alcohol,[45] and that forced examination of the content of jokes significantly reduced the subjects' assessment of how funny they were.[46]

These experiments take on a more serious aspect when connected with experiments carried out on the effects of nonhumorous violent fantasies. A noted study by Berkowitz, disputed by Singer,[47] found that subjects who had seen violent films tended to administer larger electric shocks to a "victim" than those who had seen nonviolent films—in other words, the violent fantasy was not cathartic but protreptic. And recent work on social learning theory has tended to support Berkowitz's findings, making the idea of catharsis much less tenable. Bandura,[48] in his description of "aggression elicitors" (cues that trigger aggressive behavior), cites several studies in which repeated verbal and pictorial stimuli changed subjects' emotional and sexual responses—especially the work of McGuire, Carlisle, and Young, which connected deviant sexuality with fantasies accompanied by masturbation.[49] If this hypothesis is correct, then presumably the "normal" release of sexual humor and invective, with their accompanying fantasy-stereotypes, conditions "normal" sexuality. Findings along these lines support feminist theories on pornography, and the structural similarities between sexual humor and violent sexual fantasy explain why feminist theories on pornography can so readily be applied to sexual humor, particularly to satire.

This is evident on examination of feminist definitions of pornography: pornography is a depiction of "sex in which there is clear force or unequal power," where the viewer "must identify with either conqueror or victim."[50] Such depictions are typical of Roman sexual humor. Further definitions point out that pornography "describes degrading and abusive sexual behavior so as to endorse and/or recommend" it.[51] Longino points out that the root *porne-* is important, since the woman who participates is viewed as a whore who takes money in return for doing what the man wants; then this view is generalized, so that the woman comes to be perceived as Everywoman. Again, this describes the women both in Roman erotic writing and in Roman sexual humor.

The element of dominance is not only central to this definition but reflects circumstances in the society as a whole. Longino traces a connection between pornography and xenophobia, seeing in pornography "another tool of capitalism" that reinforces white male supremacy.[52] An ex-model for pornographic movies perceives herself as a "marketable commodity"[53] and comments on the use of words denoting sweet food as names for women in these movies (p. 62; cf. pp. 66–67). The use of children in pornographic movies parallels the use of women; basically sexless themselves, they submit to male gratification.[54] And Ron Sproat, an ex-writer of pornographic movies, gives a formula for the exploitation of children in pornography: "Emphasize hairlessness—tiny privates, lack of tits."[55] This tallies exactly with the Roman erotic ideal.

But the element of violence is also important and is what troubles feminists most. Some see a connection between the amount of pornography and the amount of sadism prevalent in a given society[56]—an issue that has been at least raised for Roman society.[57] Robin Morgan connects rape with the patriarchal society, calling it "the ultimate metaphor for domination, violence, subjugation, and possession" in a "phallocentric culture."[58] The application to the *Carmina Priapea* is obvious: they are hymns to phallocentrism—not serious, of course.[59] Morgan further points out the use of rape as a form of communication in war.[60]

The next question is, why rape, or why use violent fantasy as a substitute? Susan Griffin attempts to explode the whole complex by postulating that "underneath violence is the desire to appear violent" (p. 142).[61] She sees in scientific explanations of aggression and territorialism an exaltation of violence, a "hysterical" argument that uses violent fantasy as a threat. By means of a sort of empty self-denial ("the shining glow . . . of real rape and murder, to be forever denied") men are able to cling to the fantasies themselves (which are thus, as Huizinga said, the true end rather than the means). The "catharsis" of pornography, Griffin claims, is an illusion: "It is dangerous to confuse the therapeutic experience with the experiencing of the symptoms of one's illness." Less sophisticated, but still cogent, theories suggest that fantasies of violence are directly harmful, as, for example, the use of loaded sexual language perpetuates biased social systems.[62] Susan Lurie, using a psychological approach,[63] traces the need for violent sexual fantasy and behavior to male perceptions of male and female genitalia. If a fantasy must originate to "combat a disappointing, hostile reality," for what disappointment does pornography compensate? Lurie's answer is that male fears about the vulnerability of the penis in early childhood, and the fear and lack of knowledge of the vagina, lead men to produce a fantasy that both denies female sexuality and silences the woman. This might tie in with the idea that in patriarchal societies women are always aligned with nature (through childbirth) and men with culture; since culture dominates nature, the sexual function of women must be derogated.[64]

A minor defect in most feminist thought on pornography is that it assumes that the relation between violent sexual fantasy and violent sexual behavior is one of cause and effect. Although psychologists have long labored to prove or disprove even the partial truth of this idea, surely it is logical to assume that violent fantasy and violent behavior are both products of the same cultural characteristics, each perhaps capable of inflaming the other. Nevertheless, feminists have amply demonstrated the harm inherent in socially accepted modes of humor, art, or sexual fantasy that promote one sexual role at the expense of all others. Even where the victims of such modes "go along with" them or laugh at them, they must thereby acknowledge the established roles. To say "I am not like that" is to define yourself in terms of "that."

The arguments in favor of humor and against it reach no conclusion. All seem flawed in some respect; probably the question is not capable of an answer. The most obvious facts about humor contradict each other: laughter makes people feel good; hostility and aggression, sometimes extreme, provide the structure for most humor. For the purposes of understanding Roman sexual humor, Freud's descriptive model will do very well, with the addition of the model of Priapus. Yet the prescriptive models are thought-provoking, some disturbing; it is impossible to ask the question "What end does this humor serve?" without wonder and unease. If it is true that genres of literature are functions of states inherent in particular cultures, then Roman sexual humor provides distressing insight into Roman society.

Caesar in Cicero's *De Oratore*, offering a prefatory *apologia*, remarks (*De Or.* 2.217):

> Ego vero . . . omni de re facetius puto posse ab homine non inurbano, quam de ipsis facetiis disputari . . . qui eius rei rationem quandam conati sunt artemque tradere, sic insulsi exstiterunt, ut nihil aliud eorum nisi ipsa insulsitas rideatur.
>
> As a matter of fact, I think that a not unsophisticated man can talk about anything more wittily than about wit itself. Those who have tried to teach some kind of theory or technique of this business have made such fools of themselves that nothing of theirs got a laugh but their foolishness.

This does not prevent him from going on to analyze the use of humor in rhetoric, with a final descriptive breakdown of kinds of jokes not unlike Freud's (2.289). But his *apologia* accords well with the real problems inherent in the analysis of humor, and thus it is hard to agree with a further remark he makes in passing (2.219)—"quippe leve enim est totum hoc risum movere," "indeed, this whole business of raising a laugh is a light one."

CHAPTER 4 Graffiti, Gossip, Lampoons, and Rhetorical Invective

Perception of the simplest level of Roman sexual humor is complicated and hampered by the fact that we cannot directly record Roman verbal and colloquial humor and abuse. This makes it somewhat difficult to determine what were appropriate levels of language for different levels of society and different social situations. However, a great many graffiti preserved randomly afford a sort of control. In addition, a large body of material preserved in published letters, in histories and biographies, and in speeches provide examples of political lampoons, current gossip, and even of conversational sallies. The material as a whole shows great consistency in choice of subject; even if the more formal sources use periphrasis rather than direct obscenity, graffitist and orator are saying the same thing.

Graffiti

Graffiti show a full spectrum of the sort of sexual values in which the virile male is the norm; the nature of Roman graffiti certainly implies that most, if not all, were written by men. The graffiti discussed here all come from Pompeii[1] and show various levels of sophistication: some are mere name-calling, some are prostitutes' advertisements from the brothels, many include variant spellings or forms of Greek letters, and some are written in verse, usually elegiac distich (also a common meter for political lampoons).

A graffito written by a lover curses rivals (Diehl 600):

> si quis forte meam cupiet vio[lare] puellam,
> illum in desertis montibus urat amor.

> If anyone may wish to lay hands on my girl,
> may love burn him in the mountains of the wilderness.

Similar poems wish that rivals will be eaten by bears (601) or threaten Venus with a beating (27); cf. Diehl 583–612. Graffiti concerning intercourse are not always positive; they are sometimes written against the female partner, as, for example (Diehl 615):

hic ego nu[nc f]utue formosa fo[r]ma puella
laudata a multis, set lutus intus erat.

Here I have now fuckid a gril beatiful too see,
praised by many, but there was muck inside.

The girl may be a prostitute, as this graffito is similar to one specifying a price (469) and to a come-on perhaps written in a public latrine (470); but such boasts are common, cf. Diehl 613–21, 625, 1086, 1090.

The elements of threat and boasting are prominent in all these graffiti; their mechanism is in fact much safer than that of sexual humor in literature or even in conversation. The speaker is anonymous or, even if he includes his name, is not present himself to make his statement. The victim can thus be attacked by name. The audience has no choice but to read, if the graffito is prominently displayed; thus the audience is both assaulted by the graffito, which acts as a sort of verbal cat's-paw for the speaker, and excused for participating. This mechanism is particularly marked in the graffiti comprising specific personal messages, especially when these are insults. With the graffiti on heterosexual intercourse cited above can be compared those related to homosexual affairs and to oral intercourse. Some are greetings to lovers, straightforward and boastful (Diehl 540):

fonticulus pisciculo suo plurma salut.

Fonticulus [Little Fountain] sez a big hi to his little fishie

(Cf. Diehl 545, 1091.) Others are insults, statements that another person is a pathic homosexual (Diehl 648):

Cosmus Equitiaes magnus cinaedus et fellator est suris apertis

Equitias' slave Cosmus is a big queer and a cocksucker with his legs wide open

(Cf. Diehl 582, 623, 626–28, 1102.) Most of the graffiti concerning oral sex are of this type, simply asserting the practices of their victim (Diehl 649–50, 657–60, 1104–08), occasionally with comment (Diehl 659):

Sabina felas, no belle faces

Sabina, you give blojobs, you don do good

Many graffiti list a price (Diehl 451, 455–70), for example, Diehl 467:

Lahis felat a.II

Lahis gives blojobs for $2

Direct threats in graffiti are less common but paradigmatic of the relation between the graffitist and the viewer (Diehl 504):

me me mentulam linge

lick me [= my] prick

Most threats just direct the addressee to perform cunnilingus (Diehl 501a–502) or fellatio (501, 503, 1103). The reversal of roles in which the speaker is emasculated is exemplified by crude name-calling:

656 Antus ψωλή

Antus [is a] schmuck

667 imanis metula es

your a big prike

In the first case the insult identifies the victim with a threatening phallus—as if that is all he is, and as if he has raped the writer. In the second case the victim and audience are identified with each other as threatening phalli. Several graffiti include drawings of phalli; these threaten (Diehl 1092) or identify reader with phallus (1078). Some waggish graffiti state that the act of reading implies perversion (582) or will be punished (1093, 1094).

The only other class of obscene graffiti that exists apart from this model is that of scatological graffiti; yet these, too, are generally threats, warnings not to defecate or urinate in that place. Presumably many were written on tombs or other delimited places. Some (698) are in verse, some (696a) are plain. Outside this context, mention of excrement occasionally appears in graffiti for comic effect, as in this famous couplet (Diehl 702):

mixims in lecto. fateor, peccavimus, hospes,
si dices quare? nulla matella fuit.

We have pissed in the bed. I admit, we were wrong, my host,
if you ask why? There was no chamber pot.

This poem forces the news of the wet bed on (presumably) a later guest and casts aspersions on the facilities of the lodging place. The writer of the verse sounds proud of himself. This sort of bragging about actions normally considered shameful is typical of the hostile, boastful attitude of Roman sexual humor and possibly also typical of the provenance of this graffito.[2]

Gossip

> more hominum invident, in conviviis rodunt, in circulis vellicant . . .
>
> —Cicero, *Pro Balbo* 57

The kinds of things that Romans reported saying to each other as gossip or circulating as jingles were couched in nicer language than were graffiti and depended on implication rather than on direct statement. Perhaps literate Romans did call each other names, but if so they did not like to record their slanging matches. Even so, the gossip and anecdotes preserved in various authors make by implication many of the same statements made by graffiti. Although the exact sexual activities are left unnamed, women are branded as prostitutes and adulteresses while men are said to be adulterers and cuckolds, or else it is hinted that they are too fond of boys, or of other men, or are effeminate. It is instructive to note with what freedom the Romans maligned men who were afterward deified or venerated and how many of these stories survived for a long time.

It can be assumed that the only vaguely reliable source of gossip for its own sake is the letters of Cicero, even if they have been edited for publication. Pliny generally places himself above gossip in his letters; and other types of sources, though full of rumors, deal in material that has survived the day-to-day attrition of the scandal mill usually for definite political reasons. While such works provide a rich assortment of rancid allegations, Cicero's letters display the products of a more private and spontaneous malice.

After Cicero tells Atticus the juicy story of the fop Vedius, in whose luggage were found portraits of five Roman ladies, and makes jokes on their husbands' names (*Att.* 6.1.25), he concludes, "sumus enim ambo belle curiosi," "for we are both awfully nosy." This seems to have been quite true. Although Cicero, like most people writing to a best friend, usually shows more interest in his own money, family, and personal prospects than in anything or anybody else, the letters are peppered with society scandal. Cicero indeed observes a certain urbane restraint: in accordance with his *recusatio* of obscenity in *Fam.* 9.22, he leaves out the four-letter words; but he can still be quite crude. He suggests the adultery of Memmius with Lucullus' wife, framed in terms from Greek epic (*Att.* 1.18.3):

> instat hic nunc annus egregius. eius initium eius modi fuit ut anniversaria sacra Iuventatis non committerentur; nam M. Luculli uxorem Memmius suis sacris initiavit. Menelaus aegre id passus divortium fecit. quamquam ille pastor Idaeus Menelaum solum contempserat, hic noster Paris tam Menelaum quam Agamemnonem liberum non putavit.

> Here now an egregious year is at hand. Its beginning was of such a sort that the annual rites of Youth were not undertaken; for Memmius initiated Marcus Lucullus' wife in his own rites. Menelaus [= M. Lucullus, the less important brother], taking this badly, divorced her. Although the Idaean shepherd had insulted Menelaus alone, this Paris of ours [= Memmius] treated as lackeys both Menelaus and Agamemnon [= L. Lucullus, the famous brother, who eventually divorced his wife Servilia for committing adultery].[3]

Cicero drops dark hints about Caesar and Servilia (*Att.* 2.24.3), and Postumia and

Pomptinus (*Att.* 5.21.9), and follows the progress of the divorce of Metella, one of his son-in-law's mistresses (*Att.* 11.23.3, 12.52.2, 13.7). Caelius' news of adulteries is put in a more gossipy tone (*Fam.* 8.7.2), but he says no more than Cicero was wont to say to Atticus; Cicero asks him for more details (*Fam.* 2.15.5).

Cicero reserves his worst venom for the vices of his enemies. He is surprisingly gentle, merely snide, about Antony and Cytheris, though her travels with Antony were a thorn in his side (*Att.* 10.10.5, 10.16.5, 15.22). For Clodius and Clodia he pulls out all the stops. Chagrined references to the affair of Clodius and the rites of Bona Dea keep recurring (*Att.* 1.12.3, 1.13.3, 1.18.2–3, 2.4.2); in a formal letter to Lentulus Spinther (*Fam.* 1.9.15) he rants about Clodius—"illa furia . . . qui non pluris fecerat Bonam Deam quam tris sorores," "that scoundrel . . . who had held the Bona Dea of no more account than his three sisters [said to be his mistresses]." And this after Clodius' acquittal. Cicero liked to give nicknames to the brother and sister: Clodia he called *βοῶπις*, "ox-eyed" (*Att.* 2.9.1, 2.12.2, 2.14.1, 2.22.5); she was indeed noted for her beautiful eyes (*Har. Resp.* 38, *Cael.* 49—cf. Catullus 3.18, 43.2), but *βοῶπις* was the epithet of Hera, who was married to her brother Zeus.[4] According to Cicero, he even went so far as to tax Clodius with this famous incest, and crudely at that (*Att.* 2.1.5):

> "sed soror, quae tantum habeat consularis loci, unum mihi solum pedem dat." "Noli," inquam, "de uno pede sororis queri; licet etiam alterum tollas." "non consulare" inquies "dictum." fateor; sed ego illam odi male consularem: "ea est enim seditiosa, ea cum viro bellum gerit," neque solum cum Metello sed etiam cum Fabio, quod eos nihili esse moleste fert.

> "But my sister, who has so much of the consular section [at the games], is giving me only one foot." "Don't complain about one of your sister's feet," says I; "you can always get her to lift the other [= Engl. colloq. "you can always get her to spread her legs"]." "Not the words of an ex-consul," you will say. I admit it; but I hate that consul's non-lady: "for she's a treacherous one, she wages war with her man," and I don't mean only with Metellus but also with Fabius, because it bothers her that the two of them are doing no good.[5]

The charge of incest was the one Cicero most favored against Clodius, but this does not stop him from using another common insult: impugning Clodius' masculinity. He calls him "Appuleia" at *Att.* 4.11.2, a double joke: the name is a reference to the proverbially seditious L. Appuleius Saturninus, but the feminine form implies that Clodius is effeminate. Cicero makes use of the same kind of insult at *Att.* 1.14.5 about the younger Curio: "concursabant barbatuli iuvenes, totus ille grex Catilinae duce filiola Curionis," "All the goatee'd youth came running, that whole crowd of Catiline's, with Curio's little girl as their general." It is notable that the short beard was, from Cicero's point of view, a sign of moral degeneracy that included both effeminacy and promiscuity of all kinds. Cicero casts similar aspersions several times, with the fairly clear implication that he means them only as insults, but letting stand the insinuations as to the actual sexual proclivities of his target. In a fit of pique he comments on Pompey's foppishness (*Att.* 2.3.1); later, Q. Cicero comments even more explicitly to Tiro on the effeminacy of the consuls-elect Hirtius and Pansa (*Fam.* 16.27.1)—"quos ego penitus novi, libidinum et languoris effeminatissimi animi plenos," "whom I know through and through to be full of the lusts and languor of the most effeminate mind." This sort of thing could be taken much further. In 50 B.C. Caelius engaged in a vendetta with the censor Appius Claudius and wrote about it to Cicero (*Fam.* 8.12.3, 8.14.4). He first scoffed at Drusus' hearing cases under the lex Scantinia (which seems to have punished intercourse between men and freeborn youths), Drusus apparently being in no position to censure others; then he found himself accused under the law. In retaliation, he accused Drusus' ally Appius under the same law.

This case of Caelius' shows how invective could be given concrete political form. There are myriad examples of Roman political or politicized invective in all forms, but they are mostly preserved by later biographers and historians who are quite obviously, sometimes consciously, repeating what had become a kind of party line. In other words, this invective is fossilized, kept alive by political motives that have long outlived the protagonists of the stories. Besides simple rumors and insults of the sort recorded by Cicero, such invective includes political speeches whole or fragmentary, jokes and apocryphal tales that have relatives throughout Indo-European folklore, serious political pamphlets, and verse lampoons.

Lampoons

The crudest sort of invective was a political institution at Rome. There are frequent mentions in Cicero's letters of the unpleasant fate that awaited a politician out of favor: any public appearance, especially at the games or at the theater, would be greeted by a public outcry, *clamoribus et conviciis et sibilis*, "with shouting and insults and hissing" (*Att.* 2.18.1; cf. *Fam.* 8.1.4, 8.2.1; *Sest.* 115, 117–18, 126). Such displays were not peculiar to the turbulent first century B.C.: Dio describes the foolhardy Tarentines as singing scurrilous verses and defecating on a Roman envoy (9.39.7–8); Marcus Servilius, in the time of Aemilius Paulus, was exasperated enough to bare his posterior to the crowd (Plut. *Aem.* 31). In the first century this sort of thing could affect even a consul: Bibulus (Plut. *Pomp.* 48; *Cat. Min.* 32) had dung thrown at him as well as insults.

Typically, mudslinging might have been carried out by claques, as in the case of Clodius and Pompey described by Plutarch (cf. also Dio 39.19.1–3, 21.3). According to Plutarch, Pompey was at one point harassed at every public appearance by a crowd of hecklers shouting in unison, "Who is the degenerate general?

Who is the man who scratches his head with one finger? Who is the man who seeks another man?" (Plut. *Pomp.* 48.7). The same joke about touching the head with one finger was made against Caesar by Cicero (Plut. *Caesar* 4); this gesture was part of the stereotype of effeminacy (Calvus, *FPL* 18 Morel; Sen. *Ep.* 52.12; Juv. 9.133). An eyewitness account survives of Pompey's involvement with Clodius in a slanging match at Milo's trial, in which Clodius' hecklers attempted to keep him from speaking by shouting, *convicio et maledictis*, to which Pompey's claque replied with over an hour of jeering and yelling, ending with verses on Clodius and Clodia. The Clodians replied with an hour of heckling led by Clodius, after which they began spitting at the Pompeians; the meeting ended in a brawl (*QFr.* 2.3). Cicero's description of the method used by Clodius and his gang, a sort of question-and-answer routine, tallies with Plutarch's.[6]

Where men were accused of effeminacy, women were accused of unchastity. In general the women of whom we read were the wives of prominent political figures of the first century B.C. and, later, members of the imperial family or of the surviving aristocratic families. Rarely is anything said of them other than that they have committed adultery with a certain man, or that such an adultery is the reason for their divorce; an exceptional figure was the elder Julia, about whom a whole cycle of jokes survived to the time of Macrobius. An example (Macrob. *Sat.* 2.5.9):

> Cumque conscii flagitiorum mirarentur, quo modo similes Agrippae filios pareret, quae tam vulgo potestatem corporis sui faceret ait "numquam enim nisi navi plena tollo vectorem."

> When those who knew of her sins were expressing their wonder that she gave birth to sons who looked like Agrippa [her husband], when she made such public property of her body, she said, "Why, I never take on a passenger until the ship is loaded."

Although these stories are apocryphal, they do give Julia what almost no other of the supposed adulteresses of contemporary gossip had: a personality and a milieu. In most of the stories she gets the better of her interlocutor, despite her hopelessly besmirched character; it is Julia who is the "heroine" of these jokes, and so their purpose is not a simple one. True, they degrade the "First Daughter"; they also show ideological opposition to the policy of moral reform, as well as a cynical amusement at the notorious disparity between Augustus' policies and his family's behavior.

The cases in which men were accused of effeminacy or licentious pederasty are far too numerous to analyze here case by case. Fossilized in the pages of ancient biography are slurs against Lucius Quinctius Flamininus, for sadism and pederasty (a great scandal; Plut. *Flam.* 18, *Cat. Mai.* 17); against the poet Terence, for being the *puer* of Scipio and Laelius (Suet. *Poet.* 1); against Sulpicius Galus by Scipio Aemilianus (Gell. 6.12); against the Roman youth in general, and the son of a candidate in particular, also by Scipio (Macrob. *Sat.* 3.14.6–7); against Hortensius, apparently commonly (Gell. 1.5, Macrob. *Sat.* 3.13.3–5); against Caelius by Cato (Macrob. *Sat.* 3.14.9); against Sulla (Plut. *Sulla* 2, 36); against his son-in-law Piso by Cicero (Macrob. *Sat.* 2.3.16); against Maecenas, seemingly commonly (Sen. *Ep.* 114.4–6) and by Augustus (Macrob. *Sat.* 2.4.12); against Vergil, of exclusive pederasty (Suet. *Poet.*, *Verg.* 9–10); against Sejanus as an ex-*puer* (Dio 57.19.5); against Nymphidius Sabinus (Plut. *Galba* 9); against Seneca (Dio 61.10.3–6); against Otho (Plut. *Otho* 4, 9; Dio 63.8.3). These slurs, in their context, arise from various motives. Established and conservative political figures attack the young men of the day, as Scipio attacked the youth for dancing, Cato attacked Caelius, and Cicero attacked Catiline's crowd. Or respected intellectual figures are demeaned—but here again lurks a political motive: Terence and the great Scipio are more than just patron and poet, the powerful lawyer is a laughingstock, and Augustus' *éminence grise* Maecenas (whom Augustus was said to have cuckolded) commands little respect. In turn, the conservative or politically powerful are derided in the same terms—Otho, Sabinus, Pompey, Sulla; and Cicero attacks a son-in-law out of favor. Sexuality here is no more than a metaphor for power; Dio even has Queen Boadicea deride the Romans *en masse* as effete pederasts (62.6.4–5).

The stories about the emperors in Suetonius demonstrate that scandals about a single figure did not have to be consistent. Most of the twelve Caesars were rumored to have been licentious as both adulterers and homosexuals (not that the two were mutually exclusive, as will be seen), and Gaius and Nero were both supposed to have been adulterers, active homosexuals, and pathics. According to Suetonius, Julius Caesar was cuckolded by Clodius (*Iul.* 6, 74) but was himself so noted an adulterer that Pompey (*Iul.* 50) called him "Aegisthus" (mock epic again); and his foreign affairs were the talk of Rome and of the army (*Iul.* 49–52). The elder Curio quipped that he was "every woman's husband and every man's wife" ("omnium mulierum virum et omnium virorum mulierem," *Iul.* 52). Augustus was crushed by his daughter's goings-on (*Aug.* 65) but was supposedly a great lecher himself (for which Suetonius used a letter of Antony's as evidence, *Aug.* 69–71; cf. *Claud.* 1, a lampoon on Augustus and Livia). Julia supposedly tried to seduce Tiberius while still married, and later cuckolded him (*Tib.* 7, 10). Gaius thought he was a son of Julia's by Augustus (*Calig.* 23), and himself went in for adultery and incest (24, 36); but the descriptions of Augustus' and Gaius' behavior at parties are suspiciously alike:

Aug. 69.1:

> M. Antonius super festinatas Liviae nuptias obiecit et feminam consularem e triclinio viri coram in cubiculum abductam, rursus in convivium rubentibus auriculis incomptiore capillo reductam . . .

Antony cast up to him, besides the hurried wedding to Livia, his abducting to a bedroom a consular's wife from the dining room of her husband while he was there, and bringing her back to the dinner with her ears burning and her hair disheveled.

Calig. 36.2:

quas plerumque cum maritis ad cenam vocatas praeterque pedes suos transeuntis diligenter ac lente mercantium more considerabat, etiam faciem manu adlevans, si quae pudore submitterent; quotiens deinde libuisset egressus triclinio, cum maxime placitam sevocasset, paulo post recentibus adhuc lasciviae notis reversus vel laudabat palam vel vituperabat, singula enumerans bona malave corporis atque concubitus.

Which women, often, when he had invited them to dinner with their husbands, he used to inspect, as they walked past his feet, carefully and slowly, like a purchaser in the market, even lifting their faces with his hand, if any looked down in modesty; then whenever he was suited he went out of the dining room, when he had called the most pleasing one, and returning soon after, with the traces of lust still fresh, he either praised or reviled her, openly, detailing the individual good points and bad points of her body and their intercourse.

The structure of the episode has each man treat a respectable woman as a slave; the later episode is only more elaborate.

Claudius, a weak figure in Suetonius' pantheon, commits no adulteries of his own but countenances those of others (*Claud.* 16) and was cuckolded by both Messallina (*Claud.* 26) and Urgulanilla (*Claud.* 27). The best he could do was to get vicarious thrills; he had visitors to the palace searched and pawed about, especially women, boys, and girls ("feminae praetextatique pueri et puellae," *Claud.* 35)—like an impotent Priapus. Other weak emperors, Galba and Otho, likewise committed no adulteries of their own: Galba was approached by Agrippina (*Galba* 5), Otho had to give Nero his wife (*Otho* 3, subject of a lampoon). But Nero was, of course, a noted pursuer of women—even to debauching Vestal Virgins (*Ner.* 28)—as were Domitian (*Dom.* 1) and even (before his accession, and becoming good) Titus (*Tit.* 7). The pattern of these stories seems to be that the weaker figures have much less active sex lives than the stronger ones do; their experiences are marred by cuckoldry and impotence.

The same pattern marks the stories about homosexuality, and consequently many of the same emperors reappear in them. Suetonius devotes four lurid chapters to the tale of Tiberius' goings-on at Capri (*Tib.* 42–45), with his villas full of "spintrians" (sexual acrobats, apparently) and his grottoes full of little boys swimming. In all this, Tiberius is disgusting because senile and impotent; the prurient descriptions detail his voyeurism and the ways he contrived to be fellated. Gaius supposedly played both active and pathic parts, with the aristocrats Marcus Lepidus and Valerius Catullus, with the actor Mnester, and with anonymous "hostages" living at the the palace (*Calig.* 36); Valerius Catullus boasted of wearing himself out on the emperor. Gaius' dress was effeminate (*Calig.* 52, cf. below); yet he teased his future assassin Cassius Chaerea for effeminacy (*Calig.* 56):

> Cassius Chaerea . . . quem Gaius seniorem iam et mollem et effeminatum denotare omni probro consuerat et modo signum petenti "Priapum" aut "Venerem" dare, modo ex aliqua causa agenti gratias osculandam manum offerre formatam commotamque in obscaenum modum.

> Cassius Chaerea . . . whom, as elderly and soft and effeminate, Gaius used to single out with every kind of scorn—sometimes, when he asked the password, Gaius gave "Priapus" or "Venus"; sometimes, when he was thanking him for some reason, Gaius gave him his hand to kiss, making his hand into an obscene shape and wiggling it [i.e., with the middle finger stuck out and thrusting; cf. *Pr.* 56.1–2; Pers. 2.33; Mart. 2.28.1–2, 6.70.5; Juv. 10.53].

Any participant in the game of invective could apparently be allotted either role, Priapus or victim.

The weak Claudius had no homosexual love life, according to Suetonius (*Claud.* 33), while Galba liked grown men (*Galba* 21), and Otho, rumored to have been involved with Nero ("consuetudine mutui stupri," *Otho* 2), took great care of his appearance, including depilating himself and attempting to keep his beard from growing (*Otho* 12). On the other hand, the activities attributed to Nero were various and bloodcurdling: he seduced boys and married Sporus, to whom he played the husband (*Ner.* 28), and then married Doryphorus, this time playing the wife (*Ner.* 29). This gave rise to a joke which Suetonius claims was still current in his day (28.1):

> exstatque cuiusdam non inscitus iocus "bene agi potuisse cum rebus humanis, si Domitius pater talem habuisset uxorem."

> And there is still in circulation a fairly clever joke of someone's, "The world would have been a better place, if Domitius senior had had a wife like that."[7]

Nero supposedly raped and then had assassinated a royal youth, Aulus Plautius (*Ner.* 35), and invented sadistic pleasures—Mohocking (*Ner.* 26, *Otho* 2), "brothels" full of *matronae* and boys (*Ner.* 27; cf. *Calig.* 41), and, while dressed in an animal skin, nuzzling into the genitalia of prisoners tied to stakes (*Ner.* 29). Vitellius was also supposed to have played both active and pathic roles: he was a spintrian on Capri and had "Spintria" as a nickname all his life (*Vit.* 3; cf. Dio 63.4.2); he also had a long, stormy affair with his freedman Asiaticus (*Vit.* 12; cf. Dio 64.2.1–4.3). The good emperor Titus supposedly owned a troop of *cinaedi*, whom he abandoned, with Queen Berenice, on coming to power (*Tit.* 7).

Domitian, not a good emperor, was supposed to have played the pathic role for Claudius Pollio (on whom Nero wrote a satiric poem, *Dom.* 1) and for the future emperor Nerva. Vespasian, a very good emperor, has only a verbal connection with homosexuality: he impugns Mucianus' virility (*Vesp.* 13). Augustus, on the other hand, weak and sickly as a youth, was subjected to frequent taunts of effeminacy (*Aug.* 68; Dio 50.27.6–7).[8]

Gaius, Nero, Titus, and Domitian were all rumored to have committed incest—Gaius with his sisters (*Calig.* 24, 36), Nero with his mother (*Ner.* 28), Titus with his sister-in-law (*Tit.* 10), and Domitian with his niece (*Dom.* 22). Many thought Otho's father was Tiberius' bastard (*Otho* 1), and Gaius thought *he* was Augustus' (*Calig.* 23).

Are these stories perhaps just true? Many are supported by "evidence"—letters, eyewitness accounts—and Suetonius is famous for his enviable access to palace files. But it is obvious that most of the stories belong far more to folklore than to history, partly to the kind of tale that grows up around any famous figure and partly to the kind of tale that attributes utterly appalling sexual activities to a real-life figure no longer present.[9] The interest of an audience in such stories is prurient (often a quality to the fore in discussions of Suetonius), and their function is to feed the hostile fantasies of those who hear them. From the stories in Suetonius it would seem that the amount and kind of tales that attached to any one figure depended on the amount of charisma he had—good or bad made no difference; and Tiberius' physical withdrawal from Rome produced the most sensational stories.

If these stories owe anything to historical "documentation," it must be largely to real propaganda (like Antony's letter about Augustus' sex life) and real lampoons. Suetonius also seems to need these stories to balance his careful record of moral reform for each emperor; the implication of hypocrisy in high places adds great piquancy to each biography. The tale of stern reformers included Julius Caesar (*Iul.* 42, 43, 48), Augustus (*Aug.* 34, 37, 39, 45, 67), Tiberius (*Tib.* 33, 34, 35, 58), Gaius (who banished the spintrians, *Calig.* 16), Nero (who banished the actors, *Ner.* 16), Vespasian (*Vesp.* 8, 11), Titus (*Tit.* 6), and Domitian (*Dom.* 7–8, including reforms aimed at actors, eunuchs, adulterers, homosexuals, and the Vestal Virgins). To add to the confusion about their characters, each also, as emperor, represents the stereotype of the tyrant in rhetoric, and rhetorical tyrants always debauch helpless women and children. As a general rule, stories about vice seem to have been part of the necessary material for biography, so much so that Suetonius even drags in weak examples in the life of Titus. It must have been obvious to biographers gathering information so long after the fact that many of the stories were apocryphal or deliberate fabrications, but their genre was concerned not with truth but with edification.

It is not at all unusual, as these stories show, for the same man to be castigated both for effeminacy or interest in other men and for being an adulterer; Julius Caesar is only the most notorious example of this phenomenon. This was simply part of the Roman sexual stereotype: effeminate men were thought to be more interested in sex of any kind than were more rugged types; one might compare the transvestitism affected by singers like Mick Jagger, who have great sexual appeal to women. As has been seen, the stereotype was extended to writing style as well as personal appearance, so that it was Maecenas' "soft and dissolute" style in his letters that prompted Augustus to call him (Macrob. *Sat.* 2.4.12)

> mi ebenum Medulliae, ebur ex Etruria, lasar Arretinum, adamas Supernas, Tiberinum margaritum, Cilniorum smaragde, iaspi Iguvinorum, berulle Porsenae, carbunculum Hadriae, ἵνα συντέμω πάντα, μάλαγμα moecharum.

> my ebony of Medullia, ivory of Etruria, asafetida of Arretum, diamond of the Adriatic, pearl of the Tiber, emerald of the Maecenas family, jasper of the Iguvines, beryl of Porsena, carbuncle of the Adriatic, *et pour conclure*, *bon-bon* of the adulteresses.

Anecdotes do not always state in so many words that a man is effeminate or a pathic homosexual.[10] Where indirect insults were customary, a whole vocabulary of significant attributes was called upon to hint at underlying sexual profligacy or perversion. Besides being called *pathicus* or *effeminatus*, a man might be called *mollis*, "soft," or any of a dozen adjectives connoting weakness or delicacy. A common insinuation was that the man was too graceful in his physical movements; a joke ascribed to Cicero about his son-in-law Piso has him recommend his daughter to "walk like your husband" (Macrob. *Sat.* 2.3.16). This is similar to the bias against dancing so often expressed in Latin literature: not only were nice women not supposed to be able to dance very well, as in Sallust's famous description of Sempronia (*Cat.* 25.2), but it was a shocking thing for men to know how to dance at all. A good typical history of this idea is Furius Albinus' tirade against dancing and singing at Macrob. *Sat.* 3.14.4–15, which also explains the stigma on these activities: they were too much the property of actors and paid entertainers, and were especially reminiscent of the *cinaedi*—effeminate dancers who cut lewd capers at banquets—and of the prostitute's strut. And actors, entertainers, and *cinaedi* were commonly viewed as tantamount to prostitutes themselves.

Another mark of effeminacy was the wearing of unusual dress, especially Greek, or eccentricity in the belting of one's clothing (this last may seem overly particular until one recalls the fuss made today over hats and neckties). *Discinctus*, "unbelted," was a synonym for "effeminate" (Pers. 3.31, 4.22; Sen. *Ep.* 114.6); perhaps again the association is with the stage, since lyre players wore the ungirt tunic (Dio 63.17.5). A speech of Scipio Aemilianus (Gell. 6.12; cf. Suet. *Calig.* 52) provides a summary of the way a conservative Roman viewed unorthodox dress; the *chiridota* he mentions is explained by Gellius as a long-sleeved tunic reaching the fingers—this at a time when the Romans wore only tunics with very short sleeves, having previously worn nothing at all under the rough wool of their togas:

> Hac antiquitate indutus P. Africanus, Pauli filius, vir omnibus bonis artibus atque omni virtute praeditus, P. Sulpicio Gallo, homini delicato, inter pleraque alia, quae obiectabat, id quoque probro dedit, quod tunicis uteretur manus totas operientibus. . . . "Nam qui cotidie unguentatus adversum speculum ornetur, cuius supercilia radantur, qui barba vulsa, feminibusque subvulsis ambulet, qui in conviviis adulescentulus cum amatore, cum chiridota tunica interior accubuerit, qui non modo vinosus, sed virosus quoque sit, eumne quisquam dubitet, quin idem fecerit quod cinaedi facere solent?"

> Publius Africanus, son of Paulus, imbued in these old-fashioned ways, a man endowed with all good arts and every virtue, among the many other things he cast up to Publius Sulpicius Galus, an over-refined man, also gave this cause for blame, that he wore tunics covering his whole hand. . . . "For a man who daily is adorned before his mirror, covered with perfumes, whose eyebrows are shaven, who walks around with his beard plucked out and his thighs depilated, who as a very young man at dinner parties lay curled up against his lover dressed in a leotard, who is not only a wine fancier but a man fancier—does anyone doubt about him, that he did the same thing that *cinaedi* do?"

But even the great orator Hortensius was supposed to have been similarly particular about his dress; a story was told that Hortensius took his colleague to court for *iniuria* because he had disarranged a fold of his toga (Macrob. *Sat.* 3.13.5), and that Hortensius' rival in a court case, Lucius Torquatus, jeered at him for his effeminacy (Gell. 1.5), calling him "Dionysia" after a famous danseuse of the time. To this Hortensius was said to have replied, "Dionysia malo equidem esse quam quod tu, Torquate: ἄμουσος, ἀναφρόδιτος, ἀπροσδιόνυσος," "I really prefer to be Dionysia than like you, Torquatus—*sans Muse*, *sans Aphrodite*, *sans Dionysos*."[11] Hortensius' idiosyncratic and melodramatic speaking style is well known from critics who basically admired him;[12] it is noteworthy that, although he exactly fits the stereotype of the foppishly dressed man with elaborate vocal tricks and gestures, the stories told about him are not entirely hostile.

Most of the political and literary greats of Rome figure in stories like these. Macrobius' collection of Cicero's famous witticisms includes one about Caesar's effeminate belting of his toga (*Sat.* 2.3.9; cf. Dio 43.43). Antony was notorious for his connection with the younger Curio (Cic. *Phil.* 2.44–47; Plut. *Ant.* 2), while his followers taunted Caesar for his indulgence in pederasty (Plut. *Ant.* 59), and he or his party must have been the source of the letter to Augustus teasing him for his many adulteries (Suet. *Aug.* 69.2). Tacitus repeats a story (*Ann.* 14.60.4) against Tigellinus, in which one of Octavia's slaves bravely withstood torture rather than bear false witness against her mistress; she defied her tormentor, saying, "castiora esse muliebria Octaviae quam os eius," "[My mistress's] genitals are purer than [your] mouth"—a heroic taunt, unfortunately more likely to be apocryphal than true. And the poet Lucan, whose involvement with and subsequent betrayal of the anti-Neronian party must have been notorious, was said to have displayed his feelings egregiously by declaiming the following verse of Nero's while breaking wind loudly in a public latrine: "sub terris tonuisse putes," "you might think it was thundering below the earth" (Suet. *Vita Luc.*).

Besides the tales of political claques, and stories whose very neatness makes them suspicious, there is ample evidence that the wholesale manufacture of scurrilous propaganda was a favorite Roman political activity. An outstanding example is the attack on Cicero's reputation: the speech attributed to Q. Fufius Calenus by Dio (46.1–28)—which says, among much else, that Cicero pimped his wife and treated his daughter as his mistress (46.18.6)—is dubious not only from the evidence of Cicero's own letters but from Dio's general rabid hatred of Cicero and most of his contemporaries. The little invective tract of pseudo-Sallust against Cicero and the equally spurious reply include their share of sexual innuendoes (ps.-Sall. *in Cic.* 2, 5; ps.-Cic. *in Sall.* 1–3, 7, 9–10, 13–15, 16, 21): "Sallust" claims that Cicero had used his body to gain his rhetorical training and then had committed incest with his daughter, "Cicero" claims that Sallust had been a prostitute as a boy and had gone on to become a notorious adulterer.[13] But the use of propaganda long antedates the Roman revolution and at least in part belonged to an honorable and ceremonial tradition: the songs of soldiers ridiculing their general at his triumph. That this was a form of apotropaic and cleansing magic (above, chapter 1) may explain why so many politicians went along with the tradition cheerfully—although Roman politicians were usually glad to pay any price for fame.

The soldiers presumably always sang; reports of this exist for Aemilius Paulus (Plut. *Aem.* 34) and Caesar (Suet. *Iul.* 49, 51; Dio 43.20.2–4). Sulla put up with verses on his looks and his marriage, as well as with another military tradition, jeering from the walls of a besieged town (Plut. *Sulla* 2, 6, 13); Pompey engaged in political pamphleteering (Plut. *Pomp.* 49). Dio remarks on the annoying meter used by Alexandrian demonstrators (65.8.4–7). The stoical Cato, cut out in his courtship, actually wrote iambics against Scipio Metellus; later, common lampoons were written on his son's supposed affair with the wife of a Cappadocian (Plut. *Cat. Min.* 7, 73). Cicero claims that lampoons about Verres and his mistress Pipa were written over the praetor's bench (*Verr.* 2.3.77; cf. 2.5.81, 2.5.94). Caecina wrote a "very libelous" *(criminosissimo)* book against Caesar during the Civil War (Suet. *Iul.* 75), both Caesar *(Fam.* 9.16.4) and one Gaius Melissus wrote books of jests (Suet. *Gram.* 21), and someone must have collected Cicero's jokes for Macrobius to have picked them up (he attributes the collection to Tiro, *Sat.* 2.1.12). Lampoons were written about Tiberius (with serious results, Dio 57.22.5), Nero (Suet. *Ner.* 39), Otho (*Otho* 3), and even Vespasian (Dio 65.11.1–

2). Quintus Cicero wrote an epigram on the *lex Aurelia*, discomfiting Pompey (*QFr.* 1.3.8), and the rhetor Sextus Clodius endeared himself to Antony with an epigram on Fulvia (Suet. *Rhet.* 5). Calvus wrote scazons against the disreputable Tigellius, of which a fragment remains: "Sardi Tigelli putidum caput venit," "the stinking head of Tigellius the Sardine is for sale" (*Fam.* 7.24; *FPL* 3 Morel; cf. Plut. *Rom.* 25.5). He also wrote a lampoon on Pompey that puts the chant of Clodius' claque into verse (*FPL* 18 Morel). The letter of Antony's on which Cicero bases *Phil.* 13 is of dubious provenance, to say the least. And the comic theater was a potential political battleground; Paetus wrote a mime (*Fam.* 9.16.7), and Cicero warns Trebatius that a "Briton-attorney" may cut a ridiculous figure on the comic stage if Trebatius does not return soon (*Fam.* 7.11.2). The publicity of the theater made it a convenient place for the crowd to confront political leaders: when Caesar shamed the *eques* and mimographer Laberius (Macrob. *Sat.* 2.7.1–9), Laberius chided him from the stage, in verse, and tradition held that the people "turned their faces to Caesar alone, marking his lack of power pelted by such smart talking" (*Sat.* 2.7.5; for a similar episode, cf. Suet. *Aug.* 68—but such episodes are the stuff of ancient biography).

The lampoons form a sort of subliterary genre; they are in verse, and while some are crude, some are cleverly constructed. Quite a few are extant. One, ascribed to Augustus, is quoted by Martial (11.20):

> Caesaris Augusti lascivos, livide, versus
>   sex lege, qui tristis verba Latina legis:
> "Quod futuit Glaphyran Antonius, hanc mihi poenam
>   Fulvia constituit, se quoque uti futuam.
> Fulviam ego ut futuam? quod si me Manius oret
>   pedicem, faciam? non puto, si sapiam.
> 'Aut futue, aut pugnemus' ait. quid quod mihi vita
>   carior est ipsa mentula? signa canant!"
> absolvis lepidos nimirum, Auguste, libellos,
>   qui scis Romana simplicitate loqui.

> Jealous man, read six sexy verses of Augustus Caesar,
>   you who read good Latin words with a long face:
> "Because Antony fucks Glaphyra, Fulvia has set
>   this penalty for me, that I fuck *her* in turn.
> Shall I fuck Fulvia? What if John Doe should beg me
>   to bugger him, would I do it? I doubt it, if I've any sense.
> 'Either fuck me, or let us fight,' she says. What if my prick
>   is dearer to me than my life? Let the trumpets sound!"
> You certainly absolve my frivolous books, Augustus,
>   who know how to speak with Roman straightforwardness.[14]

Few extant lampoons are as long or as elaborate as this. Most are in the form of epigrams, while the soldiers' songs were set in the trochaic septenarius, like the one from Caesar's Gallic triumph (Suet. *Iul.* 51):

> urbani, servate uxores: moechum calvom adducimus.
> aurum in Gallia effutuisti, hic sumpsisti mutuum.

> City men, save your wives; we're bringing back our bald adulterer.
> [Caesar,] you've fucked away the gold in Gaul, here you've floated a loan.

At the same triumph the soldiers sang about Caesar's affair as the *puer* of Nicomedes of Bithynia (Suet. *Iul.* 49.4), which was also lampooned by the irrepressible Calvus (*Iul.* 49.1). Most lampoons were also two lines long, like this one on Nero (Suet. *Ner.* 39.2):

> Quis negat Aeneae magna de stirpe Neronem?
> sustulit hic matrem, sustulit ille patrem.

> Who would deny that Nero springs from the great line of Aeneas?
> The one made away with his mother, the other made off with his father.

Rhetorical Invective

> Est plane oratoris movere risum.
> —Cicero, *De Oratore* 2.236

The same categories of insult, the same mechanisms for insinuations, are found in the most highly formalized sort of invective—courtroom character assassination. The speeches of Cicero notoriously contain scurrilous attacks on several important opponents—most notably Clodius in the *De Domo Sua*, *De Haruspicum Responsis*, and *Pro Sestio*; Clodia in the *Pro Caelio*; Piso and Gabinius in the *In Pisonem* and *Post Reditum in Senatu*; Verres in the *Verrines*; and, as has been seen, Antony in the *Philippics*, especially the second.[15] Indeed, most of the *exempla* in Cicero's own exposition of the use of humor in oratory constitute ad hominem repartee (*De Oratore* 2.220–91 passim). Jests cited as brilliantly funny include: a play on Catulus' name (220); a series by Crassus against Brutus involving Brutus' squandered patrimony, some baths Brutus had sold, and Brutus' father, concluding that it was Brutus' *libidines* that had wasted his money (222–25); two on adultery (263, 275); three imputations of pathic homosexuality (256 [by Cato], 265, 277); and a crudely elementary attack on a deformed man (262):

> . . . L. Aelius Lamia, deformis, ut nostis, qui cum interpellaret odiose: "Audiamus," inquit, "pulchellum puerum," Crassus.

> . . . Lucius Aelius Lamia, a misshapen man, as you know; when he kept interrupting annoyingly, Crassus said, "Let's hear the lovely little boy."

In most of these anecdotes the pleasure of the audience comes partly from hearing home truths (or rumored truths) about the participants given utterance, but equally from the contest between the two speakers. Libo accuses Servius Galba of packing his jury, Galba turns around and accuses Libo of chronic adultery (263); Quintus Opimius twits a man for effeminacy, who neatly turns the charge back on Opimius (277). The whole system seems more of a game than earnest—at least as it is recalled by the successful participants.

The abuse in Cicero's orations falls easily into familiar categories. He paints all women connected with the opposing party as wildly unchaste: Clodia, who (he hints) murdered her husband, made herself available to the youth of Rome, framed Caelius, and committed incest with her brother;[16] Sassia, who (he claims) seduced her daughter's husband, married his murderer, and framed her son Cluentius;[17] Fulvia, successively the wife of Clodius, Curio, and Antony (whose mistress Cicero suggests she was while married to Clodius);[18] the actress Volumnia Cytheris, Antony's mistress;[19] Chelidon ("Swallow"), Verres' mistress;[20] and Verres' other mistresses in Sicily—Tertia, daughter of a mime actor;[21] Pipa, whose husband was spirited off to collect protection money;[22] and Nice, whose husband was sent to sea while she feasted with Verres and the other two.[23] Cicero (*Clu.* 199) calls Sassia *uxor generi*, *noverca filii*, *filiae paelex*, "her son-in-law's wife, her son's stepmother, her daughter's husband's mistress"—the last phrase being picked up by the author of the *Invectiva in Ciceronem*, reversed, and applied to Cicero's own wife and daughter. The adjective most commonly used of these women, both courtesans and adulterous *matronae*, is *meretricia*, "whorish."

Cicero claims his opponent and men allied with him are effeminate in dress, manner, or style of recreation. The basic idea was that the victim was a woman in comparison with real men, and so Cicero sets Clodius off against Milo: "tamen mulier inciderat in viros," "nevertheless this woman had fallen upon men" (*Mil.* 55); "ut homo effeminatus fortissimum virum conaretur occidere," "that an effeminate person should try to kill a most brave man" (*Mil.* 89). The elder Curio's dictum on Caesar seems to have been a common sort of joke: Cicero says of Clodius, "contra fas et inter viros saepe mulier et inter mulieres vir fuisset," "against all that is holy, [he] had often been both a woman among men and a man among women" (*Dom.* 139); of Verres, "At homo inertior, ignavior, magis vir inter mulieres, impura inter viros muliercula proferri non potest," "But a more impotent, cowardly man, one more a man among women, a dirty little woman among men cannot be found" (*Verr.* 2.2.192). Unorthodox dress shows decadence,[24] and foreigners (e.g., Juba, *Leg. Agr.* 2.59) are effeminate. It is an insult to estimate your enemy in war as a woman (*Mur.* 31); Cicero applies this principle to invective, explicitly calling Gabinius "Semiramis" (*Prov. Cons.* 9) and comparing Antony to Helen of Troy (*Phil.* 2.55).[25]

Cicero used Clodius' invasion of the rites of Bona Dea over and over again in the orations of the 50s,[26] and often the point of the reference is the allegation that

Clodius then wore women's clothing (e.g., *Har. Resp.* 4, *muliebri ornatu*). Where Cicero makes no elaborate attack, he likes to throw in insulting epithets in passing, and several of his favorites imply effeminacy: "curly haired" (*cincinnatus*) or "marked by the curling iron (*calamistrum*),"[27] often paired with the phrase *unguentis oblitus*, "smeared with unguents" (as for a banquet);[28] and, the strongest, *saltator* ("dancer"),[29] frequently applied to the ex-consul Gabinius—at *Dom.* 60, for example, Cicero attacks Piso *cum saltatore conlega*, "with your co-consul the dancer." More violent attacks state that the opponent prostituted himself or had an older lover in his boyhood;[30] the highest insult was to claim that the victim was still pathic as an adult, and Cicero only hints this about Gabinius,[31] though he is willing to be cagily explicit about Clodius (*Har. Resp.* 42):[32]

> iam robustus provinciae se ac rei militari dedit atque ibi piratarum contumelias perpessus, etiam Cilicum libidines barbarorumque satiavit.

> when already grown up he gave himself to his province and to the army and there allowed the insults of pirates, and even satisfied the lusts of the Cilicians and the barbarians.

Some of the same victims were claimed to be licentious pederasts—the license stemming from their attachment to *ingenui*, even to social equals. There is no consistency; it all depends who is to be insulted—the man to be insulted is said to be a pathic. Cicero insinuates that the Fonteius who adopted Clodius was really his *puer* (*Dom.* 36)—largely on the basis of the difference in their ages. On the other hand, at *Pis.* 65 he implies that Piso was using Clodius in this way, and he makes similar, more or less explicit allegations about Piso throughout the speech.[33] Cicero depicts Piso as gloomy and boorish, the image of rustic virility and the opposite of his effeminate colleague; thus, in his province, he forces his *legati* (*Pis.* 88), like Catullus' Memmius (see below).[34]

The stereotypes attack all extremes equally; if it is bad to be effeminate, it is just as bad to be a savage satyr like Piso, making indiscriminate sexual attacks on all who should be chaste. This accounts for accusations of rapes and seductions, especially of respectable *matronae*, by the man as governor of a province.[35] Sometimes the man attacked had henchmen who procured women for him, like Verres' Timarchides (*Verr.* 2.2.134) and Apronius (*Verr.* 2.3.22–23, 60, 65, 134, 140, 158); Cicero insinuates that the latter was more to Verres than just a procurer (*Verr.* 2.3.65). Even Gabinius was linked with adulteries (*Sest.* 20). The idea is that a man who would commit one kind of sin would commit any (*Phil.* 14.9):

> Refugit animus, patres conscripti, eaque dicere reformidat, quae L. Antonius in Parmensium liberis et coniugibus effecerit. Quas enim turpitudines Antonii libenter cum dedecore subierunt, easdem per vim laetantur aliis se intulisse.

> My mind shrinks back, senators, and shudders to name those things which Lucius Antonius did to the children and wives of the men of Parma.

> Whatever foul acts the Antonii have willingly undergone to their shame, they are delighted to have inflicted upon others by brute force.

This idea produces the stock description of the debauch, in which anyone to be branded as vile participates; the events are left fuzzy but the identifying marks are always the same—unguents, wine, an early hour for starting the feast, and consequent hangovers.[36] These revels are usually luxurious; Cicero reserves special scorn for the squalid drunk, for Piso wallowing in *popinae* and Antony vomiting in public.[37] He finds Piso particularly horrifying because of his rustic facade; that he was a hypocrite makes his secret crimes all the worse (*Red. Sen.* 14):

> Idem domi quam libidinosus, quam impurus, quam intemperans, non ianua receptis sed pseudothyro intromissis voluptatibus!

> The same man, at home how randy, how dirty, how unrestrained, with his pleasures not let in by the front door but smuggled in the back way!

"His sins were hidden by the walls of his house" ("flagitia parietibus tegebantur," *Sest.* 22); although an Epicurean, he is certainly a forerunner of the secretly pathic Stoics of Martial and Juvenal.

The idea of secret infamy is the force behind another sort of accusation: that the victim has the *os impurum*. This attack, particularly vile to a Roman, Cicero reserves for the lowly, less powerful victims. Chief among them is Sextus Cloelius, henchman of Publius Clodius, who was the butt of a series of double entendres in several speeches, especially *De Domo Sua*.[38] Cicero, addressing Clodius, calls Cloelius *praegustatori libidinum tuarum . . . qui sua lingua etiam sororem tuam a te abalienavit*, "the fore-taster of your lusts . . . who, by his tongue, stole even your sister away from you" (*Dom.* 25; cf. *Dom.* 47). At *Dom.* 83 Cloelius is to be found at Clodia's house: "invenient hominem apud sororem tuam occultantem se capite demisso," "they'll find the man at your sister's house, hiding himself, with lowered face." Clodius' *os impurum* is part of his sacrilege (*Dom.* 104); Dolabella's is vague, part of his general sadistic depravity (*Phil.* 11.5, 7); and Gabinius' certainly relates to his effeminacy (*Pis.* 20)—while it is insinuated that Sextus Cloelius is a cunnilinctor, Gabinius is felt to be a fellator. Cicero lets Clodia herself be accused by the figure of Appius Claudius Caecus, a famous prosopopoeia (*Cael.* 34; cf. *Priapea* 30). Vatinius' foulness is manifest (*Vat.* 39); his warts, says Cicero, have left his mouth for other parts of his body.

The foulness of the *os impurum* is similar to that implicit in a group of epithets related to inherently foul occupations. Where *cincinnatus* and *saltator* imply effeminacy, *leno* ("pimp")[39] and *gladiator*[40] imply uncleanness. Both *lenones* and *gladiatores* were *infames*, that is, they not only had limited civil rights but were "untouchable," each condition feeding off the other. It is noteworthy that both epithets were applied to widely different types of people, sometimes linked with effeminate attributes (as at *Red. Sen.* 12), sometimes with aggressively heterosexual ones. Each has obvious links with the complex of stereotypes outlined so far—*leno* with procuring for adultery and with the boys who sell themselves, *gladiator* with the sort of bloodthirsty rape practiced by bad governors—but Cicero uses the terms with only roughly these connotations. The gravity of these implicit accusations makes it surprising that the profession of acting had the same connotations, and the word *mima* or *mimus* is as strong as *meretrix* or *leno*. Association with actors or actresses was damning,[41] as in the case of Volumnia Cytheris and Tertia; and Cicero says, discreetly but firmly, that his client Roscius the comic actor was such a good man that he was worthy never to have gone on the stage at all (*Quinct.* 77–78; *QRosc.* 17). Cicero always depicts the retinues of his opponents as consisting largely of actors, pimps, prostitutes, and gladiators;[42] the description of part of Catiline's following combines several standard motifs (*Cat.* 2.22–24):

> Postremum autem genus est non solum numero verum etiam genere ipso atque vita quod proprium Catilinae est, de eius dilectu, immo vero de complexu eius ac sinu; quos pexo capillo, nitidos, aut imberbis aut bene barbatos videtis, manicatis et talaribus tunicis, velis amictos, non togis. . . . (23) In his gregibus omnes aleatores, omnes adulteri, omnes impuri impudicique versantur. Hi pueri tam lepidi ac delicati non solum amare et amari neque saltare et cantare sed etiam sicas vibrare . . . didicerunt. . . . num suas secum mulierculas sunt in castra ducturi? . . . idcirco se facilius hiemem toleraturos putant, quod nudi in conviviis saltare didicerunt! (24) O bellum magno opere pertimescendum, cum hanc sit habiturus Catilina scortorum cohortem praetoriam!
>
> Moreover, the last sort is not only in its position but even in its very nature and life what is closest to Catiline, to his liking, rather even of his embrace, of his bosom; whom you see with combed hair, greasy, either beardless or heavily bearded, with tunics down to their fingertips and toes, wearing sails, not togas. . . . (23) In these flocks all gamblers, all adulterers, all dirty men and sluttish men are tumbled about together. These boys, so charming and delicate, have learned not only to love and be loved, not only to dance and sing, but even to brandish daggers. . . . They aren't going to bring their little ladies with them into their bivouac? . . . they think they'll bear the winter more easily, because they've learned to dance naked at dinner parties! (24) A war greatly to be feared, when Catiline will have this praetorian cohort of whores!

Only rarely does Cicero resort to the use of specific animal names as epithets: he calls Verres' companions dogs (*Verr.* 2.1.126), and Piso a dog (*Pis.* 23) and a pig (*Pis.* 19, 37)—and he does not resist the temptation to pun on Verres' name. He insults Vatinius for his ugliness (*Vat.* 10), but this, again, is rare.[43]

All this considered, it is not surprising that the orations include a great deal of xenophobia. Cicero does not use ethnic physical stereotypes to provide him with epithets, as is the common modern practice. Rather, he bases several orations on the argument that the national group represented by his opponent is widely known to be untrustworthy and ignorant.[44] When it suits him, he extends this principle to freedmen.[45]

It will be seen that not only are the topics the same here as in informal invective, the techniques are the same. Giving your opponent a female name, the use of epithets or strings of epithets, insinuations, combinations of seemingly contradictory vices—all can be found in graffiti and gossip as well as in the orations. But the loftier genre has its peculiarities, some of which it shares with other lofty genres, like satire.

First, it emerges from the mass of various insults that there was a *locus communis* on the boyhood of the opposing party in a court case. Almost every case of Cicero's in which one or both clients were male involved accusations about their misspent youth (the *Pro Archia* is perhaps the only exception). This is clearly a subsection of the argument from the person of the opponent[46] and could be used by the advocate for either side; Cicero several times delivers defenses of the purity of his client's boyhood, obviously (though discreetly) in reply to an attack by the other side.[47] The accusation is not always of pathic homosexuality: Plancius was accused of taking a male to his province *libidinis causa* and of molesting an actress (as Cicero tells it, *Planc.* 30); a large part of Caelius' problem was, of course, Clodia (e.g., *Cael.* 29, 30—but cf. *Cael.* 15); the unchastity for which Rabirius was supposed to have been fined involved both his own and that of others, probably women; and the lack of specificity about Verres' boyhood seems to stem from the notoriety of his excessive heterosexuality (*Verr.* 1.11, *Verr.* 2.1.32–33). But a peculiar recurring accusation was involved with homosexual debauchery: this was a claim that the victim had danced naked at a dinner,[48] and Cicero actually has to counter such a claim in the case of King Deiotarus (*Deiot.* 26, 27, 28). The idea was that a man who would do such things was a bad man and would have stooped to whatever the case was about—and vice versa; whole cases depended on such arguments (e.g., *Rosc. Am.* 38–39, *Mur.* 11). But Cicero, naturally, cuts his coat to fit his cloth: at *Sest.* 138 he states that young men going into politics should be chaste, while much of the *Pro Caelio* is an endorsement of the wisdom of sowing wild oats. The great weapon of this sort of attack is the *praeteritio* (e.g., *Flac.* 34, *Phil.* 14.9, *Verr.* 2.1.32–33); the passage from the second Philippic discussed above (chap. 1) demonstrated the implications of a *praeteritio* for the speaker's attitude toward the obscene. If one were to begin to accept Cicero's sincerity at *Phil.* 2.47, it need only be compared with *Phil.* 11.9, on the sadism of Dolabella:

> alteri a puero pro deliciis crudelitas fuit, deinde ea libidinum turpitudo, ut in hoc sit semper ipse laetatus, quod ea faceret, quae sibi obici ne ab inimico quidem possent verecundo.

> To the other, cruelty was his favorite thing from boyhood, and finally such a foulness of lust, that he himself was always delighted by the fact that he had

> done things which could not be cast up to him by anyone with any sense of modesty, even an enemy.

The conceit seems to have pleased him.

More disturbing is the light these cases shed on the connection between invective and reality. The repetition of the same epithets and vague anecdotes erodes the reader's belief that there is any connection at all and begins to produce the feeling that all governors were accused of corruption, all politicians of vice. Unfortunately for this illusion, in the case of Verres Cicero adduces a great deal of circumstantial evidence; it is always possible that he fabricated it for the published speeches, but the sheer length of the parade militates against such a possibility. Verres' crimes are appalling, as incredibly sensational as the stories from Nazi Germany and as inescapably real. In Verres the figure of Priapus comes alive, the living equivalent of Catullus' *irrumator praetor*. This stereotype, at least, had a correlative in the realities of Roman society. But usually Cicero does not bring in much evidence at all, and he was quite capable of arguing the other side, as in the *Pro Murena*; a good deal of the time, then, this sort of behavior was just played down.

The position of the advocate, as noted above, resembles the position of the satirist. His attitude incorporated ambivalence—he could attack contradictory vices in the same breath or take contradictory attitudes in consecutive cases: the Cicero who belittles Greeks in the *Pro Flacco* adores them in the *Pro Archia*, the man who pooh-poohs the Sardinians' grievances in the *Pro Scauro* carefully explains, for the *In Verrem*, how far superior the Sicilians are to other Greeks (*Verr.* 2.2.4–11). It is interesting that he restricts his attack on Piso and Gabinius to the speech he made to his equals *(Post Reditum in Senatu)*; in the *Post Reditum ad Populum* he mentions them only with neutral courtesy. The advocate's attitude involves an even more fundamental paradox: the exploitation of sensational material. Throughout the indignant orations, like the Verrines and Philippics, the idea is that "we good men must preserve our homes, and the purity of our women and children." Yet the speeches themselves exploit impurity as much as possible; if the material seems repetitive and ridiculous when collected together, in context and aloud it would have enlivened the rhetoric and woken up the jury (as Cicero was well aware, *De Or.* 2.236). The Verrine orations have the morbid appeal of all narratives of atrocity and resemble the sadistic pornography discussed in chapter 3. The *praeteritio* is in fact a highly significant mask, representing the whole riddle of the stance of the accuser/moralist/satirist. Is he leaving it out or emphasizing it? Is he, is his audience, disgusted or fascinated? Is he inculcating aversion or pandering to a need to hear about the activities he deplores, a need to hear them presented as deplorable—and in as much detail as possible?

It is a far cry from graffiti on a wall in Pompeii to Cicero's orations, but it is easy to see that the same principles of objurgation were used in both; indeed, inasmuch as Cicero's speeches normally depended for their effect on the presence and consequent direct public shaming of the victim, they are a less sophisticated form of invective than graffiti and must have required great gall on the part of the speaker. Yet the speeches are generally considered great literature, equivalent in quality to the best Latin poetry, despite their inclusion of invective. The next chapters will examine the place of invective and obscenity in Latin poetry. And the last evidence for subliterary genres to be considered here concerns something that is a major issue for literature: free speech.[49]

Clearly the issues were not quite the same for the satirist and the man who wished to call someone names on the senate floor. But for subliterary invective, there is a startling accumulation of evidence of strongly enunciated societal attitudes toward verbal invective. It might best be phrased in the publicist's maxim that any publicity is good publicity—better to be the man singled out for scorn than a nonentity.[50]

Roman politicians were proud of their ability to take abuse; at the same time, it is clear that such magnanimity could not always be relied on. Plutarch remarks on Sulla's liking for insult matches (*Sulla* 2); Antony, too, was easygoing in his attitude toward raillery (*Ant.* 24). And that personal recriminations between bitter rivals were expected is underscored by Plutarch's comment on the lack of personal abuse between Tiberius Gracchus and the tribune Octavius (*Ti. Gracch.* 10). The Romans seem to have considered verbal abuse, claques, brawls, and graffiti to be valid means of political expression,[51] and they took them seriously; historians recorded graffiti encouraging Tiberius Gracchus (Plut. *Ti. Gracch.* 8) and Brutus (Plut. *Brut.* 9; cf. Cic. *Phil.* 1.36). Such exhortations or threats made an impression on the public and on the great politicians, and perhaps filled the place that polls and the press and other media fill today; the whole phenomenon certainly impressed biographers long after the events—what was scrawled on the walls of Rome weighed in the account.

Thus the significance of two stories about Augustus, preserved together (with innocent lack of comment) by Macrobius, can be understood in context. One story comments on how well Augustus took jokes on himself (*Sat.* 2.4.19), and an example of such a joke is later given (*Sat.* 2.4.29): after Actium, Augustus rewarded a man who had trained a crow to say "Hail Caesar, our victorious ruler!" The man's rival, jealous, told Augustus that the man had another crow trained to say "Hail Antony, our victorious ruler!" But Augustus took this calmly. Yet the following bon mot (*Sat.* 2.4.21) hints at an underlying danger:

> Temporibus triumviralibus Pollio cum Fescenninos in eum Augustus scripsisset, ait "at ego taceo. non est enim facile in eum scribere, qui potest proscribere."

When, in the time of the triumvirate, Augustus had written Fescennine [i.e., ribald] verses against Pollio, Pollio said only, "I, on the other hand,

> will hold my tongue; for it is not easy to write against a man who can write—your name on the proscription list."

The relationship between invective and power is as essential to nonsexual as to sexual material. And, overwhelmingly, the material in this chapter that is not sexual is either political or military. These interconnected preoccupations continue in poetry of all qualities.

CHAPTER 5 Literature Based on Invective: Invective against Old Women, Priapic Poetry, and Epigram

> Locus autem, et regio quasi ridiculi . . . turpitudine et deformitate quadam continetur: haec enim ridentur vel sola, vel maxime, quae notant et designant turpitudinem aliquam non turpiter.
>
> —Cicero, *De Oratore* 2.236

> Moreover, the place and, as it were, the area of the ridiculous is bounded by ugliness and a certain sort of misshapenness: for either the only, or the most outstanding things which are laughed at are those which mark and describe some ugliness in no ugly manner.[1]

After the grand bastinadoes of Ciceronian character assassination, it is disappointing to turn to the first sort of invective poetry that can reasonably be considered literature: epigram. The link between political lampoons as seen above and the art of the epigrammatist is obvious and close; on the other hand, literary epigram has a very different set of premises from those of political lampoon and invective. The relationship between aggressor, victim, and political audience is replaced by one in which the poet, as aggressor, writes for a general audience at the expense of a victim who is almost never explicitly identified with a real person. Occasionally, especially in Catullus, it is clear that the *redender Name* or type name assigned to the victim is meant to be identified with that of a real person, and the audience is meant to guess at or know the identification; but the epigram is always supposed to be able to be admired on its own, as a beautifully crafted piece. The implication is that the audience has a new motive: without that of seeing a politician shamed by his rival, the motive can only be pleasure in the hearing or reading of the invective itself. Thus this invective is an art form; as such, its attraction for its audience will have been both form and content (as well as presentation and delivery, attributes lost to us today), and in this case the content is a sort of hypothetical invective addressed to imaginary victims. The great amount of time devoted by Martial and Catullus to this form can perhaps be even better understood in the light of the Roman fondness for reality-based invective as seen above; imaginary invectives are only a refinement on real ones, and the audience is perhaps even freer to enjoy them since the victims are not powerful and dangerous politicians but sexual or ethnic types who can safely be docketed as vague "others" rather than as existing neighbors.

This model being defined, it can further be understood why this sort of invective (in satire as well as in epigram) is so often more salacious than the poetry described as "erotic" in chapter 2. A certain prurient interest is built into the model of poet-victim-audience; the audience is interested in hearing taboos broken, not only by means of attacks on vices usually not spoken of but by means of language used elegantly in a poem when it is usually not used in polite conversation. There is no question of romantic ideals or of love—quite the reverse; all positive literary images, including the ideal of beauty, are fair game for invective. The victims of invective are exposed as ugly and/or wanton; sexual freedom here forms part of a fantasy of vice, not a fantasy of pleasure. This situation might seem paradoxical or the satirist a hypocrite if the author of literary invective were viewed as a stern, angry reformer who really loathes the vices he describes; if he does loathe them, why does he wallow in elaborate fantasies of lust and profligacy? No, although a feeling of loathing can be present in invective and accounts for the ugliness of some pictures or the cynicism of the comments made on them, enjoyment of obscene ideas and language is clearly the major ingredient in invective.

The approach of different authors varies, depending on the persona each adopts. In particular, the feeling of prurience increases with the author's pretense of censoriousness. The satirists form an instructive comparison for the epigrammatists here. Horace's touch in the *Sermones* is light, and his depictions of even the most explicit scenes are rather frothy or sunny in tone; Juvenal stands, in his sixth satire, in condemnation of women's vices, and, consequently, when he launches into descriptions of gross sexual misbehavior, he achieves a lurid, as it were torchlit effect. In fact, most such scenes in Juvenal are set at night, with special attention given to their lighting; the description of Messallina (6.114–32) is an outstanding example of salacious invective:

> quid privata domus, quid fecerit Eppia, curas?
> respice rivales divorum, Claudius audi
> quae tulerit. dormire virum cum senserat uxor,
> sumere nocturnos meretrix Augusta cucullos[2] 118
> ausa Palatino et tegetem praeferre cubili 117
> linquebat comite ancilla non amplius una.
> sed nigrum flavo crinem abscondente galero
> intravit calidum veteri centone lupanar
> et cellam vacuam atque suam; tunc nuda papillis
> prostitit auratis titulum mentita Lyciscae
> ostenditque tuum, generose Britannice, ventrem.

excepit blanda intrantis atque aera poposcit,
continueque iacens cunctorum absorbuit ictus.
mox lenone suas iam dimittente puellas
tristis abit, et quod potuit tamen ultima cellam
clausit, adhuc ardens rigidae tentigine volvae,
et lassata viris necdum satiata recessit,
obscurisque genis turpis fumoque lucernae
foeda lupanaris tulit ad pulvinar odorem.

It worries you what private households have done, what Eppia's done?
Look at the rivals of the gods, hear what Claudius
had to bear. When his wife knew her husband was asleep,
the empress/hooker, daring to put on her small-hours cloak
and to like an old mattress better than her Palatine chamber,
used to leave with no more than one maid for companion.
And, hiding her black hair in a yellow wig,
she entered the hot whorehouse by the rag-quilt door,
and a room empty, all her own; then, naked,
she stood before her door, with gilded nipples,
pretending on her placard that her name was "Foxy,"
and bared the belly that held you, well-born Britannicus.
Sweetly she greeted those entering and asked for money,
and lying down at once she cushioned the blows of all.
Soon, when the pimp was already sending his own girls home,
she went away sadly, and (the most she could do),
at least closed her room last, still burning
with the hard-on of her stiff womb,
and went away, tired by her men but not yet sated,
and, foul with her darkened cheeks and soiled with lantern smoke,
she brought the smell of the whorehouse to the holy pillow.

The scene is set at night *(nocturnos . . . cucullos, fumo . . . lucernae)*, and the details grow more and more specific and obscene: the sleeping emperor; the cloak, the mat, the single maid, the wig with slave-colored hair; the horrible brothel, hot and shabby; and finally the *cella* of the "imperial prostitute," where she stands with painted nipples and naked belly, under a sign bearing the name of a Greek whore. The lily gilding that follows is typical of Juvenal: not only does she engage in such activities, she cannot bear to stop, and is more eager for her work than are the real prostitutes. Juvenal concludes with a vivid and almost unique description of her sexual arousal, returning her at last, smelly and smudged from the smoke of the brothel, to her husband's pillow (for which he uses the technical term for the cushions on which statues of the gods were placed, recalling line 115, *rivales divorum*). The cycle from her departure to her return climaxes with her violent and pounding intercourse, and all takes place in darkness; the reader/audience/interlocutor lies in the place of Claudius and, with him who should be semidivine, is defiled by cuckoldry and by the return of the stained wife; even the son with the military hero's name is defiled.

Such sybaritic and cosmic disapproval is a sophisticated effect, beyond the reach of most epigram. When Martial attempts a tour de force of obscene invective, the effect is usually puerile; the pleasure he takes in obscene language and situations stops short of any vivid imagining of the idiosyncrasies of scene or personnel. The following poem achieves its only point in its obscenity (11.61):

> Lingua maritus, moechus ore Nanneius,
> Summemmianis inquinatior buccis;
> quem cum fenestra vidit a Suburana
> obscena nudum Leda, fornicem cludit
> mediumque mavult basiare quam summum;
> modo qui per omnes viscerum tubos ibat
> et voce certa consciaque dicebat
> puer an puella matris esset in ventre,
> (gaudete cunni; vestra namque res acta est)
> arrigere linguam non potest fututricem.
> nam dum tumenti mersus haeret in volva
> et vagientes intus audit infantes
> partem gulosam solvit indecens morbus.
> nec purus esse nunc potest nec inpurus.

> Nanneius, husband with his tongue, adulterer with his mouth,
> filthier than red-light lips—
> when dirty Leda sees him naked
> from her 42nd Street window, she closes the cathouse
> and would rather kiss his middle than his mouth—
> who, until recently, used to go through all the tubes of the guts
> and used to say with a firm and knowledgeable voice
> whether a boy or a girl was in the mother's belly
> (rejoice, ye cunts, for your work is done),
> cannot erect his tongue that does his fucking for him.
> For while he was stuck, plunged in a swelling womb
> and was listening to the babies crying inside,
> a nasty disease weakened his gluttonous part.
> Now he can't be either clean or dirty.

The poem's outstanding feature is the outlandish and childish hyperbole. Nanneius' mouth is more unclean than those of prostitutes; even "Leda" (again, epic travesty, and probably a reflection of real practices)[3] avoids his visits and feels she would sully her mouth less by fellating him than by kissing him (a sort of *adynaton*). His tongue actually reaches into the wombs of pregnant women and can tell (as if it had eyes) the sex of the fetus. Yet the poem is illogical: Nanneius' activity does not supersede anything that women normally do, but the poem says he is doing the work of *cunni* (line 9); and his disease, or perversion (*morbus* has both meanings), strikes him, for no reason, in mid-act (lines 10–13). The joke is that his tongue, like a penis, has become impotent; the punch line plays on *purus esse*, "be clean" (he cannot, because of his past), and *impurus esse*, "be unclean," that is, "perform cunnilingus"—which he cannot do because of his impotent tongue. All the humorous elements are laboriously contrived in order to examine the obscene elements as fully as possible. Leda, looking out the brothel window, is made interesting by this human action (the only mention in Roman literature of this architectural element in a brothel), but she quickly disappears in the heaping of foul details on the otherwise featureless Nanneius.

Martial's epigrams, and all Roman sexual humor, are pervaded by ideas that appear in their purest form in two subgenres, Priapic poetry and invective against old women.[4] The latter is found in abundance in Greek literature, but it is so thoroughly entrenched in Latin literature that it cannot have been a strain to borrow it; possibly it did not have to be borrowed at all. On the other hand, and oddly enough, although the god Priapus was borrowed from Lampsacus, by far the greatest amount of Priapic poetry surviving is in Latin. And the two genres are by no means exclusive: Priapic poetry includes some invective against old women, and there are many invectives against old women and Priapic poems outside the *Priapea*. Many known authors wrote Priapics, still extant, in several lyric meters, even in hexameter (Hor. *S.* 1.8).

Invective against Old Women

The outstanding examples of invective against old women in Latin are, surprisingly, by Horace—*Epodes* 8 and 12. The two poems are not only the longest and most personal attacks on old women, they are also even more than usually savage. But at the same time they do include the chief elements of the genre: statement of the woman's great age; explicit description of repulsive physical deterioration (elsewhere focused on the genitals); accusation of sexual insatiability; rejection of the woman as a sexual partner. Another common theme in the genre, the bibulousness of old women, appears in Latin invective (as it very commonly does in Greek); but since it normally appears separately from invective against their sexuality, it will not be considered here.

Epod. 8:

> Rogare longo putidam te saeculo
>   viris quid enervet meas,
> cum sit tibi dens ater et rugis vetus
>   frontem senectus exaret,
> hietque turpis inter aridas natis
>   podex velut crudae bovis?

sed incitat me pectus et mammae putres,
  equina quales ubera,
venterque mollis et femur tumentibus
  exile suris additum.
esto beata, funus atque imagines
  ducant triumphales tuum,
nec sit marita, quae rotundioribus
  onusta bacis ambulet.
quid quod libelli Stoici inter sericos
  iacere pulvillos amant:
illiterati num minus nervi rigent?
  minusve languet fascinum,
quod ut superbo provoces ab inguine,
  ore allaborandum est tibi?[5]

You, foul by your long century, ask
  what unmans my strength,
when you've a black tooth, and old age
  plows your brow with wrinkles,
and between your dried-out cheeks gapes filthy
  an asshole like a dyspeptic cow's?
But your chest and decaying tits arouse me,
  like mare's udders,
and your soft belly and your skinny thigh
  on top of swollen shins.
Congratulations, and may images of great men
  precede your funeral train,
nor may there be a wife who walks
  laden with rounder pearls.
And so what if Stoic booklets like to lie
  between your silk pillows?
Do unlettered cocks harden less for that?
  Or does that phallus droop less,
which you have to work on with your mouth
  to raise from its proud crotch?

This tirade follows on the epode against Antony and Cleopatra and precedes one on the triumphant drinking of wine upon Cleopatra's defeat, creating comic transitions of images at both ends of the poem. The woman's antiquity and her failure to arouse the narrator are established in the first two lines; the next eight lines (3–10) comprise a catalogue of her ugliness. Black teeth, wrinkled face, gaping and excrement-stained anus, pendulous breasts, flabby stomach, and misshapen legs are all perversions of the qualities usually named as attractive in beautiful women—except that the anus rarely appears at all in the praise of women. This old woman is rich (lines 11–14); she wears pearls, and her dead male ancestors were successful Roman generals (lines 11–12). The narrator turns up his nose at her money and high lineage (imagined, appropriately, as part of her funeral)—a scenario often, though by no means always, found in invective against old women; it appears, for instance, in deprecation of *captatores* of old women (e.g., Mart. 4.5). The poem's last section belittles the woman's literary and philosophical pretensions, suggesting that all her lovers, literati and ordinary men alike, are impotent with her. For the opening image of the Stoic books in her luxurious bed, it must be remembered that *libelli* could be roll-shaped, and the book roll occasionally represents the phallus (e.g., Juv. 6.337–38). The genitalia of all males, and their poetry, refuse to respond to this woman, who degrades herself by fellating them, and who is soon to die. *Epode* 12 outdoes *Epode* 8:

> Quid tibi vis, mulier nigris dignissima barris?
>   munera quid mihi quidve tabellas
> mittis nec firmo iuveni neque naris obesae?
>   namque sagacius unus odoror,
> polypus an gravis hirsutis cubet hircus in alis,
>   quam canis acer ubi lateat sus.
> qui sudor vietis et quam malus undique membris
>   crescit odor, cum pene soluto
> indomitam properat rabiem sedare; neque illi
>   iam manet umida creta colorque
> stercore fucatus crocodili, iamque subando
>   tenta cubilia tectaque rumpit!
> vel mea cum saevis agitat fastidia verbis:
>   "Inachia langues minus ac me;
> Inachiam ter nocte potes, mihi semper ad unum
>   mollis opus. pereat male, quae te
> Lesbia quaerenti taurum monstravit inertem,
>   cum mihi Cous adesset Amyntas,
> cuius in indomito constantior inguine nervus
>   quam nova collibus arbor inhaeret.
> muricibus Tyriis iteratae vellera lanae
>   cui properabantur? tibi nempe,
> ne foret aequalis inter conviva, magis quem
>   diligeret mulier sua quam te.
> o ego non felix, quam tu fugis ut pavet acris
>   agna lupos capreaeque leones!"

> What do you want, woman best fit for black elephants?
>   Why do you send me gifts, why letters,
> I who am no firm youth, nor of unrefined nostril?
>   Indeed, I alone can sniff out more sagely

whether an octopus or a heavy goat lurks in hairy armpits,
  than can a keen dog sniff out where the boar hides.
What a sweat on her shriveled limbs, and what a bad smell
  grows everywhere, when (after my cock is limp)
she hurries to quiet her unconquered lust; nor does
  her wet powder stick now, her blush
painted on with crocodile dung, now by being in heat
  she breaks the taut bed and the covers!
Or she tries to arouse me from disgust with savage words:
  "For Inachia you droop less than for me;
you can do Inachia three times in a night, for me you are always
  soft for one job. May she die badly, that Lesbia
who pointed motionless you out to me as a bull,
  when I had Coan Amyntas by me,
who had a joint in his unconquered groin stiffer
  than a new tree that sticks in the hills.
For whom are these fleeces of wool redone in Tyrian purple
  being hastened? For you, no doubt,
lest there be a dinner guest among your comrades
  whom his own woman loves more than she loves you.
O unhappy I, whom you flee as the lamb fears
  cruel wolves, as kids fear lions!"

Following on a rueful meditation on love (*Epod.* 11), Horace here launches again into invective. The great age of the woman in *Epod.* 12 is not clearly specified, as is normal in such attacks; but the situation is similar to that in *Epod.* 8, with the poet's rejection of the woman being even more physically immediate. Again the poet begins by scornfully questioning the woman's vain attempts to arouse him, this time by gifts and letters as well as by sexual athletics (lines 1–3, 8, 11–12). As in *Epod.* 8, he follows his opening question with a list of the woman's physical flaws, mostly concentrating on smell (lines 1, 3–12). He uses bizarre and monstrous animals as vehicles of comparison for her—an unusual technique but one he has used before (*Epod.* 8.5–8).[6] The second half of the poem (lines 14–26), a speech by the woman (another rare technique; *vetulae* are rarely imagined as saying anything), stresses her greed for sex and her resentment of the poet's lack of sexual interest in her (lines 14–17). Her speech includes the information, lest anyone doubt the narrator's potency, that he is exceptionally able with another mistress, of whom the *vetula* expresses her jealousy. The speech ends in travesty: the final couplet (lines 25–26) is the sort of thing usually said by a male lover about an elusive beloved—a mockery in the mouth of a sexually repulsive woman. In her lofty simile she is the wolf/lion, her lover the lamb/kid; in her lover's eyes she resembles goats, elephants, pigs. And, as in *Epod.* 8, Horace relates the woman not only to animals but to the dung of outlandish animals (line 11). Her eagerness, while a source of scornful amusement in the poem (her whole speech is undercut by the introduction to it, and by its bluntness), is in itself repulsive *(rabiem, subando)*; still, it is largely her physical ugliness that repels the poet (though he has certainly been with her in bed), and the ugliness brought on by her *rabies*.

The construction of the poems is neat, even elegant,[7] and the language vivid and striking; all the same, they express loathing of their victims and characterize the narrator as superior principally because he withholds his own sexual arousal from a woman he describes as frantic and old. It is thus somewhat startling to find a major critic of the *Epodes*, comparing Horace's invective against old women with Martial's, conclude, "Horace's essentially moral indignation is lacking in the epigrammatist."[8] This is an important fallacy; here, as in Cicero's orations as well as in satire, there is no question of moral indignation. It simply does not arise. Or perhaps it would be better to speculate that all moralists attack their familiar cavalcade of vices for reasons similar to those that motivate invective—fear, hatred, and the desire to dominate. But, speculation aside, Horace clearly enjoys in *Epodes* 8 and 12 a thorough stare at ugliness, wallowing in the foulness he creates and rejects. Both the poem and the situation it records are perfectly ambivalent: the narrator loathes the woman, yet he is her sexual partner; the poet perceives the situation as ugly, yet he imagines and describes it in explicit detail.

Horrible old women appear throughout Latin literature, like those who attempt to rape Encolpius in the *Satyricon* (134–38). Occasionally they are not only hags but witches, like Meroe in Apuleius *Met.* 1.13, with grand literary relatives in the African sorceress in *Aeneid* 4 and Erictho in Lucan 6. At other times they are compared to the reverend women of epic and tragedy—old nurses, and women like Hecuba or the Sibyl. It seems at least possible that invective against *vetulae* constitutes a sort of apotropaic satire that attempts to belittle and control the power of old women, pitting the phallus against the threat of sterility, death, and the chthonic forces.[9] Ovid, for one, attributes his temporary impotence to witchcraft (*Am.* 3.7.27–36, 79–80). At any rate, the poet's stance is always the same vis-à-vis the old woman, and she always remains a loathsome and slightly uncanny other.

Poets other than Horace often use two forms of invective in their attacks on old women that do not appear in *Epodes* 8 and 12—degradation of the traditionally respected *exempla* of old women and befoulment of the victim through description of her genitalia as disgusting. The degradation is achieved subtly, through a technique borrowed from mock epic: the comparison of an unlikely subject with an exemplar from epic. Often these attacks begin with an assessment of the woman's birth as contemporaneous with the age of heroes; she is a coeval of Hecuba, the Sibyl, Tithonus, Priam, Nestor, etc., not just as old as they lived to be. A typical example is *Pr.* 57:

> Cornix et caries vetusque bustum,
> turba putida facta saeculorum,

quae forsan potuisset esse nutrix
Tithoni Priamique Nestorisque,
illis ni pueris anus fuisset,
ne desim sibi, me rogat, fututor.
quid si nunc roget, ut puella fiat?
"Si nummos tamen haec habet, puella est."

Crow and decay and old tomb,
made putrid by the crowd of centuries,
who perhaps could have been the nurse
of Tithonus, Priam, and Nestor,
if she hadn't been an old woman when they were boys,
asks me that I not desert her as a fucker.
Suppose she should ask to be made a girl?
"But if she has money, she's a girl."

Again, the woman is not only old and decaying but a walking tomb, the embodiment of the ages; her sterility antedates the boyhood of the proverbial old men of mythology. But more than that, both they and she are degraded by the picture of such a crone giving suck to the great kings in their infancy and praying to Priapus for sexual satisfaction. The epic figures are, elsewhere, women, as at *Pr.* 12.1–4, where the randy, ragged old woman is called *soror . . . Sibyllae*, "the Sibyl's sister." And the same technique can be used more actively: in 10.90 Martial manages to conjure up the picture of Hecuba depilating her crotch (and here again he lets the *mentula* reject the woman's *cunnus*).[10]

The last line of *Pr.* 57 brings in another anomalous element in old women that serves as a focus for satiric rage: their use of money to buy sexual favors. As in Horace *Epod.* 8.11–16, where the rejected woman is wealthy and aristocratic, or 12.2, where she sends the poet gifts, here the old woman can try to buy the status of attractive woman *(puella)* from the scornful and condescending god. Such arrogation of the initiative rankled with Martial (9.37; cf. 11.29), who includes *arrigere ad vetulas*, "getting it up for old ladies," in a list of scams beneath the dignity of a poor but proud man (4.5). Juvenal, performing variations on Martial's list, links old women's lusts explicitly with the practice of *captatio* (1.37–44). Although the childless in general were the targets of *captatores* (thus Eumolpus' charade at Croton), the *orbae* (as at Juv. 3.129–30) were also *vetulae*, and so their power is doubly resented by satirists, a woman both old and moneyed being doubly anomalous.

Martial's metaphor using Hecuba (10.90) unites degradation of *exempla* with the technique of shaming the woman by calling attention to faults in her genitalia. The outstanding example of this motif is a section of a Priapic poem from the *Virgilian Appendix* (83 Bücheler, pp. 151–53 Oxford). Inveighing against his impotent phallus, the narrator threatens it as follows (lines 26–37):

bidens amica Romuli senis memor
paratur, inter atra cuius inguina
latet iacente pantice abditus specus
vagaque pelle tectus annuo gelu
araneosus obsidet forem situs.
tibi haec paratur, ut tuum ter aut quater
voret profunda fossa lubricum caput.
licebit aeger, angue lentior, cubes,
tereris usque donec, a, miser, miser
triplexque quadruplexque compleas specum.
superbia ista proderit nihil, simul
vagum sonante merseris luto caput.

A two-toothed mistress who remembers old Romulus
is ready, amidst whose dark loins
lies a cave hidden by a flaccid paunch,
and, covered by skin wandering in yearlong cold,
cobwebbed filth obstructs the door.
She's ready for you, so that three or four times
this deep ditch can devour your slimy head.
Although you'll lie there weak, slower than a snake,
you'll be ground repeatedly until—o wretch, wretch,
you fill that cave three times and four times over.
This pride of yours will get you nowhere, as soon as
your errant head is plunged in her noisy muck.

The improbably old woman bears the epithet *bidens*, "two-toothed," usually applied to sacrificial animals, like sheep. She is represented to the penis, appropriately, by her vagina, which is dark and hidden *(atra, latet, abditus, tectus)*, flabby *(iacente pantice, vaga . . . pelle)*, enormously loose *(specus, profunda fossa, specum)*, cold *(annuo gelu)*, and filthy *(araneosus . . . situs, sonante . . . luto)*. What is more, it will eat up and grind the penis *(voret, tereris, merseris)*, making repulsive noises the whole while (line 37; this flaw is the subject of Mart. 7.18). Paradoxically, this will not destroy the penis but will cause it to become erect (lines 34–35). The narrator, who is addressing his penis directly here, also personifies it *(caput)* and expresses reproachful sympathy *(a, miser, miser)*. This form of humor clearly depends on a strong identification between the reader and the male narrator, represented by his genitalia, and a concomitant willingness to regard the woman's genitalia, when penetrated, as an unknown territory, dark and forbidding. (In the preceding section [lines 19–25] the narrator tells the penis it will be deprived of attractive boys and women, whose orifices are not mentioned and whose bodies are accorded complimentary adjectives—*tener puer*, "tender boy"; *mobilem natem*, "mobile ass"; *puella iocosa*, "charming girl"; *levi manu*, "light hand"; *lucidum femur*, "shining thigh.") The depiction of women's genitalia here, as usual, is restricted to strongly negative contexts, often connected with repellent old age.[11] This theme is part of the motif of the *vagina dentata*, common in western European folklore[12] and linked with the worldwide belief that male genitalia are preferable to female.[13]

Priapic Poetry

Indeed, personification of the phallus, like that in the poem from the *Virgilian Appendix*, is found in various contexts. Horace gives the *muto* a voice at *S.* 1.2.68–71, where it has an indignant conversation with the man to whom it belongs; likewise, Martial says his penis protests when he refuses to buy a *puer* at a high price: "hoc dolet et queritur de me mea mentula secum," "my prick grieves over this and complains to itself about me" (1.58.3). Elsewhere, Martial lets his penis see, in order to reject an ugly woman for him (9.37.10). The god Priapus can himself be construed as a talking phallus; conversely, some poems compare a man's phallus, or the man himself, to Priapus (Antipater *AP* 11.224; probably Catullus 53; Juvenal 6.375–76; Mart. 11.51, 11.72). The exposed phallus can be a source of applause, like Ascyltos' in the baths (Petron. *Sat.* 92.6–11; cf. Mart. 9.33). Catullus develops this trope to its fullest when he calls Mamurra *Mentula*, as, in a different way, did Augustus in calling Horace *purissimum penem* (Suet. *Vita Horati*)—here a term of endearment.[14]

The address to the impotent phallus is something of a topos in Latin literature. Petronius makes of this theme an opportunity for mock epic (*Sat.* 132.7–15), with the wretched Encolpius passionately upbraiding his penis, breaking into a Vergilian *cento* (132.11), and comparing himself to Odysseus in conference with his heart (132.12–13):

> nec minus ego tam foeda obiurgatione finita paenitentiam agere sermonis mei coepi secretoque rubore perfundi, quod oblitus verecundiae meae cum ea parte corporis verba contulerim, quam ne ad cognitionem quidem admittere severioris notae homines solerent. (13) mox perfricata diutius fronte "quid autem ego" inquam "mali feci, si dolorem meum naturali convicio exoneravi? aut quid est quod in corpore humano ventri male dicere solemus aut gulae capitique etiam, cum saepius dolet? quid? non et Ulixes cum corde litigat suo, et quidam tragici oculos suos tamquam audientes castigant?

> And when so foul an excoriation was over, I began to feel no little remorse for my speech, and became suffused with a secret blush, that, forgetful of my modesty, I should have bandied words with that part of my body which men of a more serious stamp do not usually even admit to their cognizance. I repeatedly beat my brow, but soon, "What evil, then," I say, "have I done, if I have lightened my grief with a natural outburst of annoyance? Or what about the fact that, in the human body, we are accustomed to accuse the

stomach or the throat or even the head, whenever they hurt? Well? Does not Ulysses argue with his heart, and certain tragedians chastise their eyes as if they had ears?

Ovid's use of the theme in *Amores* 3.7 probably served as the jumping-off point for the Priapic poem from the *Virgilian Appendix* discussed above, although Ovid's treatment of the theme is far more gentle. *Am.* 3.7 had enough status as a serious poem to be parodied in the *Priapea*:

Ovid *Am.* 3.7.1–2:

At non formosa est, at non bene culta puella,
at, puto, non votis saepe petita meis?

But isn't the girl pretty, but isn't she well dressed,
but hasn't she, I ask you, been often sought by my prayers?

Pr. 80.1–2:

At non longa bene est, at non bene mentula crassa
et quam si tractes, crescere posse putes?

But isn't it a good long prick, but isn't it a good thick one,
and one which, if you'd handle it, you'd think could grow?

Throughout 3.7 Ovid restricts himself to the mildest euphemisms and says little more than that a girl he had desired was in bed with him at last; he was impotent; she tried to arouse him (kissing him deeply, putting her thigh against his, whispering exciting endearments); finally she tried manual stimulation, and when this failed she became angry and left. He refers throughout to his impotent member euphemistically as *pars* (lines 6, 69) or describes it dramatically as *truncus*, *iners*, *species*, *inutile pondus* (line 15). He repeats the idea that he has shown himself "not a man" (lines 20, 43, 59, 60).

Two passages in this poem are closely related to an epigram of Philodemus (*AP* 11.30).

AP 11.30.1–2:

Ὁ πρὶν ἐγὼ καὶ πέντε καὶ ἐννέα, νῦν, Ἀφροδίτη,
ἓν μόλις ἐκ πρώτης νυκτὸς ἐς ἠέλιον

What I could do before five or nine times, now, Aphrodite,
scarcely once from nightfall to the sun

Ovid *Am.* 3.7.23–26:

at nuper bis flava Chlide, ter candida Pitho,
ter Libas officio continuata meo est;
exigere a nobis angusta nocte Corinnam,
me memini numeros sustinuisse novem.

But recently blond Chlide twice, fair Pitho three times,
three times Libas was done in succession by my services;
I remember when Corinna demanded it of me in a narrow night,
I brought the count up to nine.

AP 11.30.5–6:

ὦ γῆρας, γῆρας, τί ποθ' ὕστερον, ἢν ἀφίκηαι,
ποιήσεις, ὅτε νῦν ὧδε μαραινόμεθα;

O old age, old age, what will you do later,
if you come at all, since now I am dying away so?

Ovid *Am.* 3.7.17–18:

quae mihi ventura est, siquidem ventura, senectus,
cum desit numeris ipsa iuventa suis?

What [kind of] old age is to come to me, if it is to come at all,
when youth itself falls short of the mark?

The tally recalls the one at Hor. *Epod.* 12.14–16, and here has the function of contrasting the golden age of the narrator's sexual prowess with his present comparative failure. Ovid, Philodemus, and Encolpius, who use the theme in self-reproach, write here in the elegiac mode; Martial brings the theme back into the mainstream of invective in his version (11.97):

Una nocte quater possum: sed quattuor annis
si possum, peream, te, Telesilla, semel.

I can do it four times in one night; but I'll be damned
if I can do it to you once in four years, Telesilla.[15]

Here, as in *Epod.* 12, the narrator's sexual ability remains as strong as ever, and lapses only in the face of a woman he wishes to reject.

Ovid's address to his phallus (*Am.* 3.7.69–72) is brief and dignified:

quin istic pudibunda iaces, pars pessima nostri?
sic sum pollicitis captus et ante tuis.
tu dominum fallis, per te deprensus inermis
tristia cum magno damna pudore tuli.

Why do you lie there full of modesty, o worst part of me?
So I have been taken in by your promises before.
You're cheating your master; caught weaponless because of you
I have paid a sad price with great shame.

Inermis is suggestive of the Priapic poems, as it was particularly Priapus who described his genitalia as his weapons (see esp. *Pr.* 9, 20; also 11.3, 25.7, 31.3, 43.1, 55.4). On the other hand, Ovid addresses his phallus not as a god or even as an equal but as a slave who has cheated him *(tu dominum fallis)*; Ovid is the *dominus*.

And the wording of this passage is genteel, markedly different from that of the episode at Horace *S.* 1.2.68–71, in which the poet gives the *muto* an appropriately coarse speech of its own:

> huic si mutonis verbis mala tanta videnti
> diceret haec animus: "quid vis tibi? numquid ego a te
> magno prognatum deposco consule cunnum
> velatumque stola mea cum conferbuit ira?"

> To him seeing such evils if the spirit of his cock
> should put this into words: "What do you want? Do I ever
> demand from you a cunt descended from a great consul
> and wearing a matron's dress, when my anger seethes?"

As in the Priapic from the *Virgilian Appendix*, the penis perceives women in terms of their genitalia; lineage, standing, and clothing have nothing to do with physiology. The *muto* refers to its desire as *ira*, "anger," and uses the obscene term *cunnus* rather than any periphrasis or euphemism. The same bluntness characterizes the Priapic from the *Virgilian Appendix*, even though its premise is the same as that of *Am.* 3.7; the phallus in the *VA* Priapic is referred to as *iners penis* (line 5), *fascinum* (line 8), and *sceleste penis* (line 19), and, as has been seen, the poet vividly re-creates the act of intercourse from the point of view of the penis—as punishment for it.

The Priapic poem from the *Virgilian Appendix* is not just an imitation of Ovid, nor even a more obscene version of Ovid's lament; it incorporates an address to the god Priapus, and one of exceptional beauty (lines 6–18):

> placet, Priape, qui sub arboris coma
> soles, sacrum revincte pampino caput,
> ruber sedere cum rubente fascino?
> at, o Triphalle, saepe floribus novis
> tuas sine arte deligavimus comas,
> abegimusque voce saepe, cum tibi
> senexve corvus impigerve graculus
> sacrum feriret ore corneo caput.
> vale, nefande destitutor inguinum,
> vale, Priape: debeo tibi nihil.
> iacebis inter arva pallidus situ,
> canisque saeva susque ligneo tibi
> lutosus affricabit oblitum latus.

> Are you pleased [by my impotence],
> Priapus, who under the tresses of a tree
> like to sit, red, with your reddening phallus,
> your holy head bound about with vine tendrils?
> But, o Thrice-penised, often with new flowers
> I have tied back your tresses, without art,

often I have driven them away with my voice, when
    an ancient raven or busy jackdaw
was striking your holy head with his horned mouth.
Goodbye, unspeakable deserter of my loins,
goodbye, Priapus: I owe you nothing.
You will lie in the fields, pale with mold,
and the wild dog and the pig, covered with mire,
will rub against your wooden, forgotten flanks.

It has been remarked[16] that many poems in the *Priapea* begin from one of the main principles of Roman religion, *do ut des*—"I sacrifice so that you will grant my prayer." This principle has a peculiar resonance in Priapic poetry, for when the poet/narrator asks for potency rather than a good harvest, he asks the god for a personal, physical, and yet frivolous boon, which the god himself is carved to represent. *Do ut des* implies the power of the mortal to influence the immortal, impatience and exigency coupled with reverence and awe. The poem from the *Virgilian Appendix* demonstrates well the relationship between the man and the god. The man has worshiped in the past, bringing garlands to the red-phallused god in the garden and protecting him from birds.[17] In the future he will desert the god who has deserted him and will let animals befoul the god, who is, after all, made only of wood. The poet here increases his ridicule by modeling his rejection of Priapus on Catullus' rejection of his *puella* (Cat. 8). But the beauty of the picture of the god among trees and flowers, and the god abandoned in the fields, endows the god and his powers with high significance.

This significance prompted many authors to write Priapic poetry, among them the author or authors of the collection known as the *Carmina Priapea.*[18] The *Priapea* contains by far the widest variety of themes for Priapic poetry, some of which are especially crude in both language and content, while others match the Priapic from the *Virgilian Appendix* in elegance of expression. The cruder themes include word games (7, 54, 67); invective against an old or a young woman (12, 32, 46, 57; cf. 78); description of a dancing girl (19, 27); and the most prevalent type of theme in the collection, threats against thieves,[19] which make up 46.3 percent of the poems in the *Priapea.*

The word games, unusual in Latin,[20] tease the reader into drawing Priapus' phallus or forming an obscene word. At the same time, they threaten:

7 Cum loquor, una mihi peccatur littera; nam T
    P dico semper blaesaque lingua mihi est.

When I speak, one letter is confused by me; for "T" [you]
    I say as "P" [I bugger] always and my tongue is lisping.

54 CD si scribas temonemque insuper addas,
    qui medium volt te scindere, pictus erit.

If you write "CD" and put a beam on top of it [CD],
   what wants to split the middle of you will be drawn.

67 Penelopes primam Didonis prima sequatur
   et primam Ca†ni† syllaba prima Remi,
quodque fit ex illis, tu mi deprensus in horto,
   fur, dabis: hac poena culpa luenda tua est.

Let the first syllable of "Dido" follow the first of "Penelope"
   and the first of "Remus" follow the first of "Canus"
      [= PE + DI + CA + RE, "bugger"];
that which is made of them, you, caught by me in my garden,
   will give, thief; this penalty must be paid for your crime.

In all three poems the reader, addressed as *tu/te*, decodes a message that tells him Priapus wishes to rape him—a sort of double rape. The fiction is that these little poems, and all the *Priapea*, are offerings tacked onto the god's image in the garden—which in turn pretend to be the god's own words. The reader thus is supposed to be standing in front of the god's statue as he reads, that is, he is in Priapus' garden, and as such, he is either a worshiper or a potential thief.[21] Hence the god's threats are always potentially directed at the reader himself.

The threats are quite limited in range. Although the god threatens with the sickle he holds in his hand (e.g., 6.2, 11.2), the greater threat comes from his *mentula*: female thieves will be raped by it, adult male thieves will suffer irrumation, and boys will suffer anal rape. This distinction is made clear in a group of poems differentiating the three sorts of punishments (13, 22, 74). But most of the poems threaten anal rape (6, 11, 15, 17, 25, 31, 41, 51, 52, 64, 69, 76, 77), sometimes in combination with oral (28, 35). Oral rape is the sole threat only occasionally (30, 44, 56, 59, 70), and the rape of a woman is the sole subject of a poem only twice (66, 73). Priapus also curses those who bilk him of verses, promising rape (41) or sexual frustration (47; cf. 23).[22]

Although the threats are usually extremely violent—Priapus claiming he will ram the thief's very vitals—several poems state that thieves come just for the pleasure of being raped (51, 64) or show Priapus bargaining with the thief (3, 5, 38)—*do ut des* (5):

Quam puero legem fertur dixisse Priapus,
   versibus hic infra scripta duobus erit:
"quod meus hortus habet sumas inpune licebit,
   si dederis nobis quod tuus hortus habet."

The law which Priapus is said to have stated to the boy
   will be written here below in two verses:
"What my garden has you may take with impunity,
   if you give me what your garden has."

The powerful and attractive worship Priapus' *mentula* while thieves must fear its blows (25):

> Hoc sceptrum, quod ab arbore est recisum,
> nulla iam poterit virere fronde,
> sceptrum, quod pathicae petunt puellae,
> quod quidam cupiunt tenere reges,
> cui dant oscula nobiles cinaedi,
> intra viscera furis ibit usque
> ad pubem capulumque coleorum.

> This scepter, which was cut from a tree,
> will now be able to grow green with no leaf,
> this scepter, which pathic girls seek out,
> which certain kings desire to hold,
> to which aristocratic fags give kisses,
> will go into the guts of a thief all the way
> up to my crotch and the hilt of my balls.

The poem begins with epic travesty, describing Priapus' *mentula* in the terms used of the scepter of the Greeks at Troy (*Iliad* 1.234–39). Priapus lays stress on the fact that he is only carved of wood; still, he has eminent worshipers. Yet he degrades them; they here form a threefold receptacle for him, like the thieves divided into vaginal–?anal–oral. It is a joke for a king to wish to hold this kind of scepter, and the phrase *nobiles cinaedi* is a contradiction in terms. The last two lines typify Priapus' rapes, which are hyperbolically thorough; the scepter so highly valued by girls, kings, and nobles is also a sword (so *capulum* implies).

Yet his disdain for those he rapes extends to a refusal to rape those who desire him—a refusal reminiscent of those in invective against old women. In 45 Priapus mocks a *cinaedus*; in 64 he rejects a pathic male who comes to him:

> Quidam mollior anseris medulla [=Cat. 25.1–2]
> furatum venit huc amore poenae:
> furetur licet usque: non videbo.

> A certain man softer than the marrow of a goose
> comes here to steal from love of the penalty;
> let him go right on stealing; I won't see him.

And in his invective against women Priapus rejects them in the same way—old women in 12 and 57, young women in 32 and 46. They have prayed to him to service them (12.7, 32.11–12, 57.6)—although perhaps this means they pray to him for lovers (cf. 58.3–4). He sends away the women in 12 and 46 but admits the possibility of intercourse, horrid though it would be, with the women in 32 and 57. For the first three he paints repellent pictures of their physical ugliness, including their genitalia. The woman in 12 is ancient, shabby, toothless, and ill, and he commands her (lines 10–15):

> "tolle" inquam "procul et iube latere
> scissa sub tunica stolaque russa,
> ut semper solet, et timere lucem
> qui tanto patet indecens hiatu,
> barbato macer eminente naso,
> ut credas Epicuron oscitari."

> "Take it far away," I say, "and order it to hide
> under your torn slip and your rusty dress,
> as it always does, and fear the light—
> that thing which gapes unlovely with such a gap,
> skinny, with its bearded nose sticking out,
> so that you'd think Epicurus was yawning."

Here the clothing that covers the genitalia is important, since it is tattered and cheap; the genitalia are shamelessly exposed and gape unattractively. They are hairy, unlike the carefully depilated genitalia of young women,[23] and an excrescence, perhaps her clitoris, protrudes. The iconoclastic comparison to a bearded philosopher makes an unpleasant connection between mouth and genitalia, an identity that pervades Latin invective.

The woman in 32 fares no better; she is fantastically thin and dried out, so that intercourse with her is like metal scraping on horn (32.13–14). As for the woman in 46, she is black, perverse, short, hairy, and loose (i.e., her vagina is lax); Priapus comments (lines 7–10):

> nam quamvis videar satis paratus,
> erucarum opus est decem maniplis,
> fossas inguinis ut teram dolemque
> cunni vermiculos scaturrientes.

> For although I might seem to be well enough prepared,
> I would need ten handfuls of [aphrodisiac] colewort,
> for me to rub the ditches of your groin, and beat
> the swarming worms of your cunt.

Again the narrator is potent, the woman simply too disgusting to be acceptable. This picture of the woman's genitalia infested with worms is the harshest in Latin and shows not only the violent hostility of the god's performance *(teram, dolem)* but his fear and loathing of what lies within the woman.

Conversely, the god praises his own phallus. Sought by the pathic, as in 25, it can fill any woman (18) and (in the Ovidian travesty of 80) is even too large for some. Making an allusion to semen (rare in Latin humor), the god claims that the wetness of his *mentula* is not dew or frost but "what comes out spontaneously, when I think of a pathic girl" (48.4–5). The power of this phallus is like that of a mortal, although Priapus remains linked with his natural setting *(ros, pruina)*; he is also linked with the mortal as poet, as in 79:

> Priape, quod sis fascino gravis tento,
> quod exprobravit hanc tibi suo versu
> poeta noster, erubescere hoc noli:
> non es poeta fascinosior nostro.
>
> Priapus, because you are heavy with your stretched phallus,
> and our poet casts this up to you in his verse,
> don't blush at this:
> you aren't bigger-phallused than our poet.

Priapus and his worshiper-creator here share their salient characteristic.

Considering the savage, if joking, hostility of the poems in which Priapus threatens interlopers, the attitude of another group of poems is quite surprising. Here the god is a figure of fun, apologizing for his rude, wooden shape (10), making comparisons between himself and the Olympian gods (9, 20, 36, 39, 53, 75), complaining about the weather and other problems (26, 33, 47, 55, 61, 63). Worshipers bring offerings and pray to him (4, 16, 21, 27, 34, 37, 40, 42, 50, 53, 65, 80a), but they are more concerned to praise (or apologize for) their offerings and themselves than to propitiate the god. At his most refined, the god discusses problems of literary theory, in *apologiae* (1, 2, 49; cf. 66) and in a tour de force of mock epic that makes a series of obscene puns on Homeric Greek (68).

In 10 Priapus defends himself against a girl who comes and laughs at him:

> Insulsissima quid puella rides?
> non me Praxiteles Scopasve fecit,
> non sum Phidiaca manu politus;
> sed lignum rude vilicus dolavit
> et dixit mihi "tu Priapus esto."
> spectas me tamen et subinde rides:
> nimirum tibi salsa res videtur
> adstans inguinibus columna nostris.
>
> Extremely silly girl, what are you laughing at?
> Not Praxiteles nor Scopas made me,
> I'm not polished by the hand of Phidias;
> but a gardener hewed raw wood
> and said to me "You be Priapus."
> Yet you look at me and burst out laughing;
> I suppose this thing looks funny to you—
> the pillar standing at my loins.

The veiled threat is more than counterbalanced by the shamefaced excuses Priapus makes for himself. Unlike the expensive marble statues that often adorned gardens, he is just a homemade wood carving. A lowly servant hacked him out of wood, in effect created him; and not only does he have a servant for a parent, but a girl laughs at him. The idea that Priapus is subservient appears often in the poems of dedication, some of which come from the owner or manager of the garden in which Priapus stands (16.7, *dominus florentis agelli*; 42.1, *vilicus*; 65) and most of which make only the most modest of offerings (especially 53, which calls Priapus *dive minor*).

This pose, however, cannot be a denial of the god's importance and power, so strongly enunciated in the poems incorporating threats. The poems that laugh at Priapus do not reject him; they express dominance over him, superior power over his wooden form. He remains a symbol of mastery, especially sexual, in the rich setting of his garden. His rusticity is like that of the shepherds of pastoral poetry, who proclaim their simplicity in well-turned verses. Even his boorishness is a pose, as in 68, where the god begins by announcing his ignorance and goes on to create a long (34 lines) and brilliantly lewd travesty of the *Iliad* and *Odyssey*:

Rusticus indocte si quid dixisse videbor,
  da veniam: libros non lego, poma lego.
sed rudis hic dominum totiens audire legentem
  cogor Homeriacas edidicique notas.
ille vocat, quod nos psolen, ψολόεντα κεραυνόν,
  et quod nos culum, κουλεόν ille vocat

If I, a rustic, seem to say anything illiterate here
  forgive me; I cull not books but fruit.
But, crude as I am, I am forced to listen to my master reading here all
    the time,
  and I have learned Homeric letters.
He calls, what we call "schmuck," "smoldering thunderbolt,"
  and what we call "ass," he calls "scabbard"

The puns work both in sound and in sense: phallus = thunderbolt, buttocks = sheath. The poem goes on to describe Helen as *Taenario . . . cunno*, and Agamemnon's *mentula* as the cause of the whole war; Ulysses' travels were motivated by lust, his *mentula* (rather than his *mens*) the wonder of the world, while Penelope, a randy *vetula* (line 27), kept her house full of adulterers.

The *Priapea*, then, violates not only the sexual territory of men, women, and boys but the boundaries between serious poetry and the obscene, between ethereal religion and the reverence for the sexual. "Nos vappae sumus," "I'm a good-for-nothing," says Priapus, inviting lovers into his garden (14); they need not fear him and his shrine, he says, as they fear *caelitibus . . . severis*, "stern heaven-dwellers," for "stamus sub Iove coleis apertis," "I stand under Jupiter [=in the open air] with my balls exposed." Women (4, 27, 34, 40) as well as men (37, 50) make dedications, with prayers for sexual luck, to him; but the women are prostitutes (34, 40) and a street dancer (27), and the prayers are not for lovers but for customers. The *Suburana* Telesina gives Priapus a wreath after she has earned her freedom by her labors—which she enjoys (40); the dancer Quintia prays that her crowd will always be as erect as the god (27); and a nameless girl makes a dedicatory tally (34):

> Cum sacrum fieret deo salaci,
> conducta est pretio puella parvo
> communis satis omnibus futura:
> quae quot nocte viros peregit una,
> tot verpas tibi dedicat salignas.

> When it was the festival of the lusty god,
> a girl was hired for a small fee
> to be shared as enough for all;
> who, as many men as she got through in one night,
> dedicates that many willow-wood dicks to you.

The women who venerate Priapus are women in the service of men.

Several authors best known for other kinds of poetry wrote Priapics as well. A fragment of a formal dedication by Catullus survives (fragment 1); it has plausibly been connected with his trip to the Greek east,[24] since it mentions the cities around the Hellespont, Priapus' home. Horace makes Priapus the ludicrous hero and narrator of *S.* 1.8, the battered custodian of Maecenas' new gardens who frightens away two old witches by farting; here again Priapus is the enemy of hags. As in some poems of the *Priapea*, the god gives his own genealogy, an embarrassing descent from a block of wood (lines 1–5); a carpenter made him, and it was a toss-up whether he carved the wood into Priapus or a bench. "Deus inde ego," Priapus says (line 3)—not very impressive. But he represents normalcy, in comparison with the two fearsome witches, and he concludes the satire by putting the reader in his own place—"cum magno risuque iocoque videres," "you'd have seen this all with great laughter and jesting."

Tibullus makes of Priapus a creature of love elegy, an adviser for love affairs (1.4). For him Priapus' lack of physical beauty is a source of wonder as to how he manages to attract beautiful boys (lines 3–6), and he asks the god how he does it. Priapus replies with a discourse on boys and advises strict compliance with boys' whims; he curses the boy who first took a gift (lines 57–60) and urges boys to love the poets. With a touch of humor, he reminds them that it is poetry alone that made Nisus and Pelops famous (lines 63–64), an early version of Horace's *vixere fortes ante Agamemnona*. This Priapus is a shadow of his Priapic self, and is only an excuse for Tibullus to lament his lack of success with Marathus.

The three Priapic poems from the *Catalepton* (84–86 Bücheler = Oxford pp. 131–33) are much closer to the *Priapea* and to Martial's Priapics. Like samples, each takes a different meter—1 in elegiac distich, 2 in scazons, 3 in priapeans. In all three poems the god again flaunts his modesty: in 1 he fears the cold, for farmers may use him for firewood; in 2 he is a dry stump who guards a diminutive garden (line 3, *agellulum*; line 4, *villulam*, *hortulum pauperis*) for his master (line 4, *eri*) in return for modest offerings (lines 6–15); in 3 his situation is the same (line 1, *villulam*; line 5, *domini colunt me*; line 6, *pauperis tuguri*; offerings of garlands, small sacrifices, lines 10–18). In 2 his *mentula* is meant to frighten a passerby; when it does not, the god suggests the gardener will break off the *mentula* and use it as a club (lines 16–21). The Priapus in 3 is similarly feckless; warning off boys, he only urges them to go next door where the Priapus is rich and negligent (lines 19–21). This is a feeble Priapus; yet the lists of offerings are beautiful, and the garden is an idyllic spot, a sort of annex to the pleasantly humble world of bucolic imagery.

It is remarkable that this is the Priapus Martial adopts for his Priapic poems—the wooden bumpkin in danger of combustion, guardian of a pitiable plot. In these poems Martial belittles and mocks Priapus,[25] but again this constitutes an assertion of power over the god, as well as a kind of mock hymn. Priapus is a god who can be mocked in his physical manifestation, a divine buffoon; yet Martial cannot have despised him, as he chose him to help present his Saturnalian pieces to his friend Juvenal (7.91):

> De nostro, facunde, tibi, Iuvenalis, agello
> Saturnalicias mittimus, ecce, nuces.
> cetera lascivis donavit poma puellis
> mentula custodis luxuriosa dei.

> From our little field to you, eloquent Juvenal,
> look, we send you Saturnalian nuts.
> The other fruits have been given to sexy girls
> by the extravagant prick of the guardian god.

Epigram

In what way are invective against old women and Priapic poetry the model for satire and invective epigram? Obviously they represent the quintessence of the castigation of female sexuality and the praise of the male, as well as identifying male sexuality with dominance. What is important, and what is easy to lose sight of, is that both are kinds of sexual *humor*, which would be recognized as such by the author's audience. This means that both incorporate norms of the obscene, as discussed in chapter 1; both constitute explicit statements of what was normally left unsaid, as well as staining of the normally sacrosanct (women, boys, gods).

Without a real victim, the breaking of taboo and the staining of an ideal become the main object of the humor. And the amatory ideal in which the lover eternally pursues becomes the invective ideal in which the Priapic male eternally rejects. In real life Priapus' threat of rape was the punishment enacted by a cuckolded husband on his wife's lover caught *in flagrante delicto*, while he had the right to kill his wife (below, appendix 1); in a society that valued chastity and virility, Priapus' threat is a suitable fantasy. A sexual humor that includes both invective against old women and Priapic poetry can logically be expected to include diluted versions of both; in fact, invective epigram and satire consist largely of just that. And the principle of *variatio* is as strong in invective as in other kinds of Latin poetry: poets borrowed freely from each other in the creation of literate and elegant billingsgate.

The influence of the ideas and attitudes behind invective against old women and Priapic poetry becomes apparent when one begins to analyze the mechanisms and categories of Martial's sexual invective. As invective against old women and Priapics are directed at types, so are Martial's poems; by far the greatest number of Martial's invective poems attack women and male homosexuals. The difference is that Martial is able to shift his persona so that he is not always threatening or sneering; in addition, he can react against positives in literature (the erotic ideal) as well as against "real" positives. At times he carries over the benevolent attitude of erotic poetry into poems whose essential content is hostile or critical, producing a sort of invective in which the attacker seems to approve the actions of the victim (really no more than saying, "Now I'll get dirty with you"). But by and large the epigrammatist stands as the mouthpiece for his vitriolic invective; he himself is either invisible, an abstract norm that scorns aberrants, or present, in which case he physically threatens victims with exposure or rape or rejection.

Both Greek and Latin invective epigram attack flaws other than sexual. In general, the Greek poems are more diversified; Catullus restricts himself almost entirely to sexual or scatological invective, while Martial's nonsexual invective does not fall as readily into set categories as the Greek does.[26] The Greek themes include flaws of character (folly, cowardice, meanness, fickleness, ignorance, stinginess, laziness) as well as of skill or physiology (slow running, slow boats, leaky boats, bad doctors, silly philosophers, physical defects like long noses [including one, *AP* 11.418, by the emperor Trajan], skinniness, and lameness). What sexual or scatological invective there is in Greek epigram concerns itself mostly with four areas: the *os impurum*; invective against old women; pathic homosexuality; and bad breath, occasionally tied to the *os impurum*, more often given a scatological or scatophagical reference.[27] Other, less common themes include cuckoldry, physiological gibes usually involving male genitalia, and taunts of impotence.[28]

The poets Lucillius and Nicarchus together are responsible for sixteen or seventeen of this group of forty-odd epigrams from *AP* 11. Four (five, including 415) of their epigrams, those on bad breath, are very close to Catullus'. These poems compare the breath of their victim to excrement (239, 241, 242, 415) or to a he-goat (240); they play on the analogy between mouth and anus, claiming that the breath smells like a fart (241, 242, 415). Poem 241, by Nicarchus, can serve as an example of this topos:

> Τὸ στόμα χὼ πρωκτὸς ταὐτόν, Θεόδωρε, σοῦ ὄζει,
> ὥστε διαγνῶναι τοῖς φυσικοῖς καλὸν ἦν.
> ἦ γράψαι σε ἔδει ποῖον στόμα, ποῖον ὁ πρωκτός.
> νῦν δὲ λαλοῦντός σου ⟨βδεῖν σ' ἐνόμιζον ἐγώ⟩.

> Your mouth and your asshole smell the same, Theodorus,
> so much so that it would be a good trick for doctors to tell them apart.
> You should certainly have made a sign saying which was your mouth,
> which your asshole.
> Just now when you were gabbing, I thought you'd farted.

With this compare Catullus 97.1–4:

> Non (ita me di ament) quicquam referre putavi,
> utrumne os an culum olfacerem Aemilio.
> nilo mundius hoc, nihiloque immundius illud,
> verum etiam culus mundior et melior.

> I didn't think, so help me God, it made any difference,
> whether I smelled Aemilius' mouth or his ass.
> The latter is no more clean, the former no more unclean,
> in fact the ass is rather cleaner and better.

All three poets are embroidering on a theme that was apparently a favorite in invective. The use of first-person verbs (*olfacerem*, cf. *AP* 11.242.1) fixes the speaker as a direct experiencer of the victim's flaws, yet the victims are not very clearly identified. Catullus is fond of attacking people under names that seem to be pseudonyms of his acquaintances, but the Greek names tend to be anonymous or amusing (Theodorus, in this context), and Martial follows suit. His victims have stock names, or *redender Namen*, as in 6.93, where he uses the topos of bad smell:

> Tam male Thaïs olet quam non fullonis avari
> testa vetus media sed modo fracta via

> Thaïs smells as bad as not the old crock
> of even a greedy fuller does, only just broken in mid-road

Here "Thaïs" is used for comic effect, since ordinarily the name connotes an attractive courtesan, after the famous Thaïs of Athens.

Greek invective epigram, then, is comparable to Latin invective epigram in subject matter. The major difference between Greek epigram of all kinds and Latin epigram is in language. Use of obscene language of any kind is rare in Greek epigram, and limited to a few common words, most often βινεῖν, "to fuck," πυγή, "ass," and βδεῖν, "to fart." The only authors to use obscenities consistently in invective are Nicarchus and Lucillius, who may have served as models in this respect for Martial.[29] Their language is noteworthy also for their use of mock epic and metaphorical obscenities, for example, Nicarchus' poem 11.328, describing the division of an old prostitute among three customers:

Τὴν μίαν Ἑρμογένης κἀγώ ποτε καὶ Κλεόβουλος
ἤγομεν εἰς κοινὴν κύπριν Ἀριστοδίκην·
ἧς ἔλαχον μὲν ἐγὼ πολιὴν ἅλα ναιέμεν αὐτός·
εἷς γὰρ ἕν, οὐ πάντες πάντα, διειλόμεθα.
Ἑρμογένης δ' ἔλαχε στυγερὸν δόμον εὐρώεντα,
ὕστατον εἰς ἀφανῆ χῶρον ὑπερχόμενος,
ἔνθ' ἀκταὶ νεκύων, καὶ ἐρινεοὶ ἠνεμόεντες
δινεῦνται πνοιῇ δυσκελάδων ἀνέμων.
Ζῆνα δὲ θὲς Κλεόβουλον, ὃς οὐρανὸν εἰσαναβαίνειν,
τὸ ψολόεν κατέχων ἐν χερὶ πῦρ, ἔλαχεν.
γῆ δ' ἔμενε ξυνὴ πάντων· ψίαθον γὰρ ἐν αὐτῇ
στρώσαντες, τὴν γραῦν ὧδε διειλόμεθα.

Once Hermogenes, Cleobulus, and I took
one Aristodike for our common love.
Of her, I myself got her white sea to dwell in;
we divided her up, one part for each, no switching.
Hermogenes got her broad "hateful abode,"
finally stealing into the secret place
where are the shores of the dead, and windy wild fig trees
whirl in the blast of shrill-screaming winds.
Then count Cleobulus as Zeus, who got to go to heaven,
holding his smoldering thunderbolt in his hand.
The earth stayed common to all. Strewing on it
a rush mat, so we divided the old woman.[30]

Here Nicarchus uses heroic metaphors not found elsewhere: the "white sea" is the woman's vagina; the part described as Hades is her anus, where "fig trees" (perhaps the figs/anal warts of Latin invective, otherwise possibly hairs) are stirred by the blast of farts.[31] "Heaven" is the woman's mouth, so called not because it is heavenly but because it is her highest part (cf. *summus*, *Pr.* 74.2, Mart. 11.46.6, 11.61.5); Cleobulus' "thunderbolt," described as his ψολόεν πῦρ, is his phallus (ψωλή), which he guides to the woman's mouth. The projection here of the parts of the cosmos onto the body of an old woman recalls Bakhtin's analysis of satire; but here the intent is surely not constructive, and the effect is a soiling of the epic conventions along with a vivid depiction of the woman's body as foul. The passage is a specific and close travesty of *Iliad* 15.187–93, in which Poseidon tells of the division of the world among the three divine brothers, Zeus, Poseidon, and Hades—hence the doubly destructive analogy: the three gods are like three men penetrating an old woman; the old woman is as grossly physical as the earth, spread out below the three god-likened men.

Buchheit, who refers to the conceit as a *triporneia*, points out an analogy between the threefold use of the woman and the threefold threat of Priapus.[32] Apparently the concept of the power of the phallus as orifice-filling tool prompted both fantasies: Priapus reduces all comers—that is, the whole world other than himself—to a procession of orifices, while the *triporneia* reduces the woman to a sort of orifice-riddled surface (as in the American slang term "punchboard"). It is noteworthy that in the close description in the *triporneia* the orifices are decidedly unattractive, the anus dirty and the vagina salty; the speaker scorns what he boasts of using.

The fantasy of simultaneous use of several of a woman's orifices[33] appealed to other epigrammatists as well; both Martial (10.81; cf. 9.32.4) and Gallus (*AP* 5.49) wrote poems on this conceit:

Mart. 10.81:

> Cum duo venissent ad Phyllida mane fututum
> et nudam cuperet sumere uterque prior,
> promisit pariter se Phyllis utrique daturam,
> et dedit; ille pedem sustulit, hic tunicam.

> When two had come to Phyllis for a morning fuck
> and each wished to be first to take her naked,
> Phyllis promised she'd give herself equally to each,
> and she did: one raised her legs, the other her slip [i.e., from behind].

Gallus 5.49:

> Ἡ τρισὶ λειτουργοῦσα πρὸς ἓν τάχος ἀνδράσι Λύδη,
> τῷ μὲν ὑπὲρ νηδύν, τῷ δ' ὑπό, τῷ δ' ὄπιθεν,
> "εἰσδέχομαι φιλόπαιδα, γυναικομανῆ, φιλυβριστήν.
> εἰ σπεύδεις, ἐλθὼν σὺν δυσί, μὴ κατέχου."

> Lyde, doing a job quickly for three men at once,
> one above her belly, one under, one higher up, said,
> "I take on the pederast, the womanizer, and the pervert.
> If you're in a hurry, even when two others are here, don't hold back."

The two poems are much less elaborate and more flippant than Nicarchus' extravaganza; yet, even at this level, there are notable differences in the technique of the two authors. Not only has Gallus gone Martial one better by fitting three customers into his four-line epigram, he also explains the situation through a speech, making of the prostitute a character with a voice of her own. This tactic is almost totally lacking in Martial; he prefers to describe, or, if there is a voice, it is "his" voice, the words being spoken by the narrator of the poem.

While Catullus' invectives are fairly restrained in language (if not in imagery), Martial often uses extremely obscene language; sometimes a great deal of it in a single epigram, sometimes a single word to create a shock. Even in epigrams that draw much of their attraction from clever construction, Martial will also freely use primary obscenities, some of which have no equivalents at all in Greek epigram. For example, in his fantasy of group sex he gets in only two customers but manages to use the supine form of the verb *futuo*. In 2.28 Martial neatly accuses his victim of being a *fellator* or *cunnilinctor*, studiously avoiding these words by using the process of elimination. In the course of this process, however, Martial ticks off the vices not present, by name—not a *cinaedus*, not a *pedico*, not a *fututor*. *Irrumator* alone is expressed in a periphrasis:

Rideto multum qui te, Sextille, cinaedum
  dixerit et digitum porrigito medium.
sed nec pedico es nec tu, Sextille, fututor,
  calda Vetustinae nec tibi bucca placet.
ex istis nihil es, fateor, Sextille: quid ergo es?
  nescio, sed tu scis res superesse duas.

Go ahead and laugh at the man who calls you a queer,
  Sextillus, and give him the finger.
But you aren't a bugger, Sextillus, no, nor a fucker,
  nor does the hot cheek of Old Mama give you pleasure.
I confess you aren't one of these, Sextillus: then what are you?
  I don't know, but you know two things are left.

Martial's poetry is the richest single source of Latin invective. In addition to conventional themes, he brings in topical ones—over twenty epigrams on adultery,[34] many relating to or hinting at the revival of the *lex Julia de adulteriis coercendis* by Domitian; five epigrams on illegitimate children and their status (1.84, 6.39, 8.31, 10.95, 10.102). On conventional themes he is inexhaustible. He has several poems against lesbians (below), a topic untouched by Greek epigram; against male homosexuals he has over forty epigrams,[35] dealing with such repeated themes as hypocritical Stoic/pathics, sore anuses and anal warts, depilation, homosexual prostitution, and infibulation. There are nearly sixty epigrams deriding indulgence in oral sex,[36] eight accusing a man of impotence,[37] several against circumcised men (7.55, 7.82, 11.94). His poems vary widely in tone, from the very coarse (like the Nanneius epigram discussed above) to the circumlocutory, which avoid direct statement of obscene language or topics.

Martial also writes a class of epigrams that are simply insults in sexual terms—invective lists against a victim, with insulting comparisons often including sexual aberrations (1.41, 6.64, 7.10, 9.57, 11.66).

1.41:

Urbanus tibi, Caecili, videris.
non es, crede mihi. quid ergo? verna,
hoc quod Transtiberinus ambulator,
qui pallentia sulpurata fractis
permutat vitreis . . .
. . . .
quod de Gadibus inprobus magister,
quod bucca est vetuli dicax cinaedi

You seem witty—to yourself, Caecilius.
You're not, believe me. What then? A house
slave,
same as a Trasteverine peddler
who exchanges pale matches
for broken glass . . .
the same as a lewd captain from Cadiz,
the same as the witty lips of an old fag

This may be the most rudimentary type of invective to appear in Latin poetry and is similar to the Eskimo and Arabic satires quoted by Elliott:[38]

Arabic:

Negroes are better, when they name their sires,
Than Qahtan's sons, the uncircumcised cowards;
A folk whom thou mayst see, at war's outflame,
More abject than a shoe to tread in baseness:
Their women free to every lecher's lust,
Their clients spoil for cavaliers and footmen.

Eskimo:

She [my wife] who was snatched from me
By a prattler, a liar . . .
That lover of human flesh,
Cannibal, miscreant,
Spewed up from starvation days.[39]

Martial's analogical or direct insults include ones directed at single flaws: personal appearance (1.83, 2.33, 3.42, 3.53, 3.74, 10.83), sexual appeal and ability (3.79, 11.23, 11.62, 12.27, 12.79), smell (6.93).

Martial's invective against women varies a great deal in its tone. Some, jocose or ribald epigrams revolving around women's wantonness,[40] are comparable in tone to his erotic epigrams and occupy a sort of borderline area; their acerbity places them close to invective, though they have an urbanely anecdotal air. For example,

6.67 insults both woman and interlocutor, while the whole has an air of being contrived, since it is difficult to believe in this epigram as a reply to the question it claims to be answering:

> Cur tantum eunuchos habeat tua Caelia, quaeris,
> Pannyche? volt futui Caelia nec parere.

> You ask why your Caelia has only eunuchs for servants,
> Pannychus? Caelia wants to be fucked and not give birth.

In this epigram the gullible Pannychus has supposedly expressed surprise that "his Caelia" has only eunuchs as slaves; the poet rudely explains what this means. The woman is attacked for her cynical use of an ill-regarded sort of slave; her wish to avoid having children marks her as a bad woman, the opposite of the traditional *matrona*. At the same time, the use of *futui* abruptly exposes her; and *volt futui* is a statement appropriate only for prostitutes, whereas "Caelia" is apparently someone's wife or mistress, probably an aristocratic woman. On the other hand, her husband or lover is given the peculiar and quasi-religious Greek name "Pannychus" ("All-night"); such a combination, as well as the question and answer, is very much removed from real life. And Martial sets up the poem in the form of a gossipy interchange, without explicitly condemning the situation.

The vices for which Martial attacks women can be reduced to a single common element: too much interest in sex. Most frequently the women are adulteresses, that is, they betray their husbands; sometimes they are just extravagant in their indulgences, actively pursuing their hoped-for lovers. Other women are ugly, smelly, or dirty; old women try to look young (*Pr.* 57; Mart. 4.20, 8.79, 9.37, 10.39; Juv. 4.36, 6.191–96); young women try to conceal their flaws.[41] These are the themes of invective against old women, and here again women are targets for satire when they are imagined as adopting the role of pursuer rather than pursued. The poet reserves the right to reject such women and to approve or disapprove of their bodies.

Martial is one of the few Roman writers to mention lesbians at all (1.90, 7.35, 7.67, 7.70); he both attacks them and draws attention to the mechanics of their lovemaking. The two most specific poems define their subjects as counterfeit men (1.90.8; cf. Sen. *Controv.* 1.2.23), to the point of exceeding male capabilities (7.67.2–3, Philaenis "bangs" eleven girls each day). Remaining a spectator at a distance, Martial expresses horrified disgust at Bassa in 1.90 (*pro facinus*, line 6; *monstrum*, line 9) but revels in details about Philaenis (7.67), who "buggers boys" (line 1), works out in a bathing suit, vomits at dinners (lines 9–10), and prefers cunnilingus to fellatio, as being more "manly" (lines 14–17). Juvenal, who adapts parts of 7.67 for *Satire* 6 (lines 246–64, 425–33), keeps only the nonsexual elements, and elsewhere has a female speaker deny the existence of lesbianism (2.47–49); Martial is clearly fascinated by what he depicts as an encroachment on male sexuality.

Martial's invective against male homosexuals manifests a similar ambivalence. As has been noted, his erotic poems to *pueri* are often humorous and/or rueful, and some of his depictions of pederasts and even of pathics are sympathetic in their satire. But the element of threat against the abnormal = less virile = inferior is often felt, and is not restricted to purely sexual invective. It is quite jarring to find that 3.82, an excoriation of the effete host of a too-luxurious dinner party, ends with Martial suggesting to a fellow guest that they rape the host:

> Conviva quisquis Zoili potest esse,
> Summoenianas cenet inter uxores
> curtaque Ledae sobrius bibat testa:
> hoc esse levius puriusque contendo.
> iacet occupato galbinatus in lecto
> . . . .
> hos Malchionis patimur inprobi fastus,
> nec vindicari, Rufe, possumus: fellat.

> Whoever can bear to be the guest of Zoilus,
> let him dine among the wives of 42nd Street
> and drink sober from Leda's broken bottle:
> I take that to be a lighter and purer thing.
> For Zoilus lies clad in chartreuse, taking up a whole couch
> . . . .
> And we endure these insults of the vile Pasha,
> nor, Rufus, can we be avenged: he sucks.

Martial portrays himself and Rufus as the moderate guests of an extravagant host; likewise, they are manly where he is effeminate, and they would like to prove this by forcing him to play the pathic for them (cf. 11.63). They are insulted even by witnessing his behavior. The rejection of Zoilus even as a candidate for rape is similar to the rejection of old crones by Priapus; the similar typology of the Norse *Edda*, in which warriors threaten to rape their opponents, includes one statement that not only will the opponent play the female, he is a "disgusting hag" (stanza 38).[42]

As was evident in the survey of Martial's pederastic poems, he was capable of treating the erotic ideal of the *puer* roughly. Several times he reproaches a boy for his coyness, saying he will masturbate as a substitute for enjoyment of the boy. In 11.58 he compares the boy to an extortionate barber whose legs he would break; by masturbating, "lota mentula laeva / λαικάζειν cupidae dicet avaritiae," "my prick, when my left hand is washed, will tell your grasping greediness to *fous-moi la paix*." Here the left hand replaces the boy, while the *mentula* speaks for the poet—a form of synecdoche not unusual in Martial (cf. 1.58.3, 9.37.9–10). In 11.73 Martial again says his hand is a substitute for the boy: "succurrit pro te saepe sinistra mihi," "my left hand often serves me in your place." This sheds light on the complaint to a wealthy and selfish friend, 2.43.13–14:

> grex tuus Iliaco poterat certare cinaedo:
> at mihi succurrit pro Ganymede manus.
>
> Your flock could have competed with the Trojan fag—
> but my hand serves me instead of a Ganymede.

The double entendre is obvious, and coarse in its context (a dinner at which the complaining poet feels cheated); the introduction of Ganymede, the standard referent for boys to be praised, as *Iliaco . . . cinaedo* is highly irreverent (cf. Mart. 11.43, 11.104), and the poet portrays himself as one who has not only no Ganymede, but no boy at all. A hand will do as well; compare *Pr.* 33, *fiet amica manus*. As with his deflation of the romantic image of women, Martial achieves distance by looking at the boy as someone else's, not his own.

When Martial writes satirically of the *pueri* of other men, his tone becomes that of the objective observer rather than of the rueful sufferer. He lays great stress on the venality of the boys, how they will pass to other masters and make love to them as well. His tone is indulgent but cold-blooded (12.16):

> Addixti, Labiene, tres agellos;
> emisti, Labiene, tres cinaedos.
> pedicas, Labiene, tres agellos.
>
> You sold three fields, Labienus;
> you bought three fags, Labienus.
> You're buggering your three fields, Labienus.[43]

The use of the word *cinaedus* (rather than *puer*) for the high-priced sexual toy marks the poet's distance from the situation; he would never say "emi cinaedum." Extravagant pederasty in another can be a source of amusement, while the poet takes his own love affairs more seriously, with no sign of embarrassment—chagrin, yes; shame, no. Significantly, when he writes poems on pederasty to identifiable addressees—for example, Domitian—it is only to praise the boy; and in his long poem to Juvenal praising the delights of rustic life in Bilbilis (12.18), he boasts of the sexual attractiveness of his servants there (lines 22–25). The satirical epigrams on pederasty do not give details that would link them with a real man and usually sound like complete jeux d'esprit.

Martial's tone in addressing pathic homosexuals is not so indulgent. He likes to make effeminate characteristics the main constituent of his invective (2.29, 3.63, 5.41); he specifically differentiates an effeminate man from himself (10.65):

> Cum te municipem Corinthiorum
> iactes, Charmenion, negante nullo,
> cur frater tibi dicor, ex Hiberis
> et Celtis genitus Tagique civis?

an voltu similes videmur esse?
tu flexa nitidus coma vagaris,
Hispanis ego contumax capillis;
levis dropace tu cotidiano
hirsutis ego cruribus genisque;
os blaesum tibi debilisque lingua est,
nobis ilia fortius loquentur:
tam dispar aquilae columba non est
nec dorcas rigido fugax leoni.
quare desine me vocare fratrem,
ne te, Charmenion, vocem sororem.

Since you boast that you are a townsman of the Corinthians,
Charmenion, and no one denies it,
why am I called your "brother," I, born from Iberians
and Celts, a citizen of Tagus?
Do we seem to be similar in looks?
You wander about, with your waved hair glistening,
I have stubborn Spanish hair;
you are smooth with your daily depilatory,
I have shaggy shins and cheeks;
your lips are lisping, your tongue is weak,
my loins will speak more strongly;
a dove is not more unlike a hawk,
nor a fleeing gazelle to a stiff lion.
So stop calling me "brother,"
lest I call you, Charmenion, "sister."

The opposition is a strong one and contains a veiled sexual threat. Martial is a Spaniard while "Charmenion" is a Greek (often stereotyped as effeminate); Charmenion uses hair oil and a curling iron and depilates his body and face (all part of the stereotype of the *cinaedus*), while Martial's hair is neglected and his body shaggy. The comparison between the victim's effeminate speech (cf. Pers. 1.17–18, 35) and Martial suggests a threat of irrumation, while the last line and the epithet for the lion suggest a threat of anal rape.[44] The animal similes reinforce the threat of violent physical abuse, as well as the male/female contrast—*columba/dorcas/soror* versus *aquila/leo/frater*. Here again the pathic is closer to romantic love than the active male is: the narrator aligns the dove, the bird of Venus, with the pathic, rejecting its softness. Animal similes are much more commonly used in poems about women, as in the wolf/lamb contrast in Hor. *Epod.* 12.25–26 (above).

Both the poem and the stance—comparison of the virile poet with a despised enemy—owe a great deal to Catullus, but there are important and basic differences between the situations of the two poets. Where Catullus' invective is keyed in to events in his life and to particular people he knew, Martial here strongly identifies the self of the poem with his real self—the Spaniard—but "Charmenion" could be any effeminate Greek. Martial here sets "himself" up against a stereotype; in most of his invective against effeminates the comparison is left unspoken, but the stereotype of the effeminate easterner is a constant.

The humor Martial finds in the mechanics of pathic homosexuality often depends solely on the exposure of his victim, who is trying to conceal his predilections (2.54, 2.62, 3.71, 4.48, 9.57, 11.88, 12.33). But this humor has its violent side, and the exposure of the victim is perhaps no more than an extension of the fantasy of anal rape. A poem expressing mock sympathy for one Charinus is strongly reminiscent of the threats in the *Priapea* (Mart. 6.37):

> Secti podicis usque ad umbilicum
> nullas relliquias habet Charinus,
> et prurit tamen usque ad umbilicum.
> o quanta scabie miser laborat!
> culum non habet, est tamen cinaedus.

> Of his asshole, cut up to his navel,
> Charinus has no remains,
> and yet he itches with lust up to his navel.
> O with what a great mange the poor man suffers!
> He has no ass, yet he's a fag.

Martial's comic sympathy for the man is the equivalent of direct mockery: the last line, a typical epigrammatic paradox, also contains a common insult (cf. the graffiti above). To say "he has no ass, yet he's a fag" is a different statement in kind from, for example, "he has no razor, yet he's a barber," since the "yet he's . . ." element in the former constitutes a straightforward slur. Moreover, although the poet does not overtly threaten "Charinus," the poem bears a strong resemblance to *Pr.* 6, where the god threatens to penetrate a would-be thief up to his seventh rib, and *Pr.* 77, where the god remarks that he used to penetrate the *podices* of thieves *usque et usque et usque.*[45] The fantasy of the pathic with his anus slit to his navel, yet wanting more, projects a sadistic desire of the active male onto the body of the imagined pathic. And the penetration, sexual in the fantasy, would if actually carried out be a mortal wound, like that of a sword or spear.

Martial reserves his strongest invective in this area for men who pretend to be especially old-fashioned and severe but are actually pathics. Usually this severity takes the form of a pretense of being a Stoic philosopher (cf. *AP* 11.155, 157).[46] The hypocrisy of such a sham excites both Martial and Juvenal to orgies of disgusted and hilarious exposure, as if the thought that an especially virile-looking man might be eager for anal penetration was particularly fascinating to both them and their audience. The physical stereotype of the hypocritical Stoic bears a strong resemblance to Martial's portrait of himself in 10.65. One of his poems against the false Stoics, while it does not stress the hypocrisy angle, illustrates a major perceived difference between *cinaedi* (both open and hypocritical) and a "real man" (7.58):

> Iam sex aut septem nupsisti, Galla, cinaedis,
> dum coma te nimium pexaque barba iuvat.
> deinde, experta latus madidoque simillima loro
> inguina nec lassa stare coacta manu,
> deseris inbelles thalamos mollemque maritum,
> rursus et in similes decidis usque toros.
> quaere aliquem Curios semper Fabiosque loquentem,
> hirsutum et dura rusticitate trucem:
> invenies: sed habet tristis quoque turba cinaedos:
> difficile est vero nubere, Galla, viro.

> Already you have married six or seven fags, Galla,
> while [long] hair and a combed beard please you excessively.
> Finally, when you've experienced their flanks and their groins
> most like a wet thong, nor made to stand by your weary hand,
> you leave unwarlike bedrooms and a soft husband,
> and you fall all over again into the same kind of bed.
> Look for some man always talking of the Curii and Fabii,
> shaggy and savage, with harsh country manners:
> you'll find him: but the somber crowd also has its fags:
> it's difficult to marry a real man, Galla.

Here the trait that makes *cinaedi* unsatisfactory husbands is impotence, presumably the opposite of what Martial assumes in a "real man." The *cinaedi* have well-kept long hair and beard; they are soft *(molles)* and unwarlike (*imbelles*, a term that must apply both to their lovemaking and their way of life), like their beds (*toros* = "cushions")—and their genitals. Once again, the genitalia represent the man. On the other hand, the seemingly "real" man speaks of the Curii and Fabii (as opposed to being *imbellis*) and has unkempt hair and manners, which apparently go with being a proper husband. Yet "Galla" finds her series of effeminate husbands attractive and has to be directed toward men of a sterner stamp; in fact, a few jokes in Martial depend on the reverse of the hypocritical Stoic idea—namely, that men who seem effeminate are really adulterers.[47] Martial's perception of effeminates is thus not monolithic; he expresses varying ideas of what effeminate behavior means, as it suits him, while his only strong, consistent aim is to differentiate effeminacy from virility and from the persona of the poet.

It seems reasonable to suppose that epigrams were generally popular, what with Martial's many books, the Greek anthologies, and suggestions of other, lost collections. Not only was there an audience for them, it was even fashionable or chic to write them, according to Pliny's apology (above, chapter 1); well-known and distinguished Romans from the time of Catullus to Pliny's own day took pride in their ability to turn a neat and racy distich. Pliny's point that this included all the best people as well as the riffraff of literati, snobbish as it is, is a valuable bit of information, if only because it shows how epigram permeated even the top levels of Roman society. Only elegance of wording separates these epigrams from the graffiti distichs. Epigram, of course, provided an ideal setting for *sententiae* and neat or ingeniously contrived ideas; the same epigram could be written over and over, with new twists. An age that doted on rhetoric, educated in the *scholae*, must have found in epigram a perfect form of elegant recreation; the breaking up of the book into short, unrelated poems, each encapsuling a fragment of beauty, wit, or squalor, was highly congenial to the post-Augustan and rhetorical tendency to diffracted structure. And men accustomed to political lampoons might have enjoyed making an art form of them.

Still, although everyone considered these poems to be amusements, and although the Romans, proud or not, thought of them as *nugae*, it seems a pity that Martial and others devoted a whole career to them. It is true that the composite picture offered by Martial's poems is a more complete portrait of contemporary Rome than even that of Juvenal's satires; his erotic and invective poems, taken together, afford an irreplaceable spectrum of the sexual attitudes found only piecemeal in other authors, and it would be hard to see clearly how it all fits together without the evidence of Martial. But the poems themselves are unsatisfying, soulless—even the graffiti and political lampoons produced by soldiers and nameless loiterers have more life in them. The whole genre is a curiosity; the noninvective sorts of epigram are so different one from another, while invective epigram itself as written by Martial is nothing but the elevation of street invective to a level of abstraction higher than that of satire. The narrator is abstract and omniscient or, if identified with the author, appears only fleetingly. The victims are effigies.

Priapic poetry, invective against old women, and invective epigram taken together add to the evidence already seen in oral invective demonstrating that sexual invective has more than sexual implications. The main victims of sexual invective—women, old women, and pathic homosexuals—represent by their sexual behavior the social behavior that the narrator wishes to dissociate from himself. Presumably this is one reason for the blanking out of lesbianism from Roman literature: lesbians are perceived, as in Martial, as fake men, and a female Priapus makes an uncomfortable stereotype. In political invective an attacker might accuse his male opponent of effeminacy or his female opponent of promiscuity; he means not only to shame the opponent but to assert his power over him or her. The phallus is the source of both interpersonal dominance and sexual mastery, as at Hor. *S.* 1.2.44, where the servants punish the adulterer by urinating upon him; the penis contains and ejects both urine and semen, stain and seed.[48] Conversely, Priapus threatens rape, a sexual punishment, against thieves, committers of a nonsexual crime that yet infringes on Priapus' property. Sexual threat is thus a metaphor for assertion of a questioned dominance over personal property. This dynamic underlies the audience's enjoyment of invective poetry, since (as has been shown) the main thing the audience enjoys here is the invective for its own sake; to enjoy such poetry, the reader must pick up the feeling in the invective (hostile threat or rejection) and translate it into his own experience, identifying it with his own similar feelings, which may or may not have sexual targets. This dynamic also produces one of the main frameworks in the poetry of a man who used it with originality, consistency, and brilliance—Catullus.

A second aspect of Priapus, and one that was seen to be puzzling in its use by Martial and others, is his status as a ridiculous god, a god to be mocked—something of a contradiction in terms. He is the source of threats, god of the phallus, yet he is also a shabby wooden idol to whom poets give ridiculous speeches (as in Hor. *S.* 1.8, for an early example). In him Zeus' ψολόεις κεραυνός is transformed into the ψωλή. This ambiguity in Priapus' status parallels an important line of thought in satire, the questioning of the gods' relations with man—a question that, among the Romans, was most insistently put by Ovid.

APPENDIX: The Date and Authorship of the *Carmina Priapea*

The most sustained attempt at assigning a provenance to the *Priapea* is that of Vinzenz Buchheit (*Studien zum Corpus Priapeorum*, Munich 1962 = *Zetemata* 28), who argues for single authorship on the basis of the stylistic unity and the content of *Pr.* 1 and 2, which he compares most pertinently with the double-barreled opening of Strato's *Musa Puerilis*. He then counters the evidence that the *Priapea* is an anthology, most notably the title in the oldest manuscript, *Diversorum auctorum Priapeia*, and the apparent attribution of *Pr.* 3 to Ovid by the elder Seneca. (Buchheit is unwilling to attribute the whole *Priapea* to Ovid, which means he cannot accept Seneca's attribution. He also rightly observes that the poems share words and themes with Catullus and Martial as well as with Ovid, but this does not indicate anything about authorship one way or the other.)

It is hard to believe that Ovid, whose bibliography was subjected to such a lurid glare in his own lifetime, is responsible for the *Priapea*, but it is much harder to dissociate him from *Pr.* 3. In fact, the attribution of *Pr.* 3 to Ovid is the key to the question of single or multiple authorship of the *Priapea*, and arguments against it are not strong. Buchheit suggests simply that Seneca's words, *Ovidianum illud inepta loci* (for the passage in full, see above), are quoting a line from a poem by Ovid now lost. This is not convincing, although Scaurus' odd choice of words to quote seems to support it: as noted above, *loci* does not really depend on *inepta*.[1] Perhaps there was a lost poem of Ovid in which the two words appeared together, syntactically connected, and *Pr.* 3 reuses them, though breaking the connection. But the context in Seneca demands that the line be an elliptical reference to anal intercourse with women, especially between husband and wife. And *Pr.* 3

concerns the practice, or fantasy, in which a bride allows anal intercourse on her wedding night out of fear for the "wound" of her maidenhead. If there was a lost poem of Ovid, it must have been on exactly the same subject as *Pr.* 3; but poems that imitate wording generally change the context, and vice versa. To allow Buchheit's hypothesis, it would have to be admitted that Ovid had written a poem containing the words *inepta loci* in a context that Scaurus cleverly applied to his *controversia*, and that these words were also picked up by the author of the *Priapea* and reused in the same context in which Scaurus had used them. It seems much more probable that Scaurus was in fact quoting *Pr.* 3 and that Seneca believed Ovid to have written the poem.

Thus the *Priapea* can be taken to have been written by a single author only if that author is Ovid. Other improbabilities aside, it is certainly unlikely that Ovid wrote *Pr.* 80 (see above), which is a rather nasty parody of *Am.* 3.7.1–2. If not 80, then perhaps not others. But, in any case, the poems in the *Priapea* are uneven in quality (cf., e.g., 1 and 2 with the very awkward 24), and an attribution of the whole to Ovid is not at all convincing.

The third possibility, that the poems are a collection made during or after Ovid's lifetime—the old standard theory, dismissed by Buchheit (pp. 14–15)—thus remains at least as strong as Buchheit's theory. His argument that *Pr.* 1 and 2 demonstrate the poems to have been written by a single author is a stronger one—not on the grounds of stylistic consistency (the fact that two poems have similar structures is surely no proof that they were written by the same poet—though it is often used to show that one poem is an imitation of another) but simply because of the content of *Pr.* 2, which says plainly, "ludens haec . . . carmina . . . scripsi non nimium laboriose," "playing at these poems, I have written none too carefully" (lines 1–3), and further, "quicquid id est quod otiosus / templi parietibus tui notavi," "whatever it is that, at my leisure, I have marked on the walls of your temple" (lines 9–10). This, certainly, as an introductory poem, seems to refer to the rest of the poems in the collection and to claim authorship for them; attempts to refer *ludens*, *scripsi*, and *notavi* to the act of anthologizing strain the Latin. And most introductions to anthologies elaborate on the art of collection and the process of selection (*AP* 4.1, 4.2, 12.256 and 257), as Buchheit notes (p. 23, n. 1). As Buchheit also notes, it would be strange to move directly from an assertion of authorship in *Pr.* 2 to a poem by Ovid in *Pr.* 3 if Ovid is not the author. On the other hand, *Pr.* 49 is certainly an introductory poem (contra Buchheit, p. 13, n. 3); what is it doing in the middle of the book?

But this is not the only oddity. Why is there no attribution, no ancient reference to the book, and (if it is an anthology) no attributions of individual poems? Even the editors of the *Greek Anthology* preserved the labels on their myriad epigrams as best they could, although the labels are surely the most fragile part of the poem. The total lack of credible attribution may well mean that the book originally appeared without one; or perhaps the wide late attribution to Vergil (Buchheit, p. 15; cf. p. 66, n. 2) is in fact the original one, and the book was brought out under Vergil's name, which might have served double duty as pseudonym and shield.

Cultural considerations (the vogue for Priapus in the late Republic and early Empire)[2] and a stylistic consideration (the simplicity of the poems' structure and their lack of syntactical ornamentation) would seem to place the collection early, or perhaps during the revival of Atticism that began under Nero. One hypothetical scenario would be that Ovid was the editor (*Pr.* 80 is believable as a joke taken in good part) and that the collection was unfinished when he left the country and was brought out after he departed, but anonymously—perhaps under a pseudonym that included the fiction of single authorship. A less glamorous possibility is that the book came out at another time of moral rectitude in high places, the reign of Vespasian, or even of Trajan. It would have formed part of the series of anthologies and collected works that included the *Garland* of Meleager (ca. 90 B.C.), the *Garland* of Philip (mid-first century A.D.), the poems of Martial (late first century A.D.), and the *Musa Puerilis* of Strato (?Hadrian). There must have been many other such works, now lost, at the time, as witness the survival of the Neronians Lucillius and Nicarchus in the *Greek Anthology*.

The fact remains that the poems cannot be dated. They tell little of the circumstances in which they were written and have no references to identifiable people (perhaps another sign of troubled times); the only datable thing about them is (perhaps) a fragment of *Pr.* 3. Since the attribution of *Pr.* 3 to Ovid is so difficult to decide, and this presents a stumbling block to speculation, perhaps the question of the date is best abandoned, except to note the close relationship between the *Priapea* and Catullus, Ovid, and Martial. That interrelationship, at least, is certain and in itself illuminating.

CHAPTER 6 Catullus, Ovid, and the Art of Mockery

That invective need not be soulless is evident from the number of great Roman writers who made it their métier. For the satirists, invective formed a basic element of the genre, one that provided the genre with not only content but structure—attacker, victim, audience. But an even more elemental strain in invective, the specifics of Priapic threat and the desire to degrade, provided material for two highly individualistic poets who cannot be classified as satirists: Catullus and Ovid. Indeed, it is hard to classify them at all; but sexual themes were important for both of them, both made invective or mockery a major part of their poetic art, and they in turn served as models for many who came after them.

Catullus

Catullus stands at the height of an era, a creator of highly sophisticated personal verse in an age that valued individualism. Yet his Alexandrianism was something of a fad, something he shared with a select erudite few; he can give the impression of being *lepidus* always, polished and witty. It is difficult to find a poem of his that is not constructed with perfect elegance; then again, the poems ring with vitality, and a great many depend on ideas or images that are not elegant at all. Out of all the polymetrics and epigrams, sixty-two—well over half—include invective or sexual material, some of the coarsest in Latin verse. Quintilian was no more than accurate in describing Catullus as a poet in the iambic manner (10.1.96).[1]

The first thing that stands out in Catullus' invective and sexual poems is how many are concerned with theft and are framed as threats against a person who has stolen or might steal something of Catullus'. Of approximately forty invective poems, ten excoriate thieves of one sort or another,[2] while several others threaten sexual rivals of the poet or people who have been unfaithful to their lovers.[3] Some of the poems complain of the theft of quite commonplace things—money, table napkins, notebooks. Most of these are similar in tone to the poems against thieves of love: the girl who has taken Catullus' notebooks is a *putida moecha* (42), while the faithless Lesbia is reduced to the activities of a street whore (58); the man who has taken Catullus' bric-a-brac is a *cinaedus* of hyperbolic effeminacy (25) whom Catullus will "scrawl" with lashes, while he will punish Lesbia's lovers by irrumating them (making pathics of them) and scrawling all over the housefront (37).

The similarity between this attitude and that of the god in the Priapic poems is evident and close. Most significant in this regard are Catullus' threats to irrumate Lesbia's lovers, combined with other suggestions that their virility is questionable or will be forced to submit to his own (cf. 74); his threats to irrumate or otherwise rape men who would take his boy; and the sort of insults he directs against women, as being whorish or physically repulsive. All these poses are characteristic of the persona of Priapus, who is particularly concerned to keep thieves out of his garden and who does so by means of rape, or threats of rape. In addition, the bipolar perception of women as either beloved or ugly and sluttish is typical of Priapic invective against women and seems to reflect the options of the potentially aroused male, to accept or reject a woman as sexually worthy.[4]

Yet Catullus bases another group of poems on the reverse of this attitude; in them he decries others who adopt a Priapic pose. Sometimes he sneers at a Priapic figure, like the domineering and niggardly commander Piso (*verpus . . . Priapus*, 47.4); sometimes the poet himself is the victim, as when he describes his irrumation by Memmius (28.9–10).[5] In the famous poem against Caesar and Pompey (29), they are both protectors and dupes of Mamurra; they are addressed successively with the words *cinaede Romule, haec videbis et feres*,[6] while Mamurra = *mentula* (29.13). Catullus' anti-Priapic stance produces the whole series of poems against Mamurra under the name of Mentula (94, 105, 114, 115; cf. 57)[7] as well as less specifically antiphallic epigrams against sexual profligacy, especially the series against "Gellius" (80, 88, 89, 90, 91), although the description of Gellius' penchant for fellatio in 80 amounts to an irrumation of him by the poet. Catullus portrays himself as victim less often than as master, but he finds the counter-Priapic stance useful for showing his enemies as brutes; he adopts a similar pose when depicting himself as brutally injured by Lesbia, for example, at the end of 11, when he compares himself to a flower (normally associated with brides) cut down by a plow (normally a phallic image) at the meadow's edge.[8]

Thus Catullus' two poses: in one he espouses the brutal, violent attitude of Priapus toward a world composed of his own garden and of thieves subject to rape; in the reverse, Catullus finds it useful to decry the Priapism of others. Mamurra, for instance, nicknamed Mentula, is typified by lust for money (29), land (114–15), other men's wives (57, 94), and poetic fame (105), all of which are goods defended by Catullus when he himself plays the part of Priapus. Nowhere is the ambivalence of this schema, and Catullus' consciousness of it, clearer than in 16, a poem that explains his attitude toward all his sexual poetry.

Pedicabo ego vos et irrumabo,
Aureli pathice et cinaede Furi,
qui me ex versiculis meis putastis,
quod sunt molliculi, parum pudicum.
nam castum esse decet pium poetam
ipsum, versiculos nihil necesse est;
qui tum denique habent salem ac leporem,
si sunt molliculi ac parum pudici,
et quod pruriat incitare possunt,
non dico pueris, sed his pilosis
qui duros nequeunt movere lumbos.
vos, quod milia multa basiorum
legistis, male me marem putatis?
pedicabo ego vos et irrumabo.

I will bugger you and I will fuck your mouths,
Aurelius, you pathic, and you queer, Furius,
who have thought me, from my little verses,
because they are a little delicate, to be not quite straight.
For it is proper for a pious poet to be chaste
himself, but there is no need for his little verses to be so;
which only then have wit and charm,
if they are a little delicate and not too clean,
and can arouse a lewd itching,
I don't mean in boys, but in these hairy men
who can't move a hard groin.
You, because you have read "many thousands
of kisses," think me not quite a man?
I will bugger you and I will fuck your mouths.

His verses themselves are *molliculi* (lines 4, 8); like pathics, *cinaedi*, they (as it were) waggle their asses at the reader (*parum pudici*, line 8; cf. Cat. 1.1–2) and cause the reader to become aroused (lines 9–11). And like the agile dancing girls (cf. *Pr.* 19.4–5, Mart. 6.71, 14.203), they can arouse even the impotent; they appeal even to males usually pathic—"hairy men" who are not sexually able (cf. Martial's Stoic/pathics). On the other hand, the meretricious nature of his lines (a joke) and, what is more serious, the vulnerability of his proclamations of love (lines 12–13) do not imply that he himself is not fully virile (*parum pudicum*, line 4; *male . . . marem*, line 13); and so he threatens his putative critics with both the rape Priapus reserves for youths and the rape he reserves for older men (lines 1, 14) and calls them *pathice* and *cinaede* (line 2). His direct address to Aurelius and Furius both shows the humorous intent of the whole poem and recalls the appearance of Furius and Aurelius as companions of the poet in his most vulnerable moment (11).[9]

Catullus' direct address to Furius and Aurelius in 16 is also typical of his invective poetry as a whole. The invective poems tend to fall into verbal patterns, most common of which is the beginning with direct address of the victim by name, often introducing a question or series of questions. Two closely related techniques are the satiric dialogue, as in the two dialogues with prostitutes (10, 42; cf. 55), and the use of rhetorical questions. This pattern helps to make the poem lively, especially since the reader finds himself in the position of the victim; the reader is simultaneously confronted with the vocative case, which identifies him with the victim, and reassured by the naming of a specific other person who is the "real" victim. As a literary technique this has many relatives in other genres.[10] But its liveliness surely derives from one of its less respectable family connections, as will be seen (for example) from the following, the beginning of 88:

> Quid facit is, Gelli, qui cum matre atque sorore
> prurit et abiectis pervigilat tunicis?
> quid facit is, patruum qui non sinit esse maritum?

> What does a man do, Gellius, who itches with lust with his mother
> and sister, and stays up all night with underwear cast aside?
> What does a man do, who doesn't let his uncle be a husband?

The pattern of damaging question and obvious answer (unspoken by the poet) is the same as that adopted by the claqueurs who were Catullus' contemporaries, in fact, by the hateful Clodius himself.[11] As noted above, both Plutarch and Cicero describe the taunts with which Clodius vexed Pompey. An eyewitness account (Cic. *QFr.* 2.3.2):

> versus denique obscenissimi in Clodium et Clodiam dicerentur. Ille furens et exsanguis interrogabat suos in clamore ipso quis esset qui plebem fame necaret. Respondebant operae: "Pompeius." Quis Alexandriam ire cuperet. Respondebant: "Pompeius." Quem ire vellent. Respondebant: "Crassum."

> finally, the most obscene verses against Clodius and Clodia were recited. So he, raving and pale, put questions to his own supporters, in the midst of this uproar: "Who was it who was killing the people by starvation?" The claque answered: "Pompey!" "Who wanted to go to Alexandria?" They answered: "Pompey!" "Whom did they want to go?" They answered: "Crassus!"

According to Plutarch, the catechism was not always so political in its subject matter but made insinuations about Pompey's effeminacy. The technique of forcing the audience into participation in an obscene dialogue is also similar to the workings of graffiti, in which the passerby is forced to see invective addressed either to another victim or to any passerby. The crudest type of invective in

Catullus' poetry, name calling (e.g., 25), resembles verbal abuse even more than it resembles graffiti and is closely related to the sort of face-to-face confrontation of billingsgate which was so common a political event in Catullus' Rome.

In turn, it seems possible that the false names assigned by Catullus to some of his addressees evolve out of a sophistication of this penchant for name calling, that is, renaming the victim. The pleasure derived from this name substitution is the same as that derived from riddles, where the addressee has to identify a person or object by several absurdly connected attributes, and the technique was one of which colloquial Latin was fond.[12] The substitution of "Mentula," "Prick," for the name "Mamurra" is the prime example in Catullus, and he makes the name/thing/name connection explicitly in 115.8, "non homo sed vero mentula magna minax"—"Not a man, but truly a big bad prick." Such riddles and word games can be found in Priapic poetry (7, 54, 67) and in epigram (e.g., Martial's identification of Philaenis with a phallus, 2.33).[13] (In contrast, the poet's own name recurs again and again, undistorted, insistent, and upstage.) The other famous name substitution in Catullus is that of Lesbia for Clodia, with its literary and Hellenizing resonances; but the substitution of Lesbius for Clodius (79) can hardly have been meant to be complimentary. Considering the scabrous nature of most of Catullus' invective, it is only surprising that more of his victims are not addressed by obviously fictitious names; presumably a man who felt no inhibitions in castigating Caesar and Pompey was not hindered by other social scruples.

Other characteristics of Catullus' invective poetry are not peculiar to him. With all writers of Latin invective he shares a preoccupation with smell and disgusting physical details, and a loathing of pathic homosexuality, prostitutes, oral sex (he barely mentions cunnilingus [?frag. 2]), and excrement, especially feces. In his descriptions of prostitutes and sordid sexual intercourse he does return to one special image, that of the streets and alleyways: Lesbia's lovers are *semitarii moechi*, "back-street adulterers" (37.16), while she debases herself *in quadriviis et angiportis*, "in the crossroads and alleyways" (58.4), and other prostitutes are encountered in the city streets (10, ?42.7–9, 55.6–7).

But in combining food, sex, excreta, money, and literary fame[14] into a series of connected, reverberant images, Catullus puts his own stamp on one of the main complexes of Latin invective. The relation between eating and depravity is general in Roman culture as reflected in literature, as for example in the distaste for the *popina* (e.g., Lucil. 11 Marx; Hor. *Epist.* 1.14.21; Juv. 8.171–82), a sort of lower-class restaurant, and in the normal association of dinner parties and feasting with sexual activity. And the hungry parasite is a constant figure of fun in Roman comedy, who hopes for a meal as his patron hopes for a girl, and who occasionally has a quasi-sexual name, like Peniculus in the *Menaechmi*. On this simplest level, Catullus connects his good feeling of satiety with readiness for violent, active penetration, in the Ipsitilla poem (32.7–11): the poet describes himself as both *pransus*, "having eaten," and *satur*, "full," while his penis is aggressively erect (line

11). The same sort of sexual and material gluttony is what the poet deplores in his enemies, as in 29, where Mamurra commits infinite adulteries (lines 6–8) and steals infinite amounts of money (lines 14, 17–20, 22); Catullus combines the three ideas of money, sex, and food throughout poem 29, as in lines 13–14:

> ut ista vestra diffututa mentula
> ducenties comesset aut trecenties?
>
> so that that fucked-out prick of yours
> may eat up two or three hundred thou?

Mamurra (with those who tolerate him) is *impudicus* ("promiscuous"), *vorax* ("hungry"; cf. *devorare patrimonia*, line 22; *vorax adulter*, 57.8), and *aleo* ("a gambler"); that is, they all have excessive appetites for sex, food, and money. Conversely, lack of money equals unsatisfied hunger, as in 28 (*famem*, line 5) and 47, where Catullus attacks Porcius, Socration, and Piso (*fames mundi*, line 2; *verpus . . . Priapus*, line 4), who unjustly have "elegant feasts" (*convivia lauta*, line 5), while Catullus' friends Veranius and Fabullus are outside *in trivio*, "at the fork in the road" (line 7), the place of the outcast.

At the same time, the abuse of enemies is both sexual and oral. This is carried to an extreme in 108, where Cominius, his "old age befouled by unclean morals" (an insinuation of sexual perversion, oral [cf. 99.10] or anal), will be torn apart by the mob and the various parts of his body given as food to wild animals—first of all, his "tongue, enemy of good men" (*inimica bonorum / lingua*, lines 3–4). Memmius irrumates Catullus (28.9–10), who is here *supinus* as he was in 32; likewise the master of Veranius and Fabullus abuses them by "stuffing" them (*farti estis*, 28.13) with his penis (insultingly specified as a circumcised one [*verpa*], line 12). Similarly, when Aurelius seduces Catullus' *puer*, Catullus calls Aurelius *pater esuritionum*, "father of hungers" (21.1; cf. Furius in 23) and complains he not only wants to "bugger" the boy (*pedicare*, line 4) but is teaching the boy to "be hungry and thirsty" (*esurire / . . . et sitire*, lines 10–11). The sexual dimension of this brings in Catullus, who says he will irrumate Aurelius (line 8), that is, will fill his mouth for him (emphasizing the sexual element in the anal/oral "hunger" Aurelius was teaching the boy); if Aurelius were *satur*, "full," Catullus "would be silent" (*tacerem*), line 9.

Irrumation, logically, forces the victims to be silent as well, as in the absurd double entendre in 74 (lines 5–6, "quamvis irrumet ipsum / nunc patruum, verbum non faciet patruus," "though he should fuck his uncle's own mouth, his uncle wouldn't say a word"—naturally). Hence the special applicability of Catullus' threat to irrumate his critics in 16. The sexual/oral/verbal threat is most fully worked out in 116, which has been recognized as programmatic.[15] Here Catullus says he has tried to "soften" (*lenirem*, line 3) Gellius, so that he would not "send hostile missiles against my head" ("tela infesta ⟨meum⟩ mittere in usque caput," line 4); *tela* = poems, but *tela . . . mittere . . . in . . . caput* is also a recognizable double entendre for *irrumare*, as in the claim attributed to Julius Caesar (Suet. *Iul.* 22), "insultaturum omnium capitibus," "that he would abuse the heads of all." Catullus concludes 116 by warning Gellius that punishment in kind awaits him, "at fixus nostris tu dabis supplicium," "but pierced by mine you will undergo your punishment" (line 8)—strongly recalling the structure of the threat in 21 (lines 7–13) and the wording of 15, which also threatens Aurelius:

> ut nostrum insidiis caput lacessas 16
> ....
> quem attractis pedibus patente porta 18
> percurrent raphanique mugilesque.
>
> that you should beat me about the head with your ambuscades
> ....
> [you] whom, with your door open and your feet drawn apart,
> horseradishes and mullets will run through and through.

As Catullus threatens to "scrawl" a beating on the effeminate Thallus (25) and to draw phalli on Lesbia's house (37.10), so in 116.8 *nostris* = weapons = poems = phallus.

This identification in turn may help to explain another facet of Catullus' oral imagery: his focus on the mouths of his beloved and of his enemies, and the way he degrades those of his enemies. Catullus' best known poems are those in which he counts the kisses of his lovers, both Lesbia (5, 7) and Juventius (48; cf. 99); even here he contrasts these sweet things with the *mala lingua*, "bad tongue," of the world (7.12). Juventius' kisses are compared with food: honey (48.1), wheat (48.5), ambrosia (99.2). But in his invective Catullus consistently insults enemies and rivals by assimilating their mouths to excretory orifices. The objectionable Egnatius, a frequenter of Lesbia's house in 37, brushes his teeth with urine (37.20), specified as his own at 39.18–19; but Catullus takes this further, saying Egnatius' white teeth show "hoc te amplius bibisse . . . loti," "how much more piss you've drunk." In other words, Egnatius not only deliberately washes out his mouth with urine, he ingests urine. This, foul enough in itself, also connotes oral-genital contact, as in 99, where Juventius wipes off Catullus' kiss "as if [it were] the foul saliva of a pissed-on whore" (*tamquam commictae spurca saliva lupae*, line 10)—a phrase which here implies that the woman's mouth is tainted because she performs fellatio. It seems probable, on this basis, that at least for Catullus, the foulness of the *os impurum* stems from the contact between mouth and penis as outlet for urine.

Similarly, in 97.2 Catullus says there is no difference between Aemilius' mouth (*os*) and buttocks (*culum*; here = *podex*); the mouth looks and smells like a *ploxenum* (possibly a basket used to carry night soil,[16] lines 5–6), or like the vagina of a mule in heat urinating (lines 7–8). Catullus derides Aemilius' plentiful intercourse with women (line 9) and claims that any woman who would have sexual intercourse with him would be willing to "lick the ass of a sick hangman" (*aegroti culum lingere carnificis*, line 12). Again, Catullus creates an image of a thoroughly revolting mouth, but by likening the mouth to excretory orifices also used sexually (*culus*, *cunnus*—here made to stand for the whole crotch), he suggests this function for Aemilius' mouth as well. An image that supports this connection, and unites it with the sex/hunger/property complex discussed earlier, is the description (33.4) of the thief "Vibennius filius" as *culo . . . voraciore*, "with a hungrier ass." A similar case is that of "Rufa" in 59, who is not only a *fellatrix* (line 1) but frequents graveyards (line 2), like the lowest prostitutes (cf. Mart. 1.34, Juv. 6.O.15–16), and eats bread she steals from funeral offerings (lines 3–4), for which she is beaten or raped by the (untouchable) undertaker's man (line 5). The things stolen from Catullus (money, tableware, notebooks) now seem significantly connected.

In this respect as well, the verbal function of the mouth connects with the derided function: Victius (98), one of the "wordy and stupid" (*verbosis . . . et fatuis*, line 2), could "lick asses and creaking gum boots with that tongue of yours" (*ista cum lingua . . . culos et crepidas lingere carpatinas*, line 4). The soiled mouth is like the irrumated mouth: mouth (speaker/eater) = anus = receptacle for the Priapic phallus. This in turn suggests that the epithet of the famous *cacata carta* of 36 denotes not only their worthlessness but the anal/oral receptivity of their author. Conversely, in 16 Catullus selects *milia multa basiorum* to represent all the poetry he wishes to defend.

Catullus' sexual and invective poems can be divided into several categories, some overlapping.[17] One group of rather lighthearted poems might be labeled "sympotic," since all have to do with dinner parties or friendly meetings. In these poems the element of threat is minimal, and the sexuality is usually jolly. Most innocuous is 45, the Acmen and Septimius poem, redeemed from Hellenistic saccharinity by its tongue-in-cheek air. Likewise 13, the invitation to a nonexistent feast, makes no threat worse than that of forcing the guest to provide the food, while the poet's loving mistress provides perfume; the essential kindness of such a poem is exemplified by the positioning of a similar one in the choral resolution of *Lysistrata*.[18] Poems 6 and 55 both address a friend suspected of a secret liaison; 6 adduces the evidence of Flavius' groaning and spavined bed,[19] while 55 describes a search through the city during which the poet had to interview the streetwalkers in order to find his friend. In these poems the suggestion of sexuality is coarse but jocular; Catullus creates a similar tone in 10, in which he has a long conversation with a woman. While she flatters him, his estimation of her goes up; when she makes him out a liar, he begins to think of her as a whore. Here the poet's interaction with the woman becomes that of an adversary, so that he is in a position to threaten her. The most threatening poem in this sympotic context is 32, to

Ipsitilla, in which the poet begins by flattering and cajoling the girl to come to him, and ends with a violent image of sexual readiness, similar to the wording of several Priapic poems:

> sed domi maneas paresque nobis
> novem continuas fututiones
> ....
> nam pransus iaceo et satur supinus
> pertundo tunicamque palliumque.
>
> but stay home and prepare for me
> nine fuckings in a row
> ....
> For I lie here, having dined, and full, flat on my back,
> I'm poking through my shorts and my trousers.

The invective poems against Lesbia (11, 37, [39], 58, [79]) share the double attitude of 32, in which the poet first pleads and then threatens. In 11 and 58 the poet appeals to his friends, in 11 with beautiful imagery, in 58 with touching *geminatio* of Lesbia's name; then he blasts Lesbia for acting like the cheapest sort of prostitute.[20] In 11 he concludes with a sad image of himself struck down by her. Poem 37 consists entirely of castigation of Lesbia as a whore and threats to irrumate her myriad lovers; the staining of Egnatius' mouth in 39 is only a refinement of this. Catullus' attitude here is considerably different from that in the noninvective poems in the Lesbia cycle, in which he views Lesbia's personality and his own reactions to her on many different levels.

The Juventius poems and the invective associated with them demonstrate an important difference from the cycle about Lesbia.[21] It is not so much that the feelings Catullus expresses for Juventius (24, 48, 81, 99) cover a narrower range than those in the poems about Lesbia. True, Catullus shows few sides of Juventius' personality, and Juventius is like the boys of epigram—pretty, coy, and fickle; but still, Juventius, like Lesbia, is beloved. The difference lies in the invective poems: there are many threats against those who would seduce Juventius (15, 21; perhaps 40), but these poems never blame Juventius or suggest that he is sluttish for going off with these men. The only poems that show any malice toward a *puer* are 106[22] and the enigmatic 56. In comparison with the Juventius poems, it seems best to understand the *puer* of 56 as the male equivalent of Ipsitilla, since the tone of jolly savagery is the same as in 32; Catullus does not write of Lesbia as he does of Ipsitilla, likewise the *puer* in 56 is not likely to have been conceived to be Juventius.[23]

An enormous list of poems remain that seemingly have little in common but their invective. These fall into several groups; perhaps only because of our lack of information, some of the poems seem less "real" than others, seem to be attacking types or effigies rather than victims with individual personalities. Some poems against men—69 on Rufus' smell, 71 against an unnamed rival, 78 on Gallus, 97 on Aemilius' smell, 98 on Victius', and 112 on Naso's perversion—demonstrate this quality. The victims are described in the filthiest terms—tongue identified with anus, mouth identified with the vagina of a urinating mule, mouth identified with the anus of a diseased hangman—but they have no other identity, at least in Catullus' poems. Although attempts have been made to identify them, and although all have common Roman names, it is possible that all the names are false; some, like "Rufus" (cf. 59; also Catullus' friend Caelius), "Gallus" (= "eunuch"), and "Naso" (= "Nose-man"), have the ring of *redender Namen*. If these were real people against whom Catullus was expressing his hate, they are unidentifiable. The same is true of the poems against guests who have acted as thieves (25, 33). The old man of Colonia (17)[24] and the incestuous family behind the talking door (67) are laden with concrete but nonspecific details, and several women remain mysterious. Is the Ameana attacked in 41 and 43 really Mamurra's mistress? Who is the Rufa attacked so violently in 59, immediately after the worst attack on Lesbia? Are the pimp Silo (103) and the girl Aufillena, attacked in 110 and 111, stereotypical sexual figures like Ipsitilla in 32? All these figures have in common the poet's hatred and contempt for them, and his feeling that they have cheated him or someone else. They are attacked occasionally for things they have done outside the context of the poem, but the circumstances are usually so trivial as to do little to reinforce the victim's personality (what made the girl in 42 keep, or take, Catullus' *codicilli*, and what exactly were they?). It is as if the poet is writing only for those who know the daily history of his life. Some of the victims, especially the men, are attacked in such primitive invective that they and their crimes fade into the background: such are the list invectives in 23 (against one of Catullus' close friends) and 25, and the scatological/homosexual taunts of 33, 69, 71, 97, 98, and 112. The content of some of these poems amounts to a stream of vituperation and primary obscenities, beautifully structured.

The impression of deliberate obscurity presented by these poems is the more marked in comparison with the other invective poems, which attack famous people by name, with scurrilous details. The most noted, and the ones that caused the greatest furor at the time, were the poems against Mamurra,[25] both the cycle in which he is labeled *Mentula* (94, 105, 114, 115) and the poems linking him to Caesar and Pompey (29, 57). Caesar and Pompey are further ridiculed in 54 and 113; other victims include the historian Volusius (36), the politician Cominius (108), and the military leaders Memmius and Piso (28, 47). Not only are these men attacked for specific vices and crimes closely tied to their public activities; they are all the same kind of men—important politicians and generals who abuse their wealth and power. In return for this Catullus paints them as, at one and the same time, pederasts, cuckolds, adulterers, rapists, pathics, effeminates, boors, gluttons, and good-for-nothings, a sublime exchange between poetry and politics. The freedom that was allowed to him by these men, and that he allowed to himself, stands in startling contrast to the practices of later satirists.

The high topicality of these poems and of the Lesbia poems that touch so closely on the notorious Clodia and Clodius seems to extend to the cycle against Gellius (74, 80, 88–91), another member of the Roman nobility being excoriated for his sins against Catullus.[26] The whole phenomenon recalls E. F. Benson's depiction of society caricature:

> He was working hard, he had told her, to finish his little gallery of caricatures with which he annually regaled London, and which was to open in a fortnight. He was a licensed satirist, and all London always flocked to his show to observe with glee what he made of them all, and what witty and pungent little remarks he affixed to their monstrous effigies. It was a distinct cachet, too, to be caricatured by him, a sign that you attracted attention and were a notable figure. He might (in fact, he always did) make you a perfect guy, and his captions invariably made fun of something characteristic, but it gave you publicity. She wondered whether he would take a commission: she wondered whether he might be induced to do a caricature of Peppino or herself or of them both, at a handsome price, with the proviso that it was to be on view at his exhibition.[27]

There are many shades of sophistication and relation to real circumstances in Catullus' invective; this is not to say that the more elemental invective is worse poetry. On the contrary, it is among the best constructed and most vivid poetry Catullus wrote, with its air of magical incantation; for example, 25 has a grotesque beauty which the more specific poems lose by their very circumstantiality:

Cinaede Thalle, mollior cuniculi capillo
vel anseris medullula vel imula oricilla
vel pene languido senis situque araneoso
idemque, Thalle, turbida rapacior procella,
cum diva †mulier aries† ostendit oscitantes,
remitte pallium mihi meum quod involasti,
sudariumque Saetabum catagraphosque Thynos,
inepte, quae palam soles habere tamquam avita.
quae nunc tuis ab unguibus reglutina et remitte,
ne laneum latusculum manusque mollicellas
inusta turpiter tibi flagella conscribillent
et insolenter aestues, velut minuta magno
deprensa navis in mari, vesaniente vento.

Faggot Thallus, softer than bunny hairs,
or than downmost goose, or than earlobe tiplet,
or than the cock of an old man, drooping and cobwebby with filth,
likewise, Thallus, more thieving than a turbulent whirlwind,
when the holy [woman] points out gaping [rams],

give me back my cloak, which you pilfered,
and my Spanish handkerchief and my painted-up Bithynians,
you fool, which you like to have openly as if they were your heirlooms.
Now unglue these from your fingernails and give them back,
lest the branding whip foully scribble over
your woolly little flanks, your soft little hands,
and you bob as you are not used to, like a little
ship caught in a big sea, when the wind goes crazy.

The poem is remarkable for both structure and imagery.[28] It begins with a five-line section on Thallus' (= "Fleur") effeminacy and thievishness; Catullus, as in so many other poems, addresses the victim directly in the first two words and spends several lines describing him. The next section (lines 6–8) completes the first sentence with an imperative, demanding that Thallus return what he has stolen—again, a common pattern. The final section of five lines balances the first section; in it, Catullus threatens to beat Thallus if the things are not returned—also a common pattern, the ending with a threat. The three sections have several verbal links, especially *mollior* (line 1) and *mollicellas* (line 10); *turbida . . . procella* (line 4) and *velut . . . vento* (lines 12–13). Thus the first section and the last are tied together by images both of effeminacy and of storms, opposed images. The middle section is tied syntactically to the first and verbally to the second: *remitte* (line 6) – *remitte* (line 9); *soles* (line 8) – *insolenter* (line 12). The lines are loosely tied together by a series of end rhymes or near rhymes: *capillo* (line 1) – *oricilla* (line 2) – *procella* (line 4); *oscitantes* (line 5) – *involasti* (line 6); *avita* (line 8) – *remitte* (line 9); *mollicellas* (line 10) – *conscribillent* (line 11); *magno* (line 12) – *vento* (line 13). There is a great deal of alliteration throughout the poem, most notably in the interlocking *velut . . . vesaniente vento / minuta magno . . . mari* (lines 12–13); in addition, the name Thalle in the first line is repeated in the same metrical position in line 4.

All these devices are obvious, if not childish, but they suit the content. The initial listing of disgusting objects to which the victim is compared is like a charm or chant, similar to the Arabic and Eskimo satires cited above. The jingling rhymes recall the speech play of children and of the men of Chamula, discussed above. The series of animal similes is characteristic of all Latin invective, although here Catullus contrives disgust through association of things usually innocuous or attractive (rabbit fur, goose down, spiderweb; cf. 13.8) with repulsive people and things (a *cinaedus*, mold). The two startling physiological human similes show a similar absurd and uncomfortable juxtaposition—the harmless earlobe and the old man's genitals, a subject for mockery in invective against old men and of pious shame in epic poetry. The final threat picks up on the images of softness, especially the unusual images of downy things, in line 10, and goes on to promise a beating: Catullus will scrawl Thallus' sides over with whips, a peculiarly vivid picture in which we see the curving red weals (cf. 37.10). At the same time, the idea that Catullus will write weals on the body of his victim is an expression of what the poem itself does. The conclusion shows Thallus as a skiff tossed about in a sea of blows, whereas before he had himself been likened to a whirlwind; now Catullus is the whirlwind, *vesaniente vento—vesanus* being a word he applies to himself elsewhere, as at 7.10.

Thus the poem is made with language and sound effects suitable to its content, with some sophistication in the shifting of the storm image from Thallus to Catullus. It also exhibits two features common in Priapic poetry: it threatens a man characterized as effeminate with a beating for theft, and it identifies the threatened punishment with the poem itself, through the use of the word *conscribillent*. It may not offer the insight into Roman politics that forms such a feature of poems like 29, but it is a strong poem and in itself represents what Catullus was doing with invective poetry.

Ovid

Ovid is perhaps the most difficult Latin poet to triangulate; as with so many other genres, it seems that Ovid's writing does not really belong with sexual and invective poetry. His one proto-invective, the *Ibis*, is no more than an erudite list of mythological sufferings, and his promise of iambi there (53–54, 641–44) carries little conviction. It is safe to say that his closest link is to the erotic poetry discussed in chapter 2; although he never seems to take any of his loves very seriously, his poetry fits well with that of the elegists and writers of erotic epigram. But it is an uneasy solution, and Ovid over a distance of two thousand years demands to be considered separately. The important fact about his place as a satirist is that he is flippant. It was not for Ovid to make poetry out of crude and foul images; his specialty, the satirical skill at which he excelled, was mockery, especially mock epic.[29]

Many satirists imitated him, and he was certainly not the first to put crude ideas under an epic veneer.[30] His use of mock epic is so telling and so wicked, however, that he stands out from the rest. In fact, it is possible to see the same tongue-in-cheek use of great tales from antiquity throughout the *Metamorphoses*, and it seems quite likely that this caused part of Augustus' irritation with Ovid. For, as has been suggested above, parody is as much a staining of ideas and words as invective is a staining of a victim; the noble saga of Troy, in some part at least a constituent of the *dignitas* of the Caesars, had lost some of its shine when Ovid was through with it.

This is particularly true of Ovid's treatment of the progenetrix of the Julian house, the goddess Venus herself. His description of the capture of Venus and Mars *in flagrante delicto* (*AA* 2.561–92), adapted from the *Odyssey* (8.266–366), exhibits a prurience largely lacking in the epic original. Whereas Homer carefully explains the lawlessness of the act, Ovid offers the story as an illustration of the maxim *crescit amor prensis*, "love increases in [lovers] who are caught," advising men to feign ignorance of their beloved's infidelities.[31] He begins and ends the story as if recounting a gossipy anecdote: "fabula narratur toto notissima caelo" (2.561), "a story is told, notorious all over heaven"—here *urbe* could easily be substituted for *caelo*, "all over town." Ending the tale, he moves from direct address of Vulcan (589–90) to the second person, "saepe tamen demens stulte fecisse fateris," "but often, maddened, you confess you acted stupidly" (591), and so back to the narrative voice, "teque ferunt artis paenituisse tuae," "and they say you repented of your craft" (592). Venus is a sophisticated (*nec . . . rustica*, 565–66), pleasure-loving (*neque . . . mollior ulla*, 565) woman, who puts no difficulties in the way of Mars; and Mars, father of the Quirites, "de duce terribili factus amator erat" (564), "from a terrifying general had been made into a lover." Hardly in line with the normal Augustan ideal. Moreover, Venus mocks her husband's deformities, charmingly (567–70).

The affair, says Ovid, was originally secret (572): "plena verecundi culpa pudoris erat," "their sin was full of chaste modesty"—an amoral oxymoron; likewise, Ovid hints to the Sun, who informed on the lovers (*indicio*, 573), that he should have had the sense to blackmail Venus into buying his silence with her favors (575–76). The section's climax is the capture of the lovers by Vulcan's golden net (579–84), six lines that totally expose the entangled pair to the reader. Ovid begins with six choppy sentences:

> fingit iter Lemnon; veniunt ad foedus amantes;
> impliciti laqueis nudus uterque iacent;
> convocat ille deos; praebent spectacula capti;
> vix lacrimas Venerem continuisse putant

> He pretends a journey to Lemnos; the lovers come to their troth;
> tangled in the nets they each lie naked;
> he calls the gods; the captives present a show;
> they think Venus hardly held back her tears

The hexameters are made up of half-line sentences, with Vulcan in the first and the lovers in the second half of each line. Each pentameter makes up a single long sentence describing the lovers. Ovid makes the whole scene happen in the space of four lines, broken into six segments; this after a decidedly leisurely buildup (561–78). The next two lines mark time, keeping the focus on the naked lovers in the net; the phrases lengthen even more (583–84):

> non vultus texisse suos, non denique possunt
> partibus obscenis obposuisse manus.

> They cannot have covered their faces, and, most of all,
> they can't have placed their hands over their obscene parts.

By emphasizing this difficulty, Ovid ensures that the reader imagines the genitalia of the gods without the covering of a hand; he effectively uncovers them. The scene goes on, quoting the ribald, laughing comment of some bystander (585–

86), the indignation of Neptune, and Vulcan's reluctant loosing of the net; then, in less than a line, the lovers have flown away, Mars to Thrace and Venus to Paphos (588). The moral (589–90): "quod ante tegebant / liberius faciunt," "what they used to cover up / they do more freely." Ovid has exposed here not only Venus' promiscuity but also her body, not as something holy but as something frivolous and immoral, *obscena pars*; and he has deliberately chosen two gods to illustrate a decidedly immoral maxim.

Considering the tone of this portrait, Ovid's later caricature of Venus at the end of the *Metamorphoses* is not surprising. The structure and perhaps the tone of the episode may come from the epic original in *Iliad* 5, but Venus has political affiliations unknown to Aphrodite. On behalf of her beloved Caesar, about to be assassinated, she buttonholes all the gods as they go about their business (*Met.* 15.764–65) and complains at length (765–78). The gods, unable to change the course of events, put on a show of omens in the clouds and on earth (783–98). Venus, distrait, gets out the old cloud with which she had rescued Paris and Aeneas (804–06). Jupiter makes a long speech to her, foretelling Augustus' greatness (807–42); the words are scarcely out of his mouth when Venus pops (invisible) into the senate house, snatches up Caesar, and flies up to heaven with him, although she drops him when he gets too hot (843–48). The final praise of Augustus as equivalent to Jupiter (858–60) and prayer that he not die for a long time to come (861–70) are sadly undercut by the last lines of the poem—Ovid's claim that his work is stronger than Jupiter (871) and that his own name will be deathless (875–79).[32]

Ovid's power as a poet thus surpasses that of gods, emperors, and epic poets; he makes an *amator* out of Mars and a silly adulteress out of Venus. If she is such, then what of her progeny? The action of this sort of mockery manifests itself in the opposite and equal reaction of Ovid's exile.

The same kind of travesty pervades the *Ars Amatoria* and *Amores*. In his description of the most becoming positions for intercourse (*AA* 3.769–808, one of the few explicit references to intercourse in the whole poem), Ovid has the audacity to use Andromache as an example of a tall woman (*AA* 3.777–78):

> parva vehatur equo: quod erat longissima, numquam
> Thebais Hectoreo nupta resedit equo.

> Let a short woman "ride on horseback"; because she was very tall, never
> did the bride from Thebe sit on her Hectorean horse.

The runner Atalanta is given as an example of a woman who does well to place her legs on her lover's shoulders (775); the woman whose stomach is scored with stretch marks from giving birth is recommended to straddle her lover backward, like a Parthian horseman (785–86), a vehicle of comparison borrowed from serious lyrics honoring military exploits. Ovid concludes this section with advice on how to achieve—or fake—orgasms (793–804), including unparalleled comments on the signs of female orgasm and on the importance of sexual pleasure for women as well as men. All an odd context for Hector's chaste wife; Ovid's excuse, with which he prefaces this section (769–70):

> ulteriora pudet docuisse, sed alma Dione
> "praecipue nostrum est, quod pudet," inquit "opus."

> I'm ashamed to teach what lies beyond, but my guardian, Dione,
> says, "That work is especially ours, which makes for shame."

At *Am.* 2.14.9–18 Ovid reproaches his mistress for having an abortion and asks what would have happened if Thetis, Ilia, and Venus had had abortions. Very amusing, except that he is suggesting that Venus might have wished to abort the Julian *gens*.

Martial borrows two of these ideas directly from Ovid, the one about abortion in 9.41 (leaving Venus out of it and switching the theme to masturbation) and the one about Andromache in one of his longest and most lively epigrams, in which the narrator appeals to his wife to be more lascivious (11.104.13–22):

> masturbabantur Phrygii post ostia servi,
> Hectoreo quotiens sederat uxor equo,
> et quamvis Ithaco stertente pudica solebat
> illic Penelope semper habere manum.
> pedicare negas: dabat hoc Cornelia Graccho,
> Iulia Pompeio, Porcia, Brute, tibi;
> dulcia Dardanio nondum miscente ministro
> pocula, Iuno fuit pro Ganymede Iovi.
> si te delectat gravitas, Lucretia toto
> sis licet usque die; Laïda nocte volo.

> The Phrygian slaves would masturbate behind the door,
> whenever his wife sat on her Hectorean horse,
> and though the Ithacan was snoring, his chaste Penelope
> always used to have her hand down there.
> You won't let me bugger you; Cornelia gave this to Gracchus,
> Julia to Pompey, Porcia, Brutus, to you;
> before the Dardanian servant mixed the drinks,
> Juno served as Ganymede to Jove.
> If you like seriousness, you can be Lucretia
> all day if you like, but I want Laïs at night.

The image of the most famous and virtuous of Roman women allowing their husbands anal intercourse is a striking addition to the more usual mock-epic comparisons. The words of the comparison to Andromache are closely adapted from Ovid, but the point is changed to make a much more straightforwardly prurient image, including voyeurism within the poem to match the voyeurism of the reader.[33]

The technique of giving mundane situations epic trappings is, of course, a great source of humor. It is found in nonsexual situations, as for instance Hor. *S.* 2.5 (Ulysses as *captator*) and Juvenal 3.198–99, a description of a fire that alludes to the one at Vergil *A.* 2.311–12. Throughout the *Satyricon* situations are borrowed from the *Odyssey* and analogies are drawn between its characters and Odysseus. Lichas recognizes Encolpius by his penis, as Eurykleia recognized Odysseus by his scar; and Encolpius addressing his phallus compares himself to Odysseus addressing his heart. Giton is dragged out from under the bed, where he had been hiding like Odysseus under the ram in the Cyclops' cave; the first sight of Trimalchio is like the first sight of Nausikaa; and so on. Most of these cases have a cross-sexual or phallic joke as their point.[34]

Mock epic uses epic language in inappropriate places, as well as putting heroic characters into comic situations. The epic language and Vergilian *cento* in Encolpius' address to his impotent phallus ridicule both Encolpius and epic poetry itself; in epigram, Nicarchus' use of Homeric phrases in his description of the prostitute serving three men at once constitutes a notable cheapening of lofty language. Juvenal emphasizes the effeminacy of Otho by describing his makeup mirror in words borrowed from Vergil's description of a spear: *Actoris Aurunci spolium* (Juv. 2.100, Vergil *A.* 12.94).

But the closest parallel to Ovid's use of mock epic is a far lesser work, Seneca's *Apocolocyntosis*. Most of the jokes in this short travesty of apotheosis depend on the most physical sorts of humor: scatological jokes referring to Claudius' flatulence (§§3, 4, 7, 10); xenophobic digs at Claudius' extension of citizenship and his unintelligible speech (§§3, 5, 8); simple mockery of his physical deformities (§§5, 8). Of more interest are the depictions of the gods as venal and vulgar (§§9, 14), with recognizable personalities (§10, Augustus); the council of the gods is nothing but a contentious meeting of the senate (§§8–11), the judgment in Hades that of an everyday Roman court (§§14–15). And Seneca writes elemental satire when he reiterates the identification of king and fool (§§1, 3, 6, 8, 9, 14, 15); Claudius is to be treated like a gladiator (9) or a slave to be beaten (15), and his proper holiday is the Saturnalia (8). All these features strongly recall the positive value Bakhtin put on the comedy of the death of the king, and Claudius' progress in the *Apocolocyntosis*—from earth to heaven to hell—also figures in Bakhtin's system. And Seneca certainly praises the new, young king (§4). But it is hard to see a joyous affirmation of the renewal of life in the *Apocolocyntosis*; it reads much more like a splenetic attack by a man who was exiled against the man who recalled him from exile. The immersion of Claudius in ordure and darkness is the main point of the satire; appropriately, the oafish god Diespiter, proposing that Claudius become a god to eat turnips with Romulus, asks that a record of his achievement be inserted in Ovid's *Metamorphoses*.

The difference in the ways these authors use mock epic lies in the complexity with which each adapts the technique to his own art. Martial's variations on Ovid's themes are experiments in form; he wishes to recall Ovid's elegant, iconoclastic wit and give it a new twist. As an epigrammatist, he can have no consistent pose, but while he is being Ovidian he tries to out-Ovid Ovid. He greatly increases the obscenity, but the fact that obscene epigrams occupy a licensed niche in the world of poetry vitiates the shock of the whole; Martial is not professing to teach any *ars*, while Ovid titillates by draping his stories in a see-through veil of didacticism. Martial's *ars* lies entirely in his *variatio* and his license.

The *Apocolocyntosis* uses mock epic in a similarly simple way, this time as straightforward political invective (against a dead man, rather safe); here at least there is some personal motive to enliven the conceit. If Seneca meant no all-encompassing blasphemy in his satire, he certainly succeeded in degrading Claudius and in staining the image of gods who would consider such a man for godhead. But the picture of the divine and infernal worlds as exaggerated versions of his own world does not so much ridicule the Olympians as cast doubt on the possibility that a man, and one known familiarly, could actually go to heaven or hell; viz. the speech of Janus (§9) and Seneca's allusions to the senatorial witness to Drusilla's ascension who was suborned by Caligula (§§1, 5). The *Apocolocyntosis*, in the broadest interpretation, thus stands only as an indictment of the concept of deification of the emperor.

The fact remains that mock epic and the comedy of kings form a common part of rituals of reversal, rituals that can validly be claimed to have strong positive functions in their societies (above). The degradation and staining of powerful patriarchal figures played a large role in, for example, the comedies of Plautus;[35] these plays, hardly harbingers of rebellion, surely served the cathartic/conservative function of Saturnalian festivals, in which gods look silly but keep their power. (As with the heckled *triumphator*, the gods themselves remained glorious.) Likewise, the free political invective of the late Republic seems to have served a salutary political purpose, although on at least one occasion (that observed by Cicero, above) the catcalls were only the prelude to violence and the breakup of the meeting.

Catullus, preeminently, used this social aspect of mock epic in his poetry, on at least three levels: personal, political, and literary.[36] The Priapic pose, as has been seen, allowed him to jeer at his enemies, arrogating to himself virility or innocence as it suited him and setting his sexually depraved enemies in contexts of degraded epic: "glubit magnanimi Remi nepotes" (58), "she peels back the grandsons of greathearted Remus"; "salax taberna . . . / a pilleatis nona fratribus pila" (37), "randy hangout . . . / the ninth doorpost from the brothers in the pillbox hats." Priapic political mockery feminized the Roman hero (29): "cinaede Romule, haec videbis et feres?" "faggot Romulus, you see this and bear with it?" And the literary Priapus pimps his book, *pumice expolitum*, "clean-shaven" (1.2); threatens his critics with rape (16); and, conversely, pooh-poohs the literary efforts of the boor Mamurra:

105 Mentula conatur Pipleium scandere montem:
Musae furcillis praecipitem eiciunt.

Mr. Prick is trying to climb up the mount of poetry;
the Muses push him out headfirst with their pitchforks.

115.8 non homo, sed vero mentula magna minax.

not a man, but truly a big bad prick.

In the first poem the Priapic figure opposes the Muses, and in this case is ignominiously rejected by them; as the Muses eject the would-be poet, so their *furcillae* push out the *Mentula*. In the second poem Catullus lifts a line from Ennius (*Annales* 264 Ernout), *machina multa minax minitatur maxima muris*. Surely the application of the *mentula* to epic poetry is, in literal terms, the rape of epic poetry. Yet not the rape but the poet is the important thing here: Catullus' art is a domain as much his as the garden is Priapus'.

And, as has been seen, the *Priapea* often repeat an identification of god with poet, *mentula* with poetic power, garden with poetry. Poets hang verses on the god's statue (61.13–14), his master reads poetry to him (68); he himself is a stump, a *codex*, his phallus the shape of a *libellus*; he excludes the Muses from his garden (2), as Catullus says the Muses exclude Mentula from their mountain, but Priapus has his own kind of poetry. He stands as a powerful symbol not only of sexual norms in society but of the relation of literature and humor to those norms.

Hence the significance of his adoption by Petronius as the god of the *Satyricon*;[37] he represents not only the hero's lost virility but the novel's rejection and staining of the values of epic. Encolpius, a shoddy Odysseus at best, wanders through a chaos that ludicrously recapitulates the Odyssean world; he has (or seeks, along with everyone he meets) *mentula* instead of *mens*, with no now-recognizable *nostos* in store, a failed gladiator rather than a brave soldier. And his view of the world parallels the novel's comments on literature: debilitated, emasculate, degenerate, the new epic poetry (as represented by Eumolpus) is nothing but ridiculous bombast, resembling the new oratory in its inflation and tawdry glitter. The *Satyricon* uses mock epic both as content and raison d'être.

Ovid, as always, is the most difficult to understand and to explain. Certainly he connects mock epic with his own literary credo, as in the preface to the *Ars Amatoria* (above). But if it is ever right to take him at his word or to take him seriously, perhaps it is right to connect his mockery of epic with a further, deeper denial: the mockery of religion. The deep pessimism of the *Metamorphoses*, and even of the *Ars Amatoria* (which takes faithlessness and lack of feeling so much for granted)—the despair that underlies the poet's flippancy—predates his exile. The gods of the *Metamorphoses* are peculiarly spiteful, like Athena with the artist Arachne, or peculiarly deaf, like the gods to whom Philomela cries out unanswered; they rape, and they allow and even stimulate the most terrible changes in human beings. The great men of the past that Ovid selects are such that he must cry out at them, "Pro superi quantum mortalia pectora caecae / noctis habent," "o gods above, how much blind night the hearts of mortals hold!" (*Met.* 6.472–73). This universe has no good order to it; Ovid's mock epic rejects the belief in divine wisdom without putting anything in its place, and reveals evil and vulgarity where wisdom was thought to be. This attitude lies at the heart of satire and constitutes the theology of satire; after all, the degradation of figures of authority must include the degradation of God. Yet it must not be forgotten that this leaves God squarely in the limelight.

CHAPTER 7 Sexual Satire

Although Catullus and Ovid are two writers who stand apart from classifications of genre, the nature of their work still can illuminate the nature of Roman satire. Sexual themes and invective were important for both writers, particularly Catullus, who made a whole idiosyncratic kind of poetry out of the ideas and language common in graffiti. Invective not only provided a rich vein of material for Catullus but also determined the poet's stance and the structure of many poems, especially the insulting dialogue and the tirade (list of foul qualities). What invective was to Catullus, it was to the whole genre of satire. Although it is certainly true that satire deals with many topics besides sexuality, an analysis of the place of sexual themes and invective in Roman satire goes far toward explaining both the subject matter and the structure of most Roman satire.

Lucilius

That the Romans, educated Romans, took even doggerel invective seriously can be seen from the way they linked it with the work of Lucilius. Not only did most Roman satirists explicitly claim to follow in his footsteps, professing to revere the freedom he represented; this freedom could be invoked even for the ordinary sort of insult. Trebonius, commenting on a scurrilous lampoon he has written against someone he hates (Cic. *Fam.* 12.16.3), remarks, "deinde qui magis hoc Lucilio licuerit adsumere libertatis quam nobis?"—"then why should Lucilius have been allowed to take this kind of liberty more than I?" The grammarian Pompeius Lenaeus, who had studied Lucilius with a noted Lucilian scholar (Suet. *Gram.* 2), wrote an invective which Suetonius dignifies with the name of *satura* (Suet. *Gram.* 15):

> Lenaeus, Magni Pompei libertus et paene omnium expeditionum comes . . . tanto amore erga patroni memoriam exstitit, ut Sallustium historicum, quod

eum oris probi, animo inverecundo scripsisset, acerbissima satura laceraverit, lastaurem et lurconem et nebulonem popinonemque appellans, et vita scriptisque monstrosum, praeterea priscorum Catonisque verborum ineruditissimum furem.

Lenaeus, freedman of Pompeius Magnus and his companion on almost all his campaigns . . . continued to feel such reverence for his patron's memory that he lacerated the historian Sallust with a satirical work of the most bitter nature, because he had written that Pompey had a clean mouth but a dirty mind. Lenaeus called him a gigolo and a guzzler, a good-for-nothing and a barfly, and a pervert in his life and in his writings; in addition, he called him a highly illiterate thief of the writings of our forefathers, particularly of Cato's.

This "satire," as reported by Suetonius, is no more than an invective tirade; the interlinking of sexual and dietary depravities with faults of literary style only recalls similar connections in Catullus as well as in the literary critics: *talis oratio, qualis vita*. Yet Lenaeus, the student of Lucilius, was presumably influenced by the great satirist's style.[1]

To later satirists Lucilius stood for freedom of expression in satire, including the freedom to attack famous men by name. The extant fragments of his work demonstrate that he not only did do this, he occasionally heaped sexual ridicule on his victims, much as Catullus was later to mock Caesar and Pompey, and with the same unspoken excuse for his effrontery: he came from a good family.[2]

Some of the surviving gibes are directed against Scipio and relate primarily to his military and political career; for example, a complaint presumably put in the mouth of Scipio's indolent quaestor: "ille, ut dico, me exenterat unus," "he, as I say, is the one who's disemboweling me" (470 Marx;[3] cf. Cat. 28.9–10). By the same token a speaker who must be Scipio himself calls his quaestor a *nebulo*, "good-for-nothing" (467–68). Scipio's policing of the camp's morals is the subject of a comment (398–99) that he "threw all the dirty-mouthed out of the camp like dung." Lucilius also twits Scipio for his squabble with a man from his political retinue, whom he labels a *cinaedus* (1138–40). Another praetor (Scipio again?) is scolded for his affair with Lucilius' *puer*, who Lucilius says will come back to him (Gentius, 273; cf. Macedo, 275); this moved Apuleius, long afterward, to expostulate (272):

Et quidem C. Lucilium, quamquam sit iambicus, tamen improbarim quod Gentium et Macedonem pueros directis nominibus carmine suo prostituerit.

And indeed, even though Gaius Lucilius be an iambic poet, still I would reprove him for prostituting the boys Gentius and Macedo by their real names in his poetry.

Besides his freedom in directing invective at important men, Lucilius also provides the earliest examples of the major kinds of sexual and invective themes exploited by later Roman satirists; some of these passages were even imitated by later authors. Although it is often difficult to establish the context of an extant line, it is still easy to perceive the common presence of two complex themes, sexual interaction with women and homosexuality, as well as, less commonly, satire on prostitution, adultery, scatology, and oral sex.

Lucilius apparently included in his satires material that later became the province of elegy and epigram. At least, according to Porphyrio *ad* Hor. *C.* 1.22.10, the sixteenth book of Lucilius was called "Collyra" because it was about his mistress *(amica)* Collyra (Lucil. 517 Marx). There are indeed several fragments dealing with heterosexual intercourse from an erotic rather than a satirical standpoint; 925–27 is especially reminiscent of Ovid *Am.* 1.5:

⟨Cretaea nuper⟩, cum ad me cubitum venerat
sponte ipsa suapte adducta ut tunicam et cetera
reiceret[4]

Cretaea recently, when she had come to me to go to bed,
was led of her own free will to throw off her underwear
and everything else

But there are gradations in the attitude expressed in Lucilius' poems; in many mentions of women or intercourse he chooses images of violence. He uses the word *vannere*, "winnow," of both a man and a woman:

278 . . . illam autem ut frumentum vannere lumbis
. . . and to winnow her with your loins, like grain

330 crisabit ut si frumentum clunibus vannat.
She will shimmy as if she were winnowing grain with her haunches.

He has a character speak the line "nemo istum ventrem pertundet," "no one will poke through that belly/womb of yours" (1071),[5] and Donatus cites his usage of *pugna*, "fight," for *stuprum*, "rape" or "sex" (1323). The poet shows repugnance for women's genitalia (73, *bulgam . . . pilosam*), describes their yelps of pleasure (285; cf. Juv. 6.64), and in a long fragment enumerates the flaws even in renowned beauties like Alcmene or Helen (540–46). As a concomitant of this attitude, he describes the erect phallus in comically alarming terms (303):

cum poclo bibo eodem, amplector, labra labellis
fictricis conpono, hoc est cum psolo copumai

when I drink from the same cup, I embrace [her], I place
my lips to the lips of the sculptress, that is, when I burst
with my hard-on

Lucilius uses the old words *mutto* (307) and *moetinum* (78)[6] for the phallus and finds animal and vegetable similes for it (279–81, probably 1022), as well as describing in detail a ram's testicles (534–36). The *mutto* in 307 is personified, said to have "tears" wiped away by the left hand/mistress[7]—presumably a description of masturbation to ejaculation. Lucilius even (possibly) describes a wet dream.[8]

It is thus no surprise to find examples of invective against old women in Lucilius' writings. He mocks at the old woman's proverbial bibulousness (766–67):

> "hinc ad me, hinc, licet":
> anus russum ad armillum.

> "here to me, here, please":
> the crone to the rust-red wine jar.

He also jeers at the sexual repulsiveness of old women; in 279 –81 the protagonist apparently cheats an old, randy woman who has done him wrong in some way by castrating himself:

> hanc ubi vult male habere, ulcisci pro scelere eius,
> testam sumit homo Samiam sibi, "anu noceo" inquit,
> praecidit caulem testisque una amputat ambo.

> When he wants to vex her, to be avenged on her sin,
> the man takes a Samian sherd to himself, says, "I hurt the crone,"
> cuts his stalk and testicles both off at once.

Another fragment seems to react against such an extreme proposal (282–83):

> . . . vetulam atque virosam
> uxorem caedam potius quam castrem egomet me.

> . . . me, I'd bang a little old man-hungry wife
> rather than castrate myself.

Two more old women may be witches (1065–66):

> illo quid fiat, Lamia et Bitto oxyodontes
> quod veniunt, illae gumiae vetulae inprobae ineptae?

> So what, if Lamia and Bitto the acudentate
> are coming, those little old, bad, no-account gluttons?

But the impotence of old men also comes in for ridicule (331–32):

> quod deformis, senex arthriticus ac podagrosus
> est, quod mancus miserque, exilis, ramice magno

> that he is deformed, old, arthritic and gouty,
> crippled and wretched, thin, with a big rupture[9]

These fragments show that, besides including erotic attitudes found in writers of elegy and epigram, Lucilius' heterosexual satire expressed hostile attitudes common in invective poetry.

The fragments on homosexual themes demonstrate a similar range of feeling. Although there are no fragments of romantic poetry to *pueri*, there are several passages that, if ribald, at least manifest a positive attitude. Line 1267 seems to be a general commendation of anal intercourse:

> podicis, Hortensi, est ad eam rem nata palaestra.
>
> asshole wrestling, Hortensius, was created for the same purpose.[10]

Lucilius made use of the same sort of mock loftiness by which Martial was later to compare boys to Ganymede, comparing them instead to Hyacinthus, Apollo's beloved (276, cf. 895–96); according to Servius he even had Apollo refuse to be called *pulcher*, as being too effeminate a term (23)—the same kind of play on words inherent in Catullus' rejection of the epithet *mollis* (cf. Marx *ad loc.*). The loves of Socrates formed the subject of a similarly half-lofty comparison (830–33).

Lucilius praised a woman for resembling a boy (296–97) and invented a vocabulary for pederasty as Catullus was to do for kissing: *pedicum* (74);[11] *subpilo*, *pullo*, and *premo* for men who chased young boys (967). He made jokes about depilation, the standard characteristic of effeminates:

> 845 "Gnato, quid actum est?" "depilati omnes sumus."
>
> "Gnatho, what's going on?" "We've all been plucked!"
>
> 264 rador, subvellor, desquamor, pumicor, ornor,
> expilor,⟨ex⟩pingor
>
> I'm shaved, plucked, de-scaled, pumiced, decked out,
> polished, and painted[12]

Jokes about depilation in later authors are generally found in contexts hostile to homosexuality, in which effeminates are being castigated. There is much evidence of such invective in Lucilius, for example, in this violent image of anal intercourse (72):

> si natibus natricem inpressit crassam et capitatam
>
> if he has pressed a thick, headed water snake into your butt

The identification of phallus with snake is almost unique in Roman satire (cf. only Oxford *VA* "Quid Hoc" 33) and manifests distaste for the active as well as for the passive partner. Elsewhere Lucilius twice links violent imagery of heterosexual intercourse with violent imagery of pederasty. The line in which he uses *vannere*, "winnow," to mean *futuere* reads in full (278):

> hunc molere, illam autem ut frumentum vannere lumbis
>
> to grind him in a mill, but to winnow her like grain with your loins

This line is matched by one citing the disadvantages of both sorts of intercourse (1186):

> haec inbubinat, at contra te inbulbitat ⟨ille⟩
>
> she be-bloods you, but then he be-merdes you[13]

These images of filth directly connected with anal or genital intercourse were not to be picked up by later authors, with the exception of a few associations of feces or loose bowels with anal intercourse (*Pr.* 68.8, 69.4; Mart. 9.69.1, 11.88, 13.26; Juv. 9.43–44); mentions of menstrual fluid are extremely rare outside this passage. It seems that Lucilius at times espoused and could legitimately articulate an explicitly savage disgust with both women and boys as sex objects. The tone, as was remarked for Catullus above, is savage and jolly at the same time, taking pleasure in playing with gross words and fearful images.

Again, Lucilius uses outlandish or invented vocabulary, possibly slang, in homosexual invective. He calls someone a *halicarius* (496), supposedly after the prostitutes who worked the grain mills. He talks of *scultimidoni* (1373), "asshole-bestowers"; uses *maltam* as an epithet (732), apparently an equivalent for *μαλακόν*; and invents a sexual oxymoron, *inberbi androgyni*, *barbati moechocinaedi* (1058), "beardless androgynes, bearded adulterer-faggots." He sneers at dancing as effeminate, the business of *cinaedi* (32), and laughs at Scipio's quarrel with a *cinaedus* (1138–42). He lists the effeminate mannerisms that continued to be the target of satire after him (882–83):

> hic me ubi videt
> subblanditur, ⟨sub⟩palpatur,[14] caput scabit, pedes legit.
>
> when he sees me
> he chats me up, he feels me up, he scratches his head,
> he shuffles his feet.[15]

Lucilius satirized several other areas of sexual activity: adultery, telling the story of Cipius who pimped his wife (1223); oral sex, twice making of it a casual insult (398, perhaps 1167); and prostitution (206, 271, 891, 1271). It seems likely that he drew a connection between old women and prostitution, as in 334–35:

> si nihil ad faciem et si olim lupa prostibulumque
> nummi opus atque subit
>
> If she has no face, if as an old whore and prostitute
> she needs cash and goes down[16]

What is perhaps more significant, it seems likely that he wrote a good deal of scatological humor, some of it as inventive as his homosexual terminology. He made a few jokes about the *latrinae*, the public toilets (253, 400), and discussed the intimate parts of the house, making a list full of jarring juxtapositions (312):

> pistrinum adpositum, posticum, sella, culina

with the bakehouse nearby, the backhouse, the toilet, the kitchen

A similar repulsive oral-anal juxtaposition enlivens a metrical proverb (659):

mordicus petere aurum e flamma expediat, e caeno cibum

granted, it's useful to pull gold from the fire with your teeth—or food from the dung heap—

And another list not only places the reader in filth but names various species of filth (1018):

hic in stercore humi fabulisque, fimo atque sucerdis

here in dung on the ground, in goat dung, in manure and pig dung

Some of the qualities that have emerged here as characteristic of Lucilius' sexual satire are only those traditionally associated with his style, like the use of lists and of inventive language. Moreover, it has always seemed likely that any modern view of these qualities in his work must be exaggerated by the process that preserved it: lines containing unusual words were noted by grammarians and so survived. These lines contain a good many sexual terms, which are themselves rare in extant Latin. Nevertheless, the language and the lists were present in his work and must have given it the slangy, racy, colloquial tone that all his successors adopted, each in his own way. But as his satire is more personal than that of almost any of his successors—more a product of the scandal of the moment—so his language sounds more dated than anything that came after it. His language is poetry made of current speech, only some of which is of a literary level. Most of his successors used colloquialisms only as a conscious ornament for their literary creations.

This, as it were, street poetry makes a good setting for the sexual attitudes expressed by Lucilius—attitudes that typify the matter and structure of all later satire. The single common element in Lucilius' attitudes is that of staining. Just as mock epic involves a staining or degradation of epic, so the lists that include jarring juxtapositions in effect stain the innocent elements by associating them with foul ones—an effect that Juvenal in particular was to adopt. This is especially evident when the juxtaposition is oral/anal (later a favorite of Catullus'); but Lucilius' probably abundant use of scatological themes in his satire amounts to a befoulment of the reader, an immersal in dung. That this is one assessment he makes of sexual intercourse (*inbulbitat ille*) ties this mechanism of befoulment with the tone of jolly savagery. Marx takes lines 1022–23, "hic ut muscipulae tentae atque ut scorpios cauda / sublata," "here like taut mousetraps and like a scorpion with raised tail," to be the satirist's standard boast, "Beware of me"; these images are surely not only hostile but also phallic (cf. *Pr.* 6.5, 68.16; Hor. *S.* 1.2.45, 2.7.49). The connection between humor in violence and befoulment of the reader or victim formed the basis for much of Roman satire. Lucilius' *exemplum*, along with the tradition it fostered, was not simply one of freedom.[17]

Serious attempts have been made to reconstruct the content of Lucilius' satires and to trace the sources that influenced him as well as his own influence on later authors.[18] Although the extent of these reconstructions depends largely on subjective assignment of one-line fragments to possible contexts, critics still have isolated several strains indisputably present in Lucilius' satire, strains which are immediately relevant to the discussion at hand and which certify that the areas attested by Lucilius' language were not only present but central to his satire.

First, the authorial boasting probably exemplified by the image of the mousetrap and the scorpion's tail (1022–23) amounts to an *ars satirica* valid not only for sexual satire but for all satire. The identification of people with animals, and lowly animals at that, and the idea that the satirist will trap people/mice, or that the scorpion/satirist will sting people, are both coupled with the image of the satirist, phallus erect, threatening his victims with rape in the form of sexual degradation. Marx connects the literary theory with the scatological threats;[19] he aptly compares the image of mousetrap and scorpion to Horace's analogies between satirist and bull (*S.* 1.4.34), and between satire and the sword (*S.* 2.1.39–46). Marx believes that Lucilius in books 26 and 30 explained and defended the "ratio satiricae poesis." He identifies 1014–15, "idque tuis saevis factis et tristibus dictis / gaudes" ("and so you delight in your savage deeds and your severe words") as an opponent's reply, while the list of various kinds of dung (1018) imagines his opponent satirized.[20] The use of *cinaedus* as an insult in Lucilius' satire (32, 1058, 1140) makes it clear that he perceives men as either virile/good or effeminate/bad, so that the identification of his own writing as virile/good and his victims as effeminate/bad is natural. Likewise he portrays the hero Scipio as powerful and angry as opposed to the impudent *cinaedus* in his entourage (1138–42)—a contrast that has been aptly likened to Horace's annoying encounter in *S.* 1.9.[21] Thus Lucilius, the archetypal Roman satirist, feels the need to justify his work, to boast of his power in physical terms, to align himself with the wielders of political and military power, and to differentiate himself from the effeminate. From this it is in turn clear that the role of satirist implies fear that the writer is not enough of a soldier or politician, the belief that his work sets him apart from his society, and fear as well as hatred of effeminate men.

From this defensive self-justification seems to stem the iconoclasm that produces mock epic. Perhaps the best efforts at reconstructing Lucilius are those directed at his *concilium deorum*, which was attested by Lactantius (*Div. Inst.* 4.3.12) and by Servius (*ad A.* 10.104; 3 Marx). Lucilius' *concilium* apparently did for Scipio's enemy Lucius Cornelius Lentulus Lupus what the *Apocolocyntosis* did for the emperor Claudius. But, like the *Apocolocyntosis*, its predecessor is more than an ad hominem attack. It treats the gods with profane jocularity and, above all, perverts semisacred literary traditions.

As Cichorius pointed out,[22] Lucilius uses the setting of the *concilium deorum* to let the gods revile Lupus for him. The satire, presumably written immediately after Lupus' death, begins with Lupus still alive; the gods decide he must die for the good of Rome, though the gods themselves are laughable. Cichorius suggests that Apollo's sensitivity about being called *pulcher* belongs here (23) and that Romulus' character as a bumpkin (Sen. *Apocol.* 9; cf. Mart. 13.16) goes back to Lucilius. Like Augustus in the *Apocolocyntosis*, a speaker who may be Romulus, complaining about the Hellenization of Rome, extols the good old days (12–14, 15–16). In reply (as Cichorius tenuously but possibly rightly guesses), Lupus insults both Romulus and the other gods—"stulte saltatum te inter venisse cinaedos" (32), "you stupidly have come to dance among the faggots"—if Cichorius is right, a thumping blasphemy indeed.

The relation between this satire and earlier epic poetry is fairly clear. Cichorius notes that both Naevius and Ennius had written serious versions of the *concilium deorum*, and he believes that Lucilius here probably parodies Ennius' *concilium* in book 1 of the *Annales*. Fiske goes back further to draw comparisons between specific lines of Lucilius and passages in Homer;[23] for instance, Neptune's statement of regret at having been away (27–29) recalls the opening of the *Odyssey*. Most important of all, however, is Fiske's comparison of Lucilius' *concilium* with the mock-epic Σίλλοι of Timon of Phlius. These Homeric parodies, naturally enough, were cast in dactylic hexameter, and Fiske hypothesizes that the Σίλλοι may have prompted Lucilius to choose hexameter as a meter for satire. If so, this means that the very meter of satire was originally meant to recall the completely different style and ethos of epic; the meter was a tool to remind the reader of the iconoclasm of what he was reading. Originally the use of the meter of the *Iliad* for cynical, obscene, and irreverent material must have constituted a most striking literary heresy and surely constitutes a staining even more basic than the staining of words. And since epic continued to be written as long as satire was written, the savagery of the echo can never have been wholly lost. The two genres comprise major and opposed modes in which human beings think about themselves and their life; their shared meter reinforces their complementarity.

Fiske also draws attention to another mock-epic episode in Lucilius—the retelling of the return of Ulysses (book 30), in which Ulysses becomes a "Cynic-Stoic hero." This, in turn, as Fiske notes, may have prompted Horace's *nekuia* in *S.* 2.5.[24] Ulysses occupies a special position in Roman satire and seems to be the ancestor of all the picaros of later literature. His sufferings and his series of romantic entanglements (from which he flees only halfheartedly) can be changed with only a shift in tone into the adventures of the satiric hero, who lives miraculously through the most cataclysmic events and whose ups and downs usually include sexual imbroglios. Thus, as Fiske suggests, Lucil. 480–83 may be the words of Ulysses telling the tale of the Cyclops to a skeptical audience (cf. Juv. 15.13–16). But the idea of the *nekuia* itself held a peculiar fascination for satirists and reappears not only in Hor. *S.* 2.5 but elsewhere: the *Apocolocyntosis* combines the *concilium deorum* with a *nekuia*, and the *cena Trimalchionis* borrows some of the structural elements of epic journeys to the dead.[25] Here again an element of major importance to epic reappears in satire; but in epic the *nekuia* gives the hero significant and serious information and direction, whereas the satirical *nekuia* gives the hero only punishment or insane or cynical advice.

A third theme in Lucilius' satire, for which two reconstructions have been widely accepted, rejects marriage and points out the many flaws of women.[26] Cichorius accepts Marx's suggestion that 678–86 constitute a reaction against the speech and promarriage legislation of Metellus Macedonicus (131 B.C.). Lucilius, an "inveterate bachelor" according to Cichorius, may have found ample scope for satire in Metellus' own words; even the lawmaker did not endorse marriage wholeheartedly (Gell. 1.6):

> Si sine uxore vivere possemus, Quirites, omnes ea molestia careremus; sed quoniam ita natura tradidit, ut nec cum illis satis commode, nec sine illis ullo modo vivi possit, saluti perpetuae potius quam brevi voluptati consulendum est.[27]

> If we were able to live without a wife, descendants of Quirinus, we would all lack that bother; but since nature has so ordained, that it is neither possible to live with them at all comfortably, nor without them at all, we must consult our ongoing welfare rather than our temporary pleasure.

Metellus' semiserious complaints point up the direction of his exhortation: he means to encourage men to seek wives, not women to seek husbands. The initiative rests with the state and with men, "Quirites." His humor expects his audience will grant his premises: that men have the initiative, that women are difficult to live with, that living with a woman is a necessary thing for a man, and that temporary sexual encounters are more pleasurable than marriage. The satirist's position depends on the second premise: Lucilius describes the ways in which wives are difficult. And he hedges slightly; Cichorius, identifying several lines as criticisms of faddish, extravagant women in comparison with the old-fashioned, frugal wife (680–85), concludes that Lucilius is writing not so much against marriage as against modern women.

Lucilius apparently expounded similar ideas in a satire on the virtues of cheap women. Cichorius assigns 851–52, 857–58, 859–60, 866–67 to this satire; the last two sets bear a strong resemblance to parts of Hor. *S.* 1.2:

> 859–60 hic corpus solidum invenies, hic stare papillas
> pectore marmoreo.
>
> here you will find a firm body, here tits standing out from a marble breast.

> 866–67 qui et poscent minus et praeb⟨eb⟩unt rectius multo
> et sine flagitio.
>
> who will both ask less and offer much more properly and without crime.

Fiske finds parallels to Hor. *S.* 1.2 in Lucilius books 29.3, 7, and 8; adducing Arnobius' statement that Lucilius wrote a satire called *Fornix* ("Bordello"), he identifies this satire with book 29.3, in which, as he reconstructs it, Lucilius opts for prostitutes as the best outlet for sexual desire. It seems at least possible that line 307, "at laeva lacrimas muttoni absterget amica," belongs in this sort of context; the line then states that the hand is a kinder *amica* than the woman, who has presumably caused the *mutto* to weep.

The reconstructed areas of mock epic and satire on women thus conform with the stance inherent in the theme of authorial boasting. The satirist undermines serious poetry, especially poetry about the gods, thereby reinforcing his own genre and his own authority. As for women, anomalies in the schema of virile = good, effeminate = bad, they wind up in the category "bad," except when they can be bought cheaply; most of them are adversaries to the poet/protagonist and his *mutto*. Of course this is a humorous attitude and does not mean that men consorted only with prostitutes, or even that Lucilius was a bachelor, and Metellus' speech affords a convenient example of the difference between practice and preaching. Deplore women though he might, Metellus was an enthusiastic proponent of marriage; presumably he closed his eyes and thought of Rome. And Lucilius' satire was there to cheer him up.

Horace

Horace revered Lucilius; the foregoing analysis of Lucilius' sexual satire lends Augustus' epithet for Horace, "purissimum penem" (Suet. *Vita Horati*), a critical application that Augustus probably did not intend. *Purissimus*, certainly—his satires thickly coated with layers of philosophy and rumination; *penis*, as well—for the content and structure of much of his satire recall the stance of his model.

Horace's *S.* 1.2 has been labeled his "earliest and most Lucilian," on account of both its language and its content.[28] The repeated words alone are striking, enough to bring Lucilius strongly to mind. The name "Maltinus" (line 25; cf. *maltus*, Lucil. 732 Marx), *permolere* = *futuere* (line 35; cf. *molere*, Lucil. 278), *perminxerunt* (line 44; cf. Lucil. 1248), *caudam salacem* = *penis* (line 45; cf. *caulem testisque*, Lucil. 281; *cauda*, Lucil. 1022)—all recall Lucilian images that are not only violent and inventive but exclusively sexual. Lucilius 29.3 may have advocated cheap and easy sex as a substitute for the pains of adultery; this is certainly the gist of Hor. *S.* 1.2.

If *S.* 1.2 is the earliest Horatian satire, it already bears the identifying marks of his later and most characteristic satires. Horace approaches the topic (the pros and cons of intercourse with various classes of women) obliquely, opening the poem with a long introductory meditation on men who run to extremes in the spending of money (lines 1–24), which concludes, "dum vitant stulti vitia, in contraria currunt," "while stupid men avoid vices, they run to the opposite ones." A coda to this section (lines 25–30) cites specific cases, all at least tangentially sexual: the man with an effeminately cut toga versus the man so rustic his toga exposes his groin, the scented man versus the goat-smelling man, men who chase *matronae* versus men who chase low prostitutes. The last *exemplum* provides the lead-in to the body of the poem, which disparages *matronae* as mistresses and touts less respectable women for that purpose. The rather discursive argument includes the following points of special interest:

words of praise (attributed to the elder Cato)[29] for young men who frequent brothels, since this spares *matronae* (lines 31–35);
two vivid descriptions of the physical punishments and degradations to be feared by adulterers (lines 41–46, 127–34);
a conversation between a rejected lover and his *muto* (lines 68–72);
a checklist of the physical points that a good prostitute exhibits for her potential customer, points that *matronae* keep hidden (lines 83–103 passim); includes an analogy between choosing a woman and buying a horse (lines 86–89);
advice to take the nearest boy or girl when desire strikes, on the principle, "num tibi cum fauces urit sitis aurea quaeris / pocula," "Do you need gold cups when thirst burns your throat?" (lines 114–27).

This cynical discourse assumes that the reader has no interest in marriage (or at least in fidelity) and views married men only as obstacles in the way of married women; Cato's statement endorses this system, giving it the imprimatur of the man who embodied Roman *virtus*. The *muto* also speaks, to confirm Horace's proposition that any woman will do to satisfy desire. The equally important corollary to this proposition points out the real hazards in the pursuit of *matronae*, as opposed to the ready availability of prostitutes; this boils down to the difference between man in control (by means of money) and man at the mercy of both the *matrona* and her husband (*S.* 1.2.41–46; 127–33):

hic se praecipitem tecto dedit; ille flagellis
ad mortem caesus; fugiens hic decidit acrem
praedonum in turbam; dedit hic pro corpore nummos;
hunc perminxerunt calones; quin etiam illud
accidit, ut quidam testis caudamque salacem
demeteret ferro. . . .
. . . .
nec vereor ne dum futuo vir rure recurrat,
ianua frangatur, latret canis, undique magno
pulsa domus strepitu resonet, vae pallida lecto
desiliat mulier, miseram se conscia clamet,
cruribus haec metuat, doti deprensa, egomet mi.
discincta tunica fugiendum est ac pede nudo,
ne nummi pereant aut puga aut denique fama.

One throws himself headlong from the roof; another
was beaten with whips to the point of death; another,
fleeing, fell into a fierce

mob of muggers; another gave cash for his bodily safety;
the kitchen oafs pissed all over another; why, it has even
happened, that a man cut off the testicles and lusty tail
with cold steel. . . .
....
Nor do I fear that, while I'm fucking, the husband may run
back from the country,
the door be broken in, the dog bark, on all sides the house
beaten by great outcries resound, oh, pale, from the bed
the woman leap down, our accomplice shout she is wretched,
and fear for her legs, the woman caught for her dowry,
I for myself.
My retreat must be beat with unbuttoned shirt, and barefoot,
so my cash won't perish, or my derrière, or even my reputation.

Both vignettes owe their theatrical force to mime, but the punishments are realistic (see appendix 1, below); the elements of the scenes are nonetheless organically related to *S.* 1.2. Caught *in flagrante delicto*, the lover loses all status and power; at best he can stave off corporal punishment, the invasion of his body, by surrendering money, that is, by diminishing his own possessions and augmenting those of the husband. Possibly the lover will suffer only accidental injury—falling off the roof, robbery in a bad neighborhood. But the husband has the right to prove his questioned manhood on the body of the captured lover—by raping him (*puga*, line 133) or otherwise defiling him (*perminxerunt*, line 44) with the aid of his household; by castrating him (lines 45–46); or by beating him with a whip (lines 41–42), a slave's punishment. The lover is in the same fix as the wife, who stands to lose her money (line 131), and the conniving maid, who may have her legs broken (lines 130–31). In having intercourse with another man's wife, the lover runs the risk of being treated as a woman himself.

But the prostitute, conveniently, "aperte / quod venale habet ostendit," "openly shows what she has for sale" (lines 83–84), wearing gauzy clothes that reveal her legs and feet (lines 101–03). The lover found in adultery, running madly away, resembles her, "discincta tunica . . . ac pede nudo," "with underclothes unfastened and with naked foot" (line 132); he is thus reduced to the dishabille so attractive in a woman—not an acceptable situation for him. The listing of parts to be checked on a horse or a thinly clad woman—*pes*, *clunis*, *caput*, *cervix* (lines 88–89), *crus*, *bracchia* (line 92),[30] *crus*, *pes* (line 102)—recalls the listing of physical punishments for the adulterer; it also recalls the listing of physical flaws in, for example, Horace's *Epodes* 8 and 12, and in fact a list of bad points appears here too: *depugis*, *nasuta*, *brevi latere*, *pede longo*, "derrièreless, big-nosed, with flat hips and big feet" (line 93). As in invective against old women, the woman is represented by her genitalia (*cunni . . . albi*, line 36; *cunnum*, line 70). The analogy between women and horses likewise smacks of invective; the reduction of women to physical parts or animals reinforces the narrator's control over them, while the *muto* retains the power to complain and direct, and speaks of its desire as *ira*, "rage" (line 71). Lack of power turns the powerless into chattel, objects of possession or violence.

No matter how much Horace here depends on Lucilius, the way in which he frames the satire depends on preoccupations of his own. Two of these reappear in many of the satires of both books: the question of control and the related question of money. (The adulterer in *S*. 1.2.133 worries first about his money, then about his derrière, and finally about his reputation, an intentionally amusing but characteristic reversal.) Apparently prompted by uneasiness over his humble origins, Horace returns again and again to musings on the importance of money and power. His other sexual satires reiterate these concerns: the slave Davus (2.7.46–74) recommends that the poet abandon *matronae*, follow his example, and take cheap and wanton mistresses; on the other hand, the Priapic satire (*S*. 1.8) portrays a poverty-stricken Priapus (lines 1–16) in a garden made of a potter's field (thanks to Maecenas),[31] who nevertheless manages to frighten away two repulsive hags.

Horace enunciates his *ars satirica* accordingly.[32] What is most striking of all, he enunciates it at great length, devoting to it three full satires (1.4, 1.10, 2.1) out of eighteen. *S*. 1.4 proposes both motive and style. Horace begins with the *exemplum* of Old Comedy (lines 1–5) and cites Lucilius but rejects his style as too rapid (*flueret lutulentus*, "he rushed muddy," lines 6–13) and too prosaic (lines 54–62). Meanwhile, he makes great claims for the power of satire: everyone fears and hates satirical poetry (line 33); the satirist, merciless, attacks friend and foe alike, like a mad bull (line 34); an accuser, like Lucilius' (1014–15 Marx), claims the poet enjoys hurting others, *laedere gaudes* (line 78); Horace threatens revenge on his recalcitrant victims (lines 140–43). The poem stands as a boast of Horace's power over other men and of his superiority to his greatest predecessor.

Whether prompted by readers or by his own second thoughts (lines 1–3), Horace in 1.10 retreats slightly from the arrogance of his position in 1.4, restating his criticisms of Lucilius. He says he admires Lucilius "quod sale multo / urbem defricuit," "because he rubbed down the city with a lot of salt" (lines 3–4). However, a satirist needs certain niceties of style (lines 7–9), not including an ability to make bilingual compounds, which Horace scorns (lines 20–35); he then offers a *recusatio* of other genres, tipping his hat in passing to the chief living exponent of each—bombastic epic (lines 36–37), theater (lines 37–39), comedy (lines 40–42), *togata* (lines 42–43), epic (lines 43–44), bucolic poetry (lines 44–45). He then states flatly that he is the greatest living satirist, though not as good as Lucilius (lines 46–49)—whose style, however, had major flaws (lines 50–71). Again Horace calls Lucilius *lutulentum* (line 50) and describes the agonies of creative writing to which the best modern poets are subject (lines 72–75). The astounding conclusion to this idiosyncratic manifesto lists Horace's friends, that is, the poets he respects, by name (lines 81–88), as the only audience he cares about; he says he is "contentus paucis lectoribus," "content with a few readers" (line 74). By means of this most extreme exercise of the satirist's exclusivity, Horace distinguishes himself not from other kinds of people but from all people except those listed by name in his poem. Normally exclusivity as a mechanism fosters a feeling of complicity between poet and reader; Horace here does not invite anyone to join his clique.

S. 2.1 only reinforces the categories established in 1.4 and 1.10. The very framework of the poem, a dialogue between Horace and the noted lawyer Trebatius Testa, immediately gives the poem an air of hobnobbing with the great and near-great, as well as insinuating that the poet needs the best legal advice to protect him from his outraged victims. The poem's conclusion is foreshadowed as early as line 17, where Trebatius recommends Horace to write poetry praising Caesar as Lucilius had done for Scipio. Then, after Horace expounds for some time on the power of satire, Trebatius expresses his fear that Horace will be short-lived and that his great friends will cut him (lines 60–62). Horace responds with an image that resonates throughout his satires: pointing out (lines 62–74) that Lucilius got away with quite vicious satires, and that Laelius and Scipio were happy to have him attack Metellus and Lupus, he describes the three men—Laelius, Scipio, and the poet—down in the country together dining on vegetables (lines 71–74). But Horace then feels the need to reiterate his claim to the friendship of the powerful: even if he is "infra Lucili censum ingeniumque," "below Lucilius' tax bracket and genius," he lives with great men; "fragili quaerens illidere dentem / offendet solido," "the man who seeks to sink his teeth into [someone] fragile will [in me] hit on [someone] solid" (lines 75–79).

As in the earlier satires, Horace here speaks of his poetry's power in physical terms. His victims "fear" and "hate" him (line 23); his satire is a sword, now sheathed (lines 39–44), but the man who provokes him "flebit et insignis tota cantabitur urbe," "will weep and, marked, be sung all over town" (lines 44–46). Horace compares his satire to other ways of hurting people—lawsuits (line 47), poison and witchcraft (line 48), unfavorable verdicts (line 49), poison (lines 53–56)—as well as to the wolf's tooth and the bull's horn (lines 52, 54–55).[33]

In short, Horace himself depicts his stance as defensive and vulnerable, dependent on politically powerful men whose acceptance he craves, with only his own provocative poetry to use as a weapon.[34] He rejects epic (lines 10–15) and modestly praises Lucilius as "better than both of us" (line 29); here Lucilius appears as an old man, confiding all his life to his books, as to trusty friends (lines 30–34). Thus Horace sets up a system in which the poet (Lucilius) and his friends (Scipio, Laelius, and the satires) attack their enemies. Apparently Horace wishes to fit his own life into this mold, and so he replies to Trebatius' warning that *mala carmina* ("curses," "slander") are illegal (line 82), that his own poems *(carmina)* are *bona*, and that he himself is *laudatus Caesare*, "praised by Caesar" (line 84). But the precariousness of this safety is shown by the reason Horace gives for his rejection of epic: Octavian, if displeased, is a man "cui male si palpere recalcitrat undique tutus," "who, if you rub him down the wrong way, can kick out on all sides with impunity" (line 20). The satirist's animal power is matched by the animal power of his protector.

These ideas reappear in other satires as given conditions of the satirist's nature. The satirist is fierce: Davus uses *insanire* as an equivalent for *versus facere* (2.7.117); Horace's retreat to the country is prompted, he says, by the furor over his satires (2.3.13). The satirist has high standards: the bore of 1.9 is a literary bore, a fount of all the literary vices (lines 23–25); Horace's journey to Brundisium (1.5) is made bearable only by the presence of his friends, and by his literary friends (lines 40–44, 48–49, 93) much more than by his patrons (lines 27–29, 31–33, 48). And his *recusatio* of epic perhaps underlies the charming fable of the country mouse and the city mouse (2.6.79–117).

Like his predecessor, Horace found mock epic greatly to his taste.[35] Although 2.5, the mock *nekuia*, is the only satire completely devoted to mock epic, the other satires are peppered with it. The woman who murders her miserly master with an ax is compared to Clytemnestra (1.1.95–100); war, lust, and misery have a long pedigree in a not-so-Golden Age (1.3.99–110); men who lived a simple, rustic life are *heroas* (2.2.92–93); and Horace and Damasippus use Ajax and Agamemnon as exemplars (2.3.187–207). The pompous, almost epic phraseology of *S.* 2.4.45–47, 73–75 draws its comic effect from the application of this language to a low topic—food. But the major examples make clear the significance of Horace's mode of undercutting epic: in 1.5.51–70 a slanging match between two slaves at a dinner takes on the air of an epic single combat; the same happens in the legal battle between Rupilius Rex and Persius of Clazomenae, characters scorned as vulgar (1.7.10–18); and the city mouse introduces the country mouse to a scene that anticipates Dido's banquet (2.6.100–07), starting from a *cum inversum* construction with epic periphrasis, "iamque tenebat / nox medium caeli spatium, cum . . .," "and now night was holding the middle space of the sky, when . . ." (lines 100–01). The two mice enter a dining room full of purple draperies, ivory couches, and rich dishes, in which the city mouse acts the part of a (greedy) slave. The lowly Rex and Persius are compared to Hector versus Achilles (1.7.12) and to Diomedes versus Glaucus (1.7.16–17, 25–26), and their squabble to a war. The quarrel between the two slaves begins with an invocation of the Muse (1.5.53) and a genealogy of each slave (1.5.53–56). In all these cases, as with the shorter examples, Horace belittles the epic matter by assigning it to small characters— slaves, foreigners, and mice.

Horace takes the opposite tack in *S.* 2.5, in which Ulysses asks Teiresias how he can repair his fortunes when he finally returns, and Teiresias advises *captatio*. Instead of attributing epic deeds to low characters, Horace here attributes low deeds to epic characters. For once in his satires Horace expresses a credo by means of advising the opposite; that is to say, he heaps scorn upon the course of action recommended by Teiresias by letting Teiresias speak his piece, rather than by directly stating, "This is wrong." The poem is full of sentiments the reverse of

Horace's usual dogma. Ulysses, using an appropriate referent, says, "et genus et virtus nisi cum re vilior alga est," "both lineage and virtue, without property, are more worthless than seaweed" (line 8). Teiresias advises him to pick up a rich and weak old man and give him food before feeding the *Lar* (line 14), and to follow him whether he is a perjurer, a nobody, a fratricide, or a fugitive slave (lines 15–17); to help a wicked but childless man before a good man with children (lines 28–41); and to take advantage of his victim's senile lusts, even to the point of giving Penelope to him (lines 70–83).

The poem also abounds in parodies of epic language. On hearing that he is to pay suit to a vile nobody, Ulysses cries out, "fortem hoc animum tolerare iubebo; / et quondam maiora tuli," "I will order my brave soul to bear this; and once I bore greater things" (lines 20–21)—exactly what he is always saying in the *Odyssey*. Teiresias, as befits a prophet, speaks in language that echoes the avant-garde epic of Horace's own day (lines 39–41); his boast of direct inspiration from Apollo is cast in traditional style (lines 59–60). Oddly enough, in the middle of all this bunkum, Teiresias uses his divine inspiration to pronounce an oracle including praise of Octavian's military exploits (lines 62–64). The seer then relates a vulgar anecdote gilded with epic epithets; presumably Octavian and others are meant to find the juxtaposition amusing.

The poem's satirical flippancy about death is best expressed in one of Teiresias' stories, about an *anus improba* ("wicked old woman") at Thebes who left orders for her corpse to be well greased and her heir to carry it over his shoulder to her funeral, because he had pressed her too hard while she was alive (lines 84–88). This anecdotal sophistication, along with the degradation of Odysseus, looks ahead to the *Satyricon*, a work with which Horace's satires share another main theme: food.

An analogy between food and both literature and life pervades Horace's satires. One of his most famous similes likens the giving of good advice to teachers' bribing schoolboys with cookies to induce them to study: "ut pueris olim dant crustula blandi / doctores, elementa velint ut discere prima," "as wheedling teachers at times give cookies to boys, so that they might wish to learn their first letters" (1.1.25–26). This is as much as to say that the satires are sugar-coated bits of serious reading. Elsewhere Horace prefers a liquid metaphor, as when he compares Lucilius' poetry to a muddy stream or in the series of images in *S.* 1.7: Rupilius' attack = *pus atque venenum*, "pus and poison" (line 1); Persius' speech, which everyone laughs at (lines 22–23), Asiatic in its exaggeration, "ruebat flumen ut hibernum fertur," "rushed as a river in winter is carried" (lines 26–27); while Rupilius' speech is like pressed wine (lines 28–31) or Italian vinegar (line 32).[36]

But food in the satires generally represents Horace's chosen mode of living, and dinners often serve as microcosms. In the first satire Horace states firmly that a man needs only enough money to buy bread, some wine, and vegetables *(holus)* (1.1.74). When the men of the Golden Age got in trouble, it was for stealing vegetables (1.3.115–17). When Horace lives in Rome, he goes to the market for vegetables (1.6.112). When Scipio, Laelius, and Lucilius got together, they ate vegetables (2.1.71–74). When Horace yearns for the rustic life, it is so that he can go and eat vegetables—beans in particular, which he whimsically labels "Pythagoras' relatives" (2.6.63–64). When the good farmer Ofellus praises the simple life, he mentions eating vegetables (2.2.117). This consistent association of vegetables with the good life greatly heightens the surprise of 2.7.29–35, where Davus the slave twits Horace beautifully by pointing out that he praises vegetables only when he has no dinner invitation.

The dinners of Horace's satires stand, sometimes explicitly, for life itself. Early on the poet sets as an ideal that we should quit life "uti conviva satur," "like a sated dinner guest" (1.1.119). At pleasant feasts the slaves have great license (1.5.51–70, 2.2.66–69, 2.6.66–67, 107–09); the pompous Catius, the gourmet, finds this disgusting (2.4.78–79). The moral difference between Ofellus and Catius shows in their attitude toward eating; Ofellus' attitude is righteous (2.2.118–21):

> ac mihi seu longum post tempus venerat hospes,
> sive operum vacuo gratus conviva per imbrem
> vicinus, bene erat non piscibus urbe petitis,
> sed pullo atque haedo . . .
>
> but whether a guest had come to me after a long time,
> or a neighbor had come through the rain to me as a
> welcome guest in my slack time,
> we did ourselves proud, not on fish sought in the city,
> but on chicken and kid . . .

Ofellus emphasizes his pleasure in his guest, where guests are rare and visits difficult. This attitude puts to shame the maxims of Catius (2.4.17–20):

> si vespertinus subito te oppresserit hospes,
> ne gallina malum responset dura palato,
> doctus eris vivam mixto mersare Falerno;
> hoc teneram faciet. . . .
>
> If a guest suddenly afflicts you toward evening,
> lest the tough hen answer badly to your palate,
> you will be wise to plunge her live in champagne and stir it;
> this will make her tender. . . .

The similar wording in the two passages strengthens the contrast. Catius is far from pleased to see his guest, nor does he even consider running to the market; any old hen will do, provided she is cooked in expensive wine.

All the even-numbered satires in book 2 deal with food: 2.2 and 2.6 with simple food and the simple life, 2.4 and 2.8 with extravagant food. The *cena Nasidieni*, at which food resembling Catius' is served and the guests ridicule the host, must have been one of the main archetypes of the *cena Trimalchionis*; odd to find the poet's patron Maecenas ensconced there, partaking of the wrong sort of food. But he, after all, is the source of Horace's dinner invitations in 2.7; and Nasidienus' guests prove their savoir faire by running out before the dinner's end. Horace, tongue in cheek, begs Catius to instruct him (2.4.88–95) and seems genuinely curious about Nasidienus' banquet; but it is the country feast in 2.6 that prompts him to exclaim, "o noctes cenaeque deum," "oh nights and dinners of the gods!" (2.6.65). The parable of the city mouse and the country mouse thus takes on a wide range of meaning: the country mouse, *pater ipse domus* (2.6.88), lives in a poor dwelling but his own, and feeds his guests on cereals; the Epicurean (line 97) city mouse takes his guest to a house not his own, where he acts the slave among epic settings. The country mouse speaks for Horace as well as himself when he bids the city mouse and his grand style adieu, saying, "me silva cavusque / tutus ab insidiis tenui solabitur ervo," "the forest and my cave safe from ambushes will console me with a slender [meal of] pea pods" (lines 116–17). In vegetables lie safety, happiness, the good life, and the right kind of poetry. The bad satirist is like a drunken parasite (*S.* 1.4.87–91).[37] This metaphor may have come from conversations close to home, for when Augustus requested Horace's services from Maecenas he used a similar one: "Horatium nostrum a te cupio abducere. veniet ergo ab ista parasitica mensa . . .," "I want to take our friend Horace from you. So he will come from that sponger's table of yours . . ." (Suet. *Vita Horati*).

Besides this highly literary construction, in which the poet reacts against more sublime genres as well as wealthier life-styles, Horace does indulge in the more personal satiric mechanisms implied in his *ars satirica*. That is to say, he does satirize other people as well as other forms of literature. He does not always reassure his reader, however; again, he sets the tone early on, directly reminding the reader of the vices he shares with the satire's victim: "quid rides? mutato nomine de te / fabula narratur," "why do you laugh? change the name, the story is told about you" (1.1.69–70). Throughout the first satire the poet uses direct address, but the identity of *tu* is constantly changing, an unsettling and thought-provoking tactic.

Still, Horace makes it clear enough that he considers some of his interlocutors and some forms of locution beyond the pale. But while his interest in attacking live and well-known victims varies, it is never strong;[38] the violent attacks he boasts of in 1.4, 1.10, and 2.1 usually find general, absent, or anonymous victims. He sneers at the provincial towns he passes on his journey (1.5.34–36, 88–92, 97–100); the obnoxious Rupilius Rex and the wealthy Persius are only a laughingstock; the bore, who writes verses quickly, dances, and sings (1.9.23–25), and who suggests he can buy his way into Maecenas' circle (1.9.45–60), makes Horace miserable. The poet is snobbish about Lucilius' use of Greek words, associating bilingualism with provincialism (1.10.20–35). Of the many dialogues in book 2, only 2.1, 2.2, and 2.6 feature speakers of whom the poet approves (Trebatius Testa and the farmers Ofellus and Cervius); the best of the rest are Damasippus, a bankrupt antique dealer turned philosopher (2.3), and Horace's own slave, Davus (2.7). The others are bad: Ulysses and Teiresias (2.5), comically out of character; Catius the gourmet (2.4); Fundanius, not bad himself but the reporter of bad living (2.8). These last two satires provide further literary parodies: Horace begins each of them like the beginning of the *Symposium*, with the poet begging the interlocutor to report to him about something he is sorry to have missed.[39] Like *S.* 2.5, 2.4 and 2.8 describe things and actions to be rejected.

There are even instances in Horace's satires of the kind of misadventures that typify satiric protagonists elsewhere. The hapless adulterer of 1.2, the impotent god of 1.8, the helpless narrator of 1.9, the taunted master of 2.7, and particularly the weary traveler of 1.5 stand with the great satiric heroes like Encolpius and Gulliver. In *S.* 1.5 the poet suffers from a whole list of minor troubles: he is ill, in both his eyes (lines 30–31, 49) and his digestion (lines 7–9, 49); deprived of a girl, he has a frustrating dream (lines 82–85). The journey pains him: Forum Appi is jammed with hooligans (lines 3–4), he goes too slowly (lines 5–6), misses dinner (lines 7–9), has an argument over a ferry (lines 11–14), is kept awake by frogs and drunken singing (lines 14–17), is run aground (lines 17–23), and is caught in a fire (lines 71–76); he struggles through the mountains of Apulia (lines 77–80), only to rest in a terribly smoky house (lines 80–81); he has to buy water (lines 88–89); the leg to Rubi is long, and it rains (lines 94–95); the road is bad (line 96). Most of the verbs for his traveling denote either crawling or hurtling. This poem, like 1.2, is thought to derive from a Lucilian model;[40] it is certainly in the mainstream of satire.

But the remainder of Horace's *sermones* are not in the mainstream of satire; that is to say, they do not resemble the other works included in the present survey. Horace's favorite means of exegesis is to use explicitly opposed pairs or polarities, or lists of extremes, a method to which he recurs throughout his satires;[41] hence his invocation of Janus (2.6.20) has special relevance. While satire, as has been seen, often works by means of polarities (for example, virile/effeminate), normally the satirist represents one extreme, his victim the other; Horace's peculiarity is to profess (at times) to espouse the middle ground, the negation of extremes. The Priapic satirist assumes the reader to be like himself; the moral Horace posits readers who wish to become moral. He makes this clear in a noted passage, the description of the method he says his father used to dissuade him from evil (1.4.104–26). Here the *exempla* represent extreme, "bad" behavior, while the youthful Horace is to represent moderate, "good" behavior. Since Horace means this to illustrate the mechanisms of his own satire, he presumably believes that satire in fact leads its readers from bad behavior to better.

This seems to be precisely the aim of the least humorous of his satires, 1.1, 1.3, 1.6, and 2.2, which offer an expressed positive to be emulated by the reader. Horace's famous invocation of the *modus in rebus*, the "middle course in life" (1.1.106), draws its strength from the fact that much of 1.1 takes public opinion as its lodestar—whether agreeing with it or not (1.1.62, 66–67, 69–70, 84–91,

95–100). The satirist is thus the establisher of norms who points out extremes of behavior—Horace setting vegetables (line 74) as the mean between wasting money and hoarding money. The poet's reminder to consider our own vices as well as those of others (1.3), his recitation of his humble origins and his gratitude toward Maecenas (1.6), and his straightforward praise of country life (2.2, 2.6) run directly counter to the tendencies of invective and satire.

In fact, they also run counter to some of Horace's own satires; it is difficult to reconcile the saintly tolerance of 1.3 and 1.6 with the elitist exclusivity of the literary satires, not to mention 1.7 and 1.9. Presumably the good advice of the pious satires is directed at the uninitiate. Perhaps the most sympathetic moment in the satires comes when Horace grants his slave the Saturnalian freedom to criticize his master, and Horace speaking as Davus brands Horace as a social climber and a would-be squire—a hypocrite (2.7.22–43). Like Tigellius, the despised singer of 1.2 and 1.3, who sometimes boasted of his simple tastes and sometimes gourmandized, Horace himself, on the testimony he puts in Davus' mouth, swings between extremes; meanwhile his patron, unlike the vegetarian Scipio in 2.1, appears only at banquets. Horace in 2.7 recognizes the contradictions between his stances, and if they are allowed to undercut each other partially the result is pleasing and human. Still, the satires do not work like other satires because they are really only about Horace himself; the humble origins he parades painfully (1.6.45–92; cf. *me consolor,* 1.6.130; *solabitur,* 2.6.117), the modest life he lives in town (1.6.104–28) or in the country, he claims to be deliberately and rationally adopted modes of living which make for true happiness, unlike the extremes of men with money. In fact, men with money clank through Horace's satires, and he makes them wield their power foolishly like frantic puppets so that he can show them up; they all waste their *patrimonia*, while Horace continues to deal out the only *patrimonium* he has—free advice. Those readers who find it possible to identify with Horace find in his elegant changes of posture a humane paradigm of the ordinary man's dilemma. But Horace's method taxes his readers in an unusual way. Like a good preacher, he asks that you not only agree with his premises but find them virtuous and act on them; other satirists generally settle for agreement, in the form of a grin, assuming that the reader already shares their views.

Critics of Horace's satires have usually wanted to justify them, one way or another; this is made difficult (as it is inspired) by the widely varying nature of the poems, demonstrated by Fraenkel in a classic comparison of 2.6 and 2.5.[42] Some have justified Horace by saying, "At least he was satirical sometimes"—pointing to 2.5 and 1.2. Others have said, "At least he grew out of nastiness like 2.5 and 1.2 into the maturity of 2.6." This sort of pull-devil-pull-baker over "the real Horace" characterizes the special pleading that a sympathetic reading of the poems demands. If they are great poems, they have a peculiar capacity for irritating their readers—though different poems irritate different readers. The only certain rule must be that, since Horace himself did not repudiate what was "Lucilian" in himself, modern critics can accept poems like *S.* 1.2 or *Epod.* 8 and 12, along with whatever personal invective exists in the satires, as *echt* Horace, and not sweep them under a carpet of *Quellenforschung*. It should be clear by now that they belong where they are.

Meanwhile, the "real Horace" awaits readers as he always has, tangled in the contradictions of his contorted self-exegesis. If he confided his "whole life" to these books, he did not do so lucidly, and this cannot be accidental; like a raconteur whose only real subject is his mysterious self, he forces the reader to wonder about the poet—not really about life, or other people. This is the same man who wrote *exegi monumentum aere perennius*. He had, of course, some justification for his self-absorption; but, as many have remarked, the format of the *Epistles* was much better suited to his temperament. There he could devote the entire poem to himself.

The end of *S.* 1.10, discussed earlier, has been approved as a graceful bow to Lucilius,[43] on the grounds that Horace here lists the few men he cares about as an audience, just as Lucilius had done. In fact the difference between Horace and his model is instructive: Lucilius, according to Cicero (*De Or.* 2.25), said, "Persium non curo legere, Laelium Decumum volo," "I don't want Persius to read [me], I do want Laelius Decumus." Cicero explains, "ea quae scriberet neque se ab indoctissimis neque a doctissimis legi velle, quod alteri nihil intellegerent, alteri plus fortasse quam ipse," "He didn't wish what he wrote to be read either by the least erudite or the most, since the former would understand nothing, the latter perhaps more than he himself"—Persius being *doctissimus*, Laelius *virum bonum, et non illiteratum, sed nihil ad Persium*, "a good man, and not uneducated, but nothing next to Persius." This is not at all what Horace says in 1.10: Lucilius cites two names as types, while Horace seems to mean the list to be taken quite literally; more important, Lucilius aims at the more modest intellect, Horace proclaims his group to be the best. It is startling and amusing to see that exclusivity like this, then as always, provoked a desire to be included (Suet. *Vita Horati*):

> Post sermones vero quosdam lectos nullam sui mentionem habitam ita sit questus: irasci me tibi scito quod non in plerisque eiusmodi scriptis mecum potissimum loquaris. an vereris ne apud posteros infame tibi sit quod videaris familiaris nobis esse?
>
> In fact, after he had read some of the *Sermones* he complained that they made no mention of him, as follows: "Know that I am angry with you because you do not have a conversation with me, rather than anyone, in several pieces of this kind. Or are you afraid that future generations will think your reputation stained if you seem to be a friend of mine?"

The writer of this letter was Augustus.

Persius

Horace's lineal descendant, the satirist Persius, uses the Priapic stance at a more abstract level than does any other satirist. Persius in his first satire makes sexuality a metaphor for literature, castigating bad literature as effeminate or pathic.[44] In this he echoes prose writers on rhetoric: the elder Seneca's lamentation on the degeneracy of current oratory implies that it is related to degenerate living, and Seneca the philosopher implies that Maecenas' effeminacy is the cause of his effete style of speaking.[45] This sort of confusion between style and life is implicit in the *apologiae* on the separation of life from work, seen above in chapter 1.

Persius' prologue and first satire contain most of what is of interest in his writings on literature. The whole is characterized by abstraction and self-consciousness, the terms and postures applied by other satirists to people here being applied to literary genres. In the prologue Persius explicitly rejects the epic tradition exemplified by Hesiod's dream on Parnassus in deliberately degrading language, using slang (lines 1–4). Likewise, in lines 5–6 he rejects the lyric tradition as lauded by his model, Horace—"quorum imagines lambunt / hederae sequaces"; compare Hor. *C.* 1.1.29. He continues the degradation of his art with the concluding comparison of the poet to the sort of bird who speaks words impelled only by the hope of a reward—no parrot he, much less swan or peacock—and the statement (lines 10–11) that he writes poetry in order to make a living: "magister artis ingenique largitor / venter, negatas artifex sequi voces," "the teacher of my art and the endower of my genius / is my belly, a master at hunting out forbidden words." Still, though this is a *recusatio* of the elevated sort of bardhood, it is not a *recusatio* of all bardhood, as the labored difficulty of the words themselves proclaims; and Persius says, in the center of the prologue (lines 6–7), "ipse semipaganus / ad sacra vatum carmen adfero nostrum," "I, half-boor, / bear my song to the rites of bards." There is a great deal of mendacity in all this, the trickiness one might expect from a devotee of Horace's satires. Persius was wealthy, not a caged bird in any physical sense, and his *recusatio*, like most, is really a profession of superiority. This *semipaganus*, like Priapus, differentiates himself from epic in order to sneer at it and stain it; in a serious way, in *Satire* 1, he criticizes the very modus vivendi of epic in his day exactly as Priapus reviles *cinaedi*.

Persius begins his first satire by plunging his audience into not just a dialogue but a rapid fire of cross talk. The gist of his exordium is that no one will read his work and that he does not care; thus he immediately brings his audience into the most intimate association with him, as each listener imagines himself included in a highly exclusive minority of two, the poet and himself, who realize how inferior all other literature is. The vagueness of Persius' words, "vel duo vel nemo" (line 3), leaves room for the reader—unlike Hor. *S.* 1.10 *ad fin.* The exclusivity and isolation of this stance and the disgust it feels or affects are expressed at line 12, "sum petulanti splene—cachinno," "I am of cross-grained spleen—I guffaw." This is the hard, mocking laughter of the self-styled renegade. In the next line Persius begins his picture of literary degeneracy in terms of sexual degeneracy (lines 13–43): the poet when reciting wears foppish clothing (lines 15–16, 32), speaks in a fluting voice (lines 17–18, 32–35), has a roving eye (line 18), and appeals sexually to the grown men in the audience (lines 18–21; cf. line 82). Paradoxically, the audience reacts in a pathic manner, as if the poetry were the poet's penis—"tremulo scalpuntur ubi intima versu" (line 21), "when their inmost parts are scratched by the trembling verse"; none of the participants conforms to the norms of virility. This softness is tied in with these poets' stupid lust for fame (lines 24–31, 40–43)—they have not the manliness to despise an audience that would praise poetry as bad as theirs.

The poem resumes the metaphor in a later section, attacking a poet/orator (line 87): "laudatur: 'bellum hoc.' hoc bellum? an, Romule, ceves?"—"he is praised: 'This is lovely.' This, lovely? Romulus, do you shake your butt?" The unthinking, effete interlocutor behaves like a pathic in accepting this purple oratory—at least, from the standpoint of Persius the satirist, who refuses to be so compliant, defying any champion of bad poetry (line 91) "qui me volet incurvasse querella," "who shall want to bend me over with his argument." The grand finale of this metaphor is a section (lines 98–106) in which Persius implies that bombastic epic is too easily done, too commonly done, and effete, and he gives some putative sample lines (lines 99–102). He concludes by asking (lines 103–04), "haec fierent si testiculi vena ulla paterni / viveret in nobis?" "Would these things happen if any bone of our fathers' balls / lived in us?" The same system of metaphors that Catullus had used for political invective, as, for example, in 29 *(cinaede Romule, haec videbis et feres?)*, Persius adopts for literary criticism.

Throughout the poem Persius continues both the exclusivity established in its first lines and the self-consciousness about his genre announced in the prologue. He expressly addresses his interlocutor as fictitious and anonymous (line 44)—"quisquis es, o modo quem ex adverso dicere feci," "whoever you are, o you whom I have made to speak the opposing argument." He rejects the crude audience that mocks the crippled, lives in obscure towns, or would laugh at a farce confronting a philosopher with a prostitute (lines 126–34)—that is, he implies his audience is composed of sophisticated Romans. In describing his yearning for freedom of speech, he appeals to the examples of Lucilius (lines 114–15) and Horace (lines 116–18), complaining that he himself seeks only a ditch into which to whisper Midas' secret; here the whole world has ass's ears (lines 119–21). Of course the "whispering" of the secret effects a broadcast of it, in the form of the satire, but the fiction lives in the flattering of each auditor and the isolation of the antibardic satirist. Persius expresses this another way (lines 113–14) by making his opponent describe the precincts of poetry as a tomb not to be urinated on: " 'pueri, sacer est locus, extra / meiite,' " " 'boys, the place is a holy one, pee / outside.' " Persius in effect, through the medium of his satire, urinates on the tomb of epic. In the rest of his satires he does the same to all non-Stoics by means not only of the content of his satires but of a grossly distorted, as it were urinary, Latin.

Persius uses the same sort of ambivalent argument in the fourth satire, where the sexual metaphor applies directly to politics. Here the bearded (*barbatum*, line 1) Socrates gives the *puer* (*pupille*, line 3; *ante pilos*, line 5) Alcibiades a lecture on political integrity; as they are differentiated in sexual status, so the main image in the poem is a sexual one, the young politician being viewed as a young prostitute. But the metaphor is mixed: beginning with foreplay ("rem populi tractas?" "do you fondle the people's thing?" line 1), the speaker first reproves the boy for an apparently active role—"quin tu . . . / blando caudam iactare popello / desinis," "why don't you stop thrusting your cock at the sweet little crowd?" (lines 14–16). But the body of the reproof, apart from an ambiguous comparison of the boy politician to an old woman selling aphrodisiacs to a depraved slave (lines 21–22), treats the boy as a pathic prostitute; if Persius can get meaning out of contradictory images, he will use them.

This imagery of pathic prostitution ranges from suggestive to explicit. The speaker repeatedly twits the boy for being too concerned for his "skin" *(cutis)* or "hide" *(pellis)*; he is "summa . . . pelle decorus," "handsome in his upmost hide" (line 14), and loves to sunbathe: "adsiduo curata cuticula sole," "your little skin taken care of with frequent sun" (line 18); "figas in cute solem," "you stick the sun on your skin" (line 33). Accusations of sunbathing do not form part of the Roman stereotype of the pathic homosexual, although the boy's suntan oil (*uncta . . . patella*, "with oiled kneecap," line 17; *unctus*, line 33) recalls the ointments and perfumes attributed to the effeminate in invective. The image becomes explicit in lines 34–41 and continues so; in order to arrive at his own direct accusation (lines 43–52), the speaker lets the first direct statement come from an imaginary stranger watching the boy basking:

est prope te ignotus cubito qui tangat et acre
despuat: "hi mores! penemque arcanaque lumbi
runcantem populo marcentis pandere vulvas.
tum, cum maxillis balanatum gausape pectas,
inguinibus quare detonsus gurgulio extat?
quinque palaestritae licet haec plantaria vellant
elixasque nates labefactent forcipe adunca,
non tamen ista filix ullo mansuescit aratro."

There is near you one unknown who'd touch you with his elbow and
spit out a harsh word: "These your morals! for a man who
    weeds his cock and the secrets
of his loin to spread his shriveling vaginas to the people.
And, since you comb that balsamed terry cloth on your jawbones,
why does that barbered corn-worm stand out from your crotches?
Five wrestling coaches may pluck those seedling beds
and undermine your well-boiled butt with their crooked forceps,
but that fern of yours won't grow tame for any plow."

The boy here, beyond simply being pathic, becomes a woman, as Persius with typical violence turns the boy's groin from depilated male genitalia to female genitalia within two lines (35–36); and not only *vulvas*, but *marcentis*, like those of an old woman. Like the hypocritical Stoic/pathics of Martial and Juvenal (Mart. 2.36, 6.56, 9.47; cf. Juv. 2.8–13), the boy has a bearded face but shaven genitalia; still, the beard is an effeminate one, *balanatum*. The boy's pathic submission becomes completely explicit in lines 39–41: his pubic hair and anus (and possibly his penis) are likened to the meadow which is the normal referent for female genitalia *(plantaria, filix)*, while those who depilate him, namely, his male lovers *(palaestritae*; cf. Lucilius 1267 Marx, *AP* 12.206, 222), attack his softened *nates* with their metallic phalli—*forcipe, aratro*. The change of roles is effected as at Catullus 11.22–24, except that here both participants are male.

Finally the speaker himself applies this metaphor to the boy (lines 43–45):

> . . . ilia subter
> caecum vulnus habes, sed lato balteus auro
> praetegit . . .

> . . . under your hips
> you have a blind wound, but a swordbelt with wide gold
> covers it up . . .

The boy's political susceptibility is both wound and vagina, camouflaged only by money. His self-esteem is only an attempt to deceive his genitalia (lines 45–47), that is, to tell himself his success derives from merit and not from self-prostitution. He still grows pale (= pathic, Cat. 80, Pers. 1.26, Mart. 1.77, Juv. 2.50) at the sight of money (line 47), he will do anything to his *penis* (line 48), he will "beat the curbstone"—that is, in a final return to the metaphor of active prostitution, he will attempt to service an imperious customer. The speaker here underscores his view of such commerce as venal by his choice of metaphor: the *puteal* was not only a curbstone but the name of the chief site for moneylending at Rome (Cic. *Sest.* 18; Hor. *S.* 2.6.35). The speaker advises the boy to "spit back what you are not," *respue quod non es* (line 51), as if in reply to *despuat* (line 35).

The system of metaphors and the kind of words chosen strongly recall *Satire* 1, especially the quasi-medical physiological terms: *patella*, not *genu*; *maxillis*, not *genis*; compare *articulis* (if the emendation is correct), 1.23. The skin, here as in the first satire (1.23), gives the addressee away: the sickness has spread to his ears as well (4.50).[46] Persius joins this persistent imagery of the infirm body with the gustatory metaphors of his model, Horace, at the end of his last satire (6.69–74):

> . . . mihi festa luce coquatur
> urtica et fissa fumosum sinciput aure,
> ut tuus iste nepos olim satur anseris extis,
> cum morosa vago singultiet inguine vena,
> patriciae inmeiat volvae? mihi trama figurae
> sit reliqua, ast illi tremat omento popa venter?

> . . . For me on the holiday dawn shall be cooked

nettle and smoked hog's jowl with split ear,
so that that grandson of yours, long sated on innards of goose,
when the captious muscle hiccups in his wandering crotch,
shall piss into a noble vagina? Shall a woof of a figure
be left to me, while his acolyte belly wobbles with fat?

Here, like Catullus, Persius expresses outrage against the usurper; the man with money has sexual potency over women, who are reduced to genitalia, the man without money grows thin and watches. It is typical of Persius that his rich man expresses his potency through semen in the guise of urine.

Petronius

The complex of themes seen so far—mock epic, Priapic boasting, misogyny—plays a great part in Petronius' *Satyricon*. Although the form is borrowed for satire by a sort of literary *contaminatio* from the Greek novel[47]—a loan amusing in itself for reasons of parody—the structure is essentially that of the satiric dialogue at its most sophisticated, for example, Horace *S.* 1.9 or 2.5, in which the fiction is that the butt has a chance to speak for himself and thereby ridicule himself. Owing to the fragmentary state of the *Satyricon*, it cannot be known whether its butt and main character, Encolpius, ever transcended his foibles and misadventures to become, like Quixote, a comic hero rather than a victim of repeated satire. In the text as it is, Encolpius is no more than a butt, endlessly experiencing humiliation only to be revived again for more of the same.

First and foremost among the characteristics of Encolpius, Ascyltos, and Giton stands their homosexuality.[48] In making them the protagonists Petronius was at once being brilliantly innovative—no butt ever had such a star role before, or would have afterward until Apuleius' *Metamorphoses*—and conforming with an essential aim of Roman satire, the exposure and ridicule of the abnormal in the form of the less virile male. This is not to say that Encolpius' homosexuality is abnormal in itself. His interest in Giton accords perfectly with the attitude toward *pueri* expressed by Martial's more sentimental epigrams, or by the *Musa Puerilis*, and he evidently has an active, if secondary, interest in women (Lichas' wife, 106.2; Tryphaena, 113.7; Circe, 126–33). His lack of virility lies only in his impotence and in his weak-kneed bluster in the face of adversity. The virile Ascyltos is actually less conventional than Encolpius, since he is not averse to the occasional bit of active prostitution (92.10). As for Giton, his age makes him a suitable sex object, and even he engages in heterosexual intercourse occasionally (25–26).

The odd thing about the three *fratres* is their ambivalence. They describe themselves and each other as *fratres* as if they were equals, equivalents of each other, although it seems that, normally, Giton fulfills the role of *puer* for both Encolpius and Ascyltos. All three will take on whatever role is most expedient, heterosexual or homosexual, an attitude that is usually a mark of low income (cf. Mart. 6.33, 11.87). Lichas' recognition of Encolpius by his penis leads the reader to suspect that Encolpius had been a concubine of his (cf. 109.3), probably active (though cf. *AP* 11.21, 22; 12.3, 207); but both Encolpius and Ascyltos accuse each other of having been pathic and/or prostitutes (9.6, 9.10, 81.4–5). Is this no more than standard invective? *Sat.* 81.5 greatly resembles *Phil.* 2.44–47 (above, chap. 1). But Encolpius does occasionally appear effeminate (110.5, 126.2); and both he and Ascyltos apparently look like prostitutes (6–8). The *fratres*, in the fleshed-out form of characters in a novel, far exceed the stick figures of epigram in complexity and idiosyncrasy.

This by no means implies that the *Satyricon* adds much depth to the stereotype of the male homosexual in Roman satire. Although the three *fratres* do have fully developed and individual characters, the novel continually holds them up to ridicule. They are cowardly, dirty, dishonest, and constantly arguing; but besides this explicit pillorying, ridicule is implicit in the satire in the chain of humiliating and harmful misadventures that the three undergo. Still, their homosexuality, while it provides one fundamental vitiation of them as protagonists, is not the foremost element in every comic description of them; for instance, though Encolpius is prone to self-aggrandizement and falls into fustian now and then, he has a normal narrative tone that is plain and pleasant.[49] The effeminacy of style castigated by Persius shows up in Encolpius only at moments of stress, and the prime examples of bombast and bad poetry are put in the mouths of the rhetor Agamemnon (5) and the epic poet Eumolpus (89, 119–24).

The most important feature of the *fratres* and especially of Encolpius is their development of the role of satiric hero.[50] Encolpius is clearly the main character, holding the central place in the novel as Aeneas did in the *Aeneid*, Odysseus in the *Odyssey*, and so on. He is a hero of sorts, but as the hero of a satire he has peculiar qualities. Foremost are his faults—cowardice, a sort of affable woolly-headedness, his besotted affection for the scruffy Giton, his pathetic attempts to be clever. The very fact that the reader is forced to identify with him, the I-figure, is a staining joke on the reader, who is torn between identifying with Encolpius and laughing at him. A second important ingredient is the long series of mishaps that assail Encolpius. Most of them are catastrophes, enough to stop an ordinary person; the satiric hero goes through one after another. Encolpius loses his way in the slums, is raped by Quartilla's aides, threatened with death at Trimalchio's feast, falls into the hands of his enemy Lichas, is shipwrecked, and beaten by witches. Not only are these adventures hazardous, they are often degrading, and Encolpius emerges from each one still moving but slightly the worse for wear. On the ship of Lichas, for example, his life is spared but he must participate in the party with shaved head and eyebrows, his face stained with a painted-on slave brand, wearing a woman's wig to make up for his lost tresses.[51] Finally, in view of Encolpius' status as an ineffectual hero, it is only fitting that the wrath of Priapus is what he flees[52] and that impotence is his curse. Encolpius lives through the punishment only threatened by the god in the garden, while the god here is only a powerful directive presence outside the narrative—quite like Petronius himself.

The joke of the wrath of Priapus brings in a secondary attribute of the novel, its use of mock epic. Secondary, because it is at least in part a self-conscious effort by the author to stain, not human figures, but a genre of literature. Thus, although an implied comparison between Encolpius and Odysseus is a good way to ridicule Encolpius, it also adds a strain of parody to the *Satyricon* that the author can drop or take up again at will. (The same can be said of the novel's relation to the Greek romance, in which Encolpius corresponds to the stalwart young hero and Giton to the blushing heroine.) Encolpius' failings make him a suitable opposite to the clever and virile Odysseus—and, if both had one god angry with them, Encolpius' lack of a countering divine protector is conspicuous. But references to the *Odyssey* on many levels abound in the *Satyricon*. Encolpius begins his extant adventures with the rhetorical brothers, Agamemnon and Menelaus. The *fratres* first encounter Trimalchio playing ball, like Nausikaa (*Od.* 6.100 ff.); then they go to a feast at his house, like the feast of Alkinoos, where, instead of telling their own tale, they hear Trimalchio butcher Homer (29.9, 39.3, 50.5, 52.1–3, 59.3–7). Fortunata has some of Arete's characteristics—"quem amat, amat" (37.7). Giton is dragged from beneath a bed where he had hung like Odysseus under the ram, throwing Encolpius into ecstasies of admiration (97). The ship of one-eyed Lichas is a Cyclops' cave for Encolpius and his companions (101.7); Lichas recognizes Encolpius by his penis as Eurykleia recognized Odysseus by his scar (105.9–10); Encolpius later has a good deal of trouble with a woman named Circe and calls himself Polyaenos, an epithet of Odysseus (127.7); he even explicitly compares himself to Odysseus, addressing, instead of his much-enduring heart, his impotent phallus (132.13). Petronius, more than any other author, was able to utilize his work to parody epic; he does this not in a consistent or allegorical way but rather expressing, through a free-form burlesque of epic plot-fragments, his characters' vitiation of the ideals of epic.[53]

Another secondary element is the literary criticism interjected by Petronius into the novel (1–5, 88). It seems peculiar to find the degraded Encolpius and the ridiculous Eumolpus or Agamemnon arguing about the reasons for the decline of oratory; in the eyes of Seneca or Persius, they are the reason for the decline of oratory. *Vir bonus dicendi peritus* is not a description of anyone in the *Satyricon*—and perhaps that is the final point of Petronius' joke. It is a joke like Horace's *Epodes* 2, in which a long argument is placed in the mouth of a speaker whose identity (as the reader discovers only in the last distich) completely undercuts his message.[54] The appropriateness of this topic for satire lies in its previous use by Horace and particularly by Persius. Where Persius, the macho narrator, equates bad literature with effeminacy, Petronius puts both bad poetry and a lament for the decline of literature in the mouths of questionable characters. It is Eumolpus' bad poem, and Agamemnon's, that suit this personality, and the reader does have the feeling that the views expressed in their tirades against literary decline are genuine views of the author. Then, too, a tirade from a character like Eumolpus provides a neat joke on Persius, whom Petronius may well have known—and Eumolpus' bad poem is a *Bellum Civile*, like that of Lucan, whom Petronius may also have known.[55] The combination of these factors suggests that all the literary criticism in the *Satyricon* is a set of jeux d'esprit only half connected with the satirical content of the novel; but the decline of words, mourned by Encolpius, certainly matches the decay in the world of the *Satyricon*.

An important characteristic of satire for which the *Satyricon* presents the first clear-cut example in Latin is the mechanism of displacement.[56] Time and again Encolpius or others get lost—in the city, and in Trimalchio's labyrinthine house; they take the wrong ship; their house becomes a *pervigilium*. This mechanism, common to satire from the *Birds* to *Gulliver's Travels* to *Alice in Wonderland*, has the effect of relaxing the laws of probability and enabling the author to move his characters from situation to situation while keeping them detached and bewildered. This element, which is so obvious in the novel form, is in fact present in verse satire in the abruptness of the shifts within dialogues and the disappearance and reappearance of interlocutors. In Petronius, and later in Juvenal, it serves as an additional means of staining or degrading the protagonist, who is always out of step or out of place; in the verse satire of Horace and Persius it is separate from whatever protagonist there is, and sometimes (as with Horace's shifting *tu* in *S.* 1.1) it acts on the reader.

The *Satyricon*, of course, satirizes more than just the *fratres* and their friends. Two of the major groups ridiculed are freedmen, in the *cena Trimalchionis*, and women, throughout the satire. The techniques Petronius uses for these two categories are much less innovative than the other aspects of his satire so far discussed, and are similar to those of other Roman satirists.

The relation of the *cena* to earlier and later comic feasts in Latin literature has been widely recognized. This recurrent topic constitutes a comic mediation of a basic societal paradox, the bad feast, as the *Iliad* is an epic mediation of the paradox of the bad king; compare the Irish satires on hospitality, and anti-invitations like those at the end of *Lysistrata* (1043–71, 1189–1215), or Catullus 13.[57] Here Petronius tries his hand at *variatio* on a traditional theme, the most eminent forerunner being the *cena Nasidieni* in Hor. *S.* 2.8. Petronius' *cena* was bound to be a tour de force in comparison with any verse version, since his medium allowed him the freedom to paint the whole scene fully and to tie it thematically with other sections of his book. Of the chief mechanisms Petronius applies here, displacement is perhaps the most important, and it crops up in the *cena* in a range of ways: the status of the *fratres* as outsiders at the feast, the freedmen's status as outsiders in Roman society, the disguise of food at the feast and its chaotic arrangement, and the way the *fratres* lose their way at the end of the feast. The theme of death, which runs as a dark current through the *cena*, is perhaps only the ultimate expression of this displacement.[58]

Still, the satire against the freedmen manifests techniques common to Catullus,

Horace, and Juvenal. Petronius mocks the way they talk, reproducing it on the page with its slang and solecisms (cf. Cat. 84). The content of their conversation is ridiculous in many ways: they are venal, uneducated, foreign born, and vulgar; when they pretend to culture they fail; they reveal their slave origins and some even boast of them. They air rivalries that stem from unworthy causes. Their wives are silly and not ladylike, and are in addition treated vulgarly by the husbands. Above all, Petronius mocks all that Trimalchio creates: his ostentatious house, which itself incorporates solecisms; the incredible (and often inedible) food; and especially Trimalchio's impersonation of a Roman landowner, in his treatment of his slaves, his references to his estates, and his contemptible poetastery. The whole is no more than a straightforward mockery of a victim perceived as inferior, through the use of an expanded dialogue form. But this mockery is not without sympathy. All the freedmen's follies can be summed up in a word: it is their insecurity that Petronius mocks. Whether it manifests itself in Hermeros' blustering defensiveness (57–58) or in Trimalchio's pretensions, Petronius bases his caricature of them on a tension that must have run strongly in these men, once and potentially always slaves.[59]

And here again Petronius undercuts the view expressed in the narrative; after all, the eyes through which the reader perceives these men are Encolpius' eyes, those of a debauched fool. Is he right to look down on them? That would be to agree that these money-grubbing nouveaux riches are worse than any fool. Or is Encolpius again ridiculous for his pretensions to superiority? He had been glad enough to be offered a free dinner. A third possibility, a vector like Swift's in *Gulliver* 4, is that there is a middle ground, an implied positive, like Horace's expressed positive; but there is no one in the extant *Satyricon* to embody it. This makes it seem that Petronius takes the stance that there is no positive, except possibly to be a satirist or a reader of satire and despise the world. The reader is duped into identifying with Encolpius, who despises Trimalchio, and Encolpius himself cuts no admirable figure.

Petronius' satire of women, like his attack on the freedmen, is wholly consonant with the standpoint of other satirists. When listed, Petronius' women form a cavalcade of stereotypes of women in Roman satire. There is the old woman who leads Encolpius to the brothel; she is randy and nasty, a typical *vetula* (with, probably, a touch of the mock epic: "divinam ego putabam," "I thought her a divinity" [7.2], as if she were Venus in *Aeneid* 1 or Athena in *Odyssey* 7). Quartilla, the priestess of Priapus, is a monster of orgiastic religiosity; together with her maids, she is far beyond the powers of the three cowardly *fratres* to resist. She rapes them by means of *cinaedi*, a novel touch, but her voyeuristic pimping of her maid Pannyche to Giton makes her a standard *lena* (or *socrus*). Fortunata and her friend Scintilla typify the gaudily bedizened wealthy harridan, loaded with jewels; Circe and her maid are normal examples of the aristocratic woman hunting for a low lover and the pert maid who likes aristocratic men. Oenothea is a witch, like all witches dangerous to virility; the old woman at Croton who goes in for *captatio* is, like Quartilla, only too willing to sell her daughter. Only Tryphaena has a certain individuality, combining features of Fortunata and of Circe; like Eppia in Juvenal 6 she is a stout sailor when she can indulge herself at the same time.

Tryphaena's most important function is as an audience for the tale of the widow of Ephesus; here again, Petronius has provided an audience who exhibits an incongruous reaction to his words. Like Encolpius at the *cena*, Tryphaena is shocked, but the joke is clearly that she is in no position to be shocked. This is important because the widow's tale cynically subverts one of the most sacred ideals of Roman womanhood, that a woman should be *univira*.[60] The widow, betrayed by death, vows to die by a living death, is talked into living and betraying her husband, and ends by giving her husband's body to save her living lover. The body replaces another body stolen from its cross. Tryphaena reacts with shock as if she were a proper Roman matron, which she is not; neither was the widow. Thus chastity and its audience are both false and presented in a story that operates by falsehoods and substitutions, and is recounted by Eumolpus, no reliable source. Earlier, he narrates the tale of the boy of Pergamum, which also explodes a myth, this time of the pure, coy *puer*; this *puer* is not only greedy but sexually insatiable.

Thus certain strains are common to all aspects of the *Satyricon*—its structure, its style, and its content. The structure continually destroys the hero, making of him a constantly restored butt and gratifying the audience with recoveries and repeated destructions. In addition, the narrative takes an occasional turn toward the self-conscious with flights of mock epic. These mechanisms, with the style, repeatedly stain victims—anti-hero(es), freedmen, women—or their language, or displace them, using a good deal of play with deceptions and disguises. Finally, the content—the impotent pederastic hero pursued by the wrath of Priapus, the kind of people he meets, and, perhaps, the views he espouses—is in itself full of contradictions, disguises, and deception. In all three aspects nothing is what it seems for long, and interpretations offered within the text are unreliable. Where the hero is an Encolpius who is perpetually humiliated in new sets of strange surroundings, there is no implied positive, and both virtue and the lack of virtue are fictions. Priapus is as ridiculous as Encolpius. Thus Petronius is wholly different from Horace, with his didacticism and his expressed positive; this produces the feeling that the *Satyricon* is both dark and somehow alien to other Roman satire, for most Roman satire leaves room for a positive somewhere. On the other hand, only Juvenal has left such sharp images of things he has seen, like still photographs taken in a clear light, full of apparently accidental beauty.

Juvenal

The last author to be discussed here epitomizes all that has gone before. In his subject matter and in his attitude Juvenal embodies the Priapic satirist; his manifold verbal borrowings from earlier satirists pale beside his amplification of their themes and the grand scale on which he makes the mask of Priapus his own persona.[61]

This persona is well established in the first, programmatic satire, even in the first few lines:

> Semper ego auditor tantum? numquamne reponam
> vexatus totiens rauci Theseide Cordi?
> inpune ergo mihi recitaverit ille togatas,
> hic elegos? . . .
>
> Am I always to be only the audience? Shall I never retaliate,
> I who have been harassed so many times by the *Theseid*
> of hoarse Cordus?
> Unpunished by me, then, shall one man write historical dramas,
> the other elegies? . . .

Juvenal is beginning a harangue similar in import to that of Persius' prologue and first satire, against the (supposedly) insipid literature of his time; the instances here are drama and elegy rather than Persius' epic and lyric, but the idea is the same. The literature is similarly bombastic and similarly ineffectual (lines 7–13). The harangue will soon (line 22) turn from lambasting literature to satirizing people, and the aliveness of this satire in comparison with Persius' abstraction is predicted by the viable and lively program implicit in the first four lines. Juvenal depicts himself as deliberately provoked by bad poets (*vexatus*, line 2) and hence called upon to strike back, to punish (*reponam*, line 1; *inpune*, lines 3, 4). The threat against bad poets is left here; in fact, the satire itself will constitute Juvenal's retaliation (lines 19–21). The threatening attitude reappears several times in the first satire:

> . . . nam quis iniquae
> tam patiens urbis, tam ferreus ut teneat se (30–31)
>
> . . . for who is so submissive
> to the unbalanced city, so ironclad that he can hold himself in

> quid referam quanta siccum iecur ardeat ira,
> cum . . . (45–46)
>
> Why need I say with how much anger my dry liver burns,
> when . . .

> nonne libet medio ceras inplere capaces
> quadrivio, cum . . . (63–64)
>
> Doesn't it seem right to fill up big notebooks
> in the middle of the crossroads, when . . .

> si natura negat, facit indignatio versum
> qualemcumque potest . . . (79–80)

> If nature denies it, indignation makes verses
> of whatever sort it can . . .

These lines have often been quoted by those who have characterized Juvenal as angry or indignant. Yet anger and indignation are misleading terms to use in connection with Juvenal; his attitude is actively hostile and threatening. His satire is not only a vehicle for the particularized listing of the things that make him angry but in itself constitutes a vengeance upon those things by holding them up to ridicule—embodied by the notebooks at the crossroads (lines 63–64). That Juvenal feels his writing to be an aggressive action (as opposed to keeping silent) is shown by the contrast he draws at lines 30–31, "quis . . . tam patiens urbis?" He (or his sympathetic listener) is not *patiens urbis*, that is, he will not submit to the city passively. The underlying idea is exactly that of Persius 1.87—"an, Romule, ceves?"—that Juvenal will not be a pathic for the city's vices, that he will rail against them as Priapus rails against thieves.

The obverse of this anger is fear. In Catullus' poetry Priapic threats were sometimes turned around, so that the poet would at one time threaten to rape his enemies as inferior to him and at another time complain of his enemies as overly Priapic, in a sense superior to or at least stronger than he. Both attitudes wind up by exposing the enemy as inferior, in strength in the first instance and in refinement in the second. The attitude as a whole is part of the perception of the world as divided into strong and less strong, dominator and dominated, the domination being motivated by a fear of being dominated. Thus Juvenal's anger against those he despises is matched by a fear that he will not be allowed to express his contempt outright. His early boasts that he will emulate Lucilius and Horace (lines 20, 51) necessitate a long coda in which, by means of a dialogue, he explores whether it is really possible for him to write as Lucilius had written (lines 150–71). E. J. Kenney has demonstrated the strong relationship between this section of Juvenal 1 and Horace *S.* 2.1.[62] But there are basic differences especially pertinent to the present discussion: whereas Horace weasels out of Trebatius' cautious arguments by making a joke, Juvenal gives a much more concentrated and anxious picture of the bad things that happen to those who offend the corrupt and wealthy (lines 153–71):

> ". . . 'cuius non audeo dicere nomen?
> quid refert dictis ignoscat Mucius an non?'
> pone Tigillinum, taeda lucebis in illa
> qua stantes ardent qui fixo gutture fumant,
> et latum media sulcum deducit harena."
> qui dedit ergo tribus patruis aconita, vehatur
> pensilibus plumis atque illinc despiciat nos?
> "cum veniet contra, digito compesce labellum:
> accusator erit qui verbum dixerit 'hic est.'
> securus licet Aenean Rutulumque ferocem
> committas, nulli gravis est percussus Achilles

aut multum quaesitus Hylas urnamque secutus:
ense velut stricto quotiens Lucilius ardens
infremuit, rubet auditor cui frigida mens est
criminibus, tacita sudant praecordia culpa.
inde ira et lacrimae. tecum prius ergo voluta
haec animo ante tubas: galeatum sero duelli
paenitet." experiar quid concedatur in illos
quorum Flaminia tegitur cinis atque Latina.

". . . 'Whose name do I not dare to name?
What does it matter whether Mucius forgives my words or not?'
Depict Tigellinus, you will shine in that torch
on which they burn standing who smoke when their throat's been stuck through,
and which draws a broad furrow down the middle of the arena."
A man who's given arsenic to three uncles, shall he then
be carried on hanging cushions and look down on us from there?
"When he meets you face to face, press your lip with your finger;
he will be considered a prosecutor who says the words, 'He's the one.'
You can safely engage Aeneas with the fierce Rutulian,
a stricken Achilles bothers no one,
or Hylas much sought after and gone with his bucket;
whenever Lucilius, burning, as if with drawn sword,
thundered, the listener blushes whose mind is frozen
with sins, his heart sweats with silent guilt.
Thence rage and tears. Therefore turn over in your mind first
these things before the trumpet sounds; once you've got your helmet on
it's too late to repent of battle." I'll try what is allowed against those
whose ashes are covered by the Flaminian and Latin roads.

His anonymous interlocutor threatens not Trebatius' court case, a suit for libel, but a crucifixion, in horrid detail (lines 155–57). Juvenal expresses not only frustrated outrage but jealousy of the luxuries enjoyed by the evil (lines 158–59), but the interlocutor advises the poet to adopt the safe genre of epic, harking back to the serious repercussions of satire he had described earlier with an epic metaphor of armed combat (lines 169–70). A direct reminiscence of Horace *S.* 2.1 occurs in the depiction of Lucilius "ense velut stricto" (line 165), the sword of satire that Horace had vowed to use only in self-defense. Here it is out of its sheath and threatening an *auditor* (line 166) who can strike back. This returns the reader to Juvenal's opening cry, "semper ego auditor tantum?" Although he can strike back by means of satire, his card is trumped by the figure he fears, leading him to conclude with the remarkable statement that he will attack only those already dead (lines 170–71). Fifteen satires are to follow; it is obvious that he expects some satisfaction from this and that the dead to be attacked are recognizably similar to the living who annoy him. Perhaps these dead are also the old targets of Juvenal's revered predecessors.[63]

Fear, as a concomitant of hostility, informs not only the satirist's statements about those above him but his jeers at those below him. The unifying factor in most of Juvenal's victims is their abnormality; that is, if the poet's persona is the norm and the epitome of his audience, those he satirizes are abnormal, excessive, and different—hence bad. The satirist takes great pains to reassure himself and his audience that he and they are good and normal. The figures who particularly arouse Juvenal's spleen in *Satire* 1 are:

a eunuch who marries (22)
a woman who hunts or fights as a huntress in the arena (22–23)
a barber who is now as wealthy as the patricians (24–25)
an Egyptian vulgarian who is now a wealthy dandy (26–29)
a lawyer who is grossly fat (32–33)
a *delator* whom all his great friends, and other *delatores*, fear (33–36)
those who earn legacies by servicing a wealthy old woman (37–44)
a guardian who has defrauded his ward (46–48)
a governor who has defrauded his province (49–50)
a husband who pimps his wife (55–57)
a potential military officer who spends all his money on horses (58–62)
a man who has become wealthy by forging a will (64–68)
a woman who has poisoned her husband and will teach other women to do the same (69–72)
corrupt new brides, adolescent adulterers (77–78)
gamblers who lose fortunes and let their slaves freeze (88–93)
wealthy freedmen who crowd both the poet and the high state officers off the doorstep (95–126)
Egyptians who have monuments put up to them (129–31)
patroni who disappoint their *clientes* of a dinner invitation, letting them eat cabbage while they dine alone on a roast boar (132–46)

It is clear from this list that, although the satire conveys an impression of a varied and colorful crowd of sinners, they all act in the same way and annoy the poet for the same reason: each one has acted contrary to the way he or she is supposed to act. What qualifies these figures to be the butt of satire is that they can be perceived as out of kilter, abnormal, and also as potentially harmful or threatening, since they are not just, for example, thieves and murderers but deceitful thieves and murderers. By pointing out these vices in a derisive way the satirist reassures himself and his audience that they themselves are not abnormal or vicious, and are not deceived by those who are.

The fear is even more specific than this, however. A recurrent strain in *Satire* 1 is the satirist's jealousy of these wicked people for enjoying wealth and security, and at his expense. The wealthy barber is one who had shaved Juvenal as a young man (line 25); the funereal Egyptian forbids the passerby/Juvenal to urinate on his tomb (line 131). Most important of all, the wealthy freedman literally takes the food out of Juvenal's mouth, as he shoves ahead of the poet in the crowd awaiting the *sportula* (lines 95–102). It is in the expression of this sort of fear and resentment that the satirist unites himself with his audience against the victim of the satire—a victim here castigated for being stronger than the satirist, for frightening him. In this description of the *sportula*, Juvenal closely unites a second-person address of the audience and/or an imaginary protagonist (*agnitus accipies*, line 99) with a depiction of himself as present at the scene (*nobiscum*, line 101). He has brought himself and his addressee physically into the poem together, imagining them both together edged off the doorstep of the *patronus* as the wealthy *clientes* press forward. Again at lines 132–41 the wealthy *patronus* takes the food from the clients' mouths, and at lines 142–46 the poet actually imagines the *patronus'* death from overeating and states how happy his angry friends (*iratis . . . amicis*, line 146) then are.

The fear is claustrophobic as well: just as Juvenal is thrust aside by the freedmen on the doorstep, so his addressee is shoved aside by the *captatores* in the street (*cum te summoveant*, line 37); he sees huge litters go by bearing the undeserving (lines 32–33, 64–66), who look down on him (lines 158–59); the poisoner runs into him (*occurrit*, line 69). The injustice and abnormality of the situation are expressed in a series of *sententiae* (lines 73–76), which can be summed up by one, "probitas laudatur et alget," "goodness is praised and shivers"; the claustrophobic positioning of the poet amongst the abnormal is summed up by his picture of himself standing at the crossroads writing in his notebook (lines 63–64). The poem makes the auditor feel he is there too, jostled, contaminated, and injured by the touch of the abnormal, yet blessedly, virtuously different from them. Juvenal's introduction adroitly places his audience in the position with which he claims he himself has grown impatient—that of auditor. He makes his satire be an expression of both his and his audience's hostility.

This view of the world's structure pervades Juvenal's satires, even the later ones classed as Horatian, as mellower than the rest. It is true that *Satires* 11–16 often recall Horace's satires; both 11 and 14 have markedly Horatian introductions, with lists of different kinds of extreme behavior. But Juvenal continues to see extravagant behavior from the viewpoint of one who cannot afford it, so that his message is, "Be good—or else!"—a wistful threat. After the tenth satire establishes the inexorable nature of Fortuna, each subsequent satire balances a more powerful (fortunate) group against a less powerful one: 11, rich (young?) man/poor (old) man; 12, *captator*/friend; 13, thief/honest man; 14, old man (father)/young man (son); 15, eaters/eaten; 16, soldier (son)/civilian (father). Juvenal provides the reader with an expressed positive much like Horace's: a farm dinner, rich in its simplicity (11.56–76); a garden (11.78, 14.319, 15.174, though rejected at 13.122–23). This way of life is clearly connected with the good old days of the Roman *maiores* (11.77–119, 14.159–72), when the gods were closer to men (11.111).

Unfortunately, the gods are no longer close to men (13.38–52, mock epic; cf. 15.70–71) and cannot be counted on to aid the righteous or punish the wicked (13.112–19). The good host of *Satire* 11 is an old man (11.203), and a pleasant dinner and sitting in the sun, as it turns out, are to console his guest for financial worries and cuckoldry (11.185–92). The bad host has voluptuous serving boys and exotic dancers (11.145–76), along with money; the soldier of *Satire* 16 can beat civilians brutally (16.7–12), humiliate them in a military court (16.13–34), go to court when he pleases while the civilian has to wait on dilatory judges (16.35–50), and make both a will and money for himself so that his father must humor him (16.51–60). The retribution of the young (son kills father, 14.246–55), of fortune (shipwreck leads to beggary, 14.265–302), and of the tardy but savage gods (13.244–49) must be the consolation of the powerless. Juvenal in these poems is no amused observer; as he remarks about his predecessor (7.62), "satur est cum dicit Horatius 'euhoe,'" "Horace was full when he said 'hallelujah.'"

The earlier satires treat the struggle for power rather than the problems of impotence. The hostility of the three sexual satires, 2, 6, and 9, can easily be understood in this light, as well as the xenophobic *Satire* 3, the political pecking order derived in 4, the relationship between *patronus* and *cliens* in 5, *patronus* and poet in 7, commoner and noble in 8. The sexual satires draw together elements common to all levels of Latin invective: the sixth satire recalls not only Lucilius but invective against old women, while *Satires* 2 and 9 contain an elemental expression of hostility on the part of the norm against the abnormal.[64]

Again, in *Satire* 2, it is deceitfulness that Juvenal claims he hates most in his victims, who are pathic homosexuals pretending to be puritanical Stoic philosophers; it is their hypocrisy that galls him most, and he claims not to mind a blatant effeminate nearly as much (lines 15–35), branching off to take a sideswipe at a similar bit of sexual hypocrisy on the part of Domitian (lines 29–33). But the satire begins with Juvenal's statement that the vice he is about to expose makes him wish to flee to the Arctic wastes (lines 1–2), a hyperbolically strong expression of disgust and of the wish to differentiate oneself from another.

All the stereotypical characteristics of pathic homosexuals are present in *Satire* 2, most of them closely echoing Martial: the shaved rump (lines 11–12), anal warts (line 13), special walk (line 17), wiggling hips (lines 20–21), use of perfume (lines 40–42), enjoyment of performing fellatio (line 50). Special mention and whole sections are devoted to womanishness and transvestitism (lines 54–57; 65–78; the orgies of Bona Dea aped by transvestites, lines 83–116; Gracchus as bride, lines 117–42). Juvenal allows a woman to upbraid these false Stoics, lines 36–63, and explicitly endorses her words, lines 64–65—itself a deliberate degradation of them, the sort of farce Persius specifically rejects (1.133). At the same time Juvenal contrasts these men with the proper, Roman, manly sort of man, first in a reproach of Mars, who has allowed his rough shepherds to degenerate so (lines 126–28), finally in a brilliant fantasy of the great ghosts of the Roman military past confronted with such a shade in Hades (lines

149–59). The horror expressed by Juvenal at pathic homosexuality throughout, and also in the xenophobe's nightmare in lines 159–70, is very much the attitude of the Priapic male; still, the almost Aristophanic invention of the confrontation in hell, also a great parody of *Aeneid* 6, hints that the satirist does not take military virility as an altogether sacred positive.

The abuse of homosexuality in *Satire* 9 is more subtle and more condemnatory of Roman society as a whole. The interlocutor, who is the only example in Juvenal of a character as developed as those in Horace, is the homosexual prostitute Naevolus ("Little Wart"). He is not, however, a pathic but a "stud" who services women as well as men (lines 25–26). The bulk of the satire is devoted to an exposition of the greed and depravity of the pathic rich man, Virro ("Manly"), upon whom Naevolus depends (lines 27–101). The complementary greed of Naevolus receives special emphasis in his whining about his circumstances, especially at the end of the satire (lines 124–50), and his conniving ways are made to recall those of Odysseus by means of warped epic allusions put into his own mouth (lines 37 [= *Od.* 16.294, 19.13], 148–50). But once again the satirist imagines the whole city of Rome as pathic, consoling Naevolus with these words (9.130–33):

> ne trepida, numquam pathicus tibi derit amicus
> stantibus et salvis his collibus; undique ad illos
> convenient et carpentis et navibus omnes
> qui digito scalpunt uno caput. . . .
>
> Don't be afraid, a pathic friend will never be lacking to you
> as long as these hills are standing and safe; from all sides to them
> gather all those, by wagon and by ship,
> who scratch their head with one finger. . . .

This mark of the pathic formed part of the taunt flung at Pompey by the opposing claque (above); in general, *Satire* 9 is more Priapic in its stance than *Satire* 2 is, since it assumes that the whole of Rome is filled with pathics suitable for Naevolus' attentions. The satirist in effect rapes Rome with Naevolus as his agent—an agent at whom he jovially sneers.

> Look, in a Latin country, and that's Paris or even Strasbourg, a woman without a man is public property. It's a whore or it's rapable. Once alone, in the street or the cafe or the train, she's regarded as belonging to anyone who takes a fancy. This attitude is one of the most primitive there is. We've barely scratched the surface. Woman is butcher's meat.[65]

The great sixth satire constitutes the single largest example of invective against women remaining from antiquity.[66] The lines from Freeling above explain, in simple terms, the use of invective against women in literature. When women appear in the fiction of a poem they are essentially alone, at the mercy of the author, able to be manipulated, open to a sort of rape; hence the frequent treatment of them as either sexually attractive or repulsive, as in erotic poetry and invective against old women. Since satire, particularly Juvenal's satire, is concerned largely with expressing fear and hostility toward threatening people, the procedure adopted in *Satire* 6 is that of denial that any woman is acceptable, even if she is beautiful (lines 142–60) or virtuous (lines 161–83), and of frequent and lascivious depiction of women as whores—the closest approximation of verbal rape, the ultimate Priapic reaction to women.

That the hostility toward women in *Satire* 6 stems from fear is easily seen. The many sections all concern women who in one way or another exceed the limits of the role of the Roman *matrona*, thereby threatening the husband. Their behavior is excessive or contradictory, that is, they do things women are not supposed to do; frequently they take on overly aggressive or traditionally male roles. This aspect of their behavior is obvious from a breakdown of the sections of the poem:

lines	
1–22	Introduction: the Golden Age, the origins of adultery
23–37	Why marry? It's an insane act.
38–59	Still even a licentious man will marry, and he wants a chaste wife; he must be mad.
60–81	Women love actors.
82–113	Eppia follows a *ludus*: aristocrat chases gladiator.
114–35	Messallina: empress = prostitute.
136–41	Rich women control their husbands.
142–60	Pretty women are soon thrown out; meanwhile they waste money.
161–83	Good women are boring.
184–99	The *Graeca vetula*: old woman = flirt.
200–30	A wife tries to run her husband's money, friends, and slaves.
231–41	Mother-in-law promotes adultery.
242–45	Litigious women
246–67	An athletic woman embarrasses her husband.
268–85	A jealous wife is really concealing her adultery.
286–300	*Locus de saeculo*
301–51	The orgy of Bona Dea (including the desecration of the altar of Chastity)
352–65	Extravagant women rent trappings for the games.
Oxford fragment (*O*.1–34)	Women keep effeminate confidant/lovers.
366–78	Women use eunuchs as their lovers.
379–97	Women take musicians as their lovers.
398–412	A woman tries to gossip with men of affairs.
413–33	A woman tries to drink and feast with men in company.
434–56	A literary woman acts superior to men.
457–73	A rich woman wears too much makeup.

474–507	A woman's daily routine: sadism, lovers.
508–11	A wife wastes her husband's money and rejects his friends.
511–91	Women are religious fanatics:
	511–41 Bellona and Egyptian gods
	542–47 Jewish seer
	548–52 Haruspex
	553–64 *Chaldaei*
	565–81 Women totally depend on seers.
	582–91 The seers of lower-class women
592–609	Upper-class women refuse to have children, or produce bastards or supposititious children.
610–26	Women bewitch their families with magic potions.
627–61	Women murder inconvenient family members.

The uncomfortable role reversal produced in this scheme is the target of several sections: lines 136–41 (rich women who run their husbands); lines 246–67 (the athlete—the husband's shame when she sells her equipment publicly, the scatological joke on her toilet habits);[67] lines 398–412 (the gossip who "boldly . . . can bear the assemblies of men and speak with cloaked generals in her husband's presence with a straight face and dry tits"); lines 413–44 (the crude, drunken woman who nauseates her husband); and of course the picture of the literary critic (lines 434–56), who evaluates the poets, forcing all male speakers and critics to be silent—also all women. Juvenal says of her (lines 445–47):

> nam quae docta nimis cupit et facunda videri
> crure tenus medio tunicas succingere debet,
> caedere Silvano porcum, quadrante lavari.

> For a woman who wants to seem too learned and eloquent
> ought to kilt her tunic up to her shins,
> kill a pig for Silvanus, and be bathed for a penny.

All these are social characteristics of men. Juvenal concludes his thoughts on literary women by crying that they should limit their grammatical corrections to the vulgar among their women friends, and let their husbands err in peace.

At the end of the satire Juvenal describes serious crimes that women commit (lines 610–61); these are crimes that threaten men. Not only do the women murder their sons (lines 627–61), they use magic potions to rob their husbands of their wits (lines 610–26), potions (lines 611–12)

> . . . quibus valeat mentem vexare mariti
> et solea pulsare natis . . .

> . . . by which she can harass her husband's mind
> and beat his butt with a slipper . . .

Here Juvenal steps into the territory of tragedy, as he himself says; the Greek tragedians liked to explore the ways in which women who murder family members manifest male characteristics.

A major subdivision of the transgressions noted by Juvenal, however, concerns adultery—the case of a wife who is promiscuous. Out of thirty-one sections in *Satire* 6, eleven deal primarily with adultery (not counting passing mentions elsewhere), for a total of 301 lines out of 695—that is, 35 percent of the sections but almost 45 percent of the lines.

The perceptions of women's sexuality in *Satire* 6 are particularly noteworthy and striking. After making the introductory generalizations that adultery came in immediately after the Golden Age (lines 1–24) and that it is impossible to find a chaste Roman matron (lines 38–59), Juvenal launches into a series of vignettes on types of women. The first three deal with women's promiscuity, with increasing specificity and prurience. In these first three episodes Juvenal focuses his satire on the "fact" that women are not just promiscuous but are especially attracted to low sorts of men. The actors in lines 60–81 and the gladiator in lines 82–113 represent a class of men who were legally *infamis*; the idea that *infames* are the men who attract women is repeated in the *O* fragment, lines 366–78, 379–97, and implanted in the infidelities of lines 268–85 and the orgies of 301–51. Thus women not only choose to give their love to those who are unworthy, thereby cuckolding their husbands, but themselves are stained by consorting with such men.

Moreover, their lust is frenzied and enormous. The Messallina episode has been discussed above; in her case one can see clearly, along with her promiscuity and inability to be satiated, the staining of herself, her son, and her cuckolded husband, who through her is physically tainted by the dirt of the brothel. This episode is paralleled by the description of the orgiastic rites of Bona Dea, standing at the exact center of the poem. Juvenal leads into the vignette with a run-of-the-mill specimen of the *locus de saeculo* (lines 286–300). Then he sketches drunken women at a feast, and the aftermath of it (lines 301–13); then begins the description of the rites themselves. The audience is immediately plunged into the orgy—flutes wailing, wine flowing, women tossing their hair in great circles and shrieking. At first, in Juvenal's story, the women content themselves with lascivious dancing, and the *matronae* surpass the prostitutes; then they call for men (lines 327–34):

> tunc prurigo morae inpatiens, tum femina simplex,
> ac pariter toto repetitus clamor ab antro
> "iam fas est, admitte viros." dormitat adulter,
> illa iubet sumpto iuvenem properare cucullo;
> si nihil est, servis incurritur; abstuleris spem
> servorum, venit et conductus aquarius; hic si
> quaeritur et desunt homines, mora nulla per ipsam
> quo minus inposito clunem summittat asello.

Then their itch can't bear delay, then woman acts her true self,
and from all equally the shout is repeated from the whole apse,
"Now it's right, let in the men." The adulterer is asleep,
she orders a boy to grab his cloak and hurry over;
if there is none, they run to the slaves; if you take away the hope
of slaves, the milkman comes, for a fee; if he
is sought and there are no men, there's no delay, for her part,
in putting her butt under a superimposed burro.

Thus the climax of women's lust, the goal of their degradation, is to copulate with animals; their lust is not human but animal.[68]

Another detail in the orgy scene of great importance in the framework of *Satire* 6 is the vignette in which the two women returning from the party pause at the shrine of Chastity (lines 306–13):

i nunc et dubita qua sorbeat aera sanna
Tullia, quid dicat notae collactea Maurae
Maura, Pudicitiae veterem cum praeterit aram.
noctibus hic ponunt lecticas, micturiunt hic
effigiemque deae longis siphonibus implent
inque vices equitant ac Luna teste moventur,
inde domos abeunt: tu calcas luce reversa
coniugis urinam magnos visurus amicos.[69]

Go now, check it out, with what a sneer Tullia sniffs the air,
and what the milk-mate of the notorious Maura says,
Maura, when she's passing the old altar of Chastity.
At night they stop their litters here, they piss here,
and fill the statue of the goddess with long squirts,
and take turns riding each other, and are moved with the Moon
for witness,
and from there they go to their homes: you, when light's returned,
tread your wife's urine on your way to visit your great friends.

Tullia, the Roman aristocrat, enjoys her disreputable outings in the company of Maura, perhaps a freedwoman (judging from her name). The goddess Chastity was last seen in *Satire* 6 in lines 19–20, fleeing the earth with her sister Justice (cf. the themes of the sections outlined above, excessive behavior and adultery). Now here she is again, a statue at an old altar, standing in the deserted streets in the moonlit night. The two women who visit her come only to sneer, and they show their contempt by urinating upon her (for this image as emblematic of Persius' and Juvenal's satire, see above), directing their urine in streams as if they were men. They complete their insult by having intercourse with each other, the ultimate removal of man; they have only the moon for a witness.[70] The lonely scene recalls the rites of the two witches in Hor. *S.* 1.8.35–36, where the moon hides and only

Priapus is witness. At last the women, like Messallina, go home, an undescribed contamination. Thus the poem has three rough structural peaks of violent emotion—the introduction, this central section, and the last section, in which women are murderous monsters.

The last two lines of this vignette remain to be discussed. Juvenal likes to cap his pictures with an unexpected final twist, an abrupt shift of angle or context that forces the reader to turn a mental corner while proceeding with the text (hence his many parentheses). The one here has great importance, for here the audience visualizes clearly how the wife's misbehavior physically stains her husband. Juvenal brings this home to his listeners by making the husband again *tu*; he then marches him right through the puddle of urine. This defilement is bad enough, but the husband is, like the poor men in *Satires* 1 and 3, up early to pay the duty calls of a humble client; and he cannot know whose urine he has stepped in. He is in all ways pathetic—humbled by powerful men, stained by his wife, and too ignorant to know what is going on. He is none other than the satiric hero, the victimized protagonist, like Encolpius in the *Satyricon*. In Juvenal this figure, looking a little like Buster Keaton, only flits through the pages—as Umbricius in *Satire* 3, for instance, or as the timid traveler at 10.19–21. In *Satire* 6, as in the lines just discussed, this figure demonstrates that the satirist's hostility is expressed against other men as well as against women; the narrator of 6 thinks women make other men fools, hence both women and the other men are the butt of the satire. This lends a certain ambivalence to the position of the audience. For instance, the *tu* at line 312 forces each man to make a sudden and uncomfortable identification with the satire's butt; resentment of this must be quickly foisted upon other husbands or on all wives.

Like the other Roman satirists, Juvenal matches this general hostility with an abuse of epic. Mock epic in Juvenal is deft and witty, like the scene at the end of *Satire* 2, which skewers both military glory and myths of Hades. Another famous send-up is the description of the fate of the man crushed by rocks in *Satire* 3 (lines 256–67); here again, myths of death are the subject of Juvenal's mockery. The specific reference of the parody to Lucretius is keyed by the questions on what has become of the matter comprising the man's body (lines 259–61), and the travesty of Lucretius 3.889–99 continues with a homely picture of the unwitting carrying on of domestic activities (lines 261–64) while the poor man shivers on the shores of the Styx without a coin to give the ferryman. It has been suggested that most of *Satire* 4 is a parody of epic council scenes, especially as in Statius;[71] this aspect of the poem enhances the straight satire of the council itself, a series of telling descriptions of real men. A final and clear example, 15.13–26, takes on a familiar epic victim: Odysseus. Juvenal imagines one of Odysseus' audience in Phaeacia, goaded by the tale of the Laestrygones and the Cyclops, coming out and calling him a liar ("ut mendax aretalogus," says Juvenal, he is "like a lying Stoic parasite"). Here Juvenal uses this mild perversion of the epic story to emphasize his own veracity, the superiority of satire over epic: he will tell an amazing tale *(miranda quidem)* but one that happened recently, and he gives the year and the place (lines 27–28).

In *Satire* 15 Juvenal elevates the Priapism in his satires to the level of theology, combining this with an elucidation of his *ars poetica*. After Juvenal has stated his superiority to Odysseus, he enlarges on the special nature of the story he is about to tell—an episode of cannibalism in Egypt (15.27–32):

> nos miranda quidem sed nuper consule Iunco
> gesta super calidae referemus moenia Copti,
> nos volgi scelus et cunctis graviora coturnis;
> nam scelus, a Pyrrha quamquam omnia syrmata volvas,
> nullus apud tragicos populus facit. accipe nostro
> dira quod exemplum feritas produxerit aevo.

> We will tell of deeds wondrous indeed, but acted
> recently, in the consulship of Juncus, beyond the walls
> of hot Coptus,
> we will tell of a crime of the people, things too serious
> for any tragic boot;
> for a crime, though you unravel all the actors' costumes
> back to Pyrrha,
> was never committed by a whole people in the tragedians'
> works. Listen to what
> an exemplar dire savagery has produced in our own age.

The passage is reminiscent of the end of *Satire* 6, where Juvenal explains that the extraordinary savagery of modern women compels him to enter precincts usually reserved for tragedy. It is as if he perceives satire as the tragedy of a people, rather than of heroes and heroines—with himself, the poet, telling true things, committing to verse what has really happened. Like Persius, he sneers at the bards but brings his own sort of poetry to the rites of bards. Hence the greatly moving end of *Satire* 15 (lines 131–74), which must be for the modern reader the finale of his work, in which he reflects that nature has given us tears and pity as our best part (lines 131–33); he asks, "quis enim bonus . . . ulla aliena sibi credit mala?"—"What good man believes any evil is alien from himself?" (lines 140–42). Juvenal makes his last comment on the bestiality of the Egyptians in *Satire* 15 by remarking on how it would revolt Pythagoras, who refused to eat any meat at all (lines 171–74); and this recalls the quiet images in the most turbulent satires. They are all there is in Juvenal of an expressed positive, like Horace's but far more elusive: the little garden, remote from the city, at 3.226–31; the man striding across the silent, frosty fields in his thick boots, at 3.318–22; the famous prayer at the end of *Satire* 10 (356–66). The quiet wish for solitude and the feeling that he was expressing the tragedies of people are perhaps a natural result of Juvenal's stated understanding of God's ways toward man. His satire, full of threats, reverberates with fear; it seems he also thought that God was to man what the satirist was to his victim (15.69–71):

> nam genus hoc vivo iam decrescebat Homero,
> terra malos homines nunc educat atque pusillos;
> ergo deus, quicumque aspexit, ridet et odit.

> For this race has waned since Homer was alive,
> and earth now brings forth bad men and puny ones;
> therefore the god, whatever one is looking on, laughs and hates.

It is perhaps too much to accept that these three lines constitute the poet's theology. But they are entirely consonant with his satire. It is an intensely horrifying and repugnant theology, tumid with despair; it has a close relative in current popular satire:

God's Song

> Man means nothing he means less to me
> Than the lowliest cactus flower
> Or the humblest Yucca tree
> He chases round this desert
> Cause he thinks that's where I'll be
> That's why I love mankind

> I recoil in horror from the foulness of thee
> From the squalor, and the filth, and the misery
> How we laugh up there in heaven at the prayers you
> offer me
> That's why I love mankind[72]

Conclusion

This study began as an inquiry into the place of sexual material in Roman satire. The proportions of the preceding chapters indicate how closely this question is tied in with the evidence from related literary and subliterary material; the body of evidence as a whole shows satire to be only the most sophisticated manifestation of a frame of thought deeply rooted in Roman society. This framework, as it happens, bears close enough resemblances to similar current complexes that Roman sexual humor can be compared validly with modern sexual humor, and even with modern nonhumorous sexual material. In addition, this framework bears on Roman institutions that are not primarily sexual, like political systems, the military, and religion. It would be wasteful indeed to write off the analysis of sexual material in Latin literature as bearing only on literature and on the sexual.

The first chapter demonstrates that Romans contemporary with the writers analyzed in chapters 2, 4, 5, 6, and 7 viewed sexual material in literature, explicit sexual language, and explicit descriptions of sexual acts as a distinct body of material. They tended to envision this material as a physical area; the term *obscenus* itself is strongly related to concepts of physical and religious taboo, opposed to the sacred and sacrosanct. Hence the existence of this verbal material is tied in with the existence of classes of people who belong in one area or the other, and the critics whose works appear in chapter 1 often align written sexual material with religious rituals and dramatic spectacles that include either a sexual element or an element of reversal, or both. Males, who are the writers, are also the only members of society normally capable of participating in both the obscene and nonobscene areas without an effect on their status. Thus the verbal sexual material was classed by the Romans themselves as part of the social framework of sexual roles, enforced by strong feelings of decorum (i.e., taboo).

The figure of Priapus, the ithyphallic god who protects his garden by threatening thieves, provides a convenient model for the situation of the humorist in Roman sexual humor. As seen in chapter 2, the physical ideal of the beloved expressed in Roman and contemporary Greek erotic poetry describes only women and boys, objects of love for adult males. These beloveds are to be pursued, and their beauty consists in attributes that contrast with those of the pursuing adult male: fragility, youth, smoothness. Whereas boys' genitalia and anuses may be admired, the part of the woman that serves to receive the male is not described at all. Only in the invective material presented in chapter 5 are women's genitalia described, and there it is with revulsion; at the same time, invective against women usually describes them as promiscuous. Thus the figure of the lover and the figure of the sexual humorist both must be dominant and aggressive; the former uses the ideal of beauty to describe the subordinate figure of the beloved, the latter uses the negative ideal of ugliness to describe those who have become insubordinate. The two ideals are interdependent, and coercive. The humorist is also capable of behavior analogous to the lover's pursuit; that is, while he rejects some victims, he rapes others, by means of verbal exposure or threats. All three roles—the lover pursuing, the humorist rejecting, the humorist raping—act out their emotion on the body of its object (desire leads to intercourse, disgust leads to perception of ugliness and refusal to penetrate, anger leads to rape). The only anomaly is that there is no positive perception of the woman's main sexual characteristics, breasts and genitalia.

The third chapter, in discussing theory, considers both nonevaluative and evaluative models of humor. From Freud the most pertinent ideas are those relating humor to social structures—both the immediate situation of the joke teller with respect to audience and butt, and the larger situation of the joke teller, audience, and butt in terms of social status. The humor classed by Freud as tendentious—and, in addition, a good deal of the humor classed by him as verbal only, including parody and some puns—can be seen to depend on the presence of hierarchies of power. This factor stands at the center of most of the other theories of humor discussed here, most clearly in the case of anthropology, sociolinguistics, and social psychology. Sociolinguists and anthropologists tend to see in humor, even in nonsense, a sort of training mechanism for keeping members of a society attuned to its norms. On the other hand, the weight of the work being done in social psychology points toward the conclusion that aggressive fantasies, of which much sexual humor is a subset, serve not only to reinforce but to exacerbate already existing aggressive tendencies. This idea is a major concern of feminist thinking on pornography and rape, and since violent pornography shares its main elements with Priapic humor, the question of the effects of such pornography applies to Priapic humor as well. The most abstract theory of humor seen in chapter 3 is also the one most directly attached to literary evidence: Bakhtin's analysis of Rabelais, which finds in his ribald humor an attempt to affirm the power of life over death. In general, the theories presented in chapter 3 suggest that aggressive sexual humor reinforces and promulgates aggressive and oppressive behavior on both the individual and the societal level.

The authors surveyed in chapters 4 through 7 all use Priapic humor in one way or another. Chapter 4, which covers the least polished of this material, demonstrates quite clearly its societal connection with two central Roman institutions—party politics and the law courts. Since both institutions depended on contests of power between individuals (men usually being the main actors), tendentious humor and invective provided the appropriate verbal weapons to be used there. They also appear, to a lesser extent, in military situations, where the opportunities for direct physical contest are more readily available. The higher literary forms of sexual humor are only refinements of this elemental humor, turned into a public or semipublic entertainment. The actual contest for power between man and man becomes abstract, with one man placed offstage. Catullus attacks his rivals in love, along with prominent politicians; Ovid attacks established religion; Lucilius, women and religion; Horace, those less refined than he; Persius, those who write badly; Petronius, women and freedmen; Juvenal, women, pathic homosexuals, prominent politicians of the past, freedmen, and social climbers; Martial, all of these, but with a much higher degree of fiction than used by any of the others. The enjoyment of a reader or audience comes from being a spectator at the exaggerated and elegant contest, without having to hear any arguments for the other side.

The questions finally arise, of what determines a hierarchy, whether a nonhierarchical structure is possible, and whether humor is possible without a hierarchy (that is, humor that does not depend on imbalances of power). On inspecting the material here surveyed, Bakhtin's ideas on Rabelais come back to mind. What could possibly impel such struggles, such a fundamental need to rank people as better or worse, and such pleasure in the statement of superiority over inferiority? Perhaps Bakhtin is right in perceiving humor as an effort to defeat death and "uncrown time"; for time, with its *cursus honorum*, fosters the hierarchical, until it brings on death, the ultimate anarchist. All the struggles of the hierarchy tend toward an assertion of the individual, an effort to "make a mark," to insist upon the importance of one player in comparison with another: if better in one respect, perhaps better in the ultimate respect, that of immortal/mortal. Hence gods/men.

The hierarchical structure bears with it certain corollaries apparently basic to human societies. Hierarchy implies polarity, since each stage in the ranking necessitates a judgment of better/worse, measured by comparison with two opposed poles (for example, beauty/ugliness). Hierarchical judgments are often enacted on the persons (= bodies) of the participants, producing institutions such as war, prostitution, property, and slavery; money can be seen as only a slightly sophisticated abstraction of this reification of power relationships.

Hierarchy also determines the humor that gets the loudest laughs. Would humor be possible without hierarchy? If such a humor existed, it would have to lie only in jokes and comic situations that had no (or no consistent, that is, stereotyped) victims. This would preserve some verbal humor and all humor in which the participants enjoyed each other without regard for a third party and without permanent assumption of roles of more or less power. Among the multiple functions of humor in the models provided here—conservatism, aggression, easing of tensions—perhaps the last holds the most promise for an anarchic humor attached to temporary situations and founded on goodwill. The suggestion that this humor, which now coexists with tendentious humor, should eventually replace it altogether is not meant to be fantastic. The figures who evoked Priapus' most savage threats and most disgusted invective—the ugly woman, the randy *vetula*, the weak *cinaedus*, the foreigner—no longer find Priapus funny; nor can Priapus be accepted as a model any more. Male and female cannot remain polar opposites. The *vetula* who says "I am not that" perhaps will found another mode, a new world without the comparative degree, in which laughter and cruelty cannot cooperate. As it is, and as it was at Rome, their cooperation creates both sexual humor and satire, and orders the garden of Priapus.

APPENDIX 1

The Evidence on the Circumstances Surrounding Adultery at Rome[1]

The sexual stereotypes of Roman humor suggest that many, both in the capital and in the provinces, and of all classes, engaged in extramarital affairs. While much evidence exists on the actual circumstances surrounding adultery in Roman society, most of it is conflicting and indirect. The punishments prescribed by law differ from those apparently prescribed by folk custom; the moral ideal of Roman womanhood coexists with all sorts of gleefully malicious gossip, some of it passing for history. Straightforward accounts of adulterous liaisons are extremely rare. Yet, though it would be useful to have more reliable evidence, the very presence and nature of these conflicting accounts tell a good deal about the significance of marriage in Roman society and about the function of various kinds of verbal material in maintaining that significance.

Satire presents a conventional picture of adultery in which "self-help" punishments play the greatest role.[2] The husband who catches another man in bed with his wife inflicts on the adulterer physical punishment and humiliation, sometimes with the aid of his household slaves. The punishments include: flogging the adulterer, castrating him, or forcing him to pay a fine;[3] mutilation by cutting off the adulterer's ears and nose;[4] raping the adulterer, either by anal penetration[5] or oral;[6] throwing a slave or freedman adulterer to the beasts (Petron. *Sat.* 45.7); killing the adulterer (Hor. *S.* 2.7.56–62; Juv. 10.316). The picture presented by satire often seems visually related to a stock bedroom farce in mime.[7] The punishment of women who commit adultery is less frequently mentioned: they must wear a toga instead of the matron's *stola* (Mart. 2.39, 10.52; Juv. 2.70) and risk marriage and dowry (Hor. *S.* 1.2.131; Petron. *Sat.* 53.10; Apul. *Met.* 9.28). A husband conniving at his wife's adultery is said to act the pimp (Juv. 1.55–57; cf. Lucil. 1223 Marx, Hor. *C.* 3.6.25–30). Only Martial makes much of the legal penalties for adultery, praising Domitian for reviving the *lex Julia* (6.2, 6.4, 9.6) and then joking about those who evade the law.[8] Juvenal does mention prosecution for adultery (2.66–70).

Unfortunately, history and anecdote preserve only a few accounts of cases in which the self-help punishments were applied, all dating from the Republic. The elder Cato states the husband's right to kill his wife if he catches her in the act of adultery (in Gellius, 10.23); the historian Sallust, whom Milo caught with his wife, was beaten and fined (Varro in Gellius, 17.18); and several otherwise unknown men are stated by Valerius Maximus to have punished adulterers with beating, castration, or rape by slaves without fear of legal repercussions (Val. Max. 6.1.13). Anecdotes of sexual misbehavior multiply during the early second century B.C., the first divorce traditionally being dated to the 230s B.C.,[9] and Metellus' famous speech promoting marriage has been noted above.[10] Litigation during this period arose from adultery only in connection with the wife's right to regain her dowry, and one story remains concerning such a case; probably not a normal case, considering that the *dramatis personae* include Marius and his rescuer Fannia (Val. Max. 8.2.3, Plut. *Mar.* 38).

Rumors of affairs were rife in the well-attested late Republic; Cicero's letters are full of current gossip,[11] some of which turns up in fossil form in Plutarch's *Lives*[12]—these being stories mentioned in passing, as true. The case of Clodius and Caesar's wife at the rites of Bona Dea received a public hearing and excited endless comment.[13] A few anecdotes attest a double standard: whereas a Roman nobleman might live publicly with a libertine mistress (Antony and Cytheris, Cic. *Att.* 10.10.5, 10.16.5, 15.22), the father of a Roman noblewoman would certainly not countenance her affair with a freedman (Atticus' daughter and the rhetorician Epirota, Suet. *Gram.* 16).

Augustus passed the *lex Julia de adulteriis coercendis* in 18 B.C. presumably to end sexual freedom among the Romans, especially the nobility.[14] The law survives only as embedded in later commentaries (*D.* 48.5, *C.* 9.9, Paul. *Sent.* 2.26), which nevertheless provide a good deal of information on its workings. Augustus established a *quaestio perpetua* to hear cases of adultery, thereby aligning it with other *iudicia publica* (like murder and treason), a significant removal of adultery from private to criminal law—a move of doubtful value at best. The husband had to divorce his wife or be liable for prosecution as a pimp; sixty days were allotted to the husband or to the wife's father to prosecute her, after which any third party could institute proceedings, within a four-month period; there was a five-year statute of limitations. The adulterer had to be accused and tried first, the wife only if he was found guilty. Any killing could be done only in the act, and only in the husband's or father's house; the father had to kill both his daughter and her lover, while the husband could no longer legitimately kill his wife and could kill the adulterer only if he were *infamis*. Accessories to adultery were culpable as principals. For punishment, the wife and adulterer were relegated to different islands; the wife lost half her property and one-third of her estates, the adulterer lost half his property (these punishments being modified, with all punishments, as the distinction between *honestiores* and *humiliores* grew marked). The woman could not marry an *ingenuus* any more, and both lovers became *intestabilis* and *infamis*. It will be noted that *adulterium* is essentially a woman's crime; a married man could legitimately have intercourse with male or female slaves or concubines, with any unmarried woman (probably of a class below his own), and with any man (except, usually, freeborn youths). A wife could not prosecute her husband for adultery until the late Empire (though it seems likely that she or her agents might have taken advantage of the third-party rule).

Anecdotes from the Empire do not help much to illustrate the workings of the *lex Julia*; most concern the imperial family or at best the way in which the *princeps* treated adulterers.[15] An exception is an odd story of a man who pleaded in court that his seeming adultery had been a homosexual assignation (Val. Max. 8.1. *Absol.* 12). The cases of Augustus' own daughter and granddaughter naturally excited a great deal of comment.[16] Other notorious (and evidently trumped-up) cases included that of another Julia and the philosopher Seneca (Dio 60.8.4–5; 61.10. 1–6) and of Octavia, wife of Nero (Suet. *Ner.* 35.1–2). That some women tried to evade the law by registering as prostitutes is attested by both Tacitus (*Ann.* 2.85) and Suetonius (*Tib.* 35.2). But Tacitus generally (and often) uses cases of adultery merely to show that noblewomen are immoral, the *princeps* cruel, and *delatores* greedy; he ties the prosecutions for adultery to the trumped-up cases of *maiestas* used for political ends.[17]

All the above reports at least pretend to objectivity; the commission of adultery in itself is not the point of the story. But in many stories it is the only point, thus showing that the stigma attached to adultery provided material for character assassination. Cicero's hints are often malicious,[18] especially in regard to Clodius and his sister[19]—which did not stop people from linking his own name with Clodia's (Plut. *Cic.* 29). Women like Servilia[20] and Fausta, the daughter of Sulla (Macrob. *Sat.* 2.2.9), had proverbially bad reputations. Hints of adulterous or amorous affairs were used against prominent men: Antony,[21] Pompey,[22] Fabius Maximus,[23] the elder Cato,[24] Cicero,[25] and Caesar.[26] Similar stories were told of the emperors: Augustus,[27] and his daughter Julia;[28] Gaius,[29] Claudius,[30] Nero,[31] Titus,[32] and Domitian.[33] That these rumors existed in oral circulation is attested by the soldiers' songs quoted by Suetonius (*Iul.* 51) and by the sling bullets from Perusia.[34]

On the other hand, idealized stories present oleographs of Roman virtues and the vices that pervert these virtues (which consist chiefly in eschewing vices). Livy contrives Lucretia (1.58) and Verginia (3.44) as *exempla* of good behavior contrasted with vice—as Dio was to do later with Plotina, wife of the exemplary Trajan (68.14.5). Tacitus found in the Germans the chastity that did not exist at Rome (*Germ.* 18–19). The anecdote collectors provide *exempla* of chastity defended.[35] The rhetoricians were fond of situations in which chastity and fidelity were violently abused.[36]

What can be concluded from this mass of evidence? Most significantly, all the material shares one point of view: that of the cuckolded husband. Adultery is defined either as a wife's betrayal of her husband or as one man's cuckolding another; the marital status of the adulterer is immaterial. Thus the stereotypes of the "cheating husband" (man who betrays wife) and of the "homewrecker" (woman who supplants wife) are missing from Latin literature. As the cuckold defines adultery, so law, satire, gossip, and moral tales amount to a defense against cuckoldry. The law is written for the use of betrayed husbands, stemming from custom which set up a family tribunal for the judging of peccant wives. Moral *exempla* provide a literary version of these tribunals. Satire, with its horrendous lists of punishments and its comic stereotypes, tells would-be adulterers that the game is not worth the candle. True, even where the message is explicit, as in Hor. *S.* 1.2, there is an assumption that male readers have experience of adultery; and erotic poetry, especially Ovid's *Ars Amatoria*, actively encourages lovers of married women. But this literature always portrays adultery as daring, never as normative. In the same way, malicious gossip establishes that one way to acquire a bad reputation is to have a reputation for adultery, yet it grants a certain cachet to both male and female sinners. Presumably this stems from the real issue involved—not marriage but power. Roman adult males must have felt as a class a fear of loss of face due to the loss of a wife to another man; hence the sexual and monetary punishments and the stress on the wickedness, and jeopardy, of the adulterer. Adultery truly amounted to stealing Priapus' fruit.

Were the self-help punishments real? Although they conform to folkloric archetypes[37] and constituted a *locus communis* in Latin literature,[38] the social and legal circumstances make a most plausible background for them. Self-help was the leading characteristic of early Roman law and custom, which began as instruments for the public coercion of opponents.[39]

As for the *lex Julia*, the sources combine to suggest that its aims were not realized. Toga-clad women were not all on islands, and marriage to them had to be forbidden. Women of ill repute were present at Rome; women looked for loopholes in the law and many were never prosecuted by their husbands, whom the law seems to have antagonized (at least at the senatorial level). The development of the *cognitio extra ordinem* and the distinction of punishments for *honestiores* and *humiliores* probably tended to protect women (and men) of the upper classes.

Finally, this material must give some indication of the nature of sexual roles within Roman marriage. The fact that no woman's voice remains to us makes it almost impossible to tell how the institution really worked. However, we can postulate a certain amount of sexual freedom for women, who were not kept from gossip, or nailed to a pedestal, and were free to hear obscene poetry. Gossip seems equally interested in both male and female peccadilloes; on the other hand, women rarely figure largely in jokes about punishments for adultery but often in melodramatic depictions of it. Presumably gossip deals in *Schadenfreude* while satire and moral *exempla* deal in personal hostility and fear. Fantasies of anger at adultery focus on the male, the adulterer, ignoring the woman's decision; her active role in fantasy is as one who rejects adultery. Verbal material thus serves as a sort of restraining net. The answer to the grimmest question of all, whether wives were physically chastised by their husbands, is that physical punishment of women at Rome was either extremely rare or extremely unmentionable. Although custom explicitly allowed a father, husband, and sometimes male agnates the power of life and death over a married woman, very few cases, if any, are recorded in which adultery was punished by death.[40] And the Romans did not make jokes about wife beating—though, as has been seen, the elegiac poets found fighting with their mistresses erotic.

APPENDIX 2

The Circumstances of Male Homosexuality in Roman Society of the Late Republic and Early Empire

The material examined above insistently raises the question of how closely the values that Latin literature assigned to different homosexual practices reflected actual practices. Scholarly exegesis has generally assessed the literary material as highly fictional;[1] a recent social historian has gone in the opposite direction.[2] The latter tactic cannot be taken in dealing with evidence that by its nature reflects the attitudes, and furthers the goals, of its writer. But precisely this axiom can be used to extract from Latin literature a fairly comprehensive schema of real Roman attitudes toward homosexuality.

Invective

To begin with invective, for which most of the available evidence was outlined in chapter 4: one of the commonest accusations in graffiti, political slanging matches, political lampoons, and courtroom attacks is that of "pathic" homosexuality. This generally denotes three sorts of behavior: having been the *puer* of an older man some years previously; continuing, as an adult, to enjoy being penetrated anally by other men; and enjoying performing fellatio. That these accusations were present at all levels of Roman society is attested by the similarities in content between misspelled and ungrammatical graffiti on the walls of Pompeii and the orations and letters of Cicero, at least on this one subject. The lampoons, anecdotes, and graffiti naturally name names, as does Cicero in his orations, since he is usually trying to discredit his opponent and paint him as all he should not be: hence, for example, the story about Curio and Antony in the second Philippic (above, chap. 1), which differs from other examples of this *locus communis* only in its invention of detail—a function of the seriousness of Cicero's intent to discredit Antony. This story can hardly be taken as evidence that homosexual marriage was a Roman institution; it simply shows, like all these stories, that a man seeking to discredit another man could do so by claiming he had been, or still was, sexually passive. Or that he had been a pander, usually of *matronae* as well as of noble youths: thus a common story of Clodius (Cic. *Att.* 1.16.5; Val. Max. 9.1.7) and a tale of decadence among the nobility (Val. Max. 9.1.8). These stories exist for a huge list of Roman politicians and emperors, and also for many poets, orators, and others. The Romans, who utilized the stories for political ends, also seem to have found them titillating in themselves (e.g., Sen. *QNat.* 1.16). Thus political invective tells nothing about its targets but demonstrates a societal preoccupation with the possibility of one male's sexual submission to another.

The stereotype of the pathic exists in literary genres as well: satire and epigram, in their tirades, include lists of characteristics considered to betray the pathic,[3] many of which are termed "effeminate" or can be aligned with the feminine. Priapus withholds his threat of rape from pathics (*Pr.* 64), Catullus uses the category "pathic" with political overtones (29, 57), and against thieves, while Petronius extracts humor from the making of the *puer* Giton into a sort of hero.

Both the stance of Priapus and the threats against adulterers seen in appendix 1 demonstrate that a threat to penetrate another male, in Latin literature and seemingly in Roman reality, was used as a sign of superior virility and power.[4] How often the actual penetration was carried out cannot now be known, except for an occasional anecdote (e.g., Val. Max. 6.1.13, carried out by slaves); the number of threats would seem to indicate that the punishment was carried out sometimes. On the other hand, accusation of having raped a (male) narrator has largely negative force; Catullus takes the pose of victim in order to insult the overly Priapic male (28). Still, this assignment of pejorative value to the stance is only temporary, as Catullus is quite willing to adopt the stance himself. In short, the threat to penetrate another male is an equation of him with the pathic; but the complaint of having been penetrated aligns the penetrator with Priapus without the victim/speaker associating himself with the willingly pathic.

It follows from this definition of the pathic that there is nothing wrong with pederasty for the older lover, and this indeed seems to have been the case. True, fondness for a boy (or too many boys) is the subject of somewhat malicious gossip; the tone is similar to that of gossip about fondness for a mistress (as in the stories about Antony and Cytheris). But this gossip shows only that the keeping of *pueri*, like the keeping of mistresses, was a common practice and one envied and emulated as much as it was talked about. Martial's wry epigrams on the cupbearers of his wealthy friends, on slaves he cannot afford, and on *concubini*[5] all attest to the normalcy of the use of *pueri*, especially when they were slaves. Catullus 61.(126)–(155) suggests a young man might be expected to put aside his *concubinus* on marriage, which Martial also implies (11.78; 12.97). These practices go back at least to the second century B.C.; Livy (39.42.8) quotes Cato describing the notorious *puer* of Flamininus:

> Philippum Poenum carum ac nobile scortum ab Roma in Galliam provinciam spe ingentium donorum perductum.

> Philip the Phoenician, a dear and noble whore, brought from Rome to Gaul in hope of large gifts.

Cato, obviously grinding an ax, nevertheless could not have made such an accusation if it had no referent. A male gold-digger must have been a recognizable type. And Plautus' sexual rule of thumb (*Curc.* 35–38) implies that love of either sex is all right as long as the beloved is not freeborn:

> nemo ire quemquam publica prohibet via;
> dum ne per fundum saeptum facias semitam,
> dum ted apstineas nupta, vidua, virgine,
> iuventute et pueris liberis, ama quidlubet.

> no one prohibits anyone from going down the public way;
> as long as you don't make a path through posted land—
> as long as you hold off from a bride, a single woman, a virgin,
> young men and free boys, love anybody you please.

A more negative aspect of the Roman stereotype of male sexuality has to do with the proclivities attributed to the effeminate man. It is true that the pathic is often claimed to seem effeminate. However, effeminate men are often claimed to be not homosexual but bisexual, in fact, overly active with both sexes. Occasionally their effeminacy is even said to be a veneer for excessive heterosexual activity, most notably in the Oxford fragment of Juvenal.[6] This literary stereotype is found in political and rhetorical invective as well, as seen in the passages from the elder and younger Seneca discussed above (chap. 1). In general, the Romans who wish to represent the *mos maiorum* attribute sexual ambivalence (goatee, not beard or clean shave; toga too long or too short, and ungirt; dancing at parties) to those they see as a threat to it—for example, Scipio to Sulpicius Galus (above, chap. 4), Cicero to Clodius and Catiline, the elder Seneca to his grandsons' coevals. In these cases the actual sexual proclivities of both sets of participants are surely side issues, each having taken on a mode of dress representing alignment or opposition to the norms of Roman patriarchy—in order to signify the determination of each to wrest power from the other.

Erotic Poetry

The norms of erotic poetry only reinforce the idea that pederasty would be acceptable in a society where the pathic is despised. The praise of beautiful boys in erotic epigram is a commonplace, as was seen in chapter 2. The presence of pederastic messages in graffiti (cf. chap. 4, above) suggests that pride in pederasty was not restricted to literature or to the highest levels of society; it might of course be claimed that the pederastic graffiti were written by men of eastern origin and that pederastic literature had the same pedigree. But, while it cannot be denied that erotic epigram has a Hellenistic form, the Greek and Asiatic influence on Roman pederasty must be seen as an augmentation, not as the basis. There is so much evidence outside of erotic epigram for the practice of pederasty that epigram cannot be discounted as the borrowing of a Greek literary form to describe nonexistent Roman practices. Catullus' Juventius may resemble Tibullus' Marathus more than he resembles Catullus' Lesbia; both boys may still very well have been drawn from life.

Some Real-Life Evidence

A sobering example of the way erotic literature and anecdotes can retreat rapidly from everyday life is the younger Pliny's story of the love poem written by Cicero to Tiro (*Ep.* 7.4; chap. 2). The very fact of the writing of this epigram may well be nothing but a joke against Cicero; still, Pliny takes it at face value, shows off his knowledge of it, and uses it as both justification and inspiration for writing an erotic epigram of his own. The question of Cicero's actual relationship with Tiro thus reaches something like a fifth remove from reality, while Pliny takes it for granted that he need have no relationship of his own in order to write love poetry.

Fortunately, Pliny does not stand alone. Dozens of epitaphs to cherished *deliciae* remain,[7] although the function of such young slaves (or servants) in life is not defined on the gravestones. But their quasi-title, as the titles *cinaedus*, *concubinus*, and *eunuchos* certainly do, may denote an occupation as sexual servant. And the best people had such servants. Where political anecdotes have an obviously slanderous point, they are not to be trusted; but Martial's poems on Earinos, Domitian's cupbearer (above, chap. 2), are not likely to have had any negative intention. With Earinos and the *deliciae* might be classed the little boys kept as pets (Suet. *Aug.* 83; Dio 48.44, 67.9.2, 67.15.3), although Suetonius classes these with the other human conversation pieces kept by Roman nobles—that is, dwarfs and cripples. The case of Antinous is too well known; his was only an elaborate version of an ordinary passion.

Whereas evidence for established and respected sexual relationships between grown men is not to be found, there is adequate evidence for pederasty and attempts to restrict it. The most conclusive evidence for the presence of pederasty in Roman society comes from Quintilian. In the most matter-of-fact way, in the midst of a lot of advice on the bringing up of children, Quintilian advises parents not to send their boys away to school, schools being a well-known hotbed of pederasty and the schoolmasters not to be trusted (*Inst.* 1.2.4, 2.2.1–5). Since no one could be less given to flights of fancy than Quintilian, this passage can be taken as evidence for the real fear underlying two satirical vignettes in Juvenal:

the students masturbating in the classroom (Juv. 7.241) and the schoolmaster bending the student over (Juv. 10.224). The point is not whether these things happened, but that serious adults of moderate means not only expected but feared that they happened. The undisciplined rhetorician Haterius even used such an accusation against a teacher in a speech—and was laughed at for his pains (Sen. *Controv.* 4.pr.11). Ellipsis was more decorous: Pliny, for example, praises a young man he knew for his moderation and chastity, only hinting at the way of life the young man might have followed instead (*Ep.* 7.24; cf. 3.3.4); a similar impulse must have prompted Augustus to set aside a block of seats at the theater for boys and their chaperons (Suet. *Aug.* 44.2). These men of wealth and position deplore pederasty when it comes to their own children, the practice apparently being enough of a presence to merit some notice.

This attitude is in turn confirmed by the legal situation with respect to the sexual enjoyment of males by other males. The *lex Julia de adulteriis coercendis* seems to have included *stuprum cum masculo* in the scope of its list of prohibited activities;[8] if so, it only reinforced the ill-attested *lex Scantinia*, which apparently made illegal the sexual use of an *ingenuus* by another male.[9] Rape existed only as a crime against the freeborn, male or female; in the case of rape of a slave, the master had recourse to the *lex Aquilia* or a praetorian action (*D.* 48.5.6.pr.). Both *stuprum* and seduction of boy, woman, or girl were accorded severe sanctions (*D.* 47.11.1.2). In these cases the adult male who corrupted an innocent youth was the one to be prosecuted. But it seems at least possible that the *lex Scantinia* allowed scope for the prosecution of an *ingenuus*, of whatever age, who allowed himself to be used, gratis, as a pathic (anyone could become a prostitute by registering with the aediles if he or she were willing to undergo *infamia*; cf. appendix 1). This is suggested by the three attestations of the law: Caelius used the *lex Scantinia* as a political weapon in a duel with Appius and Drusus (*Fam.* 8.12.3, 8.14.4); Suetonius alludes to its use by Domitian (*Dom.* 8.3); and Juvenal has the feisty Laronia in *Satire* 2 cite it in reply to the Stoic-pathic's threat of the *lex Julia* against her (2.44). In both Cicero and Juvenal the law is used to discredit opponents, identified as pathic in Juvenal; in Suetonius the law appears in a list of punishments of the unchaste, which for men usually implies playing the pathic role. One declaimer does state that "inpudicitia in ingenuo crimen est"—"unchastity is grounds for accusation in a freeborn man" (Sen. *Controv.* 4.pr.10).

As with other moral qualities, evidence of lust was used to sway the outcome of court cases. In the case of the Calidius who, found in a married woman's bedroom, claimed in court that he had come there "for love with a slave boy," the scandalized Valerius Maximus remarks, "crimen libidinis confessio intemperantiae liberavit," "the admission of intemperance freed him from the accusation of lechery" (8.1. *Absol.* 12). Another man was not so lucky: "corrupted by too much love of his little boy *{puerulí}*," he had an ox killed when the boy requested tripe for dinner. He was condemned in a *publica quaestio*, "innocent, if he had not been born in such stern old times" (Val. Max. 8.1. *Damn.* 8). And Valerius Valentinus lost his case against C. Cosconius after Cosconius adduced a *carmen* by Valerius in which he boasted, *poetico ioco*, that he had seduced a *puer praetextatus* and a freeborn maiden.[10] In all these cases the litigant's pederasty per se does not inculpate him. Instead, it weighs in with other aspects of the case: it provides a (shocking) alibi for the alleged adultery (love with a slave boy is not a crime), perhaps exacerbates the breach of sumptuary regulations, and undermines the prosecutor's credibility (love with a free boy or girl is a crime, and no joking matter).

Thus, as stated in Plautus *Curc.* 35–38, the area of illicit love, pederastic as well as adulterous, has a corresponding area of licit love. Sexual intercourse with young slave boys is not only acceptable but normal; sexual intercourse with freeborn boys is deplorable and illegal, apparently for the benefit of the boy's pride and future reputation. It is taken for granted that adolescent boys are attractive to older males, also that the older males could be attracted to women as well. Whereas the "active" position carries no stigma, and is normal and expected of an older man, the "pathic" position shames by its very subordinacy; hence the societal separation of the position from freeborn youths and maidens, the allure of young slaves, and the asexuality of wives. It seems not unlikely, in turn, that part of the social stigma attached to freed slaves derives from the possibility that they performed sexual services for their masters and/or mistresses before (and possibly after) manumission;[11] the sexual service here is entailed by the objectification of the human—slavery. The position of actors and actresses as *infames* likewise comes at least in part from their reputation for being free with their sexual favors.

Ideals

Finally, the ideal of the young man in Latin literature shows a good deal about what the reality may have been. Clearly, what bothered the Romans most in male homosexual behavior was assimilation to the female role, as witness the definition of the pathic. Roman society must naturally have harbored a fear of such assimilation, since the strong patriarchy preferred to keep all males in a family subordinate to the authority of the *paterfamilias* until his death; a Roman male was called *iuvenis* until he turned forty. The behavior of Chamula men, in a similarly strong patriarchy, makes an instructive comparison.[12] Rhetoric expressed the Roman ideal of youthful sexual behavior, most notably in the series of anecdotes on chastity in Valerius Maximus (6.1.5, 7, 9–12). Sounding wistful, Valerius recounts several famous tales in which a freeborn youth, or any of various officials on his behalf, vindicates his chastity against a corrupter. In these stories, and in the declamations,[13] bad army officers and wicked tyrants are the main source of rapes of young men; like the Priapic figure in Catullus, they are too aggressive.

As demonstrated for the concept of the obscene (chap. 1), moral ideals can be enacted on literature as well as on classes of people; thus the different genres—epigram, lampoon, satire, anecdote, declamation—describe different aspects of the situation. And so Quintilian, writing on the comic playwright Afranius, could complain that he used "foul pederastic themes" more often than was proper.[14]

Throughout this body of evidence, and in each case, it is taken for granted that men normally desire other men, especially beautiful ones. Still, the law on homosexuality, much more scantily attested than the law on adultery, seems to have aimed at limiting the pathic role to slaves. In all this literature there is no trace of a real and socially established homosexual relationship between men of the same age; this comes up only in the most extravagant invective against pathics, for example, Juvenal 2 and 9, and in anecdotes about emperors like Gaius and Nero. Seneca's Hostius Quadra is hardly presented as normal (*QNat.* 1.16.1). The invective probably implies that adult "pathic" males existed but tells us only how some other males reacted to them; the reaction was apparently not strong enough to lead to active legal persecution but strong enough to keep the "pathic" males from publishing any literature of their own. Only the rare voice of a man who was both of questioned sexuality and respected comes back to speak for himself, and in an apocryphal anecdote at that (Gell. 1.5): the great orator Hortensius, retorting, "Dionysia malo equidem esse quam quod tu, Torquate: ἄμουσος, ἀναφρόδιτος, ἀπροσδιόνυσος."

Notes

Chapter 1

1. The classic case is the Woolsey decision on Joyce's *Ulysses*, reprinted in the Vintage edition, vii–xii. In his decision Woolsey cites the legal definition of "obscene": "tending to stir the sex impulses or to lead to sexually impure and lustful thoughts." But the content of the decision itself shows how difficult it is to apply such a criterion to literature—since this also necessitates deciding what written material is "literature" and what is not. Cf. Commission on Obscenity and Pornography, *Report*, 346–442, on legal considerations related to erotica, especially the historical survey, 348–54. Even the authors of works in question are not always able to write cogently on the issue, e.g., D. H. Lawrence, *Pornography and Obscenity*. Meanwhile, obscene material has been excluded from open scholarly discussion until quite recently out of a sort of separation of styles; scholars apparently feel obscenity improper to scholarly exegesis. One discipline, folklore, made the problem the subject of a panel at its annual meeting and seems to have freed subsequent discussion considerably. The panel's papers appear in *JAF* 75 (1962); especially pertinent on theory are: Hoffman, "Panel on Folk Literature and the Obscene"; Legman, "Misconceptions in Erotic Folklore," refined by Goldstein, "Bowdlerization and Expurgation," *JAF* 80 (1967): 374–86; Legman, "Toward a Motif-Index of Erotic Humor," a fairly straightforward survey of bibliography and sources of collectanea, ca. 1459 to the present; Halpert, "Folklore and Obscenity." It also seems likely that the identification of the sexual with the female has excluded the sexual from scholarship, a traditionally male occupation. For discussion of the history of thought on sexuality, cf. Foucault, *The History of Sexuality*, vol. 1. The areas of scholarship that currently investigate obscene material most rigorously are social anthropology and sociolinguistics, beginning with Leach, "Anthropological Aspects of Language," in E. H. Lenneberg, ed., *New Directions in the Study of Language*; and Douglas, *Purity and Danger*. The significant part of Leach's article is its discussion of verbal abuse according to experiential categories and their overlaps; Douglas called for a perception of concepts of pollution as a "positive effort to organize the environment" (p. 2), hence opening the way for studies of the social function of areas such as the obscene. More recently, sociolinguistics has treated obscene humor along with nonsense and other sorts of humor with which it shares key characteristics; see especially Kirshenblatt-Gimblett, ed., *Speech Play*, who has collected an extensive bibliography and provides a detailed critical essay on this material. For a sociological treatment of the question of obscenity, cf. Alan Segal, "Censorship, Social Control, and Socialization." Recent feminist scholarship has devoted attention to the implications of the issue of pornography for the society that

harbors it; see especially Lederer, ed., *Take Back the Night*, and (a much less rigorous approach) Faust, *Women, Sex, and Pornography*. The problem of censorship in radio, television, and film is well known; see below, n. 25, for sources. Serious discussion of the content of obscene material is, with few exceptions, new in classical philology. Most notable are, in the field of social history, Dover, *Greek Homosexuality*; in philology, Henderson, *The Maculate Muse*.

2. Martial mentions several pornographers (Elephantis, 12.43.4; cf. Suet. *Tib.* 43, *Pr.* 4; Sotades, 2.86.2; Musaeus and others, 12.95.2). The works of Elephantis, at least, were illustrated (*Pr.* 4). In 2.86 Martial makes a *recusatio* of several types of verse, which have in common their trickiness—some are palindromes, some echoic, and so on. But not only is their content obscene—for Sotadics, cf. Pliny *Ep.* 5.3—Martial feels the whole genre is effete (*mollem debilitate galliambon,* 2.86.5) because it is overclever. Nevertheless, he says (2.86.6, 9, 12):

> non sum, Classice, tam malus poeta
> ....
> turpe est difficiles habere nugas
> ....
> me raris iuvat auribus placere.

That is, Martial sets his own work above the exercises of the schools, reserving his poetry for those with true delicacy of taste. Mart. 12.95 graphically depicts Martial's idea of the physical effects of reading pornography.

3. Related to the tendency of ancient biographers to depict a man's physique as a molder—or evidence—of his character; cf. Leeman, *Orationis Ratio,* 219–20; Williams, *Change and Decline,* 7–9, 12–14. For the idea in antiquity, cf. also Quintilian *Inst.* 2.5.10–12; Seneca *QNat.* 7.31–32; Pliny *Ep.* 2.14.12–13; Macrob. *Sat.* 2.4.12 (also on Maecenas).

4. Martial's *apologiae*: 1 intro., 1.4, 1.35, 2.86, 3.68, 3.69, 3.86, 4.14, 5.2, 7.8, 8 intro., 8.1, 8.3, 11.2, 11.15, 11.16, 11.20.

5. For the significance of Martial's creation of anonymous victims, see below, chap. 5.

6. People abstained from indecent speech especially in the hearing of the Vestals, Sen. *Controv.* 1.2.7; Plut. *Cat. Mai.* 20.7. For *este procul* and the clearing of the area, see Appel, *De Romanorum precationibus* (120, 122); *Reallexicon für Antike und Christentum*, s.v. Gebet I, 1156–57. Some parallels are collected by Austin *ad* Vergil *A.* 6.258. Strangers and certain types of people were banned from certain sacrifices: see Plut. *Quaest. Rom.* 60, Serv. *ad Aeneid* 8.179, Paulus ex Festo 72 Lindsay ("lictor . . . clamitabat: hostis, vinctus, mulier, virgo exesto"); Latte, *RR*, 381–82; Bömer, *Untersuchungen über die Religion der Sklaven*, 81–100. On the concept of the sacred area, see Wagenvoort, "*Profānus, profānāre*"; Benveniste, "*Profanus et profanare.*"

7. Cf. Thierfelder, "Obscaenus," in *Navicula Chiloniensis*, 98–106. Especially pertinent to the present discussion is the example Thierfelder quotes (101) from the augur M. Messala (Gell. 13.14.6), about the Aventine hill: "omnes, qui pomerium protulerunt, montem istum excluserunt quasi avibus obscaenis ominosum"; also the relationship he draws between *obscenum* and the ritual command *favete linguis* (102). These are discussed, and contrasted with Greek concepts, by Henderson, *MM*, 2–4.

8. Sources in Wissowa, *PW* 6.2751; also in Latte, *RR*, 73–74, n. 1. These games included beast shows more like modern circuses than the usual Roman beast shows, with beasts doing unexpected tricks; public largess of beans and chickpeas, flung into the crowds; a torchlight procession; and final ceremonies usually described as *iocosi*. The grand finale was a stage show in which prostitutes danced naked at the clamorous request of the

crowd (cf. esp. Ovid *Fast.* 5.349; Val. Max. 2.10.8; Sen. *Ep.* 97.8; Lactant. *Div. Inst.* 1.20.7–9). These prostitutes must have been specially hired and selected by the officials staging the games, and it must have been an honor to be chosen; this idea is at least not contradicted by Seneca and Lactantius. The whole agenda is almost a parody of more serious games—the animals do tricks instead of being killed, the crowd is sprayed with simple vegetables instead of costly gifts or favors, the procession marches at night, the finale features the lowest citizens with the enthusiastic participation of the crowd (which, despite the point of the tales [below, n. 15], included citizens like Cato and Favonius).

9. On triumphs, see Mommsen, *Röm. Staatsr.* 1:412; sources are collected in Mayor *ad* Juv. 10.36–46. The elements in the triumph that are most pertinent here are: the soldiers' participation and the obscene songs they directed at the victorious general (Suet. *Iul.* 49.4; Dio Cass. 43.20); the presence of the public slave constantly admonishing the *triumphator* and riding in the same chariot with him (Juv. 10.41–42; Zonar. 7.21); the special dress of the *triumphator* (Juv. 10.38–39, 43–44); and the ceremony in which he climbed the steps of the temple of Jupiter on his knees (Dio Cass. 43.21.2, 60.23.1). Zonar. 7.21 says the chariot was decked with a bell and a whip, the bell being the token of a man sentenced to death, who wore it so that no one would touch him and be contaminated. Pliny seems to say that the *fascinum* was hung from the chariot (*HN* 28.39). These elements constitute treatment of an exceptional individual, the general, in twofold way: giving him special marks of glory and subjecting him to exceptional humiliation. The result was lasting glory for the individual and, as Huizinga says (*Homo Ludens*, 177), the state's recuperation from the strains of war.

10. For the Saturnalia, see Macrob. *Sat.* 1.7.18ff.; Wissowa, *RK*, 204–06. Elements especially pertinent here are the liberty temporarily given to slaves and the appointment of a mock king (Sen. *Apocol.* 8.2).

11. Cf. especially Douglas, *Purity and Danger*; Levine, "Regression in Primitive Clowning"; Makarius, "Ritual Clowns and Symbolic Behaviour"; Turner, *The Ritual Process*; Abrams and Sutton-Smith, "The Development of the Trickster in Children's Narrative"; and, on comedy, Barber, *Shakespeare's Festive Comedy*; Erich Segal, *Roman Laughter*, 1–14, 42–69; on ritual jesting in the Eleusinian mysteries and elsewhere, Richardson, *The Homeric Hymn to Demeter*, 213–21. See below for full discussion.

12. That the prostitutes substituted for the actresses (*mimae*) is amply attested by the sources above (n. 8), and Val. Max. 2.10.8 (*ut mimae nudarentur*; see n. 15) need not be taken literally here; not, as Reich said (*Der Mimus* 1:171–75), because *mimae* were so highly honored and beloved by great men, but because of the special nature of the festival. Lactantius' description (*Div. Inst.* 1.20.7–9), despite its polemical quality, is strongly reminiscent of descriptions of other rituals of reversal:

> nam praeter verborum licentiam, quibus obscenitas omnis effunditur, exuuntur etiam vestibus populo flagitante meretrices, quae tunc mimarum funguntur officio, et in conspectu populi usque ad satietatem impudicorum luminum cum pudendis motibus detinentur

Compare Marriott's description of the festival of Holī, quoted by Turner, *The Ritual Process*, 186:

> the shins of the men were being most mercilessly beaten by the women. . . . The boldest beaters in this veiled battalion were often in fact the wives of the farmers' low-caste field-laborers, artisans, or menials—the concubines and kitchen help of the victims. "Go and bake bread!" teased one farmer, egging his assailant on. "Do you want some seed from me?" shouted another flattered victim, smarting under the blows . . .

The cries of the crowd are mentioned in all accounts and were probably part of the ritual (although what they seem to have been saying is "Take it off!"). For a list of *ludi scenici*, cf. Beare, *The Roman Stage*, 3d ed., 162–63.

13. On these genres of Roman comedy—*fabula togata, fabula Atellana*, and mime—see Beare, *The Roman Stage*, 128–58, and his appendices D and L (on the Oxyrhynchus Mime); for the stock mime on adultery, see Reynolds, "The Adultery Mime." On mime, see Reich, *Der Mimus*.

14. Use of obscene language, or excoriation, is often preceded by an excuse or *apologia* in ritual; cf. Ọlajubu ("References to Sex in Yoruba Oral Literature") and Turner (*The Ritual Process*), 78: "First, before singing the ribald songs, Ndembu chant a special formula . . . ('here another thing is done'), which has the effect of legitimizing the mention of matters that otherwise would be what they call 'a secret thing of shame or modesty.' . . . The same formula is repeated in legal cases concerning such matters as adultery and breaches of exogamy, where sisters and daughters or in-laws . . . of the plaintiffs and defendants are present."

15. The (obviously apocryphal) story of Cato at the *ludi Florales* is told by Valerius Maximus, 2.10.8:

> Eodem ludos Florales, quos Messius aedilis faciebat, spectante, populus ut mimae nudarentur postulare erubuit. quod cum ex Favonio amicissimo sibi una sedente cognovisset, discessit e theatro, ne praesentia sua spectaculi consuetudinem impediret. quem abeuntem ingenti plausu populus prosecutus priscum morem iocorum in scaenum revocavit . . .

Cf. Sen. *Ep.* 97.8. The use of "Cato" as a name for a hypercritical moralist apparently existed outside literature, Plut. *Cat. Min.* 19; for a collection of literary parallels, cf. Buchheit, "Catull an Cato von Utica (c. 56)."

16. Taking his cue from Cic. *Fam.* 9.22 (see below), Quintilian says the orator should avoid words or conjunctions of syllables that produce a double meaning where none is intended (*Inst.* 8.3.44–47), remarking, "Nec scripto modo id accidit, sed etiam sensu plerique obscene intellegere, nisi caveris, cupiunt."

17. On Cicero's invective oratory, cf. chap. 4.

18. The allusion is to *Pr.* 3, here attributed to Ovid. The full context (*Pr.* 3.7–8) is: *quod virgo prima cupido dat nocte marito, / dum timet alterius volnus inepta loci*. By quoting two words not syntactically connected, Scaurus forces the informed listener to reconstruct the whole line.

19. For the term *primary obscenity*, cf. Henderson, *MM*, 35–41. The weighting of certain words seems to depend on the strong association between word and thing and the learning of such words in early childhood: cf. Ferenczi, "On Obscene Words," in *Sex in Psychoanalysis*, 112–30; Bergler, "Obscene Words," especially on the connection between obscene words and feelings of aggression. The obscene word forces the hearer to imagine the thing, as technical language does not; cf. Kelling, *Language: Mirror, Tool, and Weapon*, 108–20, on the force of "real names" and the categories of words that have levels of names. It should be noted that primary obscenities in English carry an extra weight, of anger, because of their frequent use as expletives; since this use did not exist in Latin, presumably Latin primary obscenities did not connote anger.

20. Following the text and interpretation of D. R. Shackleton Bailey (*Cicero: Epistulae ad Familiares*, vol. 2).

21. The role of the auditor in construing what he hears, in the light of speech-act theory, is discussed by Crocker, "The Social Functions of Rhetorical Forms," in Sapir and Crocker, eds., *The Social Use of Metaphor*, 39–41, 43; for the mechanism of puns and related forms of discourse, cf. Milner, "Homo Ridens," 17, 22; Gossen, "Verbal Dueling

in Chamula," in Kirshenblatt-Gimblett, ed., *Speech Play*, 127–28, on the social significance of taking up double entendres.

22. Especially jocular considering that Connus is very likely a comic character, part of the body of satiric humor leveled at Socrates in his own time (so Shackleton Bailey *ad loc.*).

23. Shackleton Bailey *ad loc.* assumes a verb, *vissio* (= βδέω).

24. Shackleton Bailey accepts Münzer's identification of Aurelia and Lollia with the wives of Catiline and A. Gabinius.

25. The FCC has no list of words specifically banned from use on the air, nor even an official ruling on obscenity, although the National Association of Broadcasters does have a self-imposed code that says, "Profanity, obscenity, smut and vulgarity are forbidden . . ." (NAB radio code, sec. I.I.13–14; cf. television code, IV.8; in Kahn, ed., *Documents of American Broadcasting*, 2d ed.). But in 1973, when WBAI-FM in New York broadcast the George Carlin routine "Seven Words You Can't Use on Television," the subsequent complaint drove the FCC to rule that use of "unsuitable" material on the air during certain hours might subject a station to a fine and loss of license. This was affirmed by the U.S. Supreme Court in 1978. The FCC did not specify which words were precluded, but Carlin's list consisted of "shit," "piss," "fuck," "cunt," "cocksucker," "motherfucker," and "tits." His routine was a quasi-serious linguistic analysis of the use of obscenity, suggesting the desirability of substituting the word "fuck" for the word "kill" in violent television programs; the whole is oddly reminiscent of Cic. *Fam.* 9.22. (Cowan, *See No Evil*, 280–86; cf. 46, 135). It is instructive to compare this case with the Pacifica case (36 FCC 147), which first upheld WBAI's right to unorthodox programming, and the reservations of Commissioner Robert E. Lee concerning a program on male homosexuality (Kahn, 255–60).

26. Richlin, "The Meaning of *Irrumare* in Catullus and Martial."

27. Whereas jokes about female masturbation are not uncommon in invective against women in Attic Old Comedy (Henderson, *MM*, 221–22), there is not even a word for "dildo" in Latin.

28. On the concept of the association of dirt with a special area of life, cf. Douglas, *Purity and Danger*.

29. Cf. Richlin, "Invective against Women in Roman Satire," *Arethusa* (in press).

30. The classic statement of the process that associates feelings of disgust with genitalia is Freud's theory of the latency period, during which the young child suppresses sexual impulses and builds barriers around them (*Three Essays on the Theory of Sexuality*, 42–45). Freud comments on fellatio and oral/genital disgust, 17–18; on perceptions of the genitalia and the incentive for not regarding them as beautiful, 22, n. 2. Socialization must also play a large part in the formation of this disgust, as in the example cited by Ferenczi, "On Obscene Words," 121, of humiliation by a parent producing aversion to obscene language in a child. It has been suggested that one can deduce the thing considered most obscene in a given society by finding what is most euphemized (Bernard, "Otomi Obscene Humor," where the two ideas most commonly euphemized were fornication and pubic hair, always called "silly grasses"). The frequency of jokes on various topics certainly differs from culture to culture, and this must testify to cultural preoccupations: the Romans had few jokes or words for pubic hair, or for incest (a common source of humor in Ozark folk tales, cf. Rayna Green, in Randolph, *Pissing in the Snow*, xx–xxii), but many on homosexuality and oral sex; cf. the deductions drawn about Turkish society in Dundes et al., " The Strategy of Turkish Boys' Verbal Dueling Rhymes," and the general comments by Halpert, "Folklore and Obscenity," 191. For modern parallels on disgust with old women and female genitalia, see Legman, *Rationale of the Dirty Joke*, 369–81, 614–16; id., *No Laughing Matter*, 392–419 ("The Defiling of the Mother"); 449–57 ("The Overlarge Vagina"). For lack of disgust in Athens, cf. Henderson, *MM*, 3–6, 33, 52–53.

31. Cf. also: Lucilius 398 Marx; Catullus 78b.2; Petronius 25.5; Mart. 1.34.8, 2.42, 4.4.9, and 11.61.1–2; Richlin, "Sexual Terms and Themes in Roman Satire and Related Genres," 40–72.

32. Cf. Opelt, *Die lateinischen Schimpfwörter*, 156–57, on *impurus/improbus*; she stresses the connection of *impurus* with sacrilege.

33. For examples of disgust at kissing or eating with people who have the *os impurum*, see below.

34. Stella came from the straitlaced provincial town of Patavium and was patron not only of Martial but of Statius (*Silv.* 1.2). He was consul in A.D. 101 and *XVvir librorum Sibyllinorum* (Stat. *Silv.* 1.2.177). Like Pliny, he apparently wrote verse modeled on Catullus' (Mart. 1.7.1; 7.14.5).

Chapter 2

1. On the psychological implications of the association of ideas of physical inferiority with the female, cf. the Jungian scholar James Hillman, "On Psychological Femininity," in *The Myth of Analysis*, 215–90, esp. 231; cf. in general Vetterling–Braggin, ed., *"Femininity," "Masculinity," and "Androgyny."* For speculation on the significance of the stylishness of various body weights for women, cf. Chernin, *The Obsession*, esp. 56–65, 76–114. On perceptions of ugliness, cf. Fiedler, *Freaks*, chap. 5, esp. 137–49, on bearded women and people with strange genitalia. Feminists have attributed male perceptions of the female body to the connection between women and nature (Ortner, "Is Female to Male as Nature Is to Culture?" in Rosaldo and Lamphere, *Woman, Culture and Society*, 67–87, esp. 73–76); nature being inferior to culture, presumably the more nature is evident in the woman, the "uglier" she is. Many attributes of "beauty" are those that are signs of the relative helplessness of the beautiful one (de Beauvoir, *The Second Sex*, 177–80). For the concept of beauty in elegy, cf. esp. Lilja, *The Roman Elegists' Attitude to Women*, 119–32; for speculation on the poet's relation to this image, Sullivan, *Propertius*, 80–101; Luck, "The Woman's Role in Latin Love Poetry," in *Perspectives of Roman Poetry*. Comparative material for fifth-century Athens can be found in Dover, *Greek Homosexuality*, 57–59, 68–73, 79, 81–91, 94–99, and in Henderson, *MM*, 207; with this compare Malinowski, *The Sexual Life of Savages*, 285–309, on ideals of beauty and the concept of ugliness (= erotic repulsiveness) among the Trobriand Islanders. Malinowski lists as the constituents of ugliness cited by the Trobrianders, deformity, disease, old age, albinism—"often with the added comment: 'No one would sleep with such a one' " (289). He defines beauty in the Trobriands by means of the islanders' concept of ugliness (292).

2. On pseudonyms in Latin love poetry, cf. Williams, *Tradition and Originality in Roman Poetry*, 528–42; fantasy beloveds in the *AP*, 470; on the reality of Catullus' "Juventius," 554–55. Cf. also Page's remarks on names in Greek epigram, *The Epigrams of Rufinus*, 26–27; Sullivan, *Propertius*, 78–79. The *locus classicus* is Apuleius *Apol.* 10, also Ovid *Tr.* 2.427–28, 437–38.

3. Williams, "Some Aspects of Roman Marriage Ceremonies and Ideals"; below, appendix 1.

4. The two female poets whose work survives (in very small part) both wrote of love, but not explicitly. Sulpicia the elegist (fl. 15 B.C.), six of whose poems survive as [Tibullus] 4.7–12, does include among her conventional protestations of burning passion a tart observation that her lover, "Cerinthus," might prefer a "slut" *(scortum)* to herself, *Servi filia*. Martial praises the love poetry of a Sulpicia (10.35) as conducive to sexual contentment within happy marriages, and in 10.38 he says her marriage to Calenus has lasted fifteen years; this must, then, be the Sulpicia who wrote iambics on the breakup of her marriage to Calenus: "Si me cadurci restitutis fasciis / nudam Caleno concubantem proferat" (Probus Vallae *ad Iuv.* 6.537: Morel, *Fragmenta Poetarum Latinorum*, 134). Ovid

apparently had a friend and student named Metella (*Tr.* 2.437–38), whom, under her pseudonym "Perilla," he addresses in *Tr.* 3.7, reminiscing about their shared work and criticism.

5. By far the greatest number of poems to boys are short lyric poems or epigrams, but other genres did include some pederastic material—notably Tibullus 1.4, 8, 9, on Marathus, and Vergil *Eclogue* 2.

6. Roughly two out of three poems on boys in Martial include no coarse terms, four out of five in *AP* 12. The same is true for erotic poems about women, the ratio being four out of five in both Martial and *AP* 5.

7. The date of Strato is a much-vexed question and is tied in with the equally vexed question of the date of Rufinus (see below, n. 24). He can be no later than A.D. 250 and may well be earlier. For the purposes of this chapter, and since there is no ironclad resolution of the question, I will assume he wrote in the early second century A.D., contra Page, *The Epigrams of Rufinus*, 25–27, and in concordance with the conclusions of Cameron, "Strato and Rufinus," which I find sound and convincing. For an assessment of Meleager's artistry, cf. Gow and Page, *The Greek Anthology: Hellenistic Epigrams*, 2:591–92. On the artistry of Strato, cf. Maxwell-Stuart, "Strato and the Musa Puerilis."

8. Named as "Nemesis" in *AP* 12.12. For the theme of the pursued turned pursuer, cf. Giacomelli, "The Justice of Aphrodite in Sappho Fr. 1."

9. *AP* 11.326, 12.10, 12, 24, 25, 26, 27, 30, 31, 33, 35, 36, 39, 40, 41, 174, 176, 186, 191, 195, 204, 215, 220, 229.

10. The specificity of the metaphor (rather than taking "rosebud" = buttocks, "thorn" = hairy legs) is clear here, although it is a common romantic conceit to compare a boy to flowers, sometimes roses (*AP* 12.8, 32, 58, 151, 185 [figs], 189, 195, 205, 234, 236, 256). Apparently a rosy color was attractive, especially around the loins (12.97); cf. 11.21, where the boy's growing penis is rosy like the dawn. Hairiness was classically connected with lecherous, bestial figures likes satyrs: Dover, *GH*, 38 (and cf. 71, 144).

11. For fig = anus, see below. Cf. also *AP* 12.197, where the cucumber lying between two mounds possibly represents the boy's anus, the usual object of desire, which becomes less attractive when *πεπαινόμενος*, "ripened," i.e., "softened/coarsened." Maxwell-Stuart (216) takes it to be the boy's penis, and the *σῦς* = *χοῖρος*/*cunnus*; perhaps rightly.

12. "Prattling," τὸ λαλεῖν, is a desirable feature in a boy, *AP* 12.94, 95, 122. For touching the penis in courtship, cf. Dover, *GH* 94–97, 204.

13. This lack is further confused by rejection of the woman's anus, normal in Latin poetry, e.g., Mart. 12.96 (some Greek poems recommend anal sex with women, sometimes as a second-best substitute for a boy; see below). And, as seen above, Strato went so far as to deny women even had an anus—hyperbole on his part, presumably.

14. E.g., Sandy, "Catullus 16"; cf. Williams, *Tradition and Originality*, 551–56; also 306.

15. In addition to the link cited by Cameron, "Strato and Rufinus" (12.175=Mart. 9.25), the pentameter end in Mart. 1.45.2=*AP* 12.4.8; *AP* 12.22.7–8 draws on Mart. 11.58.11–12 and 11.73.3–4.

16. Martial's formal love poems to *pueri*: 1.46, 2.55, 3.65, 4.7, 4.42, 5.46, 5.83, 6.34, 7.29, 8.46, 8.63, 9.56, 9.103, 10.42, 11.6, 11.8, 11.26, 11.70, 12.71, 12.75 (to which cf. *AP* 12.95).

17. As in the Priapic poem "Quid Hoc Novi Est?" (Oxford *Virgilian Appendix*, 151–53), lines 32, 34.

18. *Mariscae* is also slang for some sort of anal sore, either warts or piles (cf. Juv. 2.13; more commonly, *ficus*, *Pr.* 41.4, 50.2; Mart. 1.65, 4.52, 6.49.8–11, 7.71, 12.33). This cannot be the meaning here—the contrast is clearly between a boy's anus and a woman's anus—but it does give some idea of the tone of the word. Strato in *AP* 12.204 does draw the analogy rosebud:bramble::fig:mushroom::lamb:ox::beautiful:hairy.

19. For this idea, cf. Petron. *Sat.* 92.11.

20. It is consistently assumed in Latin literature that a man is either always active or always pathic in homosexual intercourse; being active is there considered normal, while being pathic is there considered highly disgraceful. Hence the threat of anal rape is common where one man desires to prove his virility over another; see below; Henderson, *MM*, 204–20; Dover, *GH*, 104–06; Fehling, "*De Catulli Carmine sexto decimo*"; Richlin, "The Meaning of *Irrumare* in Catullus and Martial."

21. *Propertius*: 1.4.12–14, complexion, charms, hidden joys; 2.15.5–22, the beauty of Cynthia's naked breasts; 3.10, her toilette; 3.24.5–8, her complexion; 3.25.11–16, P. curses her with old age—white hair, wrinkles; 4.5.59, Acanthis points out the advantage of youth (rosy cheeks, no wrinkles). Propertius also finds Cynthia beautiful when she assaults him, as in 3.8 and 4.8.51–52. *Tibullus:* 1.1.68, hair, soft cheeks; 1.3.91–92, long hair, bare feet; 1.5.43–44, face, soft arms, yellow hair; 1.8.11–12 nails, 13–14 dress, 30 soft bosom, 33 shining arms; 1.10.61 clothes, 62 hair (both torn); 2.6.47–48, sweet voice. The poet himself has similar physical properties: graceful limbs (2.3.9), tender hands (2.3.10); and cf. Apollo in 2.3 and 2.5. Tibullus finds the image of bruised cheeks titillating (1.6.73, 1.10.55; cf. 2.5.101). His image of old age includes the need for dyed hair and smoothing the face (1.8.41–46), and wrinkles and (white) hair (2.2.20). Luck ("The Woman's Role") argues that "for a poet like Propertius, a woman is never a sex object"; the elegists certainly put a high value on the beloved and give the beloved a personality of a sort.

22. Cf. Prop. 2.2; 2.3; 2.12.23–24; 2.22.5–10; 2.25.39–45.

23. Gow and Page date the *Garland* to the reign of Gaius (*The Greek Anthology*, 1:xlv–xlix); it has recently been suggested that this date should be revised upward, to the reign of Claudius or Nero (Cameron, "The *Garland* of Philip").

24. Throughout the following section, for the sake of clarity, the numbers of the epigrams will be taken from the *Anthology*, rather than substituting Gow and Page's numbers for *Garland* authors and Page's for Rufinus.

The inclusion of Rufinus in this chapter poses similar, if not worse, problems to the inclusion of Strato (above, n. 7). Page, in his edition of Rufinus, concluded that he belonged somewhere between the *Garland* (because he was left out of it) and A.D. 400 (because Ausonius copies him). On the basis of vocabulary, Page finds the period between A.D. 50–150 doubtful for Rufinus and the latter end of 150–400 probable. He has been followed in this by Baldwin ("Notes on Rufinus"), who places Rufinus late on the basis of similarities between rare words in Rufinus and in ecclesiastical writers. Yet Cameron ("Strato and Rufinus") reached quite other conclusions, dating Rufinus soon after the *Garland* on the basis of interrelationships among Rufinus, Martial, Strato, and the *Priapea*. This argument seems sound to me, although the evidence is slender; in any case, the argument from vocabulary is basically unsound. As Cameron points out, the writers of the *Cycle* of Agathias may well have copied Rufinus in this as in much else; especially the use of vulgar words, like σοβαρός and σπάταλος, would certainly be consistent with Rufinus' inventiveness and (above all) with his subject matter. I would add that the "late compounds" in Rufinus' poems are also more likely to have been coined by him and picked up by later imitators than they are to have been traded and shared between him and someone like Gregory of Nazianzus.

25. For γαμῶν in *AP* 5.94, see Cameron, "Asclepiades' Girl Friends."

26. Line 5α presumably began with οἷα, and line 5β with τῆς Μελίτης δὲ; if 5.36 follows 5.35 in its ordering of images, as seems likely from 5.36.6, then line 5β also included φοινίσσετο or a similar verb. The difficulty of line 5 might be helped by bracketing μηρῶν; on the other hand, the difficulty of πολιῶι seems not to merit *obeli*.

27. For depilation, see Mart. 3.74, 10.90, 12.32.21–22; *CIL* 4. 1830 (Diehl 691); Henderson, *MM*, 131, #111.

28. Other double entendres in *AP* 5: Asclepiades (5.162), ἑταίρα/ἔχιδνα (whore/viper) pun, cf. Borthwick, "A 'Femme Fatale' in Asclepiades"; Dioscorides (5.138), Ilios *(ilium)* in flames; Marcus Argentarius (5.105), astrology (Dog = penis, Twins = testicles, Heavens = mouth); anon. (5.99), to a lyre player, with metaphors from the lyre; Rufinus (5.19), quoit (boy)/rattle (girl). From a later period comes the epigram by Eratosthenes Scholasticus (5.242), with an elaborate extended metaphor on folding doors/bolt/key. There are also examples of the stock metaphor of a woman as a jockey (5.202, 203, Asclepiades) or a racing ship (5.204, Meleager); cf. Henderson, *MM*, 164.

29. This epigram has been discussed at length by Schrier ("Love with Doris"), I think not satisfactorily. He took this to be a description of the position called κέλης *(mulier superior)*, as do (with reservations) Gow and Page (*Hellenistic Epigrams*, Dioscorides V), and Cameron, "Asclepiades' Girl Friends," n. 68. (This article by Cameron provides a useful overview of the kinds of women addressed by this Hellenistic epigrammatist: as Cameron argues, generally not prostitutes.) But surely the point of the poem is that Doris and the poet are doing something unusual; I would suggest that the scene describes anal intercourse (or vaginal intercourse from the rear) with the woman prone, her legs hooked over her lover's, her head turned to one side (so that her eyes are visible). Τὰ . . . πορφύρεα (lines 5–6), presumably not her eye(lid)s (δ', 5), surely refers to her buttocks, whose rosiness is stressed in line 1 and could use this further development. To take τὰ . . . πορφύρεα to represent Doris' breasts, without any other indicator, is too harsh. Floral imagery unites lines 1, 2, and 5, surely amplifying the idea of ῥοδόπυγον. With ἀμφισαλευομένης, cf. *AP* 5.35.8. The normal position for women taken from behind was standing, holding on to a low grip (Dover, *GH*, 101–04); hence the point of ἀκλινέως. For the idea of female ejaculant, perhaps intended here, cf. Ovid *AA* 3.804; modern folk parallels in Legman, *Rationale of the Dirty Joke*, 403.

30. *AP* 5.29–34, 46, 63, 101, 109, 113, 114, 125, 126, 217, 240.

31. Vow: *AP* 5.6, 52, 133, 150, 164, 165, 166, 175, 184, 250, 265, 279. Slavery: *AP* 5.22, 66, 230, 235, 249.

32. *AP* 5.13, 20, 21, 23, 26, 76, 79, 80, 92, 103, 118, 204, 227, 233, 258, 271, 273, 282, 298, 304.

33. Martial's epigrams on wanton women: 1.34, 1.57, 1.62, 1.73, 1.106, 2.9, 2.17, 2.25, 2.31, 2.34, 2.63, 3.54, 3.90, 4.12, 4.28, 4.38, 4.71, 4.81, 6.6, 6.40, 6.66, 6.71, 7.30, 7.57, 8.53, 9.2, 9.32, 9.67, 10.29, 10.68, 10.75, 11.7, 11.27, 11.50, 11.60, 11.71, 11.100, the extraordinary 11.104, 12.55, 12.58, 12.65.

34. *Illud puerile* (line 3) is probably anal sex; *improbius quiddam* (line 5) must be fellatio, so that *pollicitast* (line 6) implies the girl agreed to do it only on terms (line 8), as lines 7–8 imply she would perform fellatio only if her lover performed cunnilingus.

35. Martial's poems on sex and money: 2.34, 2.63, 3.54, 4.28, 6.66, 6.71, 9.2, 9.32, 10.29, 10.75, 11.27, 11.50, 12.55, 12.65. For the rejection of old women who try to buy the poet's favors, see below, and Richlin, "Invective against Women in Roman Satire," *Arethusa* (in press).

36. For invective directed chiefly at female genitalia, see Richlin, "Invective against Women."

37. *AP* 5.40, 54, 75; cf. Corinna's abortion, Ovid *Am.* 2.14.

Chapter 3

1. See chap. 2, n. 4, above.
2. Richlin, "Invective against Women in Roman Satire," *Arethusa* (in press).

3. As when "Mamurra" becomes "Mentula" in Catullus' poetry, or when *Bored of the Rings* (the parody of *Lord of the Rings*) changes the hero "Bilbo Baggins" to "Dildo Bugger."

4. Whereas Burt Reynolds, as a comedian, is (often) a Priapic figure, Chaplin and Woody Allen are the opposite, as is clear in the following comment on Allen by Russell Baker ("Betrayed," from *So This Is Depravity*, 60):

> If the movies created a sense of inferiority in men, they did occasionally compensate with a character so timid, so incompetent, so awkward, absurd and inconsequential, that the dreariest mouse of a man could sit in the dark and feel like a prince of lovers. Men tired of seeing Valentino get the girl could recover their self-esteem by watching Chaplin's tramp, a man so inferior he could get nothing but a nightstick over the skull. The tramp did occasionally wind up with a girl, but he was so inept at the techniques of amour that one knew he would immediately lose her to the first passing Valentino.
>
> Woody Allen has some of Chaplin's power to make us feel superior by playing the loser. He makes us laugh by being more miserable in almost every respect than the most miserable specimen of humanity in his audience. We sit laughing in contentment with our own superiority while he fails tests of manhood which the meekest of us could pass without exertion.

Cf. esp. Pollio and Edgerly, "Comedians and Comic Style," Chapman and Foot, eds., *Humour and Laughter*, 215–42, particularly 235 on the negative stereotype embodied by most comedians (minority, woman, odd weight or height, madness).

5. Demonstrated, by linguistic analysis, in Baker, " 'Pricks' and 'Chicks': A Plea for 'Persons,' " in Baker and Elliston, eds., *Philosophy and Sex*, 45–64. For some lexical support, and extended discussion of clinical implications, cf. Stone, "On the Principal Obscene Word of the English Language," esp. 32–34.

6. References are to the Norton edition (1960), translated by James Strachey.

7. Hence, in ancient literature, the sympotic epigram, and the significance of wine in Aristophanic comedy. Cf. La Barre, "The Psychopathology of Drinking Songs"; and especially Leary, "Fists and Foul Mouths," on the relation between boasting, liquor, and fighting.

8. *Tradition and Originality in Roman Poetry*, 555.

9. "Juvenal: Satirist or Rhetorician?" 718.

10. Johnson, *The Lawrenceville Stories*, 263.

11. And it has been pointed out that the very concept of obscenity depends in part on the existence of "traditional figures of public authority" (Segal, "Censorship, Social Control and Socialization").

12. Cf. Apuleius *Met.* 1.13, where Aristomenes fears the old witches will kill him, but they urinate upon him instead.

13. Elliott, *The Power of Satire.*

14. Cf. Palmer, "On Mutinus Titinus," in *Roman Religion and Roman Empire: Five Essays.*

15. See below, on William Fry.

16. See Rosenmeyer, Ostwald, and Halporn, *The Meters of Greek and Latin Poetry: versus quadratus*, 77–78; scazons (choliambic), 15, 85; cf. the system of the epode (26–27). For *iambus* = invective, cf. Hor. *C.* 1.16.22–25 and Porph. *ad loc.*; Cat. fragment 3.

17. For overall bibliography and discussion see Kirshenblatt-Gimblett, ed., *Speech Play*, 205–06. In the Dozens (black American street invective), Abrahams, "Playing the Dozens" (a skewed but seminal discussion), and cf. Elliott, *The Power of Satire*, 73–74; for Turkey, Dundes, Leach, and Özkök, "The Strategy of Turkish Boys' Verbal Dueling

Rhymes"; in southern Mexico, Gossen, "Verbal Dueling in Chamula," in Kirshenblatt-Gimblett. Such jingling can be compared with the patterns of speech characteristic of schizophrenia, where "paraphone associations" (a kind of rhyming) and "homophone associations" (pointless punning) come to substitute for textual coherence (Rochester and Martin, *Crazy Talk*, 178–79); i.e., in schizophrenia the cue takes over from the content. Cf. Stewart, *Nonsense*, 31–32. The point of departure for such rhyming is seen in children's speech play, where "the use of rhyme reduces the speaker's responsibility because the first rhyming word compels the second" (Sanches and Kirshenblatt-Gimblett, "Children's Traditional Speech Play and Child Language," in Kirshenblatt-Gimblett, *Speech Play*, esp. 72–73). For analysis of nonverbal behavior in joking in groups, see Handelman and Kapferer, "Forms of Joking Activity."

18. The device (dubbed "metatheatrics" by Slater, "The Theatre of the Mind: Metatheatre in Plautus") by which the fiction of the play is broken and an actor speaks to the audience, often as if he were the playwright, is characteristic of comedy in antiquity. It places a comic play in the same relation to a tragic one that satire has with epic.

19. For sources on the practice of recitation at Rome, cf. Mayor *ad* Juv. 3.9, 7.40.

20. For an overview, and evidence for this syndrome throughout the empire, cf. Turnbull, "The Phallus in the Art of Roman Britain."

21. E.g., Hor. *Epod.* 8, 12; *Pr.* 12, 32, 46. Cf. Richlin, "Invective against Women."

22. Legman, *The Rationale of the Dirty Joke*, 369–81; Lurie, below, n. 63. Legman adduces Henry Miller's statement that the female genitalia are "nothing," and a line he attributes to Odo of Cluny, "inter faeces et urinam nascimur." He also suggests that jokes about too loose vaginas are simply attempts to deny that the penis could be too small (377). The major psychological study on this point is Horney, "The Dread of Women"; for an extended application to Greek society and mythology, see Slater, *The Glory of Hera*, esp. 10–49.

23. *CIL* IV.10004; probably Mart. 3.72.4–7, *Pr.* 12; cf. Henderson, *MM*, 50, n. 22, on lack of slang terms for the clitoris.

24. Lévi-Strauss, *The Raw and the Cooked*, 1:269–70.

25. The standard approach to satire accepts it as natural that the satirist should set himself above the object of his mockery, and likewise accepts that satire of these objects is justified, because they are bad. This view, which sees satirists as moralists, is hampered by a basic fallacy: it treats the content of the satire as true. Some satires are more "true" than others, and it is sometimes useful to attempt to distill the sediment of truth in a particular work (see, e.g., appendix 1); but a theory that begins from this fallacy cannot go far. So (somewhat ambiguously) Northrop Frye (*Anatomy of Criticism*, 224): "The satirist has to select his absurdities, and the act of selection is a moral act." But not moral in any absolute sense; surely a highly subjective morality. Frye states that the impersonal level necessary for interesting invective implies a moral standard, and he remarks on the conventionality of humor as if the conventions (= stereotypes) were random.

26. Critics of Roman satire have concentrated on the moral aspects of satire and its relation to the truth: Anderson, "The Roman Socrates" (on Horace), in Sullivan, ed., *Satire*; Highet, *Juvenal the Satirist*, 44–45; Quinn, *Texts and Contexts*, 200–01; Ramage, in Ramage, Sigsbee, and Fredericks, *Roman Satirists and Their Satire*, 137–38, 141–43, comparing Martial's lack of purpose with the concrete recommendations of Lucilius, Horace, Juvenal, and Persius. Coffey *(Roman Satire)* deliberately excludes related genres from his consideration—genres like epigram (because Martial is a "pornographic epigrammatist"), iambi, miscellaneous abusive verse, and courtroom invective—in order to see satire without any misleading analogies. He hedges as to Juvenal's position as moralist (138–40).

Others have concentrated on the value of the satirists' reportage, again concerned about its truth. Knoche says (*Roman Satire*, 148) that *Satire* 1 shows "Juvenal's skill as an observer"; *Satire* 6 is "the greatest female character study coming from antiquity." Ramage praises Martial for similar reasons. Many critics are openly repelled by the content of the sexual satires: Mason, "Is Juvenal a Classic?" in Sullivan, ed., *Satire*; Ogilvie, *Roman Literature and Society*, 240–50. Bond, "Anti-feminism in Juvenal and Cato," closely following an idea of de Beauvoir (*The Second Sex*, 107–09), states that as the Roman women gained freedoms, they wasted them on depravities; misogynistic writers like Cato and Juvenal were "partially responsible, along with the men who shared their views, for much of the female behaviour which they so trenchantly condemned" (418). That is, satirists created self-fulfilling prophecies (446–47); the repression of female talents led to "oddities and excesses of behaviour." This method treats the content of satire as both accurate, since it shows what women are up to, and skewed, since it shows the satirist's bias. (Bond also says that Juvenal's recommendation in *Satire* 6 to sleep with a boy cannot be serious, since Juvenal condemns homosexuals in *Satires* 2 and 9; aside from the question of logic, this ignores the difference between pederasty and adult male "pathic" homosexuality.)

Notable exceptions to these trends in criticism of Roman humor are Erich Segal, *Roman Laughter*, and Rudd, *The Satires of Horace*.

27. William F. Fry, Jr., *Sweet Madness*.

28. Johan Huizinga, *Homo Ludens*.

29. Sanches and Kirshenblatt-Gimblett, "Children's Traditional Speech Play," 74; Abrams and Sutton-Smith, "The Development of the Trickster in Children's Narrative," esp. 46, on the intrinsic value of "symbolic inversion."

30. Gossen, "Verbal Dueling in Chamula."

31. Chief Oludare Ọlajubu, "References to Sex in Yoruba Oral Literature."

32. E.g., Levine, "Regression in Primitive Clowning," esp. on the use of excrement in native American clowning.

33. Makarius, "Ritual Clowns and Symbolic Behaviour"; cf. Henderson, *MM*, 13–18; Babcock-Abrahams, " 'A Tolerated Margin of Mess.' "

34. Victor Turner, *The Ritual Process*.

35. Elliott, *The Power of Satire*, 58–59, on the connection of such rites with fertility rites.

36. On the *tibicines*, see Ovid *Fasti* 6.651–714; Latte, *RR*, 164–65. They played at the *Quinquatrus minusculae* on June 14; the fifteenth was the day on which *stercus* was removed from Vesta's temple, a solemn day of restricted activities for the *flamen dialis* (*CIL* I² p. 292, with comments on p. 319; Ovid *Fasti* 6.219–34, 713–14; Varro *LL* 6.32). On phallic worship and Vesta, see Hommer, "Vesta und die frührömische Religion," 410–19.

37. Catullus 61, Macrobius *Sat.* 2.4.21. Cf. Elliott on the rites of Phales, 5–6.

38. Erich Segal, *Roman Laughter*, 1–14.

39. Douglas, *Purity and Danger*, 37; cf. her further development of the function of humor in "The Social Control of Cognition," where she holds that jokes constitute a privileged attack on social, and mental, hierarchies.

40. Barber, *Shakespeare's Festive Comedy*, 3–57.

41. Collected in Levine, ed., *Motivation in Humor*.

42. Arthur Koestler, *Insight and Outlook*.

43. Dworkin and Efran, "The Angered," in Levine, ed., *Motivation in Humor*.

44. Singer, "Aggression Arousal, Hostile Humor, Catharsis," in Levine, ed., *Motivation in Humor*.

45. Hetherington and Wray, "Aggression, Need for Social Approval, and Humor Preferences," in Levine, ed., *Motivation in Humor*; cf. La Barre, "The Psychopathology of Drinking Songs."

46. Gollob and Levine, "Distraction as a Factor in the Enjoyment of Aggressive Humor," in Levine; all the subjects in this experiment were female.

47. Berkowitz, "The Effects of Observing Violence"; discussed by Singer, 106–07. See now Russell with Lederer, "Questions We Get Asked Most Often" (25), reprinted in Lederer, ed., *Take Back the Night.* Also Diamond, "Pornography and Repression"; Russell, "Pornography and Violence: What Does the New Research Say?" These articles all respond, more or less, to the surveys reported in *The Report of the Commission on Obscenity and Pornography*, in which see esp. 7–32, 44–49, 169–308.

48. Bandura, *Social Learning Theory*, 63–64. The weakness of the theory of catharsis has been demonstrated in many recent studies; for a survey, see Gergen and Gergen, *Social Psychology*, 302.

49. McGuire, Carlisle, and Young, "Sexual Deviations as Conditioned Behaviour: A Hypothesis."

50. Steinem, "Erotica and Pornography," *TBN* 37.

51. Longino, "Pornography, Oppression, and Freedom," *TBN* 44–45.

52. She cites on this point Davis, "Rape, Racism, and the Capitalist Setting."

53. Lederer, "An Interview with a Former Pornography Model," *TBN* 62.

54. Florence Rush, "Child Pornography."

55. Quoted by Rush, 78.

56. Rush cites Pamela Hansford Johnson and George Steiner, and presents material from police records that supports this view.

57. Kiefer, *Sexual Life in Ancient Rome*, 64–106.

58. "Theory and Practice: Pornography and Rape."

59. Cf. Rankin, "Petronius, Priapus, and *Priapeum* LXVIII," in *Petronius the Artist*, on the significance of the worship of Priapus.

60. Cf. the use of the phallus on military trappings, in Turnbull, "The Phallus in the Art of Roman Britain." The feminist position on rape has been challenged by Faust (*Women, Sex, and Pornography*), who says it constitutes "misandry." Claiming that feminists oversimplify the variety of the motives behind different rapes, she explains this by saying that since black rapists suffer worse punishments than white, feminists should not attack men as a class for committing rape—that rape is a "symptom of inequities in class" (143). Her logic appears stronger in her hypothesis that rape is often intended to "show off prowess" and that the primary intention is not to humiliate a woman; but this hypothesis, one would think, is invalid where the rape has no audience, and in any case "prowess" certainly implies dominating something else.

61. Griffin, "Sadism and Catharsis: The Treatment Is the Disease."

62. Robert Baker, " 'Pricks and Chicks.' "

63. Lurie, "Pornography and the Dread of Women."

64. Cf. Ortner, "Is Female to Male as Nature Is to Culture?" in Rosaldo and Lamphere, *Woman, Culture, and Society*; and, in general, MacCormack and Strathern, eds., *Nature, Culture and Gender*; Ortner and Whitehead, eds., *Sexual Meanings: The Cultural Construction of Gender and Sexuality*.

Chapter 4

1. For the present study, the graffiti come from Diehl's edition of Pompeiian material (*Pompeianische Wandinschriften und Verwandtes*, Berlin 1930). These presumably constitute a representative sampling and at least can all be dated with certainty. Inspection of *CIL* IV showed no significant differences in kind and much supportive material; a great deal of work still remains to be done on analyzing the content of these graffiti, perhaps relating them to phallic inscriptions, etc. On, e.g., the sling bullets from the siege of Perusia, which have obscene and hostile inscriptions on them, see Hallett, "*Perusinae Glandes* and the Changing Image of Augustus." For an impressionistic portrait of Pompeii

through the graffiti, see Lindsay, *The Writing on the Wall*. The graffiti are presented in facsimile with photographs of their surroundings by Krenkel, *Pompeianische Inschriften*; cf. also Tanzer, *The Common People of Pompeii*. On the value of subliterary art as social index, see Orwell, "The Art of Donald McGill," in *A Collection of Essays*, 104–16, especially on obscene humor and stereotypes. Castleman's *Getting Up* presents an in-depth study of the graffiti of the New York subways and the boys who write them, with photographs. For comparative material in Europe to the present, and bibliography on this material, cf. Legman, *The Horn Book*.

2. Modern studies of graffiti have connected their prevalence directly with repression; e.g., Stocker et al., "Social Analysis of Graffiti." (An article *contra*, Gonos, Mulkern, and Poushinsky, "Anonymous Expression: A Structural View of Graffiti," carries little conviction.) Directly relevant to the present study is Grider, "*Con Safos*: Mexican-Americans, Names and Graffiti," who connects graffiti with territoriality, the definition of "the boundaries of a sacrosanct area." In contrast, Castleman's study shows graffiti related not to bounded territory but to movement between territories, though the connection with young male groups is still fundamental.

3. For the identifications, see Shackleton Bailey *ad loc.*

4. Here may be noted the Roman penchant for epic travesty, or witty literary allusion, in sexual invective even at the colloquial level; not only this epithet and the joke about "Menelaus" and "Agamemnon" above, but Caelius' famous nickname for Clodia, *quadrantaria Clytaemestra* ("two-bit Clytemnestra," at Quint. *Inst.* 8.6.53), all attest it; cf. Cic. *Cael.* 18. It was used in invective insinuating pathic homosexuality as well, e.g., Cic. *De Or.* 2.265: "ut cum Sex. Titius se Cassandram esse diceret, 'Multos,' inquit Antonius, 'possum tuos Aiaces Oileos nominare.' " Cf. below, chapter 6.

5. See Shackleton Bailey *ad loc.* for speculation as to the identity of Fabius; his interpretation is, however, rejected by Watt, *JRS* 1960, p. 278, and others.

6. Cf. Lintott, *Violence in Republican Rome*, 6–10, on the popular practices of *occentatio* and *flagitatio*, and for parallels for these "antiphonal insults" in comedy. Cicero's description is quoted below, chap. 6; cf. also Fraenkel, "Two Poems of Catullus." For comparative material, see Dundes et al., "The Strategy of Turkish Boys' Dueling Rhymes," and further comments by Hickman, *JAF* 92 (1979): 334–35, who points out that these insults not only constitute "primitive forms of poetry" but existed in elevated form at the courts of the Ottoman sultans. Cf. also Gossen, "Verbal Dueling in Chamula," in Kirshenblatt-Gimblett, ed., *Speech Play*; Brenneis and Padarath, " 'About Those Scoundrels I'll Let Everyone Know' "; Brukman, "Tongue Play . . . among the Koya of Southern India," in *Sociocultural Dimensions of Language Use*, ed. Sanches and Blount.

7. Cf. the joke, in oral circulation during the early 1970s, "Pull out, Nixon, like your father should have." (The reference is to the war in Vietnam.) For a Roman parallel, cf. Cic. *Phil.* 2.58 (addressed to Antony's mother): "O miserae mulieris fecunditatem calamitosam!"

8. See Hallett, "*Perusinae Glandes.*"

9. Anon., "Scatological Lore on Campus," *JAF* 75 (1962): 260–62:

> An interesting and perfectly understandable phenomenon . . . is that in time, at any one college, many of the most popular stories become associated with one particular student figure, who may or may not even have attended the school. This character seems to have attributed to him many of the scatological stories common at the time, stories that are also told at other colleges, and that were told in years gone by. Of course, the exact same sort of story adhesion happens with any legendary hero . . .

The author goes on to cite Julius Caesar as an example: "scatological" here = "obscene," as most of the tales cited by the author involve exposure of the male organ and the "gross contest." The two groups of stories make an interesting comparison: Suetonius' tales all involve sadism, exposure, and degradation of the aristocracy, the chaste, and the office of *princeps* itself; the American stories "involve extreme disregard for social behavior. . . . They are of nightmarish intensity in their antisocial attack. . . . In none of the gross tales . . . is there any idea of normal heterosexual gratification, no supernatural sex feats."

10. The Romans made a verbal distinction between active and pathic homosexuals, depending on which part was played in anal or oral intercourse: pathics were those who were always sodomized or always performed fellatio. It is rather hard to know if this behavioral pattern, which is not so absolute today, actually existed among the Romans; the distinction is consistently made both in anecdotes and in literary sources, although, as will be seen, the assignment of roles to any one person in invective often changes from place to place.

11. This exchange brings to mind the famous interchange between Oscar Wilde and the lawyer Carson in the cross-examination at the Queensberry trial (in Pearson, *The Life of Oscar Wilde*, 289–90):

C: "Apart from art, Mr. Wilde?"
W: "I cannot answer apart from art."
....
C: "I can suggest, for the sake of your reputation, that there is nothing very wonderful in this 'red rose-leaf lips of yours.' "
W: "A good deal depends on the way it is read."
C: " 'Your slim gilt soul walks between passion and poetry.' Is that a beautiful phrase?"
W: "Not as you read it, Mr. Carson. You read it very badly."

On the other hand, Hortensius never went to prison.

12. E.g., the sources cited in Leeman, *Orationis Ratio*, 93–95.

13. Cf. Carcopino, *Cicero*, 1:82–83. Carcopino suggests that the epigram to Tiro that inspired Pliny was probably a spurious product of the splenetic pen of Asinius Gallus, evidence manufactured to support an insinuation that Tiro was Cicero's *puer*. Also Nisbet, ed., *M. Tulli Ciceronis in L. Calpurnium Pisonem Oratio*, 197–99, who sees in the invective a product of the schools, and a post-Republican one at that.

14. Hallett (*"Perusinae Glandes"*) compares this lampoon (probably of the right date, n. 61) with the *glandes Perusinae* and concludes that whereas the sling bullets ridicule Octavian, Fulvia, and Lucius Antonius, Martial 11.20 represents a propagandistic effort on Augustus' part to improve his public image and make himself seem virile. Her analysis of the bellicose imagery of the poem (161–62) is particularly good.

15. On invective in rhetoric, cf. especially Nisbet's edition of the *In Pisonem*, 192–97, for an overview of the categories, with some sources; Kelly, " 'Loss of Face' as a Factor Inhibiting Litigation," in *Studies in the Civil Judicature of the Roman Republic* (with a comparison to forensic invective in Old Irish); and Geffcken, *Comedy in the Pro Caelio*, who applies Freud's theories to invective oratory, drawing largely on analogies with Roman comedy and on Bergson's cheerful view of the results of humor. She also discusses the fragmentary invective *In Clodium et Curionem* (appendix 1, 58–59), with especially pertinent remarks on the use of invective in rhetoric, on the description of Clodius in female dress in the *In Clodium*, and on transvestitism in ancient literature (75–89). On the tendentiousness of Cicero's attack on Clodia, see (for a defense of Clodia) Dorey, "Cicero, Clodia, and the *Pro Caelio*." The tradition of invective in rhetoric, of course, long antedates Cicero and is found in the fragments of earlier oratory; cf. Scipio's speech, above.

16. *Har. Resp.* 27, 38; *Cael.* 1, 18, 31, 32, 34, 36, 38, 47–49, 59, 62; cf. *Mil.* 73. Again using the technique of epic travesty, Cicero calls her *Palatinam Medeam* (*Cael.* 18). The premise of the argument in the *Pro Caelio* is that if Clodia's moral character is that of a *meretrix*, her accusations can have no weight.

17. *Clu.* 12–17, 18, 175, 176–99.
18. *Phil.* 2.11, 48, 77, 95, 113; *Phil.* 3.4; *Phil.* 5.11, 22.
19. *Phil.* 2.20, 61, 62, 69, 70.
20. *Verr.* 2.1.136, 137, 139; *Verr.* 2.2.24; *Verr.* 2.4.71, 136; 2.5.38.
21. *Verr.* 2.3.78, 79–82, 83; 2.5.81.
22. *Verr.* 2.3.77, 2.5.81.
23. *Verr.* 2.5.81–83, 86, 92, 94, 112, 131, 137.
24. *Verr.* 2.5.86; *Rab. Post.* 26–27; *Phil.* 2.76.
25. He also calls Antony "catamitum" (*Phil.* 2.77) and chides him for referring to Decimus Brutus as *venefica*, "poisoneress" (*Phil.* 13.25). Hallett (*"Perusinae Glandes"*) reads one of the *glandes Perusinae* as addressed to "Octavia" (for Octavius).
26. *Dom.* 77, 80, 104, 105, 110, 139; *Har. Resp.* 4, 8, 33, 37–38, 44; *Sest.* 116; *Prov. Cons.* 24; *Pis.* 89, 95; *Planc.* 86; *Mil.* 13, 46, 55, 72–73, 86, 87. For full treatment of the political meaning of the charges against Clodius, see Skinner, "Pretty Lesbius."
27. *Rosc. Am.* 135; *Leg. Agr.* 2.59; *Red. Sen.* 12, 13, 16; *Sest.* 18, 26; *Pis.* 25.
28. *Rosc. Am.* 135; *Verr.* 2.3.31; *Cat.* 2.5; *Red. Sen.* 12, 16; *Sest.* 18.
29. *Verr.* 2.3.23; *Mur.* 13; *Red. Sen.* 13; *Dom.* 60; *Pis.* 18 (*saltatrix*), 22, 89; *Deiot.* 26; *Phil.* 5.15.
30. *Verr.* 2.1.32–33; *Verr.* 2.3.159–62 (Verres' son); *Font.* 37; *Rab. Perd.* 9; perhaps with the other outrages at *Flac.* 34; *Red. Sen.* 11, *Dom.* 126, *Sest* 18 (Gabinius); *Har. Resp.* 42 (Clodius); *Sest.* 110 (Gellius); *Phil.* 2.3, 6, 44–47, 50, 86, 3.15, 13.17 (Antony).
31. *Red. Sen.* 10 (*Catilinam, amatorem suum*)—probably a reference to Gabinius' youth, cf. *Pis.* 20 (*Catilinae lanternario*).
32. Cf. also *Har. Resp.* 59, *Pis.* 65.
33. *Pis.* 70–71, 88, 89. *Pis.* 70–71 links Piso with the philosopher Philodemus, whose poems appear in chapter 2 above (but cf. Nisbet, ed., *M. Tulli Ciceronis in L. Calpurnium Pisonem Oratio*, 183–85, for a defense of Piso's chastity).
34. On the political uses of invective against effeminacy, see Skinner, "Parasites and Strange Bedfellows," 142 and n. 19.
35. *Verr.* 1.14; 2.1.9, 62–85; 2.2.36, 89, 110, 116, 183; 2.3.6; 2.4.116; 2.5.39; *Prov. Cons.* 6; *Pis.* 86; *Scaur.* 8; *Mil.* 76; *Phil.* 2.99 (adultery); *Phil.* 3.31, 14.9 (Lucius Antonius in Gaul).
36. *Quinct.* 93 (the opponent); *Rosc. Am.* 6, 133–35 (Chrysogonus); *Verr.* 2.3.62, 65 (Apronius), 105–06; 2.5.26–34, 40, 63, 81–83, 86, 92, 94, 112, 131, 137; *Red. Sen.* 13, 14; *Pis.* 42 (Piso); *Phil.* 2.15, 69, 104–05 (a tour de force: *ingenui pueri cum meritoriis, scorta inter matres familias versabantur*).
37. *Cat.* 2.4; *Pis.* 13, 18, 22, and especially 67; *Phil.* 2.30, 42, 63, 76, 84–87, 101.
38. *Dom.* 25, 26, 47–48, 83; *Har. Resp.* 11, 59; *Cael.* 78; *Pis.* 8. For the identification of this man as Cloelius, not Clodius, see Bailey, "Sex. Clodius–Sex. Cloelius."
39. *QRosc.* 20, 50; *Verr.* 2.4.7, 71, 83; *Cat.* 4.17; *Mur.* 74; *Red. Sen.* 12; *Sest.* 20, 26.
40. *Quinct.* 29; *Rosc. Am.* 17, 118; *Verr.* 2.3.61; *Cat.* 1.29; *Dom.* 6, 81; *Pis.* 19 (Clodius), 28 (Gabinius); *Phil.* 3.31, 5.20, 6.10, 13, 7.17–18, 12.20 (Lucius Antonius); *Phil.* 5.10, 13.40. The charge against Lucius Antonius purports to be true; Cicero repeatedly alludes to an incident in which Antonius played the *murmillo* and killed a companion dressed as a *Thrax*.
41. *Sest.* 116 (Clodius); *Phil.* 2.62, 67, 101.
42. *Verr.* 2.3.62; *Cat.* 2.7, 10, 22; *Mil.* 55 (Clodius); *Phil.* 2.57–58, 8.26, 10.22, 11.10–14, 13.26–28.
43. But cf. Nisbet, ed., *M. Tulli Ciceronis in L. Calpurnium Pisonem Oratio*, 195. On animal invective, see below.
44. *Font.* 27–36, 44, 49 (Gauls); *Flac.* 9 and passim (Asiatic Greeks); *Pis.* 53 (Gauls); *Scaur.* passim, esp. 38–45 (Sardinians); *Rab. Post.* 35 (Alexandrians); *Lig.* 11 (Greeks).

45. *Rosc. Am.* 46, 55, 57; *Phil.* 1.5, 5.14–15.

46. Leeman, *Orationis Ratio*, 38; on *vituperatio*, Nisbet, ed., *M. Tulli Ciceronis in L. Calpurnium Pisonem Oratio*, 197–99.

47. On behalf of Fonteius, *Font.* 34, 37; Flaccus, *Flac.* 5; Caelius, *Cael.* 6–7, 8, 9–11, 25–27, 28–30, 38; Plancius, *Planc.* 30; Rabirius, *Rab. Perd.* 8 (here Cicero turns the accusation against the opponent).

48. Above, *Verr.* 2.3.23 (Apronius, in front of Verres' son); *Cat.* 2.23 (Catiline's followers); *Pis.* 22 (Gabinius). Presumably this identified the victim with a *cinaedus*, who danced at feasts; nudity was a mark of debauchery or insanity, as when Antony supposedly spoke "nude" (*Phil.* 2.86 and often elsewhere).

49. On freedom of speech at Rome, cf. sources listed below, chap. 7, n. 2; esp. Williams on the case of Naevius and the Metelli, and on the immunity afforded by social status and by genre.

50. For a brief overview of invective in the late Republic and of politicians' reactions to attack, see Syme, *The Roman Revolution*, 149–52; and especially Kenneth Scott, "The Political Propaganda of 44–30 B.C."

51. Even if the Twelve Tables did outlaw *occentatio*, the practice certainly continued until the end of the Republic (sources in Lintott, *Violence in Republican Rome*, 8).

Chapter 5

1. The idea that physically ugly things should be the target of ridicule reappears throughout this section of the *De Oratore*, esp. at 239 and 266.

2. The transposition of lines 117 and 118 is Clausen's; he also brackets line 126, while early readings of lost mss. show *ac resupina iacens*, in which form the line was supported by Jachmann (Coffey, "Juvenal Report," 172, #36). The line fills out the picture of Messallina's activities, and its strong match of rhythm to sense is certainly worthy of Juvenal. The name "Lycisca" also appears in Mart. 4.17.

3. Cf. Diehl 467, "Lahis felat a. II"; at a more lofty level, the freedwoman of Volumnius Eutrapelus who was the mistress of Antony et al. bore the name "Cytheris." "Leda" is the name of the cheapest sort of prostitute at Mart. 3.82.3; in 2.63 another Leda costs 100,000 sesterces.

4. The chief works on the *Priapea* are: Herter, *De Priapo*, on the history of the religious significance of the god in life and in the plastic arts; Buchheit, *Studien zum Corpus Priapeorum*, on the date, source, and authorship of the *Priapea*, and on select problems in the text. Also of interest: Rankin, "Petronius, Priapus, and *Priapeum* LXVIII," which states that Priapus represented to upper-class Romans a certain type of brute sensuality; and especially Willenberg, "Die Priapeen Martials," which establishes, by means of extensive analysis of each poem, that Martial's Priapics constitute a cycle. Vanggaard, *Phallós*, skirts the *Priapea* but provides a good introduction to anthropological and behaviorist studies of phallic symbolism, also to the significance of the phallic threat in Norse mythology; cf. Fehling, *Ethologische Überlegungen auf dem Gebiet der Altertumskunde*, 7–38 ("Phallische Demonstration").

The *Priapea* has long provoked attempts to assign it to a single known author, as, e.g., Thomason, *The Priapea and Ovid*, refuted by Steele, *A Review of the Priapea and Ovid*; Herrmann, "Martial et les Priapées." Although it seems unlikely that either Martial or Ovid wrote the *Priapea* (see appendix at end of chapter), and it is certainly unsound to use similarities in wording to show identity of authorship, such studies provide full and interesting collections of parallels.

On invective against old women there is no in-depth study; some parallel sources may be found in Grassmann, *Die erotischen Epoden des Horaz*, 12–22, 23–34; Buchheit, *Studien zum*

Corpus Priapeorum, 88–89, and sources in 88, n. 2. Cf. also Richlin, "Invective against Women in Roman Satire," *Arethusa* (in press); Khan on Catullus 17 and the Priapic poem from the *Virgilian Appendix*, "Image and Symbol in Catullus 17"; Skinner, "*Ameana, puella defututa*." Erich Segal connects attacks on wives in Plautine comedy with the general reversal of *pietas* in the plays (*Roman Laughter*, 21–28).

5. This punctuation seems much more intelligible than that of the Oxford text. For some parallels in epigram to *Epod.* 8, cf. Weinreich, "Zu Horazens 8. Epode und Nikarch AP V 38." On the linguistic background of the words in *Epod.* 8, cf. Grassmann, *Die erotischen Epoden des Horaz*, 47–68.

6. Cf. Cat. 97.7–8, *rictum qualem . . . meientis mulae cunnus*, of a man; Mart. 11.21.10 (pelican), and a parade in Mart. 3.93:3, grasshopper, ant; 7, crocodile; 8, frogs; 9, gnat; 10, owl; 11, ram; 12, duck. For the linguistic background of the words in *Epod.* 12, cf. Grassmann, *Die erotischen Epoden des Horaz*, 70–83.

7. The structure of *Epodes* 8 and 12 has been discussed by Carrubba, *The Epodes of Horace*, 43–52, = *Latomus* 24 (1965), 591–98; Grassmann, 69–70 (8), 87 (12).

8. Grassmann, 90: "Die für Horaz so wesentliche sittliche Entrüstung fehlt bei dem Epigrammatiker."

9. Mayer, *Erdmutter und Hexe*, discusses the threat presented by witches; cf. esp. Widdowson, "The Witch as a Frightening and Threatening Figure" (note esp. physical descriptions provided by informants, 208, 209); Ross, "The Divine Hag of the Pagan Celts," esp. 146 on transformation of goddess into sexually repulsive hag; 147, hag with enlarged genitalia; and 147–49 on the female figures, possibly equivalents of Priapus, called *sheelagh-na-gigs*. For the grotesque depiction of old women in ancient drama and art, cf. Cèbe, *La Caricature et la parodie dans le monde romain antique des origines à Juvénal*, 40, 355–56, and plates II.4–6, III.2.

10. Martial's invective against old women: 1.19, 3.32, 3.93, 4.20, 7.75, 8.64, 8.79, 9.29, 9.37, 10.39, 10.67, 10.90, 11.29. Comparison with Hecuba, Niobe, other female figures: 3.32, 9.29, 10.67. Woman = corpse: 3.32, 3.93, 10.90. Woman should pay Martial for his services: 7.75, 11.29. Mart. 3.93, by far the longest of his invectives against old women (27 lines), much resembles *Epodes* 8 and 12 in comparing the woman's body to those of animals and includes many other invective themes as well (age, toothlessness, smell, promiscuity, coldness). In 4.5, 9.80, and 11.87 Martial connects *captatio* and invective against old women.

11. Esp. Laberius 139–40 Ribbeck (cf. Marx *ad* Lucil. 940); *Pr.* 12, 46; Mart. 2.34, 3.93, 10.90; in a young woman, 3.72, 7.18, 11.21.

12. On these motifs in European and American humor, cf. Legman, *Rationale of the Dirty Joke* (first series): fear of the vagina, 369–81; hatred of aggressive women, 347–55 ("Ophelia's Crime"); female insatiability, 356–60. On *vagina dentata*, Legman, *No Laughing Matter*, 427–73; Thompson, *Motif-Index of Folk Literature*, K 1222.

13. Cf. esp. Horney, "The Dread of Woman"; Millett, *Sexual Politics*, 72–78, on female genitalia and the "men's house culture"; 243–66, on the concept of "penis envy" and its implications.

14. For the similar Greek use of the term σάθων as an endearment, cf. Henderson, *MM*, 109–10 (#3).

15. Cf. Mart. 3.93, where he combines this theme with the idea that the old woman is a corpse (line 27): "intrare in istum sola fax potest cunnum," "only a funeral torch can enter that cunt of yours."

16. Buchheit, *Studien zum Corpus Priapeorum*, 64.

17. *Senex corvus* seems to substitute *corvus* for *cornix*, since crows were proverbially long-lived; in this aspect they often serve as referents for old women in invective, as in *Pr.* 57 (above).

18. See appendix at the end of this chapter for discussion of the date and authorship of the *Carmina Priapea*.

19. *Pr.* 3, 5, 6, 7, 11, 13, 15, 17, 22, 23, 24, 25, 26, 28, 30, 31, 35, 38, 41, 44, 51, 52, 54, 56, 58, 59, 64, 66, 67, 69, 70, ?71, 72, 73, 74, 76, 77.

20. Buchheit, *Studien zum Corpus Priapeorum*, 82–87, discusses these three poems and parallels, mostly Greek; esp. interesting on the significance and history of riddles using letters of the alphabet, 86, and nn. 4–5.

21. Buchheit's idea that the collection was printed in codex form and had a picture of the god on the cover, so that the book was literally a precinct of the god, although not necessitated by the content of *Pr.* 1 and 2 (Buchheit, *Studien*, 7–11), is appealing on its own merits.

22. For comparative material on anal rape as a punishment in ancient and medieval Scandinavian literature and in the medieval and modern Near East, cf. Vanggaard, *Phallós*, 71–81, 101–12.

23. For depilation, cf. Mart. 3.74; on the use of resin as a depilatory, Mart. 12.32.21–22. Depilation of female genitalia is commonly referred to in Old Comedy, Henderson, *MM*, 131, #111, where the point is that grown women remove their pubic hair to take on the appearance of prepubescent girls.

24. E.g., Buchheit, *Studien zum Corpus Priapeorum*, 62, n. 2. He rightly treats the fragments separately. Fragment 2 has been stamped Priapic as well, for insufficient reasons. It certainly concerns cunnilingus but says nothing of Priapus; Catullus might well be capable of discussing cunnilingus without Priapus, and the god elsewhere has no interest in this form of sex at all.

25. Martial's Priapic poems: 6.16, 6.49, 6.72, 6.73, 7.91, 8.40, 14.69. Willenberg ("Die Priapeen Martials") has discussed these poems fully (with the exception of 7.91), with attention to their content and purpose.

26. On the relationship between Martial's themes and those of Greek epigram, cf. Laurens, "Martial et L'Épigramme Grecque"; he argues for Martial's originality and for the realism of his characterizations (336), and cites previous bibliography.

27. *Os impurum*: *AP* 11.155, 218, 219–23, 252, 329, 338. Invective against old women: 11.65–74, 256, 297, 298, 327, 417; these concern physical flaws and great age. Especially noteworthy is 11.73, by Nicarchus, which says that an old woman will pay a man and let him do anything he pleases to her. On ugly women: 11.196, 201. Pathic homosexuality: 11.22, 155, 216, 217, 225, 272, 339. Bad breath: 11.239 (a woman), 240, 241, 242, 415.

28. Cuckoldry: *AP* 11.4, 278. Genitalia: 11.79, 197, 224, 318, 342. Impotence: 11.29.

29. Nicarchus: *βινεῖν*, *AP* 11.7; *παθικεύεται*, 73; *πρωκτός*, *βδεῖν*, 241; *βδῆς'*, 242; *πόρδη*, 395; *βδεῖς*, 415. Lucillius: *δέρεται*, *AP* 11.79; *κηλήτας*, 132; sexual/literary puns, 139; *κακοστομάτων* (play on words), 155; *δριμύς/δρῖλος* word game, 197; periphrasis for "pathic," 216, 217.

30. The elaborate conceit and threefold division perhaps influenced Rufinus in his two poems on the judgment of three women (*AP* 5.35 and 36; discussed above).

31. Cf. Buchheit, "Feigensymbolik im antiken Epigramm"; also his discussion of *Pr.* 68, *Studien zum Corpus Priapeorum*, 99–103. The distinction between vagina as sea/divine and anus as earth/satanic appears in Mailer's *An American Dream*, discussed by Millett, *Sexual Politics*, 25–32.

32. Buchheit, *Studien zum Corpus Priapeorum*, in his discussion of *Pr.* 13, 22, and 74; he adduces *AP* 11.328 and cites other parallels (on Cat. 56, cf. Buchheit, "Catull an Cato von Utica").

33. Cf. Legman, *Rationale of the Dirty Joke*, 555–56, 740–41, 747, 780–82, on the fantasy of multiple penetration.

34. Martial's epigrams on adultery: 1.73, 1.74, 2.39, 2.47, 2.49, 2.56, 2.60, 2.83, 3.26, 3.70, 3.85, 3.92, 4.9, 4.58, 5.75, 6.2, 6.4, 6.7, 6.22, 6.31, 6.45, 6.67, 6.90, 6.91, 9.6, 9.8, 10.52, 10.69, 12.93.

35. Martial's epigrams against male homosexuality: 1.24, 1.65, 1.92, 1.96, 2.29, 2.36, 2.51, 2.54, 2.62, 2.84, 3.63, 3.71, 3.91, 3.98, 4.43, 4.48, 4.52, 5.41, 5.61, 6.33, 6.37, 6.50, 6.54, 6.56, 6.64.4–5, 6.91, 7.34, 7.58, 7.62, 8.44, 9.8, 9.21, 9.27, 9.47, 9.57, 10.64 (quoting Lucan), 10.65, 11.22, 11.28, 11.87, 11.88, 12.16, 12.33, 12.42, 12.97.

36. On oral intercourse: 1.77, 1.94, 2.15, 2.21, 2.28, 2.33, 2.42, 2.50, 2.61, 2.73, 2.84, 2.89, 3.17, 3.73, 3.80, 3.81, 3.82, 3.83, 3.84, 3.87, 3.88, 3.96, 4.17, 4.39, 4.50, 4.84, 6.26, 6.56, 6.66, 6.69, 6.81, 7.24, 7.55, 7.62, 9.4, 9.27, 9.40, 9.63, 9.67, 9.92, 10.40, 11.25, 11.30, 11.40, 11.45, 11.46, 11.47, 11.61, 11.66, 11.85, 11.95, 12.35, 12.38, 12.55, 12.59, 12.85. 7.55, a curse, threatens the victim with irrumation, not by Martial but by a (circumcised) Jew, combining phallic threat with xenophobia.

37. On impotence: 2.45, 3.70, 3.75, 9.66, 10.91, 11.25, 11.46, 12.86.

38. Elliott, *The Power of Satire*, 17–18, 71.

39. Cf. the superb parody of Eskimo drum songs in Mann and Kenney, "Canadian Corner."

40. Cf. above, chap. 2.

41. Martial's attacks on women: physical ugliness, 1.72 (toothless, black), 1.83, 2.33 (bald, one-eyed), 2.41 (bad teeth), 3.42 (wrinkled belly), 3.53, 3.72 (sexual), 6.23 (her face prevents the narrator from sexual arousal), 10.84, 11.99 (buttocks), 11.100 (sexual); drinking, 1.87; breasts too large, 1.100, 2.52; smell, 6.93; genitalia, 7.18 (too noisy during intercourse), 11.21 (too loose); rejection of marriage and/or intercourse, 11.23, 11.62 (woman must pay), 11.97, 12.27, and cf. 11.104; sexual aggressiveness or promiscuity, 2.34, 3.26, 4.12, 4.28, 6.45, 6.67, 7.30, 10.68. For Martial's invective against old women, which attacks many of the same physical flaws, cf. above, n. 10.

42. The situation in the Norse *Edda* is discussed by Vanggaard, *Phallós*, 76–81 ("The Meaning of the Word *argr* in Old Norse").

43. Cf. Mart. 8.44, 8.63, 9.21, 11.70, 12.33; and below.

44. *Rigidus* = "erect," Cat. 56.7, *Pr.* 4.1, 45.1, Petron. *Sat.* 134.11, Mart. 6.49.2, 9.47.6, 11.16.5, 12.42.1. *Soror* and *frater* used of sexual partners: *frater* (heterosexual), Petron. *Sat.* 127.2, Mart. 2.4.3; *frater* (homosexual) commonly in the *Satyricon: soror*, Petron. *Sat.* 127.1–2, Mart. 2.4.3, 12.20.

45. Cf. also *Pr.* 11, 25, 31, 51.

46. Mart. 1.24, 1.96, 2.36, 6.56, 7.58, 9.27, 9.47, 12.42; Juv. 2.1–63.

47. Mart. 3.63, 5.61; cf. Lucil. 1058 Marx; Juv. 6.0.1–34.

48. Cf. the interchangeability of words for "urinate" and "ejaculate" below; for a parallel for the Horace passage, see Vanggaard, *Phallós,* 74, on similar behavior in monkeys. This whole chapter in Vanggaard, "Excursus on the Baboon" (71–75), is relevant to the present discussion.

Appendix. The Date and Authorship of the Carmina Priapea

1. On further consideration, the problem of the syntax in the excerpted words may not be so important; cf. the chunks Cicero chooses in *Fam.* 9.22.1 (above). Even in a (largely) uninflected language like English, one might conceivably quote "and kingdoms seen" or "in fealty to Apollo hold," both phrases lacking major syntactical elements; in English they would most likely have to be plugged into a correct syntactical space, but both would undoubtedly recall the first half of the line at once. This is particularly true of the practice of citing songs and poems by their opening words or first lines, e.g., "Let me not to the marriage of true minds."

2. Compare the high proportion of space devoted to Priapus by both Horace (1 out of the 10 satires in the first book) and Petronius with the 7 out of 1,162 (+ 350) epigrams in Martial, and only 2 mentions in Juvenal (6.316, 6.375). Maecenas had a Priapus in his garden, as attested by Hor. *S.* 1.8; so did Valerius Cato, as attested by Furius Bibaculus (*FPL* 1 Morel). Cf. Herter, *De Priapo*, 28, 244.

Chapter 6

1. Much that has been written on Catullus touches on aspects to be considered here; the following list can only be a selection. The most relevant general studies are: Bardon, *Propositions sur Catulle*, 65–74; Granarolo, *L'Oeuvre de Catulle*, 160–99; Lateiner, "Obscenity in Catullus"; MacLeod, "Parody and Personalities in Catullus"; and on the sources of Catullus' invective, Hezel, *Catull und das griechische Epigramm*, 39–42; Montero Cartelle, "De las *nugae* a los graffiti o del 'priapismo verbal,' " following closely Cèbe, "Sur les trivialités de Catulle." Cf. also Skinner, "Pretty Lesbius," an in-depth study of the relation between sexual and political invective in Catullus. Of the studies on one or a few poems, the following represent critical principles productive of valid analysis of Catullus' sexual imagery: Witke, "Catullus 13: A Reexamination"; Fehling, "De Catulli Carmine sexto decimo"; and Buchheit, "Sal et lepos Versiculorum (Catull. *c.* 16)"; Khan, "Image and Symbol in Catullus 17"; a group of excellent studies of Cat. 29—William Scott, "Catullus and Caesar (c. 29)," Minyard, "Critical Notes on Catullus 29," and Skinner, "Parasites and Strange Bedfellows"; the first study to emphasize *Volksjustiz* imagery in Catullus, Fraenkel, "Two Poems of Catullus (42 and 8)"; and, on Catullan invective against women, Skinner, *"Ameana, puella defututa."* Cf. also Richlin, "The Meaning of *Irrumare* in Catullus and Martial."

Useful studies of poems containing sexual imagery: Jocelyn, "On Some Unnecessarily Indecent Interpretations of Catullus 2 and 3"; M. Gwyn Morgan, *"Nescio quid febriculosi scorti*: A Note on Catullus 6"; Bertman, "Oral Imagery in Catullus 7"; Cairns, "Catullus' *Basia* Poems (5, 7, 48)"; Richardson, *"Furi et Aureli, comites Catulli"*; Sandy, "Catullus 16"; Winter, "Catullus Purified: A Brief History of Carmen 16"; Konstan, "An Interpretation of Catullus 21"; Cameron, "Catullus 29"; Gratwick, "Ipsithilla, a Vulgar Name: Catullus xxxii.I"; Tanner, "Catullus LVI"; Curran, "Gellius and the Lover's Pallor: A Note on Catullus 80"; Whatmough, "Pudicus Poeta: Words and Things" (on 16 and 97), in *Poetic, Scientific and Other Forms of Discourse*, 29–55; Khan, "Catullus 99 and the Other Kiss-Poems"; Gnilka, "Catulls Spottgedicht auf Silo," contra Lenz *RCCM* 1963, and "Lynchjustiz bei Catull"; Morgan, "Catullus 112: A *Pathicus* in Politics"; Khan, "Three Epigrams of Catullus (*Carm.*, 114, 115, 112)"; MacLeod, "Catullus 116"; Forsyth, "Comments on Catullus 116"; Housman, "Praefanda," 402. Ellis's commentary is by far the soundest on questions involving sexual material (*A Commentary on Catullus*, 2d ed.).

2. Cat. 25, 28, 29, 33, 42, 47, 59, 103, 110; cf. 12, 30.

3. His rivals for Lesbia, Cat. 11, 37, 39, 58, 71, 79, 91; his rivals for Juventius, 15, 21, ?40, 81, ?82; other adulterers, 57, 67.19–48, 113.

4. For Catullus' invective against women and its relation to conventional invective against women, cf. Skinner, *"Ameana, puella defututa."*

5. For a putative parallel in real life, cf. Vanggaard, *Phallós*, 107, who quotes T. E. Lawrence on abuse of soldiers in the Turkish army.

6. Cat. 29.5, 9. The addressees of 29 have been identified variously as: Caesar, Pompey, and the Roman people (William Scott, "Catullus and Caesar"; Young, "Catullus 29"); Caesar, Pompey, and Crassus (Minyard, "Critical Notes on Catullus 29"); and Caesar and Pompey (Cameron, "Catullus 29"). All agree on the sexual implications of the poem.

7. These seem to have been the poems that offended Caesar, cf. Suet. *Iul.* 73.

8. For the imagery of the last stanza of 11, cf. Richardson, "*Furi et Aureli, comites Catulli,*" 106.

9. Cat. 16 has been the subject of endless discussion, stemming from several problems: (a) the "reality" of the threat in 1 and 14; (b) the nature of the situation that prompted Catullus to reply to Furius and Aurelius; (c) the identity of the *versiculi* (3, 6); (d) the meaning of *molliculi* (4, 8), *parum pudicum* (4, 8), *castum* (5), *non dico* (10), *his pilosis* (10), *qui . . . lumbos* (11), *male . . . marem* (13); (e) the referent of *milia multa basiorum*—Cat. 5, 7, or 48, or all three? Problem (a) has been haunted by a red herring, the "slang" meaning of *irrumare* (cf. Richlin, "The Meaning of *Irrumare*"), and by arguments attempting to exclude the direct sexual image from consideration. Problems (b), (c), and (e) are similar to each other and not pertinent to the present discussion. Problem (c) has sidetracked several analyses, e.g., Sandy, "Catullus 16," and esp. Kinsey, "Catullus *c.* 16." Fehling, "De Catulli Carmine sexto decimo," and Buchheit, "*Sal et lepos Versiculorum,*" surmount most of these obstacles; although Buchheit attacks Fehling (346–47), the two essays together (each with modifications) constitute a complete reading of the poem. Fehling correctly adduces the theme of punitive rape and the idea of friendly insult; Buchheit, besides providing a lengthy catalog of the critical literature on 16, argues that the poem is a sort of literary allegory, all the sexual elements representing ways of writing and reading poetry. Both arguments are valid, and they are certainly not mutually exclusive. One correction: tempting as it is to compare 10–11 with Persius 1.19–21 (so Buchheit, 342–46), it is not possible to take the *pilosis* as pedicated by the *versiculi.* Although poems act as aggressive phalli elsewhere (discussed below), and Cat. 16 itself constitutes the verbal equivalent of the threat in 1 and 14, Catullus is saying that his *versiculi* have wit only if they can arouse *quod prurit . . . his pilosis . . . qui duros nequeunt movere lumbos.* The *versiculi*, as noted above, are described like *cinaedi*, *molliculi ac parum pudici*; *quod prurit* should be active rather than pathic, on the analogy of 88.1–2, *qui . . . prurit* (of Gellius with his female relations); *his pilosis* is contrasted with *pueris* and, in its context (8–9), must represent subjects difficult to arouse; thus *qui . . . lumbos* is epexegetic of *quod . . . possint*, i.e., "even when they can't . . .," while *duros . . . lumbos* is an attribute of full-grown men (cf. Juv. 6.377); finally, even if *movere lumbos* can = *movere nates*, it is a great strain to take *duros movere lumbos* = *movere nates*. (As it is, of the parallels cited by Buchheit, Pers. 1.20 *lumbum* means only "genital area" = *podex* by extension [a distortion typical of Persius]; Petron. *Sat.* 140.6 *lumborum solutorum* = "weakened groin" and in context implies impotence; and *Pr.* 19.4, *fluctuante lumbo*, describes a dancer, so that *lumbo* cannot be specifically assigned to her *nates* and would more easily denote her front side. Lucil. 278 and 330 Marx make a useful comparison [below].)

10. For a comprehensive list and discussion of the kinds of questions used by Catullus, cf. Granarolo, *L'Oeuvre de Catulle*, 310–24, 344–45.

11. The essays on Cat. 29 by Cameron, Minyard, Scott, and Skinner have all recognized this connection and developed the comparison more or less; cf. esp. the list of parallels in Minyard, "Critical Notes on Catullus 29," 177–78, and Scott, "Catullus and Caesar," 20–22, on the technique of questioning. Fraenkel, "Two Poems of Catullus," discusses Cat. 42 as *flagitatio*, a connection of Catullan matter with actual public displays of violence extended by Gnilka, "Lynchjustiz bei Catull." Quinn *(Catullus: An Interpretation)* includes a more general treatment of political poetry, 267–77.

12. Collected by Ellis *ad* 115: *non homo sed piper*, etc. The technique remains a part of oral humor, as with the parodic names of the Princeton eating clubs and the Yale secret societies: Cap and Gown = "Clap in Groin" or "Crap and Drown," Key and Seal = "Pee and Squeal," Snake and Book = "Shake and Bake."

13. Cf. chap. 5 on the personification of the phallus.

14. Parts of this complex have been discussed by critics of single poems or small groups of poems: notably, Skinner, "Parasites and Strange Bedfellows," 140–41, on

irrumation = stuffing in Cat. 28, and on hunger and thievery in Cat. 47; Minyard, "Critical Notes on Catullus 29," 179, on the connection between feasting and sexual depravity; Khan, "Image and Symbol in Catullus 17," 95–96, on the connection between "gastric and sexual hunger"; Konstan, "An Interpretation of Catullus 21," on *satur/irrumatus* in Cat. 21; Whatmough, "Pudicus Poeta," 46–47, on the recurrence of the connection between *meiere/mingere* and *dentes*; Khan, "Catullus 99 and the Other Kiss-Poems," 613, on the connection between kisses and food; Cairns, "Catullus' *Basia* Poems," 21–22, on parallels for the enumeration of kisses; Bertman, "Oral Imagery in Catullus 7," on the relationship between kisses and verbal imagery.

15. Most cogently by MacLeod, "Catullus 116"; Forsyth, "Comments on Catullus 116," adds that the connection of 116 with 65 is reinforced by the reference to Callimachus in both poems.

16. Whatmough, "Pudicus Poeta," is responsible for this interpretation of *ploxenum*. Although the bulk of his essay concerns itself with various disputes on linguistic theory, his analysis of 97 *en passant* is remarkably vivid and imaginative.

17. Lateiner, "Obscenity in Catullus," finds three varieties of obscenity in Catullus: sexual, scatological, and "jolting juxtaposition" (i.e., an appealing picture succeeded by a foul one)—a form of staining.

18. The image that concludes Cat. 13, although it certainly brings into the poem a sensuality not present earlier (cf. the construction of 32), is surely literal and not a metaphor for Lesbia's *secreta muliebria*, as has been suggested (Littman, "The Unguent of Venus"; Hallett, "Divine Unction"). Catullus does not elsewhere show any inclination to share his mistress (surely these critics do not believe he was offering to act as intermediary and smear his friend with Lesbia's juices, or that all at the dinner party were going to snuffle ecstatically in her direction), and the Romans had a general horror of female genitalia and their secretions and smells (above; cf. esp. *VA* "Quid Hoc Novi Est," 26–37, Mart. 11.21, and the concept of the *os impurum*), so that it is extremely unlikely that the promise of such an *unguentum* would be offered as an inducement. Catullus barely hints of cunnilingus elsewhere, and never mentions either fellatio or female genitalia without disgust. For full discussion, see Witke, "Catullus 13," who includes salutary, if acid, strictures on maintaining the integrity of the context of a poem. For an imaginative analysis of a possible negative picture of female genitalia in Catullus, cf. Khan, "Image and Symbol in Catullus 17," 95–96.

19. Cf. Morgan, "*Nescio quid febriculosi scorti,*" for the identification of Flavius with his bed.

20. So her station in the back streets tells us, as perhaps also her use of manual stimulation (cf. Mart. 11.29, of an old woman). On *glubere*, cf. Penella, "A Note on *(de) glubere*"; Skutsch, "Catullus 58.4–5," Randall, "*Glubit* in Catullus 58."

21. The poems on Juventius have excited an endless controversy of their own; it seems to have settled on the idea that Juventius must be as real as Lesbia. The poems are simply part of the tradition of poems to *pueri* (above, chap. 2), who are as real (and only as real) as any beloved ever is. Arguments that go beyond this point lapse into biography, viz. Richardson, "*Furi et Aureli,*" who chronicles Catullus' argument with Furius and Aurelius over the "corrupt" Juventius. There is no need to say that pederasty was "fashionable" (Richardson, 94) or even that such poems were Hellenistic in spirit, though they certainly were (Williams, *Tradition and Originality in Roman Poetry*, 549–57); pederasty was just normal, and taken for granted as such by all the poets here surveyed. Cf. appendix 2, below.

22. Perhaps a slur against Clodius; cf. 79.1 "Lesbius est pulcer" with 106.1 "Cum puero bello . . . "

23. Cat. 56 has also provoked lengthy controversy as to what the boy found by Catullus is doing when found, and what Catullus then does to him. The latter (line 7) is almost certainly anal rape; for *rigida*, cf. *Pr.* 4.1, 45.1, Petron. *Sat.* 134.11, Mart. 6.49.2,

11.16.5, 12.42.1, and esp. 9.47.6. The former depends on the construction of *puellae/trusantem* (lines 5–6); is *puellae* genitive or dative? The dative certainly packs the poem with participants, and this construction supports Tanner, "Catullus LVI," a startling but conceivable interpretation of the end of the poem as a *triplex series*. But Tanner's analogy between *puellae/trusantem* and Giton as *in promulside* (Petron. *Sat.* 24.7) is difficult to accept (better *Sat.* 113.5–8?), and the theory that *puellae* is genitive and *trusantem* = "masturbating" is supported by the close similarity between 56 and *AP* 12.13, in which Strato, having found some boys τρίβοντας (here a double entendre = *masturbantes*), uses this to lever them into submitting to him.

24. Khan, "Image and Symbol in Catullus 17," interprets the poem as using sexual-religious imagery in which the swamp represents (a) the foul genitalia of an old prostitute (adducing the Priapic from the *Virgilian Appendix*) and (b) hell. This connection, especially Khan's development of the religious aspect, strongly recalls Bakhtin's analysis of the Rabelaisian cosmos (above, chap. 3).

25. For Mamurra in Catullus cf. especially William Scott, "Catullus and Caesar," 18–20; Skinner, "Parasites and Strange Bedfellows," 144–47; and Skinner, "*Ameana, puella defututa,*" 110–11.

26. But the similarity of the grounds for attack against personal and political enemy can be seen in many cases, e.g., Cat. 112 (Naso = *pathicus*), discussed by Morgan, "Catullus 112," and 80 (Gellius = *fellator*), for which Curran, "Gellius and the Lover's Pallor," gives a complete analysis of the poem's dynamics, content, and structure.

27. Benson, *Lucia in London*.

28. The study of Cat. 25 by Bianco ("Il Personaggio del c. 25 di Catullo"), concerns itself mostly with finding another Catullan target with whom to identify Thallus. (Bianco settles on Egnatius.)

29. The present discussion can do no more than align a commonly accepted interpretation of Ovid's attitudes toward the gods with the main body of satirical writing considered here. Especially pertinent are: Otis, *Ovid as an Epic Poet*, 2d ed., 335–74; Galinsky, *Ovid's "Metamorphoses,"* 36–37, 162–73; Frécaut, *L'Esprit et l'humour chez Ovide*, 240–55, with copious discussion of earlier opinions; and Due, *Changing Forms*, 86–89 (discussion of the end of book 15). On mock epic in general, cf. Cèbe, *La Caricature et la parodie*, 67–75, 231–47, 275–82, 337, 361–65.

30. Cf. Beare, *The Roman Stage*, 3d ed., on: the phlyax farces, in which religious travesty was a common subject (335–39); Plautus' *Amphitruo* (56–57); the mime of *Anna Perenna* by Laberius (155); "burlesque of tragedy" in the literary Atellana (144). On religious travesty in Plautus, cf. also Erich Segal, *Roman Laughter*, 29–31. On mock epic in Roman satire, cf. below, on Lucilius' *concilium deorum*, Horace, and Juvenal.

31. The retelling of the story at *Met.* 4.171–90, which follows Homer much more closely, is only a preamble to a story about the Sun; even so, it includes the observation, "illi iacuere ligati / turpiter; atque aliquis de dis non tristibus optat / sic fieri turpis . . ." (186–88).

32. For an opposing opinion, cf. Williams, *Change and Decline*, 87–96, who takes the apotheosis of Caesar to be serious panegyric (92).

33. Cf. also *Am.* 1.9.33–40, *Pr.* 68; for a similar description of the position, Horace *S.* 2.7.50 (quite coarse).

34. On epic travesty in the *Satyricon*, see below.

35. Erich Segal, *Roman Laughter*, 70–136.

36. Those critics who have speculated on Catullus' positive purpose in using obscenity do not agree as to what it was. The obscene and/or pederastic poems have often been viewed as lapses in taste, at best secondary to Catullus' other poems; Rankin ("A Note on Some Implications of Catullus, 16, 11–13") is not far from this point of view in taking the

pederastic poems as "self-satire," and MacLeod, "Parody and Personalities in Catullus," comes close to this in his study of Catullus' application of conventional forms to "fictional," funny situations. Lateiner, "Obscenity in Catullus," is closest to the present study in linking obscenity with the "release of anxiety" (27) and viewing it as an outlet for aggression. The most extreme viewpoint is that of Cèbe and Bardon: Cèbe, "Sur les trivialités de Catulle," demonstrates Catullus' use of the language of obscene theater and graffiti and states this to be self-expression, the rebellion of the neoteroi against old-fashioned poetry, and an effort to "scandaliser le bourgeois"; Bardon, *Propositions sur Catulle*, sees in Catullus a renegade thumbing his nose at society, echoing his own earlier statement ("Rome et l'impudeur") that obscenity in all Latin literature and in Roman culture represents the innate Roman urge "d'être soi," "une âme sans péché" (516, 518). But this viewpoint is clearly wrong, since Catullus uses obscenity only in its traditional place in invective poetry and in negative contexts, where it would be expected—as compared with Ovid, who made an epic travesty so large it became serious.

37. Putative; see chap. 7, n. 52.

Chapter 7

1. A phenomenon often observed in classical scholars: Sir Ronald Syme, for example, writes like Tacitus, Gomme like Thucydides.

2. On the question of free speech in Lucilius, see: Rudd, *The Satires of Horace*, 122; Williams, *Tradition and Originality in Roman Poetry*, 561; Fraenkel, rev. Beckmann, *Zauberei und Recht in Roms Frühzeit*; Daube, "Ne quid infamandi causa fiat: The Roman Law of Defamation"; Smith, "The Law of Libel at Rome"; Gordon Williams, *OCD*, 2d ed., s.v. "libel."

3. Numbers throughout refer to Friedrich Marx's edition of Lucilius *(C. Lucilii Carminum Reliquiae)*.

4. As restored by Lachmann and Marx; cf. also 305, 306, 307; possibly 1296, 1297.

5. Marx takes this as part of a conversation about a fight; but cf. Cat. 32.11; Lucil. 73, "in bulgam penetrare pilosam."

6. Possibly a phallic insignia of Scaevola; cf. Marx vol. 1, xliii–xlv, for discussion and parallels.

7. Marx, *Studia Luciliana*, 2–4, takes *amica* in apposition with *laeva* on the model of Mart. 9.41.1–2 *paelice laeva, amica manus*; *Pr.* 33.6 *amica manus*; Mart. 11.22.4 *fututrici manu*.

8. 1248, if this is parallel to Hor. *S.* 1.5.84 (Dousa) and not to *S.* 1.3.90 (Marx). But the reuse of *permingo* at *S.* 1.2.44 supports Marx's view. Rudd *ad loc.* takes *permingo* = *pedico* or *stupro* (cf. Rudd, *Satires of Horace*, 55). Now *meio*, *mingo*, and their compounds can be used either solely of excretion (Cat. 97.7–8, Hor. *S.* 1.8.38, Pers. 1.114, Petron. 67.10, Diehl 696, probably Mart. 11.46.2) or of ejaculation (Cat. 67.30, Hor. *S.* 2.7.52; cf. *urina*, Juv. 11.170); sometimes the metaphor inherent in the double use is particularly clear (*commingo*, Cat. 78b.2, 99.10; *inmeio*, Pers. 6.74). Catullus certainly liked to associate urine with the mouth in invective (37, 39; discussed above), which illumines his use of *commingo*. But the Horatian passage in *S.* 1.2 focuses on the brutality of the punishments for adultery; since *permingo* for *pedico* at Hor. *S.* 1.2.44 would weaken an image instead of strengthening it, shifting from penetration to staining, it thus seems better to take *permingo* here with its primary sense, "piss all over," and likewise for the Lucilius passage.

9. Cf. Juv. 10.205–06.

10. For speculation on the identity of this Hortensius, cf. Cichorius, *Untersuchungen zu Lucilius*, 338–39, who takes him to be the father of the great orator. The imagery in this line seems to be echoed in Persius 4.39, where the *palaestritae* may be "lovers" (see below); the association of wrestling with pederasty is common in Greek epigram, cf. above.

11. Perhaps = flatulence brought on by indulgence in anal penetration, possibly attributed to Mucius Scaevola in invective, Marx *ad loc.*

12. Usually taken to refer to a female prostitute (e.g., Fiske, *Lucilius and Horace*, 270); most of these terms, however, refer elsewhere to effeminate men (esp. Pers. 4.35–41; Mart. 2.36.6, 5.41.6, 9.27.5; Juv. 9.95).

13. Paul. ex Festo 32, "bubinare est menstruo mulierum sanguine inquinari (inquinare Mueller); inbulbitare est puerili stercore inquinare, dictum ex fimo, quod Graeci apellant *βόλβιτον*."

14. So Terzaghi; Marx suggests ⟨*fur*⟩ *palpatur*.

15. Following Marx, who adduces Apul. *Met.* 10.10, "tunc pedes incertis alternationibus commovere, . . . capitis partem scalpere . . .," here a sign of guilt (hence Marx's ⟨*fur*⟩); this passage is usually taken as a description of an ingratiating slave with a guilty conscience (cf. Cichorius, *Untersuchungen zu Lucilius*, 172; Fiske, *Lucilius and Horace*, 405), but the actions surely conform with the stereotype of effeminacy.

16. *Subit* Marx for Nonius' *obsit*, adducing Juv. 2.50 *Hispo subit iuvenes*; Terzaghi supplies a Greco-Latin *obsi*.

17. The degree to which Lucilius influenced later satirists is a major question. The most useful single work on the subject is Fiske, *Lucilius and Horace*; on Horace cf. also van Rooy, *Studies in Classical Satire*, 52–55; Fraenkel, *Horace*, 150–52; and especially Rudd, *The Satires of Horace*, 97–117, 149–50, 269–70. On freedom of speech in Juvenal, cf. n. 63 below.

18. Most notably Cichorius, *Untersuchungen zu Lucilius*; Fiske, *Lucilius and Horace*; also Terzaghi, *Lucilio*; Heurgon, *Lucilius*. On Lucilius' satire on marriage, cf. also Christes, *Der Frühe Lucilius*, 53–60.

19. Marx, *Studia Luciliana*, 42–45.

20. On the connection, cf. Cichorius, 205.

21. Fiske, 331.

22. Cichorius discusses the whole *concilium deorum* at length, 219–32.

23. Fiske, 152–56.

24. Fiske, 400–05.

25. Cf. Gulliver at Glubbdubdrib, *Alice in Wonderland*. On death in the *cena*, cf. Arrowsmith, "Luxury and Death in the *Satyricon*." For forerunners and other relatives of Horace's satiric *nekuia*, cf. Rudd, *The Satires of Horace*, 235–39; Courtney, "Parody and Literary Allusion in Menippean Satire," 88.

26. Cichorius, 133–42, 157–63; Fiske, 248–74; also Terzaghi, 146–51.

27. Cf. Livy *Per.* 59, Gellius 1.6, for Metellus' law and the context of this speech; this appears to have been the speech that Augustus read out to the Senate in furthering his own moral legislation (see appendix 1), which demonstrates the persistence of Metellus' assumptions.

28. In the following notes, two critics of Horace will figure prominently. Rudd, in *The Satires of Horace*, is one of very few writers on ancient satire to analyze the content and meaning along with the form of the literature studied. Fraenkel also treats the satires (*Horace*, 76–153), but not in such depth. Rudd, although he believes Horace's aim to have been reform, which he lauds, recognizes the problems in viewing Horace as a reformer; he does see Horace as a defender of the norm and examines Horace's work in comparison with other types of satire (16, 46, 197–201).

S. 1.2 has provoked a good deal of comment, mostly defending the poem's unity. On the connection with Lucilius, see Rudd, 10–14. Critics who find a unifying theme in the poem are: Baldwin, "Horace on Sex" (the poem is a parody of the elegiac picture of love); Bushala, "The Motif of Sexual Choice in Horace, *Satire* 1.2" (a study of the relation between Horace's views on sex and those of various Greek philosophers); Curran, "Nature, Convention and Obscenity in Horace, *Satires* 1.2" (the obscene imagery = *physis*, clothing in the poem stands for *nomos*); Dessen, "The Sexual and Financial Mean in Horace's *Serm.* I, 2" (financial integrity tallies with sexual in the poem). The last two articles cited examine and analyze the poem's wording and imagery. Cf. also Armstrong, "Horace, *Satires* I.1–3: A Structural Study"; van Rooy, "Arrangement and Structure of . . . Satires 1–4," esp. 43–55; " 'Imitatio' of Vergil, *Eclogues* in Horace, *Satires*, Book I."

29. The original anecdote is given in full, with references, by Dessen, "The Sexual and Financial Mean," 201. Cf. also Rudd, *The Satires of Horace*, 31; Fraenkel, *Horace*, 83.

30. This line alludes mockingly to an epigram by Philodemus, thus constituting a direct parody of the erotic ideal of women (cf. chap. 2). Philodemus appears in person, along with his love of cheap women, at 1.2.121; for his contribution to *S.* 1.2, cf. esp. Cataudella, "Filodemo nella Satira I 2 di Orazio"; also Rudd, 31–32.

31. Rudd discusses *S.* 1.8 and its general relation to Priapic poetry without in-depth analysis of the poem itself (*The Satires of Horace*, 68–70); it was Fraenkel's opinion (*Horace*, 112) that *S.* 1.7, 8, 9 were written largely to bring the number of poems in the book up to ten. But Anderson ("The Form, Purpose, and Position of Horace's Satire I, 8") provides a full analysis of the poem, stressing the odd weakness of Priapus, the power of the witches' poison and its relation to the rhetorical *venenum* in 1.7 and elsewhere, and the function of 1.8 as a transition between 1.7 and 1.9; the whole adds up to a convincing identification of Priapus with the poet. On Maecenas' restoration of the gardens, cf. Fraenkel, *Horace*, 123, n. 2.

32. On the significance of Horace's statements about literature in *S.* 1.4, 1.10, and 2.1, cf. Fraenkel, *Horace*, 125–33 (Horace is fighting against sloppy poetry, and for morality), 142–45 (growth in *S.* 2); Rudd, *The Satires of Horace*, 81–83 (*S.* 1.9 as a statement of exclusivity), 86–131 (Horace vs. the neoterics on Lucilius, the weak threat of *S.* 2.1).

33. Most critics argue that Horace in *S.* 1.4, 1.10, and 2.1 rejects Lucilius' violent personal invective (Rudd, 114–15, 151; Fraenkel, 150–53); but the imagery Horace uses, even if it is only camouflage, is violent.

34. This pose, close to that of Lucilius, is also apparently Ennian; cf. van Rooy, *Studies in Classical Satire*, 35, on Gellius' account (12.4.4) of Ennius' description of himself as a wise and witty confidant of a great man.

35. On mock epic in Horace, cf. Rudd (*The Satires of Horace*, 31–34) on *S.* 1.9, following Anderson, "Horace, the Unwilling Warrior: *Satire* I, 9"; Rudd, 224–42, on *S.* 2.5.

36. Cf. Buchheit, "Homerparodie und Literarkritik in Horazens Satiren I 7 und I 9" (the argument in 1.7 puts forth Horace's own ideas on polemic).

37. Cf. Rudd, *The Satires of Horace*, 90.

38. On the reality of the victims of Horace's attacks, the most complete treatment is Rudd, *The Satires of Horace*, 132–59; cf. also van Rooy, *Studies in Classical Satire*, 61–71.

39. Fraenkel attributes the openings of the satires of book 2 to specific Platonic dialogues (*Horace*, 136–37); Rudd feels that the allusions are not so specific (*The Satires of Horace*, 208, 220).

40. Fraenkel (105, 108–09) points out how much less hyperbolic Horace is than Lucilius; Rudd (100), how much less wordy.

41. Most notably in the opening of 1.1; 1.1.36–100; 1.2.1–24; 1.2.25–30; 1.3.1–20; 1.4.104–26; 2.1.1–4, 47–56, 57–60; 2.2.45–64; 2.3 passim, esp. 246; 2.5.90–98; 2.7.6–20. Cf. Rudd, *The Satires of Horace*, 5.

42. Fraenkel, *Horace*, 144–45; includes discussion of earlier comparisons.

43. Fraenkel, 131–33; cf. Rudd, 102.

44. On Persius, most helpful are: Reckford, "Studies in Persius" (the use of metaphor to unify the poems, particularly *Satire* 1); Dessen, *Iunctura Callidus Acri: A Study of Persius' Satires*, esp. 58–70 (on the metaphor of homosexuality in *Satire* 4; tends to lump active and pathic homosexuality together). Bramble, *Persius and the Programmatic Satire*, discusses sexual imagery in Persius (27–66) and analyzes *Satire* 1 (67–155), focusing on the sexual metaphor; but the validity of his analysis fluctuates.

45. Above, chap. 1. For sources on this complex of ideas, cf. Buchheit, "*Sal et lepos Versiculorum* (Catull c. 16)," 334–36.

46. Cf. Reckford ("Studies in Persius") on the metaphor of diseased ears in *Satire* 1.

47. Courtney ("Parody and Literary Allusion in Menippean Satire") discusses the formal relationships between the *Satyricon* and Greek romances; especially good on reversals of sexual roles, 93. Courtney makes the important point that collection of parallels between the *Satyricon* and other ancient works should be a "means of penetrating to the real objects and aims of Petronius"—i.e., the presence of so many parodic allusions must have a significant relationship to the nature of the work.

48. The sexual themes in the *Satyricon* have received less attention than one would expect, considering that, although the extant portions include few explicit descriptions of intercourse, sexual relationships are the most important ones in the book. The major, and most controversial, study is Sullivan, *The Satyricon of Petronius: A Literary Study*, which aims at understanding Petronius' character through his writing, and finds in the text evidence of voyeurism and exhibitionism in Encolpius/Petronius. Gill, "The Sexual Episodes in the *Satyricon*," attempts to refute Sullivan and does make a useful distinction between Petronius and Encolpius, as well as some valid generalizations about the disparity between style and content in the *Satyricon* as a whole, especially in the sexual episodes (178–81). Rankin, "Petronius, Priapus and *Priapeum* LXVIII," makes a strong connection between the nature of the character of Priapus in the *Priapea* and the character of Encolpius (as victim) in the *Satyricon*, with pertinent remarks on the possible social significance of a god like Priapus. Maass, "Eunuchos und Verwandtes," 447–48, discusses the names of Encolpius, Ascyltos, and Giton as *redender Namen*.

49. Cf. George, "Style and Character in the *Satyricon*"; Veyne, "Le 'je' dans le *Satiricon*"; Auerbach, *Mimesis*, 24–49.

50. Cf. Whitman, *Aristophanes and the Comic Hero*, 21–58; Frye, *The Anatomy of Criticism*, 228–39; Welsford, *The Fool*, 218–42.

51. This sort of repeated survival of calamity is the stock-in-trade of animated cartoons like the "Roadrunner" series, in which, however, it is often the villain who undergoes this process. Encolpius is more like Donald Duck.

52. This idea, formally stated in the nineteenth century (Klebs, "Zur Composition von Petronius Satirae"), is surely plausible, even if the god's pursuit did not remain constantly in the foreground of the novel. The proposed corollary, that Encolpius was a runaway φάρμακος (Cichorius, "Petronius und Massilia"), has less to support it. A recent effort to belittle the importance of Priapus in the *Satyricon* (Baldwin, "*Ira Priapi*") is not convincing.

53. Odysseus is often chosen, in other satirists as well, to serve as the butt for mock epic; cf. *Pr.* 68; Stanford, *The Ulysses Theme*, 2d ed., 90–127 (who does not, however, discuss the satiric Odysseus).

54. Bǎgnani, "Encolpius *Gladiator Obscenus*," remarks that Encolpius is so contemptible that his views cannot be Petronius'.

55. George ("Petronius and Lucan *De Bello Civili*") sets forth the arguments against identifying Eumolpus' poem as a parody of Lucan's.

56. On the function of displacement in the *Satyricon*, cf.: Rankin, "Some Themes of Concealment and Pretense in Petronius' *Satyricon*" (secrecy and "tabu" in Roman life and

the use of deception in the *Satyricon*); Sandy, "Scaenica Petroniana" (parallels between the *Satyricon* and mime; especially good list of references in n. 1); Zeitlin, "Petronius as Paradox: Anarchy and Artistic Integrity" (esp. 654–56, on chaos in separate scenes, disintegration of episodes, and getting lost). Stewart, *Nonsense: Aspects of Intertextuality in Folklore and Literature*, 85–115, discusses the use of boundaries in fiction; her theories apply largely to self-consciously absurd literature but bear on the *Satyricon*, especially the *cena*. Particularly relevant here are her remarks on slapstick and infinite repetition (131), and on causality and the picaresque (141). Her ideas on the function of nonsense parallel those of Abrams and Sutton-Smith, "The Development of the Trickster in Children's Narrative"; their "Trickster Inventory" (32–34) includes many characteristics manifested by Encolpius, some surreal.

57. Cf. Elliott, *The Power of Satire*, 38–47, 62; Thompson, *Motif-Index*, P 327, J 1560–1577.1.

58. Cf. Arrowsmith, "Luxury and Death in the *Satyricon*."

59. Cf. Joshel, "Towards an Understanding of the Attitudes of Freed Slaves."

60. On the tale of the Widow of Ephesus in world folklore, cf. Grisebach, *Die Wanderung der Novelle von der treulosen Witwe durch die Weltliteratur*, 2d ed.; Legman, *Rationale of the Dirty Joke*, 647–49; Thompson, *Motif-Index*, K 2213.1, T 231; Aarne 1352*.

61. Most criticism on Juvenal stops at the question of his status as moral reformer; cf. chap. 3, n. 26, for typical examples. Wiesen, "Juvenal's Moral Character: An Introduction," returns to the fray to champion Juvenal's ethics. Rudd offers a sophisticated discussion in his appendix on Dryden (*The Satires of Horace*, 258–73). Dryden saw in Juvenal a "vigorous and masculine" character in comparison with the "generally grovelling" Horace; Rudd attributes this difference rather to Horace's reforming zeal and to Juvenal's "vague . . . reactionary idealism enforced by feelings of personal injustice." The emphasis here on the relative power of the two poets' personae is far more pertinent to the content of the satire than is any argument about ethics. An unusual and fruitful approach to Juvenal's motivation is Reekmans, "Juvenal's Views on Social Change," a strict sociological analysis that concludes (161): "In our opinion, his negative integration in a changing world has less to do with the moral principles of an *egregius sanctusque vir* (XIII.64) than with the preconceived opinions of an authoritarian personality." Marache, "La revendication sociale chez Martial et Juvénal," is far less specific.

62. Kenney, "The First Satire of Juvenal."

63. *Pace* Kenney, "The First Satire of Juvenal," there is not much difference between using the dead as *exempla* of wrongdoers and attacking them. But Kenney's assessment is otherwise excellent; and cf. also Griffith, "The Ending of Juvenal's First Satire and Lucilius Book XXX"; Shero, "The Satirist's *Apologia*."

64. There are few critical analyses of Juvenal 2 and 9, and most range from the uncomfortable to the savage, the critic sharing the satirist's view or intensifying it (e.g., Highet, *Juvenal the Satirist*, 59–64 ["The Faerie Queenes"], 117–21); a notable exception is Bellandi, "Naevolus *cliens*," who demonstrates Naevolus' satiric function as a put-upon *cliens* like those of *Satires* 3 and 5, drawing close formal parallels between Naevolus and Umbricius in 3. The possibly pathic gladiators of Juvenal 6.*O*.7–13 have received a good deal of attention, beginning with Housman, "*Tunica Retiarii*"; countered by Owen, "On the *Tunica Retiarii*"; more recently, Reeve, "Gladiators in Juvenal's Sixth Satire"; Colin, "Juvénal, les baladins et les rétiaires," who provides a lengthy exegesis of the Oxford fragment, adducing nonliterary evidence (esp. 329–35, 344–82).

65. Nicolas Freeling, *The Widow*, 67.

66. Juvenal 6 has received a good deal of attention, none focusing on the content of the poem as satiric poetry (most critics treat the poem as reportage or moral exhortation). Anderson, "Juvenal 6: A Problem in Structure," begins from the premise that the central problem in the poem is the relation of its structure to its contents, and he attempts to delineate a thematic structure in it; Highet (*Juvenal the Satirist*, 93–102) takes the same

approach. Nardo (*La sesta satira di Giovenale e la tradizione erotico-elegiaca latina*) traces the connection between 6 and the stock attributes of women in elegy, and notes that Juvenal keeps only the bad attributes. Bond ("Anti-feminism in Juvenal and Cato") believes the satires and the attitudes they represent forced women into the depravities the satires reprove; a deplorable cycle, fortunately attested only in Bond's article. Vianello, "La sesta satira di Giovenale," also takes Juvenal's portrait of women at face value, along with the material in *Satire* 2; he credits Juvenal with "una profunda conoscenza della psiche femminile." I was unable to see Madia, *Il fantasma della donna nella poesia di Giovenale*. Pomeroy, in *Goddesses, Whores, Wives, and Slaves*, takes parts of *Satire* 6 too literally (209–10, on 6.306–48). Opinion on the authenticity of the Oxford fragment still varies, but few accept the idea that it was lost through expurgation, considering what remains unexpurgated; the most lucid account is Griffith, "The Survival of the Longer of the So-called 'Oxford' Fragments of Juvenal's Sixth Satire."

67. This same phenomenon is specifically denied when Juvenal's interest is in attacking homosexuals, 2.51–53.

68. Cf. *Pr.* 52.9 (threat of rape [of a male] by asses); Apul. *Met.* 10.19–23 (a noble lady falls in love with ass-Lucius).

69. The text seems markedly unsatisfactory as it stands. The most recent commentator (Courtney, *A Commentary on the Satires of Juvenal*) simply notes that line 307 should be left out. Emendation seems less drastic and more helpful than transposing the lines, which removes no difficulties; Gnilka summarizes and renews the arguments for transposition, "*Maura Maurae Collactea*." The text surely should describe two women, presumably Tullia and one Maura, no more.

70. The pun on *testis*, "witness/testicle," seems at least possible here.

71. On mock epic in Juvenal 4, see Crook, *Concilium Principis*; cf. Highet, *Juvenal the Satirist*, 79, who emphasizes the parodic relation between *Satire* 4 and a poem of Statius on the German war.

72. Randy Newman, "God's Song," ©1972 Randy Newman and WB Music Corp.

Appendix 1

1. This appendix is a condensed version of Richlin, "Approaches to the Sources on Adultery at Rome." The best general sources on adultery at Rome are: Mommsen, *Römisches Strafrecht*, 688–99; Corbett, *The Roman Law of Marriage*, 127–46; Garnsey, *Social Status and Legal Privilege in the Roman Empire*, 21–24, 103ff.

2. The term "self-help," used by Mommsen, has been adopted by subsequent writers on Roman law, most notably Lintott, *Violence in Republican Rome*, q.v. for the whole question of brutality in self-help.

3. Plautus *Curc.* 35–38, *Mil.* 1395–1426, *Poen.* 862–63; Hor. *S.* 1.2.41–46, 132–34; Mart. 2.60, 3.85, 3.92, 6.2; Apul. *Met.* 9.28.

4. Mart. 2.83, 3.85; cf. Vergil *A.* 6.494–97.

5. Hor. *S.* 1.2.132–33; Mart. 2.49, 2.60, cf. 2.47, 9.67; Apul. *Met.* 9.27–28; raphanidosis (anal rape with a horseradish or other object), Cat. 15.19, Juv. 10.314–17. The use of anal (or oral) rape to humiliate another, not necessarily for the sexual gratification of the rapist, is of course not confined to the Romans; for a current overview and sources, cf. Benedict, "Men Get Raped, Too."

6. Cat. 21.7–13, 37.8; Mart. 2.47, 2.83.

7. Hor. *S.* 1.2.132–34; Mart. 2.72.3–4, 3.86.3, 5.61.11–12; Juv. 6.44. Cf. Reynolds, "The Adultery Mime."

8. Mart. 5.75, 6.7, 6.22 (cf. 1.74), 6.45, 6.91; cf. Juv. 2.29–37.

9. This was presumably not the first divorce at Rome but the first one to achieve notoriety; cf. Corbett, *The Roman Law of Marriage*, 218–24.

10. Gell. 1.6; cf. Livy *Per.* 59. For sources and references on the identification of Gellius' Metellus as Metellus Macedonicus, see Malcovati, *Oratorum Romanorum Fragmenta.*
11. Cic. *Att.* 1.18.3, 11.23, 12.52.2, 13.7, *Fam.* 2.15.5, 8.7.2.
12. Plut. *Luc.* 38, *Cic.* 29, *Pomp.* 42, *Ant.* 9, *Cat. Min.* 24.
13. Cic. *Fam.* 1.9.15, *Att.* 1.12.3, 1.13.3, 1.18.2–3; Suet. *Iul.* 6, 74; Plut. *Cic.* 28–29, *Caes.* 9–10; Dio 37.45, 38.12.1, 39.6.2.
14. See Last, *Cambridge Ancient History*; Williams, "Poetry in the Moral Climate of Augustan Rome."
15. Suet. *Iul.* 43.1, 48; *Aug.* 5, 67.2, cf. *Aug.* 45.4; *Claud.* 15.4, 16.1, 43; *Vesp.* 11. Pliny *Ep.* 6.31.4–6 is most helpful.
16. Suet. *Aug.* 65, 101.3; *Tib.* 10.1, 11.4, 11.5, 50.1; *Calig.* 16.3; Sen. *Ben.* 6.32; Dio 55.10.12–16.
17. Tac. *Ann.* 2.50, 3.25, 3.28, 3.38, 4.42, 4.52, 6.46–48, 14.60, 15.50.
18. Cic. *Att.* 2.24.3, 5.21.9, *Fam.* 9.22.4.
19. Cic. *Att.* 2.1.5, 2.4.2, 2.9.1.
20. Cic. *Att.* 2.24.3; Plut. *Brut.* 5; Suet. *Iul.* 50.2; Macrob. *Sat.* 2.2.5.
21. Cic. *Phil.* 2 passim; Plut. *Ant.* 6; Dio 45.26, 28, 30, 50.27.6–7, 51.8.1.
22. Plut. *Pomp.* 2; Suet. *Gram.* 14 (Pompey cuckolded).
23. Plut. *Fab.* 21.4 (a concubine).
24. Plut. *Cat. Mai.* 24.
25. Ps.-Sall. *in Cic.* 2, 5; Dio 46.18.6.
26. Suet. *Iul.* 49.4–52.3.
27. Suet. *Aug.* 69–71.
28. Macrob. *Sat.* 2.5.2–3, 5, 6, 9, 10; Dio 55.10.12–16, 55.13.1–1a, 56.32.4, 57.18.1a.
29. Suet. *Calig.* 24.3, 36.2, 41.1; *Poet.*, *Passienus Crispus.*
30. Suet. *Claud.* 26.2, 27.1, 43.
31. Suet. *Ner.* 26.2, 27.3, 28.1.
32. Suet. *Tit.* 10.2.
33. Suet. *Dom.* 1.3, 22; Juv. 2.29–33.
34. *CIL* XI.6721.5, 7, 9a, 10, 11, 13, 14, 34, 35, 39.
35. Val. Max. 6.1; Plut. *Mor.* 258–61; cf. Apul. *Met.* 8.13.
36. Sen. *Controv.* 1.4, 1.7, 2.7, 4.7, 7.5, 8.3, 9.1, *rhet. frag.* 1 (Quint. *Inst.* 9.2.42); cf. 1.3, 3.8, 5.6; rape, 1.5, 2.3, 3.5, 4.3, 7.6, 7.8, 8.6; Calp. Flacc. 2, 11, 17, 23, 31, 40, 48, 49, cf. 3; Quintilian *Decl.* 244, 249, 273, 277, 279, 284, 286, 291, 310, 335, 347, 357, 379; cf. *Inst.* 3.6.17, 27; 5.10.36, 39, 104.
37. For a recent cognate, cf. Sussman, "Tips and Tales from Bernie X."
38. Juvenal 10.293–317 evidently owes much to Valerius Maximus 6.1.1–2, 7, 9–12, 13.
39. Cf. Lintott, *Violence in Republican Rome*, esp. 11–16, 22–34.
40. Only two, to my knowledge: seemingly implied by rescripts of Marcus Aurelius and Commodus and of Antoninus Pius (*D.* 48.5.39[38].8). Aurelius and Commodus recommend to the court's mercy a man who killed his wife upon catching her in the act of adultery, saying this is not to be judged under the murder law; Pius recommends as punishment either hard labor for life (for a *humilior*) or *relegatio* to an island (for an *honestior*). Both rescripts may be aimed at general, not particular, circumstances.

Appendix 2

1. E.g., Williams, *Tradition and Originality in Roman Poetry*, 551–56; Quinn, *Catullus: An Interpretation*, says the Juventius poems are not "literary exercises" (246) but concludes that pederasty is less glamorous than adultery (254) and Catullus less interested in Juventius than in Lesbia (255). Lilja, *The Roman Elegists' Attitude to Women*, 217–22,

takes the opposite view with regard to Tibullus, claiming him to be more interested in Marathus than in Delia.

2. Boswell, *Christianity, Social Tolerance, and Homosexuality*, 61–87. At times Boswell ignores the difference felt by the Romans to exist between pederasty and "pathic" homosexuality (72), though he explains it himself (74–75); in his discussion of the *lex Scantinia* he speaks of "homosexuality" without distinguishing between slave and *ingenuus* (68–70), as if the sexual use of slaves implies that the sexual use of the freeborn must be legal, or socially approved. Throughout his discussion he uses invective and satiric material as if it were reportage, e.g., the statement that "marriages between males or between females were legal and familiar among the upper classes" (82), for which he adduces Cicero's description of Antony's relations with Curio, Lampridius' biography of Elagabalus, Martial's epigrams against pathics, and Juvenal 2. There is no other in-depth study of Roman male homosexuality; for related, and helpful, studies see Dover, *Greek Homosexuality*; Hopkins, *Conquerors and Slaves*, 172–96 (on eunuchs; esp. 192–96).

3. Above, chap. 4. Smooth or depilated skin: *levis*, Mart. 11.43.10, 12.18.25; Juv. 9.95, cf. Mart. 14.205.1; depilation, Mart. 2.36.6, 2.62, 5.41.6, 9.27.5, 9.57, 12.38.4; Juv. 2.12, 8.13–18, 8.114, 9.95. Gestures: Juv. 6.*O*.24, 9.133; Calvus *FPL* 18 Morel. Walk: Sen. *Ep*. 52.12, 114.4, 6; Phaedrus *App*. 8 (an unusual serious treatment of a stereotypically effeminate man). Choice of color in clothing, esp. light green: Mart. 1.96.9, 3.82.5; Petron. *Sat*. 27.2, 64.6; Juv. 2.97. Use of makeup: Petron. *Sat*. 23.5; Juv. 2.93–95, 6.*O*.21–*O*.22. Lisping speech: Persius 1.17–18, 35; Mart. 10.65.10. Cf. in general Mart. 5.41, 10.65. *Contra* Boswell (76), the word *mollis*, along with several other adjectives signifying softness or delicacy, is very commonly used as a pejorative of an effeminate and/or pathic man: Cat. 25.1; *Pr*. 64; Petron. *Sat*. 126.2; Mart. 5.37.2; Juv. 2.47 (substantive use), 8.15. Also *debilis* (Petron. *Sat*. 134.2; Mart. 2.86.5, 10.65.10), *effeminatus* (*Pr*. 58.2), *fluxus* (Mart. 5.41.1), *mitis* (Mart. 4.7.2), *pulcher* (Hor. *S*. 1.10.17), *tremulus* (Pers. 1.21; Juv. 6.*O*.2).

4. Cf. Benedict, "Men Get Raped, Too"; also discussion above, especially chap. 5.

5. Mart. 1.58, 2.43, 8.44, 8.63, 9.21, 11.22, 11.63, 11.70, 11.73, 12.16, 12.33, 12.49, 12.75, 12.97; cf. Petron. *Sat*. 27.2–6, 28.4, 64.5–12, 68.8–69.5, 74.8–75.9; Juv. 3.186–88, 6.268–72.

6. Juv. 6.*O*.1–34; cf. Lucilius 1058 Marx; Mart. 3.63, 5.61, 10.40, 12.38.

7. Aurigemma, *Dizionario Epigrafico* s.v. "delicium" (1594–1603), esp. 1602–03; cf. Plut. *Ant*. 59.4. These children, both male and female, apparently constitute a set out of which some *pueri* and cupbearers were taken; the epitaphs show them to have been esteemed on a level with close relatives.

8. *D*.48.5.9(8).pr. notes that one who lends his house for the purpose of *stuprum* or *adulterium* with another's wife or *cum masculo* is punished as an *adulter*; *stuprum* is defined as *in vidua vel virgine vel puero*, *D*.48.5.35(34).1; cf. 48.5.6.1. This law covers seduction, not forcible rape, which comes under the laws *de vi* (*D*.48.5.30[29].9, no statute of limitations; 48.6.3.4). But, as the commentators remarked, the *lex Julia* uses the words *stuprum* and *adulterium* interchangeably (*D*. 48.5.6.1; 50.16.101.pr.), and the whole enormous bulk of *D*. 48.5 concerns relations between husbands and wives, fiancées, or female concubines; no cases (even hypothetical) of seduction of males are discussed in relation to the law. Attempts at seduction, especially in public, were a type of *iniuria*; *D*. 47.10.15.15–20 defines the circumstances for women.

9. Cf. Christius, *Historia Legis Scatiniae*, for full discussion. I am indebted to John J. Winkler for uncovering this work in the library of the Kinsey Institute.

10. Val. Max. 8.1.*Absol*.8; cf. Marx *ad* Lucil. 1307.

11. Cf. esp. Sen. *Controv*. 4.pr.10 (Seneca reminiscing about Haterius): "I remem-

ber, when he was defending a freedman to whom it was cast up that he had been his *patronus' concubinus*, that he said: 'Unchastity is grounds for accusation in a freeborn man, a necessity for a slave, and *officium* for a freedman.' " (This, says Seneca, gave rise to a rash of double entendres on *officium*.) Cf. Trimalchio and Habinnas on their sexual careers as slaves, Petron. *Sat.* 63.3, 69.2, 75.11. But Callistratus opines that a freedman can be asked only for *operae* that can be performed *sine turpitudine*; even a manumitted prostitute cannot be asked to give her *patronus* sexual favors (*D.*38.1.38.pr.; cf. the discussion of *operae* and *obsequium* in Treggiari, *Roman Freedmen during the Late Republic*, 68–78). Still, considering the practice of manumitting freedwomen into concubinage (Treggiari, 211–12), it seems quite probable that a male slave might be manumitted into a similar status.

12. Gossen, "Verbal Dueling in Chamula," in *Speech Play*, ed. Kirshenblatt-Gimblett, esp. 129.

13. The tales in Val. Max. 6.1 include the story of Scantinius and Marcellus (6.1.7), repeated with different details and heightened melodrama at Plutarch *Marcellus* 2. In the declamations: Sen. *Controv.* 3.8; cf. 5.6, in which a young man raped while in woman's clothing is forbidden to prosecute and accuses the magistrate of *iniuria*; Calp. Flacc. 3, which repeats Cic. *Mil.* 9, Val. Max. 6.1.12.

14. Cf. Cichorius, *Untersuchungen zu Lucilius*, 287–91, on Lucilius and Afranius; Quint. *Inst.* 10.1.100.

Bibliography

The following abbreviations are used:

AClass	*Acta Classica* (Proceedings of the Classical Association of South Africa)
AJAH	*American Journal of Ancient History*
AJPh	*American Journal of Philology*
AncSoc	*Ancient Society*
C&M	*Classica et Mediaevalia*
CJ	*The Classical Journal*
CPh	*Classical Philology*
CQ	*Classical Quarterly*
CR	*Classical Review*
G&R	*Greece and Rome*
GRBS	*Greek, Roman, and Byzantine Studies*
IntJPsych	*International Journal of Psychoanalysis*
JAF	*Journal of American Folklore*
JRS	*Journal of Roman Studies*
LCM	*Liverpool Classical Monthly*
PP	*La Parola del Passato*
RCCM	*Rivista di Cultura classica e medioevale*
REL	*Revue des Etudes Latines*
RFIC	*Rivista di Filologia e di Istruzione Classica*
RhM	*Rheinisches Museum*
TAPhA	*Transactions and Proceedings of the American Philological Association*

Aarne, Antti Amatus. *The Types of the Folktale*. Translated by Stith Thompson. Helsinki, 1964.

Abrahams, Roger D. " 'Playing the Dozens.' " *JAF* 75(1962):209–20.

Abrams, David M., and Sutton-Smith, Brian. "The Development of the Trickster in Children's Narrative." *JAF* 90(1977):29–47.

Adams, J. N. *The Latin Sexual Vocabulary*. Baltimore, 1982.

Anderson, William S. "The Form, Purpose, and Position of Horace's Satire I, 8." *AJPh* 93(1972):4–13.

———. "Horace, the Unwilling Warrior: *Satire* I, 9." *AJPh* 77(1956):148–66.

———. "Juvenal 6: A Problem in Structure." *CPh* 51 (1956):73–94.

———. "The Roman Socrates: Horace and His Satires." In *Satire*, edited by J. P. Sullivan, 1–37. Bloomington and London, 1963.
Appel, Georg. *De Romanorum precationibus. Religionsgeschichtliche Versuche und Vorarbeiten* 7.2. Giessen, 1909.
Armstrong, David. "Horace, *Satires* I.1–3: A Structural Study." *Arion* 3.2(1964): 86–96.
Arrowsmith, William. "Luxury and Death in the *Satyricon*." *Arion* 5(1966):304–31.
Auerbach, Erich. *Mimesis*. Translated by Willard R. Trask. Princeton, 1953.
Aurigemma, A. "Delicium." In E. De Ruggiero, *Dizionario epigrafico di antichità romane*. Rome, 1895–.
Babcock-Abrahams, Barbara. " 'A Tolerated Margin of Mess': The Trickster and His Tales Reconsidered." *Journal of the Folkloric Institute* 9(1975):147–86.
Bagnani, Gilbert. "Encolpius *Gladiator Obscenus*." *CPh* 51(1956):24–27.
Bailey, D. R. Shackleton. "Sex. Clodius–Sex. Cloelius." *CQ* n.s. 10(1960):41–42.
———, ed. *Cicero: Epistulae ad Atticum*. Cambridge, 1965–70.
———, ed. *Cicero: Epistulae ad Familiares*. Cambridge and New York, 1977.
Baker, Robert. " 'Pricks' and 'Chicks': A Plea for 'Persons.' " In *Philosophy and Sex*, edited by Robert Baker and Frederick Elliston, 45–64. Buffalo, 1975.
Baker, Russell. *So This Is Depravity*. New York, 1980.
Bakhtin, Mikhail. *Rabelais and His World*. Translated by Helene Iswolsky. Cambridge, Mass., 1968.
Baldwin, Barry. "Horace on Sex." *AJPh* 91(1970):460–65.
———. "*Ira Priapi*." *CPh* 68(1973):294–96.
———. "Notes on Rufinus." *Phoenix* 34(1980):337–46.
Bandura, Albert. *Social Learning Theory*. Englewood Cliffs, N.J., 1977.
Barber, C. L. *Shakespeare's Festive Comedy*. Princeton, 1959.
Bardon, Henry. *Propositions sur Catulle*. Coll. Latomus 118, Brussels, 1970.
———. "Rome et l'impudeur." *Latomus* 24(1965):495–518.
Beard, Henry N., and Kenney, Douglas C. *Bored of the Rings*. New York, 1969.
Beare, William. *The Roman Stage*. 3d ed. London, 1964.
Bellandi, Franco. "Naevolus *cliens*." *Maia* 4(1974):279–99.
Benedict, Helen. "Men Get Raped, Too." *The Soho News*, 16 March 1982:12.
Benson, E. F. *Lucia in London*. London, 1927.
Benveniste, E. "Profanus et profanare." In *Hommages à Georges Dumézil*, Coll. Latomus 45:46–53. Brussels, 1960.
Bergler, Edmund. "Obscene Words." *The Psychoanalytic Quarterly* 5(1936):226–48.
Berkowitz, Leonard. "The Effects of Observing Violence." *Scientific American* 210(1964): 35–41.
Bernard, H. Russell. "Otomi Obscene Humor: Preliminary Observations." *JAF* 88 (1975):383–92.
Bertman, Stephen. "Oral Imagery in Catullus 7." *CQ* n.s. 28(1978):447–78.
Bianco, Orazio. "Il Personaggio del c. 25 di Catullo." *Giornale Italiano di Filologia* 20(1967):39–48.
Bömer, Franz. *Untersuchungen über die Religion der Sklaven in Griechenland und Rom*. Abhandlungen der Geistes- und Sozialwissenschaftlichen Klasse, 10: Mainz. Wiesbaden, 1963.
Bond, R. P. "Anti-feminism in Juvenal and Cato." In *Studies in Latin Literature and Roman History* (I), edited by Carl Deroux, 418–47. Brussels, 1979.
Borthwick, E. K. "A 'Femme Fatale' in Asclepiades." *CR* n.s. 17(1967):250–54.
Boswell, John. *Christianity, Social Tolerance, and Homosexuality*. Chicago, 1980.

Bramble, J. C. *Persius and the Programmatic Satire.* Cambridge, 1974.
Brenneis, Don, and Padarath, Ram. " 'About Those Scoundrels I'll Let Everyone Know': Challenge Singing in a Fiji Indian Community." *JAF* 88(1975):283–91.
Brukman, Jan. "Tongue Play: Constitutive and Interpretive Properties of Sexual Joking Encounters among the Koya of South India." In *Sociocultural Dimensions of Language Use,* edited by Mary Sanches and Ben G. Blount, 235–68. New York, 1975.
Buchheit, Vinzenz. "Catull an Cato von Utica (c. 56)." *Hermes* 89(1961):345–56.
———. "Feigensymbolik im antiken Epigramm." *RhM* 103(1960):200–29.
———. "Homerparodie und Literarkritik in Horazens Satiren I 7 und I 9." *Gymnasium* 75(1968):519–55.
———. "*Sal et lepos Versiculorum* (Catull c. 16)." *Hermes* 104(1976):331–47.
———. *Studien zum Corpus Priapeorum. Zetemata* 28. Munich, 1962.
Bushala, Eugene W. "The Motif of Sexual Choice in Horace, *Satire* 1.2." *CJ* 66(1971): 312–15.
Cairns, Francis. "Catullus' *Basia* Poems (5, 7, 48)." *Mnemosyne* 26(1973):15–22.
Cameron, Alan. "Asclepiades' Girl Friends." In *Reflections of Women in Antiquity*, edited by Helene P. Foley, 275–302. New York and London, 1981.
———. "Catullus 29." *Hermes* 104(1976):155–63.
———. "The *Garland* of Philip." *GRBS* 21(1980):43–62.
———. "Strato and Rufinus." *CQ* n.s. 32(1982):162–73.
Carcopino, Jerome. *Cicero, the Secrets of His Correspondence.* Vol. 1. Translated by E. O. Lorimer. New Haven, 1951.
Carrubba, Robert W. *The Epodes of Horace: A Study in Poetic Arrangement.* The Hague, 1969.
———. "A Study of Horace's Eighth and Twelfth Epodes." *Latomus* 24(1965):591–98.
Castleman, Craig. *Getting Up: Subway Graffiti in New York.* Cambridge, Mass., 1982.
Cataudella, Q. "Filodemo nella Satira I 2 di Orazio." *PP* 5(1950):18–31.
Cèbe, Jean-Pierre. *La Caricature et la parodie dans le monde romain antique des origines à Juvénal.* Paris, 1966.
———. "Sur les trivialités de Catulle." *REL* 43(1965):221–29.
Chapman, Antony J., and Foot, Hugh C., eds. *Humour and Laughter: Theory, Research and Applications.* London and New York, 1976.
Chernin, Kim. *The Obsession.* New York, 1981.
Christes, Johannes. *Der frühe Lucilius.* Heidelberg, 1971.
Christius, Johannes. *Historia legis Scatiniae.* Magdeburg, 1727.
Cichorius, Conrad. "Petronius und Massilia." In *Römische Studien*, 438–42. Leipzig, 1922.
———. *Untersuchungen zu Lucilius.* Berlin, 1908.
Clausen, W. V.; Goodyear, F. R. D.; Kenney, E. J.; and Richmond, J. A., eds. *Appendix Vergiliana.* Oxford, 1966.
Coffey, Michael. "Juvenal Report for the Years 1941–1961." *Lustrum* 8(1963):161–215.
———. *Roman Satire.* London and New York, 1976.
Colin, J. "Juvénal, les baladins et les rétiaires d'après le manuscrit d'Oxford." *Atti della Accademia delle Scienze di Torino, Classe di Scienze morali, storiche e filologiche* 87(1952–53): 315–85.
Commission on Obscenity and Pornography. *The Report of the Commission on Obscenity and Pornography.* New York, 1970.
Corbett, Percy Ellwood. *The Roman Law of Marriage.* Oxford, 1930.
Courtney, E. "Parody and Literary Allusion in Menippean Satire." *Philologus* 106(1962): 86–100.

———. *A Commentary on the Satires of Juvenal*. London, 1980.
Cowan, Geoffrey. *See No Evil: The Backstage Battle over Sex and Violence on Television*. New York, 1979.
Crocker, J. Christopher. "The Social Functions of Rhetorical Forms." In *The Social Use of Metaphor*, edited by J. David Sapir and J. Christopher Crocker, 33–66. Philadelphia, 1977.
Crook, John. *Concilium Principis*. Cambridge, 1975.
Curran, Leo. "Gellius and the Lover's Pallor: A Note on Catullus 80." *Arion* 5(1966): 24–27.
———. "Nature, Convention and Obscenity in Horace, *Satires* 1.2." *Arion* 9(1970):220–45.
Daube, David. "Ne quid infamandi causa fiat: The Roman Law of Defamation." In *Atti del Congresso internazionale di diritto romano e di storia del diritto* 3, 413–50. Verona, 1948; Milan, 1951.
Davis, Angela Y. "Rape, Racism, and the Capitalist Setting." *The Black Scholar* 9 (1978):24–30.
de Beauvoir, Simone. *The Second Sex*. Translated by H. M. Parshley. New York, 1974.
Dessen, Cynthia. *Iunctura Callidus Acri: A Study of Persius' Satires. Illinois Studies in Language and Literature* 59. Urbana, 1968.
———. "The Sexual and Financial Mean in Horace's *Serm.*, I, 2." *AJPh* 89(1968): 200–08.
Diamond, Irene. "Pornography and Repression: A Reconsideration of 'Who' and 'What.' " In *Take Back the Night*, edited by Laura Lederer, 187–203. New York, 1980.
Diehl, Ernst. *Pompeianische Wandinschriften und Verwandtes*. Berlin, 1930.
Dorey, T.A. "Cicero, Clodia, and the *Pro Caelio*." *G&R* 2d series 5(1958):175–80.
Douglas, Mary. *Purity and Danger*. London, 1966.
———. "The Social Control of Cognition: Some Factors in Joke Perception." *Man* 3(1968):361–76.
Dover, K. J. *Greek Homosexuality*. Cambridge, Mass., 1978.
Due, Otto Steen. *Changing Forms*. Copenhagen, 1974.
Dundes, Alan; Leach, Jerry W.; and Özkök, Bora. "The Strategy of Turkish Boys' Verbal Dueling Rhymes." *JAF* 83(1970):325–49.
Dworkin, Earl S., and Efran, Jay S. "The Angered: Their Susceptibility to Varieties of Humor." In *Motivation in Humor*, edited by Jacob Levine, 96–102. New York, 1969.
Elliott, Robert C. *The Power of Satire: Magic, Ritual, Art*. Princeton, 1960.
Ellis, Robinson. *A Commentary on Catullus*. 2d ed. Oxford, 1889.
Faust, Beatrice. *Women, Sex, and Pornography*. New York, 1980.
Fehling, Detlev. "De Catulli Carmine sexto decimo." *RhM* 117(1974):103–08.
———. *Ethologische Überlegungen auf dem Gebiet der Altertumskunde. Zetemata* 61. Munich, 1974.
Ferenczi, Sandor. "On Obscene Words." In *Sex in Psychoanalysis*, translated by Ernest Jones, 112–30. Boston, 1916.
Fiedler, Leslie. *Freaks*. New York, 1978.
Fiske, George Converse. *Lucilius and Horace. University of Wisconsin Studies in Language and Literature* 7. Madison, 1920.
Foley, Helene P., ed. *Reflections of Women in Antiquity*. New York and London, 1981.
Forsyth, Phyllis Young. "Comments on Catullus 116." *CQ* n.s. 27(1977):352–53.
Foucault, Michel. *The History of Sexuality*. Vol. 1. Translated by Robert Hurley. New York, 1980.
Fraenkel, Eduard. *Horace*. Oxford, 1957.
———. "Two Poems of Catullus." *JRS* 51(1961):46–53.

———. Review of *Zauberei und Recht in Roms Frühzeit*, by Beckmann. *Gnomon* 1(1925): 185–200.

Frécaut, Jean-Marc. *L'Esprit et l'humour chez Ovide*. Grenoble, 1972.

Freeling, Nicolas. *The Widow*. New York, 1979.

Freud, Sigmund. *Jokes and Their Relation to the Unconscious*. Translated by James Strachey. New York, 1960.

———. *Three Essays on the Theory of Sexuality*. Translated by James Strachey. New York, 1962.

Fry, William F., Jr. *Sweet Madness: A Study of Humor*. Palo Alto, 1963.

Frye, Northrop. *Anatomy of Criticism*. Princeton, 1957.

Galinsky, G. Karl. *Ovid's "Metamorphoses."* Berkeley, 1975.

Garnsey, Peter. *Social Status and Legal Privilege in the Roman Empire*. Oxford, 1970.

Geffcken, Katherine A. *Comedy in the Pro Caelio*. Leyden, 1973.

George, Peter. "Petronius and Lucan *De Bello Civili*." *CQ* n.s. 24(1974):119–33.

———. "Style and Character in the *Satyricon*." *Arion* 5(1966):336–58.

Gergen, Kenneth J., and Gergen, Mary M. *Social Psychology*. New York, 1981.

Giacomelli, Anne. "The Justice of Aphrodite in Sappho Fr. 1." *TAPhA* 110(1980): 135–42.

Gill, Christopher. "The Sexual Episodes in the *Satyricon*." *CPh* 68(1973):172–85.

Gnilka, Christian. "Catulls Spottgedicht auf Silo." *RhM* 118(1975):130–35.

———. "Lynchjustiz bei Catull." *RhM* 116(1973):256–69.

———. "*Maura Maurae collactea*. Zu Juv. *sat*. 6,306–308." *RFIC* 96(1968):47–54.

Goldstein, Kenneth S. "Bowdlerization and Expurgation: Academic and Folk." *JAF* 80(1967):374–86.

Gollob, Harry F., and Levine, Jacob. "Distraction as a Factor in the Enjoyment of Aggressive Humor." In *Motivation in Humor*, edited by Jacob Levine, 149–56. New York, 1969.

Gonos, George; Mulkern, Virginia; and Poushinsky, Nicholas. "Anonymous Expression: A Structural View of Graffiti." *JAF* 89(1976):40–48.

Gossen, Gary H. "Verbal Dueling in Chamula." In *Speech Play*, edited by Barbara Kirshenblatt-Gimblett, 121–46. Philadelphia, 1976.

Gow, A. S. F., and Page, D. L., eds. *The Greek Anthology: The Garland of Philip and Some Contemporary Epigrams*. Cambridge, 1968.

———. *The Greek Anthology: Hellenistic Epigrams*. Cambridge, 1965.

Granarolo, Jean. *L'Oeuvre de Catulle*. Paris, 1967.

Grassmann, Victor. *Die erotischen Epoden des Horaz. Literarischer Hintergrund und sprachliche Tradition. Zetemata* 39. Munich, 1966.

Gratwick, Adrian. "Ipsithilla, a Vulgar Name. Catullus, xxxii.I." *Glotta* 44(1966):174–76.

Grider, Sylvia Ann. "*Con Safos*: Mexican-Americans, Names and Graffiti." *JAF* 88 (1975):132–42.

Griffin, Susan. "Sadism and Catharsis: The Treatment Is the Disease." In *Take Back the Night*, edited by Laura Lederer, 141–47. New York, 1980.

Griffith, John G. "The Ending of Juvenal's First Satire and Lucilius Book XXX." *Hermes* 98(1970):56–72.

———. "The Survival of the Longer of the So-called 'Oxford' Fragments of Juvenal's Sixth Satire." *Hermes* 91(1963):104–14.

Grisebach, Eduard. *Die Wanderung der Novelle von der treulosen Witwe durch die Weltliteratur*. 2d ed. Berlin, 1889.

Hallett, Judith P. "Divine Unction: Some Further Thoughts on Catullus 13." *Latomus* 37(1978):747–48.

———. "*Perusinae Glandes* and the Changing Image of Augustus." *AJAH* 2(1977): 151–71.
———. "The Role of Women in Roman Elegy: Counter-cultural Feminism." *Arethusa* 6(1973):103–24.
Halpert, Herbert. "Folklore and Obscenity: Definitions and Problems." *JAF* 75(1962): 190–94.
Handelman, Don, and Kapferer, Bruce. "Forms of Joking Activity: A Comparative Approach." *American Anthropologist* 74(1972):484–517.
Henderson, Jeffrey. *The Maculate Muse*. New Haven, 1975.
Herrmann, L. "Martial et les Priapées." *Latomus* 22(1963):31–55.
Herter, H. *De Priapo. Religionsgeschichtliche Versuche und Vorarbeiten* 23. Giessen, 1932.
Hetherington, E. Mavis, and Wray, Nancy P. "Aggression, Need for Social Approval, and Humor Preferences." In *Motivation in Humor*, edited by Jacob Levine, 67–75. New York, 1969.
Heurgon, Jacques. *Lucilius*. Paris, 1959.
Hezel, Oskar. *Catull und das griechische Epigramm*. Stuttgart, 1932.
Hickman, William C. "More on Turkish Boys' Verbal Dueling." *JAF* 92(1979): 334–35.
Highet, Gilbert. *Juvenal the Satirist*. Oxford, 1954.
Hillman, James. *The Myth of Analysis*. New York, 1976.
Hoffman, Frank A. "Panel on Folk Literature and the Obscene: Introduction." *JAF* 75(1962):189.
Hommer, Hildebrecht. "Vesta und die frührömische Religion." *Aufstieg und Niedergang der Römischen Welt* I.2: 397–420.
Hopkins, Keith. *Conquerors and Slaves*. Cambridge and New York, 1978.
Horney, Karen. "The Dread of Woman." *IntJPsych* 13(1932):348–60.
Housman, A. E. "Praefanda." *Hermes* 66(1931):402–12.
———. "*Tunica Retiarii*." *CR* 18(1904):395–98.
Huizinga, Johan. *Homo Ludens*. Translated by R. F. C. Hull. London, 1949.
Jocelyn, H. D. "On Some Unnecessarily Indecent Interpretations of Catullus 2 and 3." *AJPh* 101(1980):421–41.
Johnson, Owen. *The Lawrenceville Stories*. New York, 1967.
Joshel, Sandra. "Towards an Understanding of the Attitudes of Freed Slaves." Paper presented at the annual meeting of the American Historical Association, Washington, D.C., December 1980.
Joyce, James. *Ulysses*. New York: Vintage, 1961.
Kahn, Frank J., ed. *Documents of American Broadcasting*. 2d ed. New York, 1973.
Kelling, George W. *Language: Mirror, Tool, and Weapon*. Chicago, 1975.
Kelly, J. M. " 'Loss of Face' as a Factor Inhibiting Litigation." In *Studies in the Civil Judicature of the Roman Republic*, 93–111. Oxford, 1976.
Kenney, E. J. "The First Satire of Juvenal." *Proceedings of the Cambridge Philological Society* 188(1962):29–40.
———. "Juvenal: Satirist or Rhetorician?" *Latomus* 22(1963):704–20.
Khan, H. Akbar. "Catullus 99 and the Other Kiss-Poems." *Latomus* 26(1967):609–18.
———. "Image and Symbol in Catullus 17." *CPh* 64(1969):88–97.
———. "Three Epigrams of Catullus (*Carm.*, 114, 115, 112)." In *Hommages à Marcel Renard* I, edited by Jacqueline Bibauw, 3–11. Brussels, 1969.
Kiefer, Otto. *Sexual Life in Ancient Rome*. Translated by Gilbert and Helen Highet. London, 1934. Reprint. New York, 1975.
Kinsey, T. E. "Catullus 16." *Latomus* 25(1966):101–06.
Kirshenblatt-Gimblett, Barbara, ed. *Speech Play*. Philadelphia, 1976.

Klebs, Elimar. "Zur composition von Petronius Satirae." *Philologus* 47(1889):623–35.
Knoche, Ulrich. *Roman Satire*. Translated by Edwin S. Ramage. Bloomington, Indiana, 1975.
Koestler, Arthur. *Insight and Outlook*. New York, 1949.
Konstan, David. "An Interpretation of Catullus 21." In *Studies in Latin Literature and Roman History* (I), edited by Carl Deroux, 214–16. Brussels, 1979.
Krenkel, Werner. *Pompeianische Inschriften*. Heidelberg, 1963.
La Barre, Weston. "The Psychopathology of Drinking Songs." *Psychiatry* 2(1939):203–12.
Last, Hugh. *Cambridge Ancient History* 10.443–47. Cambridge, 1934.
Lateiner, Donald. "Obscenity in Catullus." *Ramus* 6(1977):15–32.
Latte, Kurt. *Römische Religionsgeschichte. Handbuch der Altertumswissenschaft* 5.4. Munich, 1960.
Laurens, Pierre. "Martial et l'épigramme grecque du Ier siècle après J.-C." *REL* 43(1965):315–41.
Lawrence, D. H. *Pornography and Obscenity*. New York, 1930.
Leach, Edmund. "Anthropological Aspects of Language: Animal Categories and Verbal Abuse." In *New Directions in the Study of Language*, edited by Eric H. Lenneberg, 23–63. Cambridge, Mass., 1964.
Leary, James P. "Fists and Foul Mouths: Fights and Fight Stories in Contemporary Rural American Bars." *JAF* 89(1976):27–39.
Lederer, Laura. "An Interview with a Former Pornography Model." In *Take Back the Night*, edited by Laura Lederer, 57–70. New York, 1980.
———, ed. *Take Back the Night*. New York, 1980.
Leeman, A. D. *Orationis Ratio*. Amsterdam, 1963.
Legman, Gershon. *The Horn Book: Studies in Erotic Folklore and Bibliography*. New Hyde Park, N.Y., 1964.
———. "Misconceptions in Erotic Folklore." *JAF* 75(1962):200–08.
———. *No Laughing Matter*. New York, 1975.
———. *Rationale of the Dirty Joke*. New York, 1968.
———. "Toward a Motif-Index of Erotic Humor." *JAF* 75(1962):227–48.
Lévi-Strauss, Claude. *The Raw and the Cooked*. Vol. 1. Translated by John and Doreen Weightman. New York, 1969.
Levine, Jacob. "Regression in Primitive Clowning." *The Psychoanalytic Quarterly* 30(1961):72–83.
Levine, Jacob, ed. *Motivation in Humor*. New York, 1969.
Lilja, Saara. *The Roman Elegists' Attitude to Women*. Helsinki, 1965.
Lindsay, Jack. *The Writing on the Wall*. London, 1960.
Lindsay, Wallace M., ed. *Sexti Pompei Festi . . . Quae Supersunt*. Leipzig, 1913.
Lintott, A. W. *Violence in Republican Rome*. Oxford, 1968.
Littman, R. J. "The Unguent of Venus: Catullus 13." *Latomus* 36(1977):123–28.
Longino, Helen E. "Pornography, Oppression, and Freedom: A Closer Look." In *Take Back the Night*, edited by Laura Lederer, 40–54. New York, 1980.
Luck, Georg. "The Woman's Role in Latin Love Poetry." In *Perspectives of Roman Poetry*, edited by G. Karl Galinsky, 15–31. Austin, Texas, 1974.
Lurie, Susan. "Pornography and the Dread of Women: The Male Sexual Dilemma." In *Take Back the Night*, edited by Laura Lederer, 159–73. New York, 1980.
Maass, Ernst. "Eunuchos und Verwandtes." *RhM* 74(1925):432–76.
MacCormack, Carol P., and Strathern, Marilyn, eds. *Nature, Culture and Gender*. Cambridge and New York, 1980.
McGuire, R. J.; Carlisle, J. M.; and Young, B. G. "Sexual Deviations as Conditioned Behaviour: A Hypothesis." *Behaviour Research and Therapy* 2(1965):185–90.

MacLeod, C. W. "Catullus 116." *CQ* n.s. 23(1973):304–09.
———. "Parody and Personalities in Catullus." *CQ* n.s. 23(1973):294–303.
Madia, S. *Il fantasma della donna nella poesia di Giovenale*. Messina, 1957.
Makarius, Laura. "Ritual Clowns and Symbolic Behaviour." *Diogenes* 69(1970):44–73.
Malcovati, Henrica. *Oratorum Romanorum Fragmenta*. Turin, 1955.
Malinowski, Bronislaw. *The Sexual Life of Savages*. New York, 1929.
Mann, Ted, and Kenney, Doug. "Canadian Corner." *National Lampoon*, March 1979:13.
Marache, René. "La revendication sociale chez Martial et Juvénal." *RCCM* 3(1961): 30–67.
Marx, Friedrich. *Studia Luciliana*. Bonn, 1882.
———, ed. *C. Lucilii Carminum Reliquiae*. 2 vols. Leipzig, 1904–05. Reprint. Amsterdam, 1963.
Mason, H. A. "Is Juvenal a Classic?" In *Satire*, edited by J. P. Sullivan, 93–176. Bloomington and London, 1963.
Maxwell-Stuart, P. G. "Strato and the Musa Puerilis." *Hermes* 100(1972):215–40.
Mayer, Anton. *Erdmutter und Hexe. Historische Forschungen und Quellen* 12. Munich, 1936.
Mayor, John E. B. *Thirteen Satires of Juvenal, with a Commentary*. London, 1877. Reprint. New York, 1979.
Millett, Kate. *Sexual Politics*. New York, 1970.
Milner, G. B. "Homo Ridens: Towards a Semiotic Theory of Humour and Laughter." *Semiotica* 5(1972):1–30.
Minyard, John-Douglas. "Critical Notes on Catullus 29." *CPh* 66(1971):174–81.
Mommsen, Theodor. *Römisches Staatsrecht*. Leipzig, 1887–88.
———. *Römisches Strafrecht*. Leipzig, 1899.
Montero Cartelle, Enrique. "De las *nugae* a los graffiti o del 'priapismo verbal.' " *Durius* 3(1975):371–83.
Morgan, M. Gwyn. "Catullus 112: A *Pathicus* in Politics." *AJPh* 100(1979):377–80.
———. "*Nescio quid febriculosi scorti*: A Note on Catullus 6." *CQ* n.s. 27(1977):338–41.
Morgan, Robin. "Theory and Practice: Pornography and Rape." In *Take Back the Night*, edited by Laura Lederer, 134–40. New York, 1980.
Mueller, L. *Catulli, Tibulli, Propertii Carmina. . . . et Priapea*. Leipzig, 1892.
Nardo, Dante. *La sesta satira di Giovenale e la tradizione erotico-elegiaca latina*. Padua, 1973.
Newall, Venetia, ed. *The Witch Figure*. London, 1973.
Newman, Randy. "God's Song." *Sail Away*. Warner Bros. Records Inc. MS 2064, 1972.
Nisbet, R. G. M., ed. *M. Tulli Ciceronis in L. Calpurnium Pisonem Oratio*. Oxford, 1961.
Ogilvie, R. M. *Roman Literature and Society*. Brighton, England, and Totowa, N.J., 1980.
———. *The Romans and Their Gods in the Age of Augustus*. London, 1969.
Ọlajubu, Chief Oludare. "References to Sex in Yoruba Oral Literature." *JAF* 85(1972): 152–66.
Opelt, Ilona. *Die lateinischen Schimpfwörter und verwandte sprachliche Erscheinungen*. Heidelberg, 1965.
Ortner, Sherry B. "Is Female to Male as Nature Is to Culture?" In *Woman, Culture and Society*, edited by Michelle Zimbalist Rosaldo and Louise Lamphere, 67–87. Stanford, 1974.
Ortner, Sherry B., and Whitehead, Harriet, eds. *Sexual Meanings: The Cultural Construction of Gender and Sexuality*. Cambridge and New York, 1981.
Orwell, George. "The Art of Donald McGill." In *A Collection of Essays*, 104–16. New York, 1953.
Otis, Brooks. *Ovid as an Epic Poet*. 2d ed. Cambridge, 1970.
Owen, S. G. "On the *Tunica Retiarii*." *CR* 19(1905):354–57.
Page, Denys. *The Epigrams of Rufinus*. Cambridge and New York, 1978.

Palmer, Robert E. A. "On Mutinus Titinus: A Study in Etrusco-Roman Religion and Topography." In *Roman Religion and Roman Empire: Five Essays*, 187–206. Philadelphia, 1974.
Pearson, Hesketh. *The Life of Oscar Wilde*. London, 1946.
Penella, R. J. "A Note on *(de)glubere*." *Hermes* 104(1976):118–20.
Pollio, Howard R., and Edgerly, John W. "Comedians and Comic Style." In *Humour and Laughter: Theory, Research and Applications*, edited by Antony J. Chapman and Hugh C. Foot, 215–42. London, 1976.
Pomeroy, Sarah B. *Goddesses, Whores, Wives, and Slaves*. New York, 1975.
Quinn, Kenneth. *Catullus: An Interpretation*. New York, 1973.
———. *Texts and Contexts*. London and Boston, 1979.
Ramage, Edwin S.; Sigsbee, David L.; and Fredericks, Sigmund C. *Roman Satirists and Their Satire: The Fine Art of Criticism in Ancient Rome*. Park Ridge, N.J., 1974.
Randall, J. G. "*Glubit* in Catullus 58: *retractatio*." *LCM* 5.1(1980):21–22.
Randolph, Vance. *Pissing in the Snow and Other Ozark Folktales*. Urbana, Illinois, 1976.
Rankin, H. D. "A Note on Some Implications of Catullus, 16, 11–13." *Latomus* 29 (1970):119–21.
———. "Petronius, Priapus, and *Priapeum* LXVIII." *C&M* 27(1966):125–42. Reprinted in *Petronius the Artist*, 52–67. The Hague, 1971.
———. *Petronius the Artist*. The Hague, 1971.
———. "Some Themes of Concealment and Pretense in Petronius' *Satyricon*." *Latomus* 28(1969):99–119. Reprinted in *Petronius the Artist*, 32–51. The Hague, 1971.
Reallexikon für Antike und Christentum. Stuttgart, 1972.
Reckford, Kenneth. "Studies in Persius." *Hermes* 90(1962):476–504.
Reekmans, Tony. "Juvenal's Views on Social Change." *AncSoc* 2(1971):117–61.
Reeve, M. D. "Gladiators in Juvenal's Sixth Satire." *CR* n.s. 23(1973):124–25.
Reich, Hermann. *Der Mimus*. Vol. 1. Berlin, 1903.
Reynolds, R. W. "The Adultery Mime." *CQ* 40(1946):77–84.
Richardson, L., Jr. "*Furi et Aureli, comites Catulli*." *CPh* 58(1963):93–106.
Richardson, N. J. *The Homeric Hymn to Demeter*. Oxford, 1974.
Richlin, Amy. "Approaches to the Sources on Adultery at Rome." *Women's Studies* 8.1–2(1981):225–50. Reprinted in *Reflections of Women in Antiquity*, edited by Helene P. Foley, 379–404. London, 1981.
———. "Invective against Women in Roman Satire." *Arethusa*, in press.
———. "The Meaning of *Irrumare* in Catullus and Martial." *CPh* 76(1981):40–46.
———. "Sexual Terms and Themes in Roman Satire and Related Genres." Ph.D. diss., Yale University, 1978.
Rochester, Sherry, and Martin, J. R. *Crazy Talk: A Study of the Discourse of Schizophrenic Speakers*. New York, 1979.
Rosenmeyer, Thomas G.; Ostwald, Martin; and Halporn, James W. *The Meters of Greek and Latin Poetry*. Indianapolis, 1963.
Ross, Anne. "The Divine Hag of the Pagan Celts." In *The Witch Figure*, edited by Venetia Newall, 139–64. London, 1973.
Rudd, Niall. *The Satires of Horace*. Cambridge, 1966.
Rush, Florence. "Child Pornography." In *Take Back the Night*, edited by Laura Lederer, 71–81. New York, 1980.
Russell, Diana E. H. "Pornography and Violence: What Does the New Research Say?" In *Take Back the Night*, edited by Laura Lederer, 218–38. New York, 1980.
Russell, Diana E. H., with Lederer, Laura. "Questions We Get Asked Most Often." In *Take Back the Night*, edited by Laura Lederer, 23–29. New York, 1980.
Sanches, Mary, and Kirshenblatt-Gimblett, Barbara. "Children's Traditional Speech Play

and Child Language." In *Speech Play*, edited by Barbara Kirshenblatt-Gimblett, 65–110. Philadelphia, 1976.
Sandy, Gerald N. "Catullus 16." *Phoenix* 25(1971):51–57.
———. "Scaenica Petroniana." *TAPhA* 104(1974):329–46.
"Scatological Lore on Campus." *JAF* 75(1962):260–62.
Schrier, O. J. "Love with Doris." *Mnemosyne* 32(1979):307–26.
Scott, Kenneth. "The Political Propaganda of 44–30 B.C." *Memoirs of the American Academy in Rome* 11(1933):7–49.
Scott, William C. "Catullus and Caesar (*C.* 29)." *CPh* 66(1971):17–25.
Segal, Alan. "Censorship, Social Control and Socialization." *British Journal of Sociology* 21(1970):63–74.
Segal, Erich. *Roman Laughter*. Cambridge, Mass., 1968.
Shero, Lucius Rogers. "The Satirist's *Apologia*." *University of Wisconsin Studies in Language and Literature* 15(1922):148–67.
Singer, David L. "Aggression Arousal, Hostile Humor, Catharsis." In *Motivation in Humor*, edited by Jacob Levine, 103–27. New York, 1969.
Skinner, Marilyn B. "*Ameana, puella defututa*." *CJ* 74(1978):110–14.
———. "Parasites and Strange Bedfellows: A Study in Catullus' Political Imagery." *Ramus* 8(1979):137–52.
———. "Pretty Lesbius." *TAPhA* 112(1982):197–208.
Skutsch, O. "Catullus 58.4–5." *LCM* 5.1(1980):21.
Slater, Niall W. "The Theatre of the Mind: Metatheatre in Plautus." Ph.D. diss., Princeton University, 1981.
Slater, Philip E. *The Glory of Hera*. Boston, 1968.
Smith, R. E. "The Law of Libel at Rome." *CQ* n.s. 1(1951):169–79.
Stanford, W. B. *The Ulyssess Theme*. 2d ed. Oxford, 1963.
Steele, Robert Benson. *A Review of "The Priapea and Ovid: A Study of the Language of the Poems."* Nashville, 1932.
Steinem, Gloria. "Erotica and Pornography: A Clear and Present Difference." In *Take Back the Night*, edited by Laura Lederer, 35–39. New York, 1980.
Stewart, Susan. *Nonsense: Aspects of Intertextuality in Folklore and Literature*. Baltimore, 1979.
Stocker, Terrance L.; Dutcher, Linda W.; Hargrove, Stephen M.; and Cook, Edwin A. "Social Analysis of Graffiti." *JAF* 85(1972):356–66.
Stone, Leo. "On the Principal Obscene Word of the English Language." *IntJPsych* 35(1954):30–56.
Sullivan, J. P. *Propertius: A Critical Introduction*. Cambridge, 1976.
———. *The Satyricon of Petronius: A Literary Study*. London, 1968.
———, ed. *Satire*. Bloomington and London, 1963.
Sussman, Gerald. "Tips and Tales from Bernie X." *National Lampoon*, November 1979: 10–11; December 1979:13.
Syme, Ronald. *The Roman Revolution*. Oxford, 1939.
Tanner, R. G. "Catullus LVI." *Hermes* 100(1972):506–08.
Tanzer, Helen H. *The Common People of Pompeii: A Study of the Graffiti*. Baltimore, 1939.
Terzaghi, Nicola. *Lucilio*. Turin, 1934.
———, ed. *C. Lucilii Saturarum Reliquiae*. Reprint. Florence, 1966.
Thierfelder, Andreas. "Obscaenus." In *Navicula Chiloniensis: Studia Philologa Felici Jacoby . . . Oblata*, 98–106. Leyden, 1956.
Thomason, Richmond Frederick. *The Priapea and Ovid: A Study of the Language of the Poems*. Nashville, 1931.
Thompson, Stith. *Motif-Index of Folk Literature*. 6 vols. Copenhagen and Bloomington, 1955–58.

Treggiari, Susan. *Roman Freedmen during the Late Republic.* Oxford, 1969.
Turnbull, Percival. "The Phallus in the Art of Roman Britain." *Bulletin of the Institute of Archaeology* (University of London) 15(1978):199–206.
Turner, Victor. *The Ritual Process.* Chicago, 1969.
Vanggaard, Thorkil. *Phallós.* London, 1972.
van Rooy, C. A. "Arrangement and Structure of Satires in Horace, *Sermones*, Book I, with More Special Reference to Satires 1–4." *AClass* 11(1968):38–72.
———. " 'Imitatio' of Vergil, *Eclogues*, in Horace, *Satires*, Book I." *AClass* 16(1973):69–88.
———. *Studies in Classical Satire and Related Literary Theory.* Leyden, 1965.
Vetterling-Braggin, Mary. *"Femininity," "Masculinity," and "Androgyny."* Totowa, N.J., 1982.
Veyne, P. "Le 'je' dans le *Satiricon.*" *REL* 42(1964):301–24.
Vianello, Natale. "La sesta satira di Giovenale." *Historia (Studi storici per l'Antichità Classica)* 4(1930):747–75.
Wagenvoort, H. *"Profānus, profānāre."* *Mnemosyne* 4th ser. 2(1949):319–32.
Weinreich, Otto. "Zu Horazens 8. Epode und Nikarch AP. V 38." *Hermes* 77(1942):220–22.
Welsford, Enid. *The Fool.* London, 1935.
Whatmough, Joshua. "Pudicus Poeta: Words and Things." In *Poetic, Scientific and Other Forms of Discourse*, 29–55. Berkeley, 1956.
Whitman, Cedric H. *Aristophanes and the Comic Hero. Martin Classical Lectures* 19. Cambridge, 1964.
Widdowson, John. "The Witch as a Frightening and Threatening Figure." In *The Witch Figure*, edited by Venetia Newall, 200–20. London, 1973.
Wiesen, David. "Juvenal's Moral Character: An Introduction." *Latomus* 22(1963):440–71.
Willenberg, Knud. "Die Priapeen Martials." *Hermes* 101(1973):320–51.
Williams, Gordon. *Change and Decline.* Berkeley, 1978.
———. "Poetry in the Moral Climate of Augustan Rome." *JRS* 52(1962):28–46.
———. "Some Aspects of Roman Marriage Ceremonies and Ideals." *JRS* 48(1958):16–29.
———. *Tradition and Originality in Roman Poetry.* Oxford, 1968.
Winter, Thomas Nelson. "Catullus Purified: A Brief History of Carmen 16." *Arethusa* 6(1973):257–65.
Witke, Charles. "Catullus 13: A Reexamination." *CPh* 75(1980):325–31.
Young, Phyllis R. "Catullus 29." *CJ* 64(1969):327–28.
Zeitlin, Froma I. "Petronius as Paradox: Anarchy and Artistic Integrity." *TAPhA* 102(1971):631–84.

Addenda and Corrigenda

In this task I have benefited from the model provided by Henderson 1991. What I present here is mostly additional material—culled from my reading since 1983—of interest to those in the field. As will be evident, three primary sources not included in the original survey of material proved especially fruitful: Lucian, Paulus ex Festo, and the younger Seneca.

For general surveys on ancient sexuality and gender, see the articles in Grant and Kitzinger 1988 listed at the end of the Additional Bibliography.

As I remarked in the preface to the earlier edition, I regretted not being able to include a treatment of Roman comedy. Of new work in that field, most pertinent are: Konstan 1983, which provides an excellent theoretical approach to Plautus based on an analysis of power within cultural systems; Parker 1989, which deals with the issue of torture jokes in Plautus by using a Freudian approach and setting the plays in their social-historical context. See also Slater 1985 on metatheater in the plays, and Fantham 1975.

Chapter 1

On Roman concepts of the obscene and on Roman cultural phenomena associated with sexuality, see especially Barton (forthcoming). See Parker 1991 (cited in the bibliography following the introduction to this volume) on ancient concepts of the pornographic. A wealth of material from the early Christian period is provided by Brown 1988; see also Rousselle 1988, which is less reliable. For a treatment of obscene vocabulary in an influential medieval text, see Vasvari 1988. Kendrick 1988 provides a good historical overview of the issue of pornography; and see the introduction and general bibliography in Richlin 1991a (cited in the bibliography following the introduction to this volume).

pp. 5–6 **Petronius 132.15:** For a discussion and sources, see Sullivan 1968: 98–100 (cited in the original bibliography).

Correction: Petronius can, of course, claim his *sermo* is *purus* in the well-established sense of "simple and lucid"; the opposed phrases *sermonis puri* and *candida lingua* probably recall, in addition, the proper dress of a Roman male, the *toga pura* and the formal *toga candida,* both connoting a stainless whiteness. As a claim, it is still tongue-in-cheek: Encolpius' general relation to literature and rhetoric is a comic one, his immediately preceding speech (see pp. 116–17) is an epic travesty, and Petronius' text (if Encolpius is his mouthpiece here) includes the remarkable feature of the freedmen's speech, which is not *sermo purus.*

p. 9 **on *obscenus:*** Pompeius Festus says (204L): *etiam verba impudentia elata appellantur obscena, quia frequentissimus fuit usus Oscis libidinum spurcarum,* "also words uttered in shamelessness are called 'obscene,' because the use of foul lusts was very common among the Oscans." But Festus later casts doubt on the derivation (218L):

> Adicit [Verrius] etiam, quod stupra inconcessae libidinis obscena dicantur, ab eius gentis consuetudine inducta. Quod verum esse non satis adducor, cum apud antiquos omnis fere obscena dicta sint, quae mali ominis habebantur . . .
>
> [Verrius] adds also that sex crimes of forbidden lust are called "obscene," derived from the practice of this ethnic group. But I am not quite convinced that this is true, since among almost all the ancients things were said to be "obscene" which were considered of ill omen.

Both derivations of the concept of the obscene—from sexual practices considered foul, and from religious demarcation—apply to the framework suggested in chapter 1.

Elsewhere Festus gives nomenclature for the "obscene male part" in mimes (410L). See the discussion of genitalia as obscene, p. 26; see also chapter 3, p. 67. Thus the use of *obscena* as a medical euphemism; in Serenus Sammonicus *Lib. Med.* 35, a list of penis ointments (674–94) is headed *omnibus obscenis medendis.*

At Seneca *De Ben.* 3.26.2, a chamber pot is called "obscene" when in contact with a ring bearing the image of the emperor's head; see the discussion of excreta as obscene (p. 26). For the extension of the concept to the natural world, see Pliny *HN* 2.93 (a belief that a comet in the genital area of constellations betokens "obscene morals"). For a discussion of sexual decorum at Vergil *A.* 8.404–6, see Aulus Gellius 9.10.

pp. 9–10 **on rituals of reversal:** See Lucian *Pseudologistes* 16, who explains the nickname of a man known as "Seventh Day": ". . . because, like children on the seventh day of the month, he joked and laughed at things in the assemblies and turned the people's business into a children's game."

On the soldiers' songs at Caesar's triumph, compare the description at Pliny *HN* 19.144, where they are said to be sung in *alternis . . . versibus;* this suggests their structure may have been perceived to be like that of *occentatio,* as in the alternating question and answer of political claques (pp. 86–87, chap. 4, n. 6). Pliny has them singing about Caesar's stinginess in feeding them on wild cabbage at Dyrrachium.

With triumphs as rituals of reversal, compare the description (Suet. *Vesp.* 19) of how the archimimus Favor was selected to wear Vespasian's mask in his funeral procession and imitate, *ut est mos,* his *facta ac dicta;* and the jokes Favor made about Vespasian's stinginess. Presumably the coincidental recurrence of the theme of stinginess—truth value aside—marks a sense of such events as times of extravagant display; see Barton (forthcoming).

Quintilian 6.3.16 notes briefly the existence of days of special license for joking at Rome. Compare the interpretation of the significance of the Floralia attributed to Heliogabalus, Lampridius *Life of Heliogabalus* 6.5; see also 11.6.

p. 10 **Martial's *theatrum meum:*** For use of the same metaphor in the fifth century, applied to Martial and Petronius, see Sullivan 1968: 112–14 (cited in the original bibliography).

p. 18 A discussion of Quintilian *Inst.* 6.3.1–112 would be to the point here. Quintilian repeatedly insists that orators are not to use obscene language, gestures, or ideas: 6.3.25; 6.3.29, *obscenitas vero non a verbis tantum abesse debet, sed etiam a significatione;* 6.3.47 no double entendres, *neque illa obscena, quae Atellani e more captant;* 6.3.83, nothing *turpiter* either. He gives some hint of what he means at 6.3.64, with the surprise-joke *libidinosior es quam ullus spado,* for which he refuses to give the author's name to spare his modesty *(verecundia ipsius).* I would conclude that by *obscenitas* he means sexual topics.

p. 26 ***fellare*** should be translated "suck off," not "fellate," which has too elevated a tone.

Chapter 2

See now Ancona 1989, Wyke 1987a and 1987b.

pp. 36–38 In the discussion of the beauty of boys, it now seems to me that I overstated the importance of the anus in pederastic love poetry in Greek. The "rosebud" in *AP* 12.40 is surely the penis, not the anus, and the thorns are newly grown pubic hair. *AP* 12.30 (Alcaeus) and 33 (Meleager) do, indeed, specify the buttocks as threatened by hair, but the rest of the poems listed in chap. 2, n. 9 refer either to body hair in general or to the beard, face, or thighs. Some of Strato's poems do give *pugizein* as the lover's ultimate goal

(12.240, 12.243; see p. 37), one comparing *binein* unfavorably with *pugizein* (12.245) and another depicting anal sex as attainable only with boys who are mature enough (12.251; also 12.228, cf. 12.4). A few poems focus on the buttocks (12.15, 12.37 [Dioscorides], especially the talking *puga* of 12.38 [Rhianus]), and a few on the anus (12.6 and 12.7 [Strato], 12.22 [Scythinus]). But there are, in fact, just as many poems describing boys' penises (12.3, 12.207 [another lizard, this one like Aphrodite rising from the bathtub], 12.242), with which should certainly be included 12.197 (the cucumber; see chap. 2, n. 11) and 12.204 (rosebud, fig; see p. 36), and probably also 12.205 (ripening grapes) and 12.222 *(kokkous)*—all by Strato. So the remarks (p. 38) on the "idealized view of the boy's anal region" need to be modified. The whole boy is idealized, explicitly including his buttocks and genitals; the uninhibited Strato is the only one to name the anus directly in this context. This is still a far cry from the physical descriptions of women; women's genitals almost never appear in erotic poetry, and often appear in invective.

Thus in *AP* 11.329 (p. 49) the comparison is between women's and boys' pubic hair generally.

p. 36 ***Sphigkter*, "ring":** *Sphigkter* = "anus"; because it has the force of a metaphorical obscenity, I made use of the British slang term "ring" in translating. See Henderson 1991 (p. 248) on the parallel use of *daktylidion* in Aristophanes; the Latin word *anus* itself, as Cicero noted (p. 19), was another example.

p. 43 ***drauci:*** Compare Lampridius *Life of Heliogabalus* 5.3 *(bene vasatos)*, 8.6–7, 9.3, 12.2; addendum to Appendix 2 on Seneca *Ep.* 47.7. On pathics cruising the baths for men with big penises, see: Seneca *QNat.* 1.16.3 (Hostius Quadra); Petronius *Sat.* 92.6–11 (see p. 116); Martial 1.96, 11.63 (cf. 3.73, 9.27, 11.72); Lampridius *Heliogabalus* 8.6. The *drauci* in Martial's poems seem to have been (slave) males attractive to pathics because of their musculature (Mart. 7.67.5, 14.48). Thus there are two systems operating here: one (as seen in Mart. 11.63) in which a man might keep *pueri* whom he would penetrate but who were to be admired for their large penises (as in the *AP* poems discussed in the addendum to pp. 36–38); and a second in which pathics betray themselves by their choice of sex object.

Chapter 3

Work on the theory of humor continues to appear. On women's humor see the bibliography in Richlin 1992 (cited in the bibliography following the introduction to this volume). Within Classics, Branham 1989 covers some of the same ground surveyed here, offering a technical rather than a political analysis; he includes an excellent theoretical bibliography since 1983. Lucian, of course, belongs in any discussion that includes Martial and Juvenal. Likewise, Plass 1988 and 1985 take a theoretical approach compatible with the one presented here, with extended discussion of the mechanics and theory of humor. Henderson 1991 provides an updated bibliography and many additions, including remarks on theoretical approaches. Blok and Mason 1987 must be included in any reading list on ancient sexuality; see also the bibliography following the introduction to this volume. On carnival and gender, see Russo 1986.

p. 63 **curses and magic:** On the power of satire, as in Archilochus and his iambics, see the story of Hipponax and the family of Archermus at Pliny *HN* 36.12.

Plentiful material evidence on the apotropaic use of the phallus is available; see especially Johns 1982, plate 12, showing a dozen phallic amulets. See also Barton (forthcoming), especially her extended discussion of *invidia,* the phallus, and the evil eye.

p. 64 Again, a discussion of Quintilian 6.3.1–112 would be to the point here. Quintilian both gives a taxonomy of kinds of jokes and theorizes about the cause and nature of humor, especially at 6–16; 102–12 critiques Domitius Marsus' book *De Urbanitate.* Quintilian's comment *a derisu non procul abest risus* (7) accords with the general theory put forward here.

pp. 67–69 **revulsion for the female genitalia:** For a feminist analysis of the vocabulary and cultic background of the scene portraying women as pigs (playing on *choiros/cunnus*) in Aristophanes' *Acharnians,* see Golden 1988.

Chapter 4

By far the bulk of new material surveyed consists of anecdotes and rhetorical invective, to which as a category I would add the sort of philosophical *locus* on immoral practices so common in Seneca. The most comprehensive survey relevant here is Plass 1988, though its focus is on humor in general rather than on the sexual; see also Plass 1985. Baldwin 1987 and Vinson 1989 apply the analysis of invective against women, respectively, to Procopius' account of Theodora and to the historical treatment of the women associated with Domitian. Skinner 1983 includes an important formulation of the ideological use of attacks on women in Roman culture, while Skinner 1989 deals similarly with the term *cinaedus.*

The updating of Morel by Buechner (1982) provides some bibliography on individual poets.

p. 81 **graffiti:** This discussion, as well as the theoretical discussion in chapter 3, would have benefited from a consideration of material remains. Grant 1975 and Johns 1982 include many images illustrating the commonness of phallic iconography in everyday objects used in Roman households. The *fascinum* written or carved onto walls, thresholds, and corners provides a particularly clear example of the way in which the phallic presides over boundaries; perhaps sexual graffiti serve as a claim or boast in a similar way, as well as acting as a sort of vandalism, defilement, or rape of the place itself on which they are inscribed (see chapter 6 for a discussion of Catullus' inscription of phalli on Lesbia's house).

pp. 81–83 To the graffiti discussed here, add:

CIL 10.4483 (Capua), addressed to a woman: *Turtu{r Cly}mene. Caca, ut possimus bene dormire et pedicare natis candidas ceiasinos tuos. Cunnu tibi fricabo. Diciti adiuvabunt prurigin{em},* with a little sketch of what seems to be a donkey. Below is written (10.4484) *laicas eme.* This graffito is unusual for its conjunction of sweet talk, scatological themes, and heterosexual intercourse involving anal penetration and manual genital stimulation, with the addition of oral sex. See chapter 2 on the more usual attitude favoring anal intercourse with boys over that with women.

CIL 10.8145 (Pompeii): good letters painted in red on the east wall of an insula: *hanc ego cacavi;* below, a large stone phallus, also painted red. See chapter 7 (p. 169) on the association between defecation and anal intercourse in Lucilius and elsewhere; the graffito parallels *Pr.* 69.4, as Housman (1931) noted (cited in the original bibliography).

CIL 5.504a (Cisalpine Gaul, Capodistria): a herm, with a *glans* and testicles for head and arms; below, an erect phallus and the inscription *mysterium.*

Tesserae (dice) inscribed with sexual epithets are found fairly commonly, for example, among *CIL* 11.6728.5–26 (Perusia); cf. 10.8069, 8070 (Pompeii); also a mosaic dedicated to *bene futuentibus,* 11.6730.3. The article by Judith Hallett cited in chapter 4, note 1, includes a discussion of such tesserae (see p. 156).

GOSSIP AND LAMPOONS (pp. 83–96)

p. 85 ***illam odi male consularem:*** See comments in Skinner 1986 (256–57)—*male* should be construed with *odi,* not with *consularem.* But Skinner's own explication of what is wrong with Clodia shows that the force of *male* here is at least *apo koinou* with *odi* and *consularem;* the idea is that Clodia is consular and it's (in many ways) too bad she is. Note the buildup from *consularis loci* to *non consulare dictum* to *illam odi male consularem,* which Shackleton Bailey ad loc. (refusing to construe *male* with *consularem*) sees as unpolished composition (Bailey, *Epistulae ad Atticum,* cited in the original bibliography).

pp. 86–87 **public invective, claques, heckling:** Cicero's description of the brawl that developed at Milo's trial culminates with both sides spitting at each other (p. 87); a story about Aristides in Seneca (*Cons. Helv.* 13.7) provides another example of spitting in a political context. But Seneca also provides a more interesting Roman example (*De Ira* 3.38.2):

> Quanto Cato noster melius [than Diogenes]! Qui, cum agenti causam in frontem mediam quantum poterat attracta pingui saliva inspuisset Lentulus ille patrum nostrorum memoria factiosus et impotens, abstersit faciem et: "Adfirmabo," inquit, "omnibus, Lentule, falli eos qui te negant os habere."
>
> How much better was our Cato! When that Lentulus, who, in the memory of our fathers, was factious and crazy, drew up a fat glob of spittle and spat in the middle of his forehead, as hard as he could, while Cato was arguing his case, Cato wiped off his face and said: "I will attest to all, Lentulus, that they're wrong when they say you don't have any shame" [lit., "you don't have a mouth"].

As with Cicero's story about the trial, this gives us some idea of the limits of Roman public invective. Seneca chooses the younger Cato two more times to exemplify the extremes to which insult may be pushed: Cato, on his way to argue against a law, has his toga torn and is beset by obscenities, spittle, and "all the other insults of an insane mob" (*Const. Sap.* 1.3); Seneca later contrasts spit, the "purgings of the mouth," with "that sacred head" (2.3). Cf. the use of Cato as the archetype of the anti-obscene (pp. 5–6); these stories stain Cato.

A group of anecdotes about how men took various insults (Sen. *Const. Sap.* 17.1–18.3) includes further testimony to the lively atmosphere of Roman public life (17.1):

> In senatu flentem vidimus Fidum Cornelium, Nasonis Ovidii generum, cum illum Corbulo struthocamelum depilatum dixisset; adversus alia maledicta mores et vitam convulnerantia frontis illi firmitas constitit, adversus hoc tam absurdum lacrimae prociderunt. . . .
>
> We have seen weeping in the senate Cornelius Fidus, the son-in-law of Ovid, when Corbulo called him a "depilated ostrich"; in the face of other insults that tore apart his morals and life he kept his countenance, but in the face of this one, so absurd, his tears rained down. . . .

Seneca goes on to describe how Vatinius often escaped insults through self-mockery (17.3); Seneca suggests disarming insults by not taking offense at them (17.4).

p. 87 **Calvus' epigram on Pompey's effeminacy:** The correct reference should read *FPL* p. 86 Morel (= p. 112 Buechner).

pp. 87–89 **stories of debauchery:** Valerius Maximus 9.1.8 provides a parallel to several stories about the emperors; here an official prostitutes two *matronae* and a *nobilis* boy in his house (*probrosae patientiae corpora,* exclaims Valerius) for the benefit of a consul and the tribunes (see also p. 221).

pp. 88, 92 **Maecenas:** Seneca's *Epistles* include two further digs at Maecenas' virility; interestingly, both transfer epithets denoting effeminacy from Maecenas' body to his style (19.9, *enervasset, castrasset;* 92.35, *alte cinctum, virile* versus *discinxisset*). For a defense of Maecenas' dress and manhood, see *Elegiae in Maecenatem* 1.21–103, which argues that the fact that he was *discinctus* did not make him a bad soldier, and lists examples of "loose" behavior by gods.

pp. 88–89 **emperors debauch courtiers' wives:** Gaius also at Seneca *Const. Sap.* 18.2 (public comments to Valerius Asiaticus on his wife's sexual abilities).

STORIES OF MALE PATHIC BEHAVIOR (pp. 89–93)

The following story about the grandson of the orator Hortensius is told by Valerius Maximus (3.5.4), who would have been this man's contemporary:

> Iam Q. quidem Hortensii, qui . . . summum auctoritatis atque eloquentiae gradum obtinuit, nepos Hortensius Corbio omnibus scortis abiectiorem et obsceniorem vitam exegit: ad ultimumque lingua eius tam libidini cunctorum inter lupanaria prostitit, quam avi pro salute civium in foro excubuerat.
>
> Now the grandson even of Hortensius, who achieved the highest rank of authority and eloquence, Hortensius Corbio, led a life more abject and more obscene than that of all the whores; in the end his tongue prostituted itself as much among the brothels to the lust of all as his grandfather's had exercised vigilance in the forum for the welfare of the citizens.

In the introduction to the next section (3.6.intro.), Valerius goes on to say with great elaboration that he must draw back from the path on which he has set his foot lest he go too far: "I will allow the misshapen {*deformes*} shades to lie in the lowest sink of their own foulness {*turpitudinis*}." The accusation against the grandson seems to be meant more seriously than those against Hortensius himself, who was similarly attacked (p. 93); Valerius' encomium on the eloquence of Hortensia also includes a nasty sideswipe at the *virilis sexus posteri* of the family (8.3.3).

An imperial insult attributed to Gaius by Seneca (*De Ben.* 2.12.1) can be compared with the story (p. 90) about Cassius Chaerea (also at Sen. *Const. Sap.* 18.3); Seneca describes how Gaius granted the life of Pompeius Pennus but then extended his left foot, with a golden slipper on it, for Pompeius to kiss.

Seneca's comment implies that Gaius' mouth would be unsuitable for kissing (*nullam partem in corpore electurus, quam purius oscularetur*).

p. 92 **Augustus to Maecenas:** This playful effusion seems to be a sendup of some of Maecenas' own poetry; see *FPL* p. 101 Morel (= p. 132 Buechner). The word *beryllus* is also picked up in *Elegiae in Maecenatem* 1.18; see addendum to pp. 88, 92.

p. 93 **rhetorical outbursts on pathic characteristics:** Lists of pathic attributes like the one here attributed to Scipio Aemilianus were common (see sources listed at app. 2, n. 3). Not surprisingly, Seneca's *Epistles* contain several passages decrying the degeneracy of contemporary sexual *mores* (see, on women, addendum to p. 134; addenda to app. 2; see also *De Providentia* 3.13, 5.3). Even the *Quaestiones Naturales* are dotted with harangues on morality (see esp. 7.31.1–3, connecting corruption with *impudicitia* and its signs).

A fascination with the blurring of boundaries recurs in Seneca's discourse, and his sexual anecdotes outdo most others. The outstanding example is the description of the vices of Hostius Quadra (*QNat.* 1.16), which had been made into a play (1.16.1); not only did Hostius practice every sort of taboo sex, but he watched himself in mirrors while doing so. Seneca remarks that when Hostius was killed by his slaves, Augustus rightly did not avenge him—a mirrored inversion of norms, if true. Barton (forthcoming) clearly establishes how the excessive plays a central part in Seneca's world; thus Hostius takes his place next to Mamercus Scaurus (*Ben.* 4.31.3–5):

> ignorabas ancillarum illum suarum menstruum ore hiante exceptare? Numquid enim ipse dissimulabat? Numquid purus videri volebat? Referam tibi dictum eius in se, quod circumferri memini et ipso praesente laudari. (4) Pollioni Annio iacenti obsceno verbo usus dixerat se facturum id, quod pati malebat; et cum Pollionis adtractiorem vidisset frontem: "Quidquid," inquit, "mali dixi, mihi et capiti meo!" Hoc dictum suum ipse narrabat. (5) Hominem tam palam obscenum ad fasces et ad tribunal admisisti?

> Were you unaware that he used to catch the menstrual fluid of his female slaves in his open mouth? And did he even conceal it himself? Did he even want to seem *purus?* Let me repeat to you his own joke about himself, which I remember used to be spread around and received favorably even when he was present. (4) Annius Pollio was reclining, and (using an obscene word [he evidently said *"te irrumabo"*]) [Scaurus] had said to him that he would do something that he preferred to have done to himself; and when Pollio looked at him with a frown, Scaurus went on, "Whatever I've said of ill, may it come to me and my head!" [A joke on the formula

for averting the evil eye.] He used to recount this witticism of his himself. (5) And you admitted a man so openly obscene to the consulship?

Even the mention of menstrual blood in any but a medical context is extremely rare in Latin; the story of Scaurus' preferences, like that of Hostius Quadra's, goes beyond the perverse to the freakish (though Seneca mentions a similar man at *Ep.* 87.16). Seneca uses Scaurus to parallel an image of Gaius Caesar catching the blood of his fellow Romans in *his* mouth (4.31.2). These tales form an almost Sadeian development of the political rhetoric examined in chapter 4.

pp. 95–96 **lampoons:** To the collection here should be added another one on Pompey, *FPL* p. 174 Morel (= p. 204 Buechner):

quem
non pudet et rubet, est non homo sed ropio.

one
who is not ashamed and blushes, is not a man but a dong.

(Pompey was a proverbial blusher; see Sen. *Ep.* 11.4). This matches the jokes with the format "not a man but a . . . ," used by Catullus in one of the Mentula poems (115)—an appropriate parallel here (see p. 148; chap. 6, n. 12); it also ties in with the jokes in which the phallus is personified (see listing on p. 67). The verse is preserved by the third-century A.D. grammarian Sacerdos (GLK 6.461–62), who says it is "about Pompey, who was of a ruddy complexion, but an unchaste character" *(coloris erat rubei, sed animi inverecundi).* Note that this description closely follows Suetonius *Gram.* 15, quoting Sallust on Pompey—*oris probi, animo inverecundo;* see p. 165.

p. 95 **Calvus on Tigellinus:** The correct reference should read *FPL* p. 84 Morel (= p. 110 Buechner).

p. 95 **Calvus on Pompey:** The correct reference should read *FPL* p. 86 Morel (= p. 112 Buechner).

p. 96 **Caesar and Nicomedes:** Also at Suetonius *Iul.* 2. On the soldiers' songs at Pliny *HN* 19.144, see addendum to pp. 9–10.

RHETORICAL INVECTIVE (pp. 96–104)

p. 96 **what is considered legitimately funny:** Seneca implies (*Const. Sap.* 16.4, 17.2) that physical disabilities are a common source of mockery.

Again, Quintilian *Inst.* 6.3.1–112 is a major source. The question of what is proper humor for an orator motivates his whole discussion; he provides a wealth of illustrative material, naturally featuring Cicero (including remarks on his collected jokes, 6.3.5). Most of the illustrations come from performances in court.

p. 97 **attacking women's chastity:** Quintilian cites an attack by Cicero on the mother of Pletorius, Fonteius' accuser (*Inst.* 6.3.51).

p. 97 **calling an opponent by a feminine form of his name:** Add Cicero *Nat. D.* 1.93, where it is noted that Zeno always referred to Chrysippus as "Chrysippa." Q. Opimius similarly called his interlocutor by a feminine form of his name (Cic. *De Or.* 2.277); cf. "Dionysia" for Hortensius, p. 93. This form of insult is combined with a more specialized sort of joke in M. Brutus' attack on L. Crassus as *Venerem Palatinam* (Pliny *HN* 36.7). Compare Sex. Titius as Cassandra; also, for a woman, the opprobrious epithets "Medea of the Palatine" and "two-bit Clytemnestra," both applied to Clodia (see chap. 4, n. 4, n. 16). For an example in Greek, see Dio 62.6.5, where Boadicea calls Nero *hê Nerônis hê Domitia.*

p. 97 **Clodius and the Bona Dea:** On Clodius and the bribing of the jury at the Bona Dea trial, add Seneca *Ep.* 97.2–10, a lengthy theme-with-variations based on Cicero *Att.* 1.16.

p. 98 **on wicked governors:** On the idea that a man in power in a province would normally rape everyone in sight, add Valerius Maximus 4.3.1 and 2 (on Scipio and Cato). The chapter is entitled "On Abstinence"; in section 3 Drusus is singled out as remarkable for having sex only with his wife.

p. 100 **Cicero's jokes on Verres:** See Quintilian's less than enthusiastic appraisal in *Inst.* 6.3.4, 6.3.55.

p. 101 **the *locus de aetate:*** I should have noted the discussion of this phenomenon, as applied to Clodius, in Skinner 1982; cf. Skinner 1979 (both cited in the original bibliography). Examples of something similar are to be found in Lucian. In *Alexander the False Prophet* it is claimed that Alexander sold his beauty as a boy and got his training from one of his admirers (5); later the narrator tells how he forbade boys to his followers but collected the flower of the province in his household and used them as slaves, "sleeping with them and abusing them {*emparoinôn*} in every way" (41). In *On the End of Peregrinus* the speaker claims that Peregrinus, as a youth, was caught in adultery in Armenia and suffered raphanidosis before he got away, after which he corrupted a beautiful boy and escaped prosecution by the governor of Asia by paying off the boy's parents (9). This is a world more familiar from the *Satyricon* than from Martial and Juvenal.

p. 101 **dancing:** For a further—if cryptic—comment on the stigma attached to dancing, see Pompeius Festus 436L; this seems to describe those who used to dance in the orchestra, ⟨*cum gestibus ob*⟩*scaenis,* while plays were being performed onstage.

p. 103 **taking abuse with equanimity:** In the *De Ira* Seneca provides several further illustrations of the general principle that a man in public life has to be able to bear insults with equanimity (2.24.4): Antigonus (3.22.2–5), Philip (3.23.2–3), and Augustus (3.23.4–8; also at *De Clem.* 1.10.3). For the Julio-Claudians, see: Suetonius *Iul.* 75.5; *Aug.* 51, 55–56; *Tib.* 28; *Ner.* 39.

Chapter 5

Study of the *Priapea* is now furthered by the appearance of Parker 1988. In addition to a text with apparatus, translation, and brief commentary, Parker provides an extremely useful overview and categorization of all Priapic poetry in Greek and Latin, including some material missed here. As noted earlier, material evidence on Priapus in Roman culture can be found in Grant 1975 and Johns 1982. On Horace's *Epodes,* see Oliensis 1991, with bibliography, and Fitzgerald 1988. On Martial, see especially Sullivan 1991, a major study with extensive bibliography; also Sullivan 1979 and Plass 1985. The association in Athenaeus between women and food as consumables, documented by Henry 1991 (cited in the bibliography following the introduction to this volume), bears comparison with material in this chapter.

pp. 113–16 **invective against old women:** Add Varro *LL* 7.28 (Papinius *FPL* p. 42 Morel = p. 54 Buechner): a young man with an old woman. It is interesting to see that the joke, which would become a favorite of Martial's, has such a long pedigree; here the use of proper names makes the poem appear to be reality-based rather than literary invective. For a survey on old women in Attic comedy, see Henderson 1987.

p. 117 **interpretation and translation of *Pr.* 80.1–2:** Compare alternate versions in Parker 1988. I would keep my translation as is, noting that the answer implied by the rest of the poem is "No." The sense of the parody must surely follow the sense of the Ovidian original.

pp. 120–21 ***Priapea* 54:** See the discussion in Parker 1988. Judging by the material depictions of phalli, the beam is imagined as vertical, not horizontal; cf. Grant 1975: facing 31; 108, 109.

p. 127 A discussion of Ovid's tales of Priapus (*Fasti* 1.391–440, 6.319–48; cf. 2.303–58) would have been to the point here; cf. Fantham 1983 and Richlin 1991b (the latter is cited in the bibliography following the introduction to this volume). To the instances of descriptions of the statue of the god Priapus in the garden should be added Columella 10.29–34 (recommending the reader to set up a statue of Priapus—not a fancy one, but one hewn out of an old tree stump). Further Priapic poems: one found with an altar and statue of the god, *CIL* 5.2803 (Patavium; sources for debate on its authenticity are presented in Parker 1988: 19); also several of uncertain date (Parker 1988: 28–30), especially the Tivoli hymn.

p. 134 **Martial's attacks on women:** A standard list of topoi on adulteresses, much like those later found in Martial, appears at Seneca *De Ben.* 3.16.2–3. A tirade on women's degeneracy at Seneca *Ep.* 95.20–21 includes an assertion that women, *pati natae,* now even penetrate men. On this passage, and on lesbians in Latin literature and Roman life, see Hallett 1989.

p. 138 **Stoic pathics:** Compare the stories in Athenaeus on the sex lives of the Stoics (563d–e, 564f–565b, 565d–f, 605d *hoi para physin têi Aphroditêi chrômenoi*). Here they are said not to be pathics but to treat boys as sex objects past the age usually thought proper. For a close parallel to the Roman stereotype, see Lucian *Symposion, or Lapiths* 36.

A review of Lucian would have been appropriate in chapter 5; the topical overlap between him, Juvenal, and Martial is extensive. Here I can only call attention to some outstanding Lucianic examples of themes dealt with in this chapter.

The most comprehensive source is the *Pseudologistes,* in which the speaker repeatedly calls the one he is attacking a sexual pervert, most explicitly at 17: *kinaidon kai aporrêta poiounta kai paschonta,* "a queer who both performs and allows unspeakable acts." He is said to have danced in the pantomime (19), and the speaker drops hints about his goings-on with a *neaniskon* (20). This is followed by a major treatment of the *os impurum,* including an allusion to Philaenis (24); at 25, in a manner highly reminiscent of Priapic poetry, the man's tongue reproaches him for what he has made it do. This extremely explicit passage ends with the tongue saying it would have preferred to have been cut out, like Philomela's tongue, or to have been used for eating the man's children; at 26 the beard chimes in. The speaker goes on to describe the man's Polyphemus act at a party, in which the mouth substituted for the eye of the Cyclops (27); even the women know of him and say he needs a man (28).

Similar themes are found in *The Eunuch,* in which a debate between two philosophers turns into a mutual *ad hominem* attack, one of the speakers being a eunuch. This dialogue includes a statement of a theme seen in Martial (p. 139); the narrator says that if you stripped the eunuch you would find that he is only outwardly effeminate, and that he was once taken in adultery (10). As the text continues, the practice of philosophy becomes equated with intercourse; the ability to penetrate a woman becomes the mark of a good philosopher. Likewise, the *Rhêtorôn Didaskalos* includes advice on how to have sex with Rhetoric, represented as a woman (10): the ideal teacher is effeminate. Chapters 11–12 provide a description, with many of the stock characteristics of the Roman stereotype, including the idea that the effeminate man scratches his head with the tip of one finger; further details are given throughout the piece (15, 19, 23, 24). Jokes based on the stereotype also appear in *Demonax* (18, 50).

Chapter 6

On Catullus, Janan (forthcoming) provides a useful theoretical approach; see Skinner (forthcoming) on the expression of the female in c. 63 in the context of Roman male socialization. For individual poems, see Dettmer 1985, 1989; Heath 1986, Kitchell 1986, Richlin 1988, and Skinner 1989.

On Ovid, see Fantham 1983 on the rapes in the *Fasti;* Richlin 1991b (cited in the bibliography following the introduction to this volume); Myerowitz 1985 on the *Ars Amatoria* and 1991 (also cited in the bibliography following the introduction to this volume) on the relation between Ovid's love poetry and erotic wall painting.

Chapter 7

This chapter would have benefited from a consideration of Apuleius and from a better treatment of the sexuality of the characters in the *Satyricon*. On Apuleius and a wealth of related material, see Winkler 1985; his discussion of the *Life of Aesop* is most relevant here. For Lucilius, I should have made use of the edition of Krenkel 1970. On Horace's sexual attitudes, see Oliensis 1991. On Petronius, see Slater 1990 and Glei 1987 (the latter on a point in the text). On satire in general, see Henderson 1989, which is highly original and theoretically innovative. Braund 1988 focuses on questions of style and structure in Juvenal, without theoretical analysis, in response to the work of W. S. Anderson. See also Braund 1989, especially the selection by Henderson.

p. 169 **Lucilius 882–83 Marx:** The correct translation is not "shuffles his feet" but "picks his lice," as is clearly indicated by the citation in Pompeius Festus (230L). But Krenkel 1970 (ad loc.) adduces Juvenal 9.133 and Seneca *Ep.* 52.12, presumably also associating head scratching here with the effeminate stereotype (see p. 202; app. 2, n. 3).

p. 185 **Laelium Decumum volo:** Compare the version of this story at Pliny *HN pr.* 7, which includes a variant name and source plus Pliny's interpretation.

pp. 190–91 **on the sexuality of the characters in the *Satyricon*:** I would no longer argue that the sexual orientation per se of Encolpius and his friends was a central issue, nor would I describe them as "homosexuals." Not only has the use of the term *homosexuality* in connection with antiquity been called into question recently (see the introduction to this volume), but neither Encolpius, Ascyltos, nor Eumolpus falls into the single Roman sexual category that was primarily homosexual (pathic male), nor does the sexual interrelationship among the main characters provide, in Roman terms, a "vitiation of them as protagonists" (p. 191). As stated, the three follow norms of Roman adult male sexual behavior, and Giton fulfills the role of *puer*. What makes this a satiric rather than a romantic novel is the placement of romantic narrative elements in sleazy surroundings; the analogy Ascyltos (reportedly) draws between himself and Tarquin, on the one hand, and Giton and Lucretia, on the other (9.5), is funny because of the sex change *in combination with* differences in class and circumstance. Giton is no chaste *matrona* straight out of mythic history.

The mutual insults of Encolpius and Ascyltos, in which they accuse each other of pathic behavior, by and large follow conventional invective patterns, and their lapses toward prostitution do not mark a switch from active to pathic roles; likewise the parallels cited (p. 191, Martial 6.33 and 11.87) concern men who are forced by indigence to switch from penetrating boys (by choice) to women (for money). That boys are preferable to women was a theme in pederastic poetry (pp. 36–37, 41). But the real and problematic transition of young males from sex object to subject lies behind invective conventions, and Encolpius and Ascyltos do seem more ambivalent than figures in more conventional texts.

Appendix 1

See Gardner 1986. For related Greek material, consult Cole 1984. Joplin 1990 and Joshel 1991 (the latter is cited in the bibliography following the introduction to this volume) provide complementary treatments of the Roman ideological use of stories of adultery.

p. 215 **punishments for adultery:** For a mild man-caught-in-the-act-of-adultery joke, see Quintilian *Inst.* 6.3.87.

Appendix 2

I have assembled a second large group of new material here; much of it is closely related to the material added to chapter 4 in this section. See Griffin 1976, which includes an oft-cited treatment of the reality of expressions of homoerotic love in Latin poetry; see also MacMullen 1982. Lilja 1983 provides a useful collocation of sources, especially for comedy, but lacks a clearly defined model of what constituted normative sexual behavior in Rome. Oberhelman

1986 includes comparative material on Greco-Roman and Byzantine attitudes toward male homosexuality; Gleason 1990 analyzes material from the writings of the physiognomists that provides instruction in how to spot a *cinaedus.* See also the discussion in the introduction to this volume.

INVECTIVE AND THE STEREOTYPE OF THE PATHIC (pp. 220–22)

Nomenclature: Paulus ex Festo provides several examples of nomenclature applied to pathics. At Paulus 519L a man is said to be called *vinnulus* if he "carries himself softly and does anything in a way not at all masculine" *(molliter se gerens et minime quid viriliter faciens).* A usage with more sobering implications is Paulus 96L, where *inpudicatus* is defined as *stupratus, inpudicus factus*—"[masc.] having been raped, i.e., having been made unchaste." For similar cases of blaming the victim, see Valerius Maximus 6.1.1, 2, 3, 5, 6 (both male and female); see also p. 225. *Inpudicus,* as discussed earlier (pp. 28–30), often implies pathic sexuality; so, on the effects of drinking the waters of the spring Salmacis (which made men hermaphrodites), Pompeius Festus 439L: *Quam qui bibisset, vitio inpudicitiae mollesceret,* "a man who had drunk from it grew soft with the vice of *inpudicitia.*" Contamination again seems to be at issue in the definition of the phrase *inter cutem flagitatos* (Paulus 98L), literally "seduced inside the body" or "within the skin": "The ancients *{antiqui}* used so to call males who had undergone rape" (or "who had allowed themselves to be penetrated": *qui stuprum passi essent*). Compare the definition of *intercutitus: vehementer cutitus, hoc est valde stupratus*—"strongly skinned, that is well and truly raped" (Paulus 100L). The idea is of the insertion of the phallus into the body—inside the skin—of the raped male, and some context is provided by Martial 7.10, where *cutis* is used for the "body" of male characters who allow anal penetration or perform fellatio (see p. 188 on Persius 4.18, 33). More context is provided by a quotation from the elder Cato (Pomp. 208L, a speech *Against Q. Thermus* [Cato, pp. 39–40 Jordan]):

> Rumorem, famam flocci fecit ⟨inter⟩cutibus stupris obstinatus, insignibus flagitiis.
>
> A man hardened in skin rapes, in notorious sins, didn't give a rap for rumor, for reputation.

(The case against Thermus was for multiple murder.) Compare Gellius 13.8.5 *intercutibus . . . vitiis madentes,* on the familiar theme of hypocritical philosophers.

Paulus ex Festo also lists pederastic nomenclature. On the word *pullus* (Pomp. 284L): "The ancients, moreover, used to call a boy whom someone loved his *pullus.*" *Pullus* can mean the young of any animal and is often used to mean "chick" or "chicken"; it shows up in Horace as a father's pet name for a son (*S.* 1.3.45). But the definition follows the rather startling story that Q. Fabius

Eburnus, who got his cognomen "on account of his fair complexion" *(candorem)*, was called the *Pullus Iovis* ("Chick of Jupiter") "because his buttock had been struck by a lightning bolt"—presumably a birthmark. The anecdote further reinforces the point made in Appendix 2 that Roman citizen males as well as slave boys passed through a stage in life in which they would be viewed as sex objects; this Fabius became consul and censor (P-W Fabius 111). What is even more thought-provoking, this seems to be the same Fabius who killed his own son for being *impudicus* (see Val. Max. 6.1.5 and other sources in P-W).

On *drauci*, see the addendum to p. 43.

Tirades: The younger Seneca's penchant for extremes helps to define the boundaries of pathic sexuality. In a general denunciation of those who live unnaturally he includes those who "trade clothing with women" or try to look like *pueri: Numquam vir erit, ut diu virum pati possit,* "Will he never be a man, so that he may bear a man the longer?" (*Ep.* 122.7; discussed in Winkler 1990: 21, cited in the bibliography following the introduction to this volume). His poignant description of the aging Ganymede, the cupbearer who is forced to prolong his boyish appearance, includes an unusual detail (*Ep.* 47.7); the slave must stay up all night and "divide it between his master's drunkenness and his lust," *et in cubiculo vir, in convivio puer est*—"and he is a man in the bedroom, a boy at the dinner table." The suggestion that the master wants a sex partner who looks like a boy though he is mature, and then is penetrated by that boy/man rather than penetrating him, constitutes an extreme denunciation of the master's vice; it is comparable to some stories about the Caesars, to the situation depicted at length in Juvenal 9, and to similar stories of pathics and *drauci.* For reciprocal sex between adult males, see Suetonius *Otho* 2 (p. 90); Seneca *Ep.* 99.13 (*suam alienamque libidinem exercent mutuo inpudici,* in a list of types of children who do not turn out well).

In a discussion of drunkenness (*Ep.* 83.20), Seneca says it leads to the display of vice; the man who is *inpudicus* "professes and makes public his illness" *(morbum profitetur ac publicat).* Here once again pathic sexuality is marked as a disease (cf. Cat. 57.6, *Pr.* 46.2, Juv. 2.16–17, 50, 78; see also the summary of Caelius Aurelianus *De Morbis Chronicis* 4.9 in Halperin 1990: 22–24, cited in the bibliography following the introduction to this volume).

Seneca also remarks on the implicit power imbalance when a man depends on a slave's love (*De Ben.* 3.28.5). Elsewhere, confirming the ideals expressed in pederastic poetry (see chapter 2, esp. p. 44), he describes in detail how young male slaves were ranked according to their looks, including ethnicity, skin color and smoothness, and curly hair (*Ep.* 95.24). This passage smacks more of the marketplace than of the lover's eye, reminding us that the lover was also a consumer.

The tirade at *QNat.* 7.31.1–3 includes an important contribution to the evidence on the possible pathic sexuality of certain types of gladiators (see sources listed at chap. 7, n. 64). For further lists of pathic stereotypes, see the discussion of Lucian in the addenda to chapter 5 *sub fin.*, esp. *Rhet. Did.* 11–12. For pathic fantasies, see also Seneca *QNat.* 1.16 and Lampridius *Life of Heliogabalus*.

It is interesting that Seneca refers to what Hostius Quadra does as *secreta . . . quaeque sibi quisque fecisse se negat* (1.16.3)—"secret things . . . and those each man tells himself he hasn't done." Compare Dio 61.10.3, where Dio accuses Seneca of having enjoyed boys past the proper age *(meirakiois exôrois)*, and of having taught this taste to Nero. But Dio is prone to fantasy himself.

REAL-LIFE EVIDENCE (pp. 223–25)

pp. 223–24 **teachers:** See *CIL* 10.3969, epitaph to a schoolmaster, especially lines 4–5: *summa quom castitate in discipulos suos.* See Suetonius *Gram.* 23 on Remmius Palaemon.

Literary reflections: Eumolpus and the boy of Pergamum (*Sat.* 85–87); Lucian's *Symposion, or Lapiths,* in which insinuations (26–29) that the philosopher the host has engaged as tutor to his son has seduced the son (both are present and turn pale) lead to exchanges of similar accusations among the other philosophers present (32).

Correction: Haterius (at Sen. *Controv.* 4.pr.11) accuses a man of having (in his youth) masturbated his fellow schoolboys.

p. 224 **remarks in passing on the expectation that young boys are vulnerable to sexual attack:** Add Livy 2.13.10: Cloelia chooses to take the young boys *(impubes)* back with her and everyone approves of this. Not only is it maidenly of her, but it is good for "that age in particular to be freed from the enemy since it was the most vulnerable to injury" *(opportuna iniuriae).* Surely a sexual injury is implied; the use of the word *aetatem* here reinforces the suggestion (see p. 101 on the *locus de aetate*).

Authors reveal their assumptions: thus Valerius Maximus gives Ephialtes much credit for remaining firm in the face of temptation by Demostratus' son, *excellentis formae puer* (3.8.Ext.4); compare Cicero's Cotta, in *De Natura Deorum* (1.79), going on about beauty in human beings and using young men as examples. The elder Pliny cites among examples of unusual deaths two *equites* of his own day who died *in eodem pantomimo Mystico tum forma praecellente* (*HN* 7.184)—the last phrase provides (for Pliny) a reasonable explanation. An almost certain parallel is the preceding item on Pliny's list, two upper-class males who died *in venere;* Pliny got this from Valerius Maximus, who gave the incident the epithet *perridicula*—"utterly absurd" (9.12.8). We must assume from Valerius' attitudes throughout that what he has in mind here is intercourse with slave boys; the focus here is not on the penetrated bodies of *ingenui,* which incite horror (6.1.9), but on the excessive bodies of the penetrators of unnamed boys, which incite tolerant amusement—as such stories about politicians and female prostitutes still do.

p. 224 **killing an ox:** The story is clarified at Pliny *HN* 8.180, where the boy is called a *concubinus procax;* the man was exiled; the story illustrates the value of oxen in the old days. Compare Varro *RR* 2.5.4, Columella 6.pr.7, who say that killing an ox was once a capital offense.

p. 225 **homosexuality in court:** See Dio 67.11.4, where Julius Calvaster uses a pathic assignation as his defense; likewise Suillius Caesoninus in the case of Messallina, Tac. *Ann.* 11.36.5.

Notes

pp. 232–33 (chap. 2), n. 4 **Metella and Perilla:** The comments of Skinner 1986 reflect the highly problematical identity of the women in the two poems. Ovid's protégée is the Perilla of *Tr.* 3.7; *Tr.* 2.437–38 mentions another woman writer who may be named Metella and may have had the pseudonym Perilla, but she may or may not be the same person. On Roman women writers, see now Snyder 1989: 122–51 (cited in the bibliography following the introduction to this volume); on Sulpicia the elegist, see Lowe 1988; Parker 1992. On Sulpicia the satirist, see p. 134 Morel (= p. 166 Buechner).

p. 247 (chap. 5), n. 2 Correct reference should read *FPL* p. 80 Morel (= p. 103 Buechner).

p. 257 (app. 1), n. 40 **husbands killing wives:** See Valerius Maximus 6.3.9 on the man who clubbed his wife to death for drinking wine.

p. 258 (app. 2), n. 3 **gestures, Calvus:** Correct reference should read *FPL* p. 86 Morel (= p. 112 Buechner).

Additional Bibliography

The following works, most of which appeared after *The Garden of Priapus* first went to press, cover related material. This list does not repeat works cited in the bibliography following the introduction to this volume and is by no means exhaustive; I here cite only what I have found useful for the Addenda and Corrigenda.

Ancona, Ronnie. 1989. "The Subterfuge of Reason: Horace, *Odes* 1.23 and the Construction of Male Desire." *Helios* 16: 49–57.

Baldwin, Barry. 1987. "Sexual Rhetoric in Procopius." *Mnemosyne* 40: 150–52.

Barton, Carlin. Forthcoming. *The Sorrows of the Ancient Romans*. Princeton, N.J.: Princeton University Press.

Blok, Josine, and Peter Mason, eds. 1987. *Sexual Asymmetry: Studies in Ancient Society*. Amsterdam: Gieben.

Branham, R. Bracht. 1989. *Unruly Eloquence: Lucian and the Comedy of Traditions*. Cambridge, Mass.: Harvard University Press.

Braund, S[usan] H. 1988. *Beyond Anger: A Study of Juvenal's Third Book of Satires*. Cambridge: Cambridge University Press.

———, ed. 1989. *Satire and Society in Ancient Rome*. Exeter Studies in History, no. 3. Exeter: University of Exeter Press.

Brown, Peter. 1988. *The Body and Society: Men, Women and Sexual Renunciation in Early Christianity*. New York: Columbia University Press.

Buechner, Karl. 1982. *Fragmenta Poetarum Latinorum*. Leipzig: Teubner.

Cole, Susan Guettel. 1984. "Greek Sanctions Against Sexual Assault." *Classical Philology* 79: 97–113.

Dettmer, Helena. 1989. "Catullus 13: A Nose Is a Nose Is a Nose." *Syllecta Classica* 1: 75–85.

———. 1985. "A Note on Catullus 47." *Classical World* 78: 577–78.

Fantham, Elaine. 1983. "Sexual Comedy in Ovid's *Fasti:* Sources and Motivation." *Harvard Studies in Classical Philology* 87: 185–216.

———. 1975. "Sex, Status, and Survival in Hellenistic Athens: A Study of Women in New Comedy." *Phoenix* 29: 44–74.

Fitzgerald, William. 1988. "Power and Impotence in Horace's *Epodes*." *Ramus* 17: 176–91.

Gardner, Jane F. 1986. *Women in Roman Law and Society*. Bloomington: Indiana University Press.

Gleason, Maud. 1990. "The Semiotics of Gender: Physiognomy and Self-Fashioning in the Second-Century C.E." In *Before Sexuality: The Construction of Erotic Experience in the Ancient Greek World*, ed. David M. Halperin, John J. Winkler, and Froma I. Zeitlin: 389–416. Princeton, N.J.: Princeton University Press.

Glei, Reinhold. 1987. "*Coleum Iovis Tenere?* zu Petron 51,5." *Gymnasium* 94: 529–38.

Golden, Mark. 1988. "Male Chauvinists and Pigs." *Echos du Monde Classique/Classical Views* 32, n.s. 7: 1–12.

Grant, Michael. 1975. *Eros in Pompeii*. New York: William Morrow.

Griffin, Jasper. 1976. "Augustan Poetry and the Life of Luxury." *Journal of Roman Studies* 66: 87–105.

Hallett, Judith P. 1989. "Female Homoeroticism and the Denial of Roman Reality in Latin Literature." *Yale Journal of Criticism* 3: 209–27.

Heath, John R. 1986. "The Supine Hero in Catullus 32." *Classical Journal* 82: 28–36.

Henderson, Jeffrey. 1991. *The Maculate Muse*. 2d ed. New York: Oxford University Press.

———. 1987. "Older Women in Attic Old Comedy." *TAPhA* 117: 105–29.

Henderson, John. 1989. "Satire Writes 'Woman': *Gendersong*." *Proceedings of the Cambridge Philological Society* 215, n.s. 35: 50–80. Another version is contained in Braund 1989: 89–125.

Janan, Micaela. Forthcoming. *When the Lamp Is Shattered: Desire in the Poetry of Catullus*. Carbondale: Southern Illinois University Press.

Johns, Catherine. 1982. *Sex or Symbol? Erotic Images of Greece and Rome*. Austin: University of Texas Press.

Joplin, Patricia Klindienst. 1990. "Ritual Work on Human Flesh: Livy's Lucretia and the Rape of the Body Politic." *Helios* 17: 51–70.

Kendrick, Walter. 1988. *The Secret Museum: Pornography in Modern Culture*. Harmondsworth: Penguin.

Kitchell, Kenneth F. 1986. "Catullus 116.7, Amitha/Micta." *Classical World* 80: 1–11.

Konstan, David. 1983. *Roman Comedy*. Ithaca, N.Y.: Cornell University Press.

Krenkel, Werner. 1970. *Lucilius Satiren*. 2 vols. Berlin: Akademie-Verlag. Edition includes notes.

Lilja, Saara. 1983. *Homosexuality in Republican and Augustan Rome*. Commentationes Humanarum Litterarum 74. Societas Scientiarum Fennica (The Finnish Society of Sciences and Letters).

Lowe, N. J. 1988. "Sulpicia's Syntax." *Classical Quarterly* 38: 193–205.

MacMullen, Ramsay. 1982. "Roman Attitudes Toward Greek Love." *Historia* 31: 484–502.

Myerowitz, Molly. 1985. *Ovid's Games of Love*. Detroit, Mich.: Wayne State University Press.

Oberhelman, Steven M. 1986. "The Interpretation of Dream Symbols in Byzantine Oneirocritic Literature." *Byzantinoslavica* 47.1: 8–24.

Oliensis, Ellen. 1991. "Canidia, Canicula, and the Decorum of Horace's *Epodes*." *Arethusa* 24.1: 107–38.

Parker, Holt N. 1992. "Sulpicia, the *Auctor de Sulpicia* and the Authorship of 3.9 and 3.11 of the *Corpus Tibullianum*." *Helios*.

———. 1989. "Crucially Funny or Tranio on the Couch: The *Servus Callidus* and Jokes about Torture." *TAPhA* 119: 233–46.

Parker, W. H. 1988. *Priapea: Poems for a Phallic God.* London and Sydney: Croom Helm.

Plass, Paul. 1988. *Wit and the Writing of History: The Rhetoric of Historiography in Imperial Rome.* Madison: University of Wisconsin Press.

———. 1985. "An Aspect of Epigrammatic Wit in Martial and Tacitus." *Arethusa* 18: 187–210.

Richlin, Amy. 1988. "Systems of Food Imagery in Catullus." *Classical World* 81: 67–80.

Rousselle, Aline. 1988. *Porneia: On Desire and the Body in Antiquity.* Trans. Felicia Pheasant. Oxford: Basil Blackwell.

Russo, Mary. 1986. "Female Grotesques: Carnival and Theory." In *Feminist Studies-Critical Studies,* ed. Teresa de Lauretis: 213–29. Bloomington: Indiana University Press.

Skinner, Marilyn B. Forthcoming. *"Ego mulier:* The Construction of Male Sexuality in Catullus." *Helios.*

———. 1989. *"Ut decuit cinaediorem:* Power, Gender, and Urbanity in Catullus 10." *Helios* 16: 7–23.

———. 1986. Review of Amy Richlin, *The Garden of Priapus, Classical Philology* 81: 252–57.

———. 1983. "Clodia Metelli." *TAPhA* 113: 273–87.

Slater, Niall W. 1990. *Reading Petronius.* Baltimore, Md.: The Johns Hopkins University Press.

———. 1985. *Plautus in Performance: The Theatre of the Mind.* Princeton, N.J.: Princeton University Press.

Sullivan, J. P. 1991. *Martial: The Unexpected Classic.* Cambridge: Cambridge University Press.

———. 1979. "Martial's Sexual Attitudes." *Philologus* 123: 288–302.

Vasvari, Louise O. 1988. "Vegetal-Genital Onomastics in the *Libro de Buen Amor." Romance Philology* 42: 1–29.

Vinson, Martha P. 1989. "Domitia Longina, Julia Titi, and the Literary Tradition." *Historia* 38: 431–50.

Winkler, John J. 1985. *Auctor & Actor: A Narratological Reading of Apuleius's Golden Ass.* Berkeley: University of California Press.

Wyke, Maria. 1987a. "Written Women: Propertius' *Scripta Puella." Journal of Roman Studies* 77: 47–61.

———. 1987b. "The Elegiac Woman at Rome." *Proceedings of the Cambridge Philological Society* 213, n.s. 33: 153–78.

In addition to the above, the encyclopedia *Civilization of the Ancient Mediterranean: Greece and Rome,* ed. Michael Grant and Rachel Kitzinger (New York: Charles Scribner's Sons, 1988), includes the following pertinent articles:

Volume 2: Hallett, Judith P. "Roman Attitudes Toward Sex." 1265–78.
Henderson, Jeffrey. "Greek Attitudes Toward Sex." 1249–63.
Krenkel, Werner A. "Prostitution." 1291–97.
Volume 3: Dickison, Sheila K. "Women in Rome." 1319–32.
Foley, Helene P. "Women in Greece." 1301–18.
French, Valerie. "Birth Control, Childbirth, and Early Childhood." 1355–62.
Pomeroy, Sarah. "Greek Marriage." 1333–42.
Treggiari, Susan. "Roman Marriage." 1343–54.

Index of Passages Cited

Index Verborum

The following index covers both the original text and the addenda (e.g., a listing for "add. 81–83" would refer to "addendum to pp. 81–83"). The list, though not exhaustive, is meant to help the reader find discussions of common, significant, and/or notorious lexical items. (Discussions of topics are covered in the general index.) See the following for major discussions of sexual terminology in Latin and Greek (all cited in the original bibliography): Opelt 1965, Henderson 1975, Richlin 1978, and Adams 1982 (with my review in *AJPh* 105 [1984]: 491–94).

I have lumped together listings for groups of related words (e.g., *amo/amor/amator*). Generally only pages are given where the item itself appeared in a Latin text discussed. Occasionally I give a page where a related form appeared or where the word's semantic field was discussed even though the word was not; such citations appear here in square brackets.

Latin

Greek

General Index